Information Technology and Organizational Transformation

History, Rhetoric, and Practice

JoAnne Yates
John Van Maanen
Editors

Organization Science
Published in cooperation with The Institute for Operations Research
and the Management Sciences (INFORMS) and "Information Systems Review"

Sage Publications, Inc.
International Educational and Professional Publisher
Thousand Oaks ▪ London ▪ New Delhi

For information:

Sage Publications, Inc.
2455 Teller Road
Thousand Oaks, California 91320
E-mail: order@sagepub.com

Sage Publications Ltd.
6 Bonhill Street
London EC2A 4PU
United Kingdom

Sage Publications India Pvt. Ltd.
M-32 Market
Greater Kailash I
New Delhi 110 048 India

Printed in the United States of America

Library of Congress Cataloging-in-Publication Data

Information technology and organizational transformation: History,
    rhetoric, and practice / edited by JoAnne Yates and John Van Maanen.
p. cm. — (Organization science)
        ISBN 0-7619-2301-2 (cloth: alk. paper)
        1. Information technology. 2. Organizational change. I. Yates,
    JoAnne, 1951- II. Van Maanen, John. III. Title. IV. Organization science
    (Thousand Oaks, Calif.)
        HC79.I55 I5378 2000
        303.48'33—dc21   00-010588

01 02 03 04 05 06 07 7 6 5 4 3 2 1

Acquiring Editor:	Marquita Flemming
Editorial Assistant:	Mary Ann Vail
Production Editor:	Diane S. Foster
Editorial Assistant:	Cindy Bear
Typesetter:	Tina Hill
Indexer:	Kathy Paparchontis

Contents

Preface

This volume provides one of the first clear-headed assessments of information technology and organizational transformation. Its virtue is not so much in its recognition of the importance of the subject; speculation on this topic has been rampant for more than a decade. Rather, it is unusual, and unusually useful, because it avoids speculation in favor of conceptually coherent accounts grounded in empirical study of actual organizations. The chapters contained in this volume move beyond the superficial glorification of information technology as an extraordinary instrument of social change and straight to the heart of the mechanisms of change as they play out in everyday organizational life. In the process, they reaffirm that the real story of information technology in organizations is more about people than about technology. Taken together, they provide an important contribution to the intellectual foundations of one of the most interesting developments in decades.

The volume grew out of a special issue of the journal *Information Systems Research* (*ISR*), a publication of the Institute for Operations Research and the Management Sciences (INFORMS) that appeared in December 1996. This was *ISR*'s first special issue, and it was important that the issue embody the insights and intellectual rigor for which the journal is known. JoAnne Yates and John Van Maanen served as guest editors and produced results beyond expectations. In keeping with the successful partnership between INFORMS and Sage Publications, the articles of this special issue, together with four additional papers, were accepted for production as a book. Harry Briggs at Sage provided essential early support for the book project.

On behalf of *ISR* and INFORMS, I thank JoAnne, John, and Harry for their extraordinary efforts in producing this excellent volume. In addition, I acknowledge and thank the many individuals who submitted manuscripts for consideration and who helped to review these submissions. As always, the INFORMS publications staff, especially Kathye Long and Candi Gerzevitz, were of great assistance throughout the process.

John L. King
University of Michigan
Former Editor-in-Chief, *Information Systems Research*

Introduction

As we enter a new century, the pace of change seems to quicken and the talk surrounding technology and work becomes—like most everything else—increasingly apocalyptic. Predictions of major organizational upheavals, from the small independent dairy farm to the gigantic multinational corporation, from the village constable's office to the nation-state itself, have been plentiful and dramatic. All organizations, it appears, must face the so-called information age head-on and prepare for a new world order. In this time and context, the topic of information technology (IT) and its connection to what is so grandly called organizational transformation is well worth scholarly attention and empirical study. Past treatments of this connection putting forth predictions of new organizational forms are troublesome because relatively few studies call out historical precedents, worry much about the way in which causal arrows fly, or suggest very carefully how organizations actually get from here to there.

In putting together this volume, we are particularly interested in understanding how organizational transformations unfold over time, how they have occurred in the past, how they apparently are occurring today, and how interested groups draw on and refine a discourse centering on IT and organizational change. Social processes of both long and short duration are, therefore, our central concern, but these are subtle and varied and operate rather differently across time and space. Take, for example, the inflated claims currently circulating in many quarters about the Internet's power to create significant and lasting social relationships. On the surface, the World Wide Web appears to be a wonderful meeting place where like-minded souls are drawn together through on-line exchanges such that the relationships that develop electronically will broaden and deepen with time. For most of us, however, this seems hardly the case, for the Internet is not yet—and perhaps never will be—a particularly appealing, appropriate, trustworthy, and safe way in which to form close relationships. It might well be a great place to keep relationships going once they have formed, but establishing relationships on the Internet—especially good ones—is another, more problematic matter.

To gain some purchase on the problems that interest us requires, first, some definitions. By *information technology,* we mean simply those mechanisms used to organize, store, manipulate, present, send, and retrieve information. In contemporary societies, IT almost automatically brings to mind things such as computers, video games, fax machines, zip drives, high-speed printers, copiers, voice mail, modems, cell phones, CAD/CAM equipment, satellite dishes, and digital recordings. This certainly is true of the historical moment, but we must keep in mind that this is just a moment. The full and generic meaning of the phrase would include ITs as varied as libraries and blackboards, as calculators and beads, as files and piles, as reading materials and writing tools. With the recording of history, the record itself becomes a "new and improved" IT. Although we seem to talk about it so much because we have so little of it left, memory also is an IT, as is printing, painting, or telling stories. All means of human communication are ITs—the megaphone or telephone, the boom box or Walkman, the traffic light or Goodyear blimp. We also must keep in mind that the principal mode of human communication remains people speaking and listening to one another in face-to-face interaction. And this, too, may be seen as an IT.

By *organizational transformation,* we mean a shift in the way that work is done within a chartered collective. This puts a focus on the work practices of organizational members, the social structures that support and lend shape to such practices, and the ideologies and meaning systems—managerial and otherwise—that more or less legitimate such arrangements. Transformations at any level should be noticeable over time but not necessarily sudden, turbulent, or dramatic. Changes in practice may or may not be associated with shifts in the administrative architecture of an organization (and vice versa). We are more concerned, however, with changes in practice—in the ways that things are done and who does them—than with changes in organizational form or structure per se, which so often leave the work routines of most members untouched. This is not to privilege practice but rather simply to recognize that organizations exist only to the extent that they are enacted by their members—by what their members say and do. The treatment of organizational change too often relies on highly generalized and abstract representations of work—its complexity, its uncertainty, its segmentation, its authority structure, and so on. These representations equate practice with the way in which it is organized, and considerable conceptual confusion is the result. By not having a reasonably decent grip on what it is that organizational members actually do when they are at work, studies of organizational transformation at the structural level tell us little and risk conflating managerial claims about organizational form with substantive change.

What is needed empirically, we think, is a deepened sensitivity to the nature of work as it takes place on the ground and a far greater appreciation for history, context, and discourse than has typically been the case. Research of this sort is uncommon in both the application- and technique-oriented IT community and in the variable- and theory-focused organization studies community. Therefore, we have looked explicitly for studies of the past (distant and recent), studies of language use or rhetoric (official and unofficial), and studies of work communities and practices (established and emergent) to fill out this volume. Seven of the chapters presented here appeared initially as articles in a special issue (March 1996) of the journal *Information Systems Research*. Where appropriate, they have been revised to take account of subsequent events that shed new light on the particular research story told. We also have added four splendid new and previously unpublished studies to take advantage of the space a book provides as well as to more fully elaborate a theoretical and substantive category of our interest that we believe was underrepresented in the special issue—the rhetoric of IT and organizational transformation.

Taken as a whole, these studies display a broad range of sharply focused qualitative methods. They cover levels of analysis that extend from the social, political, and economic contours of the United States at the dawn of the industrial revolution to the language used by members of a small, back-room clerical team perfecting securities for a large British bank during the early 1990s. Private firms, police agencies, political parties, county governments, university research laboratories, and more serve as organizational sites of potential and, in some cases, realized transformation (although hardly in a neat, linear, and foreseeable fashion). For some authors, the close comparative analysis of text, speech, and narrative serves as a principal analytic method. Other authors emphasize ethnographic descriptions that rest on a good deal of traditional participant observation. Methods that distance researchers from the details of work practices and the use (or non-use) of IT— surveys, laboratory experiments, formal interviews with top managers—are more or less absent in this volume.

A common theme running across all the studies presented in this volume is gradualism. Contrary to the conventional (and expensive) wisdom of many futurists, technology gurus, and strategy consultants, organizational transformations—at least those tied to IT—seem not to be carefully orchestrated events, quick and sure leaps into a glorious future, or even terribly jarring disruptions of taken-for-granted practices. Change as depicted in the research that follows is slow, halting, incremental, and often ironic. Moreover, it is occurring all the time but in almost imperceptible ways. This suggests that the working men and women who make use of a new technology carve out time and space to experiment, to improvise, and to learn collectively what the technology means to them, to their work, and to their work community. In the end, they are unlikely to absorb or adopt the technology precisely as expected

xiv INFO TECHNOLOGY AND ORGANIZATIONAL TRANSFORMATION

or intended by those who design, command, and otherwise direct the implementation of new ITs. It is in this sense that the authors of the chapters here treat technology as rather unpredictable and intractable. These are, of course, the very features that make its study so engaging and valuable.

Three sets of studies follow. The first consists of studies that take an historical perspective on IT and organizational transformation. History not only points to the lessons we can learn from the past but also shows just how context and purpose make a difference in how a technology does or does not develop. Consider, for example, the production of text. The Chinese developed and used typesetting well before Guttenberg and the "invention" of the printing press in the West. Yet, print in China was for royal use, was confined mainly to matters of state, and was used primarily by mandarins of the ruling bureaucracy. Public literacy was nonexistent. In Europe, however, a market context existed such that commercial printing houses emerged and literacy grew. The two fed on each other, giving rise to a wide reading audience. History also teaches that the interweaving of technology and human use can be disturbing. Unintended consequences are common, if not inevitable, as apparently is the case with car phones that were to make our road trips more enjoyable, perhaps make them more productive, and allow us to feel secure in our vehicles. But we now know using car phones also increases the risk of traffic accidents (some say to the level of driving drunk). The point here is that the consequences of a particular IT are known only as routines of practical use emerge, and this takes time—sometimes a very long time.

The second set of studies deals with the rhetoric of IT and organizational transformation. Rhetoric concerns persuasive communication and the uses to which various forms of talk and narrative are put. We are now, for example, caught up in a public rhetoric of progress through advanced computerization giving rise to a desire for the slickest machine, the fastest modem, and the latest update. Visions of the future that rest on notions of rapid technological progress usually try to be comforting and try to evoke a sense of social change in only the most cosmetic and unthreatening ways such that any signs of struggle—between, say, the rich and the poor—vanish. Bringing rhetoric to the study of IT is to reintroduce people and their aims, relationships and ideologies, into a vision of the future in danger of being swamped by gleaming machines, disembodied voices, user dreams, and corporate missions.

Rhetoric bears on reality and surely helps to shape it, but the ways in which it does so rarely are transparent. Consider, for example, the much heralded "paperless office" that was to result from the progressive mechanization and computerization of the business world. Tools that once were thought to allow us to reduce, if not eliminate, the use of paper now have us consuming more paper than ever. There are, of course, a number of ways in which we can examine the rhetoric of IT and organizational transformation. We can examine the rhetoric of those who advocate, design, implement, manage, or otherwise push forward particular technologies. Of considerable importance here is learning what is omitted from such talk (intentionally or unintentionally). We also can examine the rhetoric of those on the receiving end—often a type of dialectic or "counter-rhetoric" stimulated and shaped by advocate claims—to learn of the sense they make of IT and how such sensemaking shapes to use. And, cutting across these fields of interest, we can examine the rhetoric of those who study and write about IT to learn of the ways in which they try to make their respective cases. Authors of the studies presented here take up each of these perspectives and, therefore, make visible the contested social terrain within which IT develops and is used.

The third and final set of chapters concerns the practices that emerge when a new IT is made available to organizational members. Do practices change? How so? These are the questions that, in our view, are central to any serious consideration of organizational transformation. Looking to practice almost guarantees that contradictions, anomalies, and unexpected results will be obtained. E-mail systems are a good example in this regard. Such systems were promoted and institutionalized on the grounds that they provide a fast and efficient means of communication within an organization and across organizations. Many of us take such claims for granted. However, we now are discovering that e-mail also serves as an attractive invitation—an offer we cannot refuse—to send more messages than ever and, therefore, force recipients (and ourselves) to sort through dozens of useless missives to discover the few that are important. A concern for practice takes us to where work is done in organizations, to a consideration of how knowledge is distributed and how the exigencies of work and relations of production are structured in everyday interaction. This is where the action is in organizational life.

Practice is, however, a collective attribute rather than an atomized trait. Practice is shaped in communities held together not by spirit or voluntarism but rather by interpersonal relations based on shared tasks and obligations. Learning on most jobs is a rich process of enculturation as newcomers become members of communities of practice. And as several generations of occupational and organizational ethnographers have documented, how work actually gets done sometimes is the best kept secret in an organization (and perhaps the society as well). Management initiatives—including especially the importation of particular ITs—often look quite odd when we learn how alien they are to the way in which work in an organization actually gets accomplished. To examine how work practices do or do not change when set against a new technology requires in situ fieldwork of a hard slogging sort that invariably results in an appreciation for the refined skills of those studied. Such study must not, of course, indulge a phenomenology of practice alone and banish the larger social, political, and economic processes that surround work such as the efforts of organizational members to protect their job boundaries or management efforts to bring these members to heel. As the authors of the studies of practice appearing in this section know well, the goal of ethnography is the close description of what the people studied do and, to the extent possible, the sense they make of these doings and the changing world around them. Corporate attempts to control workers (or vice versa) do not get lost or ignored by field-workers but rather get picked up by them as control attempts are played out on the ground in always situated ways.

The chapters that follow are, therefore, segmented by three loosely defined analytic perspectives: history, rhetoric, and practice. There is, to be sure, more than a little overlap among the three, and we had a little difficulty in casting some chapters in one category rather than another. What is clear is that the writers located in one section are sensitive to the central concerns of those located in other sections. We did not plan the volume in this way, but we certainly are struck by it now. What is perhaps novel to this collection is, then, this authorial appreciation for the multidimensional and ambiguous character of organizational change as well as the numerous uses to which IT can be put. This breeds a good deal of caution. Predictions are few in this volume, and this is, in our minds, all to the good. The one apparent exception to this rule is that all of the studies presented here imply that the near future will not look too different from the recent past. None of the authors suggests that it is now time to write the elegy for our familiar, if sometimes cursed, organizational forms. Hierarchy, specialization, and rules and regulations are here for the close and probably distant future, just as are conflict and struggle. Finally, we must note with pride that no chapter in this volume announces "the one best way" in which to bring about an organizational transformation or aims, somewhat immodestly, to bring order, rationality, and efficiency to the disorder, irrationality, and general wastefulness of most change efforts. In the end, the scholar's skepticism, trained ears and eyes, eagerness to bring back new tales from the field, and willingness to forgo the pursuit of an ever elusive one and only true theory represent, for us, the most refreshing and useful characteristics of this collection.

PART I

THE HISTORY OF INFORMATION TECHNOLOGY AND ORGANIZATIONAL TRANSFORMATION

Part I provides valuable historical perspective on information technology (IT) and organizational transformation. In today's world of rapid and recurrent upgrades of hardware and software as well as seemingly constant organizational change, we often are too immersed in the details and in apparent relationships between IT and organizational change to see the broad outlines of longer term change. Technologies (including bureaucratic technologies and equipment) that aid us in handling information have been around for millennia, from alphabetic systems to computers. Moreover, organizational forms that seem new today turn out to have been around for centuries at least. The ability to look back at change over longer periods of time provides much needed historical perspective on the interactions between IT and organizations. The three chapters in this part of the volume progress from a period of several centuries, to one of a single century, and finally to one of not quite a decade. Together, they suggest that we question some assumptions about IT and organizations that often are taken for granted.

Our first chapter, "The Role of IT in the Transformation of Work: A Comparison of Post-Industrial, Industrial, and Proto-Industrial Organization" by

Susan J. Winter and S. Lynne Taylor, uses historical evidence from the past 500 years to critique a common contemporary assertion that IT has caused particular transformations of work and organization. Recent literature, they tell us, has suggested causal links from IT to four general changes in work and organization: "1) a flattening of the hierarchy; 2) the disaggregation of functions or outsourcing; 3) an increased use of flexible, dynamic networks or partnerships; and 4) decentralization of the location of work" (p. 7). This chapter challenges these causal links based on two types of historical arguments. First, the authors demonstrate that a comparable popular argument links industrial innovations, such as improvements in mechanical devices and the harnessing of steam power, to organizational and social changes that occurred during the same period. Then, drawing on scholarship from history and social theory, they show how scholars have critiqued this analogous argument as simplistic and technologically deterministic, and they demonstrate some of the social, institutional, and economic factors that also played important roles in that earlier organizational transformation. Based on this analogous argument and its refutation, they suggest that seeking the impact of technology by itself is an inadequate approach; we also must "consider the roots and enablers of the changes, those social, political, legal, economic, and cultural factors" (p. 19) that are necessary for a better explanation of organizational transformation.

Second, Winter and Taylor turn to the organizational changes, such as the four factors just listed, that make up what often is called the "post-industrial" organization. They note that this model of work is very similar to that of the proto-industrial system of "putting out," artisan-based production, and flexible specialization—models of organization common during the early 18th century and surviving in some parts of the economy to the present day. The presence of such models before, during, and after industrialization raises serious questions about the popular link between IT and these modes of organization today. Literature on proto-industrialization suggests factors that should, the authors argue, be examined for their relationships to post-industrial organization including social movements, macroeconomics, and institutional isomorphism (for a discussion of the issue of social movements, see Iacono and Kling [Chapter 4] in Part II of this volume). Winter and Taylor close their contribution by challenging scholars of IT and of modern organizations to perform the research needed to identify nontechnological factors in organizational change and to clarify the relationships among IT, such social and economic factors, and the new organization of work.

In "Information Technology and Organizational Change in the British Census, 1801-1911," Martin Campbell-Kelly uses the history of a single large organization to make another important point about IT and organizational transformation: that information processing, which IT researchers generally see as a post-World War II phenomenon, existed and played a role in organizational change in Victorian England. His fascinating case study of a century of change in the British census—from "a decentralized manual operation, to a centralized manual activity, and finally to a fully mechanized system" (p. 35)—demonstrates that routinized, large-scale data processing characterized by extensive centralization, division of labor, and deskilling existed in the absence of any technology more complex than the bureaucratic technology of forms. Although the author's main argument is different from that of Winter and Taylor, his decade-by-decade narrative of this organization's developments in information handling demonstrates some of the nontechnological factors that Winter and Taylor urged IT researchers to examine in studying IT and organizational change, including the organization of the workforce, the nature of organizational memory in an episodic organization, and other social and cultural forces.

Campbell-Kelly shows, for example, how bureaucratic inertia and a cost-cutting mentality, bolstered by Statistical Superintendent William Ogle's resistance to mechanizing and expanding the social role of the census, led that institution to delay its adoption of office equipment—from the typewriter to punched-card tabulating equipment—for 20 years after the U.S. census adopted similar equipment. During that time, the U.S. census, motivated by a crisis in information processing driven in part by the U.S. appetite for statistical information, leaped ahead in such technology. Although the technology does not seem to have reduced cost per published page of the census reports, it increased the range of data gathered and the extent to which they were analyzed. But in spite of the U.S. lead in census technology, the author argues,

> To characterize the U.S. census as innovative and go-ahead while the British census was conservative and fossilized is too simplistic. In [each case], the response to a technological opportunity was determined by the organization's cultural heritage, its organizational goals, and the need to react to external pressure groups. (p. 56)

Here again, we see the role of nontechnological factors in shaping when and with what effect technological and organizational changes are adopted and to what extent they are linked.

Finally, this part of the volume closes with a piece of recent history. In "Texas Politics and the Fax Revolution" (originally written in 1995), historian Jonathan Coopersmith looks at the influence of facsimile transmission (or faxing) on the political organizing process in Texas during the first part of the 1990s. In preparation for this volume, the author has added a coda to update the story since that time. Although fax technology emerged as a major piece of modern (if relatively low-tech) IT only during the late 1980s, Coopersmith notes that its history is a long one, stretching back to 1843 during the earliest years of telegraph technology. Its delayed organizational adoption and influence reflect the slow speed, high cost, and lack of standards characteristic of available technology until relatively recently. During the early 1990s, fax technology was adopted and used with interesting effect in Texas politics. Although it did not change the underlying content of political organizing, campaigning, and lobbying, the author argues that it enabled the speeding up of the political news cycle. Moreover, "faxing both demands better organization and assists it" (p. 60). Structurally, fax initially had the paradoxical effect of allowing centralized organizations to look decentralized (invoking "Astroturf," rather than grassroots, campaigns) and allowing decentralized organizations to benefit from seemingly centralized coordination. Finally, Coopersmith notes that faxing contributed to an already emerging "technology gap" between the Republican and Democratic parties and related organizations in Texas, reflecting cultural and historical differences between them. This chapter again illustrates the limitations of technological determinism and emphasizes the importance of patterns of IT use in transforming organizations and, in this case, political organizing.

   In his coda, Coopersmith notes changes during the ensuing three years. The relatively low-tech fax has been joined by e-mail, the Internet (particularly the emergence of the World Wide Web), and digital cellular phones as alternative technological tools to facilitate political organizing (for a comparison, see Bazerman [Chapter 5] in Part II of this volume on use of the Web in national-level political organizing). Coopersmith also notes that the gap between political parties in their early use of fax technology in Texas has been narrowed (although not entirely eliminated) with regard to fax and all of the new technologies. With such technologies, early adoption gives a competitive advantage that might seem overwhelming to those in the middle of such a period, but that advantage fades considerably as the technology becomes a taken-for-granted necessity rather than a new toy or weapon. The technology initially has a strong symbolic as well as practical impact, signaling technological savvy. Already, however, Web technology has moved from enabling one side to appear more "modern" to being a taken-for-granted baseline for all "serious" candidates. Even the relatively brief three-year period provides added historical perspective for this story.

   This part of the volume highlights the value of looking backward as well as forward to improve our understanding of the role of IT in organizational transformation. The perspective gained from looking back over several centuries, a single century, and even a few years shifts what we focus on and makes clearer the role of nontechnical factors in shaping the adoption and use of technology. Transformations may unfold over extremely long periods—longer than the time that computers have been around. Even when the changes over a much shorter period seem dramatic, as in the case of fax, the transformation might not be an end point but simply might be a passing stage. The patience to await historical perspective, and the care in unearthing and reconstructing as much of the rich detail of context and practice as is possible, provides a payoff to the researcher. Practitioners, too, do well to lift themselves out of the moment to take a longer view. Without this longer view, they easily may become too caught up in a particular moment, seeing as static developments that are simply freeze-frames in a gradual unfolding over time.

1

The Role of Information Technology in the Transformation of Work

A Comparison of Post-Industrial, Industrial, and Proto-Industrial Organization

SUSAN J. WINTER

S. LYNNE TAYLOR

It has become commonplace in the literature on the workplace of the late twentieth century to describe the profound changes occurring as a third revolution and modern society as post-industrial (Bell 1989; Mills 1991). Four recent interrelated changes in the organization of work that seem to mark this third industrial revolution are (1) a flattening of the hierarchy; (2) the disaggregation of functions or outsourcing; (3) an increased use of flexible, dynamic networks or partnerships; and (4) decentralization of the location of work (Huey 1994; Malone and Rockart 1991; Miles and Snow 1986; *Monthly Labor Review* 1992; Nolan et al. 1988; Quinn 1992; Reich 1991; Rockart and Short 1991). This revolution is widely attributed to the increased importance of information in the economy and the attendant rise in the use of electronics, computing, and telecommunications (Applegate 1994; *Business Week*

From "The Role of IT in the Transformation of Work: A Comparison of Post-Industrial, Industrial, and Proto-Industrial Organization," by Susan J. Winter and S. Lynne Taylor, 1996, *Information Systems Research*, Vol. 7, No. 1, pp. 5-21. Copyright © 1996, Institute for Operations Research and the Management Sciences. Reprinted with permission.

1993; Webber 1993). However, the new flattened, flexible, decentralized organization of work bears a striking resemblance to the proto-industrial system found in Europe before the rise of the modern centralized organization (Goodman and Honeyman 1988; Tilly 1981) and to the form of flexible specialization found during early industrialization, both of which were common well before the rise of the information-based economy, electronics, computers, and telecommunications. This similarity calls into question the claim that advances in information technology (IT) are primarily responsible for this form of organization. A comparison between the proto-industrial, industrial, and post-industrial social and economic systems can question existing causal explanations underlying the organization of work in Europe and North America throughout the past 500 years. This historical analysis allows us to incorporate long-term longitudinal data not usually considered in studies of modern IT and organizational structure, thus building on extant research on industrialization and providing a more complete picture of the causal relationship between the two constructs. Adopting a historical perspective also encourages looking beyond the current ideological preferences that characterize the identification of organizational problems and their appropriate solutions (Kieser 1994).

Few researchers in the field of information systems have investigated, at the macro level of analysis, the relationship between the increased use of electronics, computers, and telecommunications and the changes in the way work is organized. Though the structural changes made by several individual companies have been attributed to changes in technology (see, e.g., Magnet 1992; Malone and Rockart 1991), few carefully controlled, rigorous, scientific studies have been presented to support these espoused causal relations, to rule out alternative explanations, and to illuminate contributing and inhibiting factors (but see Brynjolfsson et al. 1994 for one notable exception). Without such studies, it is difficult to determine the role of technology, even though managers and informants may state that they believe there is a relationship between IT and the changing organization of work. The perceived relationship may be just a widely held societal myth rather than reflecting the true relationship between IT and structure. Similar gaps between widely held IT myths and objective measures of the results of IT use have been found in previous research. For example, Kling and Iacono (1984) found little objective evidence of IT efficiency and effectiveness claims made by organizational informants and concluded that these claims could be considered ideologically influenced myths.

It is even more tenuous to claim that these same organizational-level causes are acting similarly at higher levels of analysis (e.g., the industry or economy level), causing IT to restructure the post-industrial economy. The relationship between IT and the organization of work is a topic that is important to information systems researchers but does not lend itself to the research methods with which most are familiar. It is a topic that would not usually be investigated by economic historians (because it is a contemporary phenomenon) but can best be researched using methods with which they are familiar. This chapter represents a collaborative effort to address the questions: What are the causes of the changing organization of work? Is the shift to a flattened hierarchy, a disaggregation of functions, a decentralized work location, and the use of flexible dynamic networks or partnerships due primarily to the shift to a knowledge-based economy and the increased use of electronics, computers, and telecommunications?

The change to industrialization had a profound impact on organizations and their workers, and the change to post-industrialization will likely have equally profound implications. This chapter investigates this change and considers some possible causes for it using historical analysis. In order to determine the causes of the post-industrial organization of work, we compare it to the industrial organization of work and the proto-industrial system of artisanal and "putting out" manufacturing. We identify strong similarities between post-industrialization, which has been attributed to the use of IT and an information-based economy; proto-industrialization, which was a goods-based manufacturing economy with little IT; and certain forms of workplace organization during industrialization. These similarities cast doubt on the argument that the organization of work is solely and causally linked to the technology. We also review the literature on the role of technology in the organization of work in all three eras to outline the support (or lack thereof) for technological determinism in each of them. Alternative causes of organizational structures are suggested, and implications for future research questions and methods are discussed.

This chapter is organized chronologically. First, we describe the popular version of modern history widely held by laypeople (nonhistorians) and its view of pre-industrial society and of the rise of the current centralized industrial organizational form, its history, and the forces that led to its widespread adoption. We then present a critique of this view based on the historical literature and review the evidence regarding the causes of industrialization. Next, we describe the widely held view of the changes associated with the post-industrial organizational form with an emphasis on the role of IT. Fourth, we present a critique of this view by drawing comparisons between the industrial and post-industrial organization of work in order to illuminate the role of technology in the organization of work and the relevance of other causal agents. Finally, we discuss the implications of this analysis for future research.

TECHNOLOGICAL DETERMINISM

Technological determinism represents a belief that technological forces determine social and cultural changes. The following discussion of technological determinism and history is informed by Smith and Marx (1994). The causal role of technology has been widely accepted in Western culture, and the role of technology as an agent of change is common in the popular view of modern history where it is usually featured in simple, plausible narratives comparing an aspect of society before and after a technological innovation and inferring causation to the sudden appearance of the technical innovation. For example, Smith and Marx (1994) write,

> The printing press is depicted as a virtual cause of the Reformation. Before it was invented, few people . . . owned copies of the bible; after Gutenberg, however, many individual communicants were able to gain direct, personal access to the word of God, on which the Reformation thrived. (pp. x-xi)

The emphasis of these stories is always on the new machine and the changes it causes, not on the forces that led to the invention of this innovation. This deterministic view of technology is a common theme in the popular discourse on such diverse technologies as the automobile (which created suburbia), the birth control pill (which created the sexual revolution), and the computer (which is restructuring the economy and the workplace). This technologically deterministic view, here called the popular version of workplace organization, is described below as it applies to industrialization and, later in the [chapter], as it applies to the post-industrial organization of work. For each of these eras, we present evidence that the popular version is inadequate and argue that social, political, economic, and cultural forces powerfully shape both technological changes and the organization of work.

HISTORICAL PATTERNS OF
ORGANIZING THE WORKPLACE

The Popular Version of Industrialization

The popular version of industrialization commonly accepted among laypersons has it that, over the course of the nineteenth and twentieth centuries, there has been an evolution in the technological and social organization of the workplace from the simple artisanal shop toward large, centralized, bureaucratic places of production structured along the lines of the factory system. The very term "industrialization" is a contentious one, for it can mean many things, but for our purposes, industrialization was the process that resulted in the mechanization of manufacturing and the concentration of labor. It has been argued that this process of industrialization was driven by advances in technology and mechanization (Hamerow 1983; Jones 1987, 1992; Landes 1969; Sussman 1973).

The extensive historical literature on the phenomenon of industrialization has branched in a number of ways including debates concerning changes in the methods of production and the impact of those on the economy and society; the organization of the workplace; the nature and manner of management; the impact of industrialization on workers, both male and (more recently) female; its impact on management; the relationship between industrialization and/or mechanization and labor unrest and organization; and the impact of technology on the workplace, economy, and society. There is much that those interested in understanding the changes in the workplace today could learn from this sizable body of work, if only to avoid the same pitfalls as well as to help frame the questions posed of the late twentieth-century workplace.

The study of industrialization began as a study of the industrial revolution, a phrase first coined by Arnold Toynbee in 1884. It was considered, first and foremost, a technological revolution, the application of mechanical power to manufacturing, which revolutionized not only the process of production but also society and the economy as a consequence. It, in many ways, set the world on the path to modernity, and it began in Great Britain, which became the standard by which other nations' industrial revolutions were measured. This school of thought was masterfully expressed in David Landes's (1969) seminal work, *The Unbound Prometheus*. In it, he defined the industrial revolution as an interrelated succession of technological changes, with material advances in three areas: the substitution of mechanical devices for human skills; the use of inanimate power, especially steam, instead of human and animal strength; and a marked improvement in the obtaining and working of raw materials, especially in the metallurgical and chemical industries. With these changes came a new form of industrial organization, the factory system, followed by the creation of the middle and working classes and, eventually, the consumer culture and market economy of today. In the words of a nineteenth-century Scottish chemist and economist, Andrew Ure,

> The term "Factory," in technology, designates the combined operation of many orders of work-people, adult and young, in tending with assiduous skill a system that is to substitute mechanical science for hand skill, and the partition of a process into its essential constituents for the division or graduation of labor among artisans. On the handicraft plan, labor more or less skilled was usually the most expensive element of production . . . but on the automatic plan, skilled labor gets

progressively superseded and will, eventually, be replaced by mere overlookers
of machines. (quoted in Hamerow 1983, pp. 3-4)

The factory system, then, was the predecessor to what Henry Ford introduced in the late nineteenth century in the United States, continuous flow
production. Essentially, it was the mechanization of production that had previously been done by hand. The efficiencies, economies of scale and scope,
and improved control over production that resulted from this new form of
organization meant that the traditional artisanal or handicraft form of production was unable to compete. A classic example of this process, and of the
industrial revolution, is the textile mills of Britain. With the advent of steam
power, textile manufacturers radically rethought the way in which the manufacture of cloth happened. They built large textile mills with huge looms and
other machinery, all powered by steam, in which they would employ hundreds, eventually thousands, of laborers. The locations of these mills were
determined, first and foremost, by the availability of either running water or
coal, the fuels necessary for the generation of steam power. For the employers, the new form of workplace organization created tremendous opportunities for reaping profits hitherto inconceivable. As a result, the traditional
form of production was gradually displaced by the factory system of production and, by the twentieth century, was supplanted.

Statistical analysis indicated that, beginning in 1780, there was noticeable
improvement in British national production levels, which the statisticians
attributed to the advent of mechanization. Thus, boiled down to its essence,
this school of thought argued that the industrial revolution was technology
driven, was unidirectional (from artisanal to factory production), and was
a revolutionary event with a distinct "take-off point." Furthermore, Great
Britain, being the first to industrialize, was the model which all others sought
to imitate, with greater and lesser degrees of success.

Thus the early historical view of industrialization was that, because of
mechanization, over the course of the nineteenth and twentieth centuries,
there was an evolution in the technological and social organization of the
workplace from the simple artisanal workshop toward large, centralized,
bureaucratic places of production providing a division of labor and structured
along the lines of the mass-production factory system. Late in the industrialization process, organizations began to integrate vertically by acquiring their
competitors and suppliers and by performing their own distribution (Perrow
1986), thus further increasing their size. They also began aggressively marketing their products and developed their own sales forces and research and
development functions, which increased both their size and the degree of differentiation in their structure as departments became more specialized in
their functions (Blau 1970; Blau and Schoenherr 1971; Chandler 1976; Child

1973). Necessarily, there was a dramatic rise in the number of supervisors and managers, often attributed to the application of scientific management and the division of labor along skill lines, which involved the deskilling of production workers and the use of skilled supervisors and managers to plan and control the work (Edwards 1979; Goodman and Honeyman 1988). Management's control of production and the growth of nonproduction functions within the large firm (e.g., marketing, sales, distribution, personnel, research and development) meant that nonproduction white-collar employment expanded considerably throughout the industrialization process, beginning in the late nineteenth century and continuing into the twentieth (Edwards 1979). These new, large, bureaucratic firms generally relied on centralized management through a hierarchy for coordination of tasks and extensive use of large, centralized workplaces. Though manufacturing was the first to adopt the centralized, industrial form, companies providing services were also generally organized along these lines.

In summary, the popular version of industrialization argues that there is a steady evolution in the structure of the workplace from that of the simple artisanal shop to the modern factory floor, from small to large firms, from simple to ponderous bureaucracies, structured along the lines of the factory system. It assumes that these organizational changes are the result of technological innovations and that the new technology required these changes. There is also a sense, in this myth, of the inevitability of progress through industrialization and through factory production as well as a dismissal of craft or artisanal production as inferior, inefficient, and pre-industrial, a hopeless throwback to a bygone era (Edwards 1979; Piore and Sabel 1984). At first glance, this seemed self-evident. Prior to the late eighteenth century, when the industrial revolution began, the European economy was overwhelmingly agrarian in nature, with only a small segment of the workforce employed in manufacturing. Mass production and assembly of interchangeable parts as we know it today did not exist. Manufacturing was largely custom and handicraft in nature, done by hand by skilled artisans, rural and urban, using simple tools, working in small shops, either alone or with a few journeymen and apprentices training with them.

Challenges to the Popular Version

This interpretation has since been challenged on a number of fronts including arguments that the British model was not the best, evidence that forces other than technology were crucial, and the realization that mechanization was not necessary or sufficient to cause the observed changes in the production process. Each of these challenges is now discussed in detail. First, it is now generally accepted by historians that British industrialization was not the only route to industrialization, nor was it a standard against which all others should be measured. Much work has been done investigating the different ways nations have industrialized; these nations emerged with very differently structured, but equally healthy and vibrant, economies as a result. Nations industrialized differently, not because they applied the British model more or less successfully but because key factors specific to each nation shaped the industrialization process, making each path a unique one specific to each country. These factors, the second challenge to the technological determinism of the popular view of industrialization, were the environment or context in which the nature of production was changing. They included a wide range of social, political, legal, economic, and cultural forces which either encouraged or constrained change in the workplace. A brief comparison of British and French industrialization may serve to demonstrate the nature of these forces.

Great Britain was the first nation to industrialize due to a favorable confluence of circumstances encouraging mass production and the development of a mass market (Kemp 1985). In Britain, the structure of feudal agrarian relations had broken down much earlier than on the continent, and in the process, a class of landless wage earners was created who were thrust into the cash economy by dint of circumstance. A large portion of the population depended for its material means of existence upon the production and sale of commodities or upon the sale of its labor power. As the standard of living slowly rose over the course of the nineteenth century, these workers became an important market for cheap, mass-produced goods such as cotton textiles. There was also a new emphasis on individual acquisition and on the rights of property. Wealth, not tradition, became the main determinant of social position, and the nature of acceptable wealth changed dramatically from a landed wealth to include one more fluid, trade based, and commerce based. The guild system had disappeared as well, making it easier to pursue innovation and removing an important barrier to the production of poorer quality, but much less expensive, mass-produced goods. Furthermore, the legal environs facilitated the efforts to engage in mass production, and an extensive credit network existed to provide the necessary capital. In addition, the topography of Britain was advantageous, for it had allowed the establishment of a dense transportation and communications infrastructure in the country, which facilitated the movement of goods. Thus British capitalist entrepreneurs operated in a hospitable environment, where their wealth was deemed socially acceptable.

France developed in a very different manner. It had many of the prerequisites considered necessary for industrialization to flourish including wealth, a growing population, and a flourishing overseas trade. But certain factors pushed French industrial development along a path different from that of Britain. The wealth in France was concentrated in the hands of a very few.

The peasantry, who made up over half of the total population throughout the nineteenth century, subsisted on small plots of land and functioned largely outside the cash economy. Any demand for manufactured goods, therefore, came from groups of nobles, as well as wealthy commoners and a few rich peasants, all of whom comprised only a small portion of the population. The remainder of the population primarily consisted of urban servants, artisans, tradespeople, laborers, and vagrants. They led a hand-to-mouth existence mostly within the cash economy (though bartering was common) and so did not have the economic means required to purchase many manufactured goods. A strong guild system enforced quality standards, preventing mass production of "substandard" goods. Such a marketplace was not conducive to the introduction of mass production. The result was an economy specializing in the production of a variety of high-quality goods in small shops using easily reconfigured, labor-intensive (as opposed to capital-intensive) production processes (Sabel and Zeitlin 1985). Also, investment capital was less available for such a shift, as most of the country's wealth was held in the form of land, and land-owners were loathe to invest in commerce. Finally, the size of France and the lack of internal waterways on the scale of Britain's made the creation of national markets difficult. Once the transportation infrastructure was in place, in which railways played a key role, development did proceed apace (Kemp 1985). Slowly, then, mass production began to develop alongside artisanal variants of production. Yet agriculture continued to dominate the French economy well into the twentieth century. Indeed, the French industrial sector did not embrace mass production wholeheartedly until after World War II, and then only with the assiduous encouragement and assistance of the state, which led the way with the nationalization of industrial firms such as Renault Motorworks as well as utilities and major banks.

So, a variety of factors shaped industrialization in these two countries and ensured that each would industrialize differently. The presence of a large, landless, wage-earning population facilitated a shift to mass production in Britain, and its absence in France acted as a brake, because such a population was needed to supply both a labor force and a mass market for mass-produced goods. The distribution and nature of wealth in each country also shaped the industrialization process. In Britain, much more wealth was available for investment purposes, both because it was not sunk into land and because those with capital were willing to invest in industrialization. The legal environment and the transportation infrastructure also facilitated this kind of venture and investment. The opposite was the case in France. Finally, in Britain, one's social status was not as closely tied to landholding as it was in France. Unlike in France, trade and commerce were considered respectable endeavors in Britain, and success was well received. This list of factors shaping the development of the two nations' economies is hardly comprehensive. Each of these points is the subject of extensive study and exhaustive debate; however, the overall point is clear. Though the technologies available were the same, the British and French experiences were very different, and they were different because of the confluence of a variety of social, political, economic, and cultural factors.

The third challenge to technological determinism has been the realization that mechanization did not always result in changes to the production process, nor were all changes to the production process the result of mechanization. In his seminal article on mid-Victorian England, Raphael Samuel (1977) convincingly demonstrates that, while mechanical power was extensively applied, it by no means reduced workers to the status of mere hands, nor did it replace human labor. Often, he argues, machinery's role in the production process was ancillary, not primary. In his article, he explores a vast array of different industries ranging from coal mining to agriculture, food processing, baking, building, railway construction, glass and pottery industries, leather and wood trades, metallurgy, and ironmongering—all of which, while harnessing steam power where practicable, remained, by and large, labor intensive and often the terrain of a skilled labor force. Ironically, the introduction of machinery often created a demand for new skills on the part of the labor force, as the machinery had to be managed, run, and maintained (Piore and Sabel 1984). Samuel (1977) suggests, then, that the organization of work was not greatly altered with the advent of mechanical power and machinery, but instead, mechanical power and machinery were adapted to the workplace.

The converse has also proven true in some areas; organizational changes to the production process have occurred without the impetus of mechanization and even well before the advent of mechanization. Recent research into proto-industrialization in Europe, however controversial the subject may be, has greatly expanded our understanding in this area (Berg et al. 1983; Houston and Snell 1984; Mendels 1972; Mendels and Deyon 1982; Mills 1982). Much of its focus has been on the putting-out system of industrial organization. Merchant-entrepreneurs purchased raw materials to sell to middlemen called factors. The factors, in turn, hired workers to transform the raw materials into a finished product and then sold the transformed product back to the merchant-entrepreneurs. The workers were paid by the factors on a piece rate from the proceeds (Goodman and Honeyman 1988). Putting out typically (but not exclusively) occurred in those rural areas where there was a large landless or land-poor rural population. Those agricultural workers who were unable to earn adequate wages in agriculture (and this was the vast majority of them due to several reasons including poor wages and the seasonal nature of employment) were the ones available for supplementary employment by the merchant-entrepreneurs. Rural industry became an important form of supplementary employment for large segments of rural populations. But proto-industrialization was more than just rural manufacture. It was nascent industrialization, with a complex and rigid division of labor geared to the international, not local, market and developed in symbiosis with commercial agriculture, or so it was argued. Whether one agrees with the notion of proto-industrialization or not, the literature has brought to light not only the putting-out system but also premechanization innovations in subcontracting, the division of labor, international distribution, cooperative and shared ventures, marketing techniques, credit arrangements, and product innovation. The presence of these innovations, as seen during proto-industrialization, thus defies the assumption that such innovation only came with the advent of mass-production processes and the concomitant changes to the structure of management, markets, and marketing (Berg 1993, 1994).

What also has become apparent as historians have explored the process of industrialization is that the stereotypical large mass-production factory was and is far from the only method of organizing work. Small craft-based firms continued to exist and thrive beside large conglomerates well into the twentieth century (Edwards 1979). Initially, Piore (1980) and others developed the theory of industrial dualism in order to explain the persistence of small firms. This theory holds that a mass-production economy required the presence of a healthy custom or craft-based sector to manufacture the specialized machinery required for mass production of interchangeable parts and to service markets with high rates of fluctuation or low levels of demand. While mass production meant the manufacture of general goods through the use of specialized resources and capital equipment, at the same time, that created a need for specialized machines and finely divided and trained labor to build them. Ironically, the special-purpose machinery required could not be mass-produced, so on the very fringe of every industry there were small firms to service the large. Yet the assumption that the backbone of the economy was mass production and the factory system remained intact.

Several historians (Sabel and Zeitlin 1985; Scranton 1991) have objected to this explanation and argued that it does not do justice to the most famous industrial districts of the nineteenth century (such as Lyon, St-Etienne, Solingen, Remscheld, Sheffield, Roubaix, Cincinnati, Philadelphia, and Pawtucket), which operated in a rather different fashion, and very successfully, at least until the world wars. These districts were hives of small firms that practiced an alternate form of industrial organization called "flexible specialization." It was a craft alternative to mass production that rejected a strategy of manufacturing large numbers of any one product and, instead, focused on creating the capacity to manufacture diverse products to fill fluctuating demand.

Those firms that practiced flexible specialization shared common characteristics. They produced a wide range of goods to suit the needs of highly differentiated regional markets at home and abroad, and they could alter the mix of goods to match changing markets and tastes and to take advantage of new opportunities as they arose. This required the flexible use of an increasingly more productive and widely applicable technology and an environment that encouraged permanent innovation. The technology had to be flexible in order to allow quick and inexpensive shifts from one product to another within a family of products and to permit the constant expansion of the range of materials worked and operations performed, facilitating the shift from one family of products to another. These firms banded together in various forms of cooperatives, dependent upon the particular characteristics of the regional society, economy, and political structure. The purpose of doing so was threefold: to stabilize the region's industry to the benefit of all; to prevent disastrous competition and, instead, promote judicious cooperation; and to facilitate the promotion of innovation, which would have been much more difficult, if impossible, for a small shop to do on its own (Best 1990; Piore and Sabel 1984; Scranton 1991).

Others, notably Maxine Berg (1994), have objected to the stark distinction drawn between small and large firms and, concomitantly, the traditional and modern industrial sectors, even by Piore and Sabel (1984). Her concern (similar to that of Williams et al. 1987) is that many manufacturers borrowed techniques from both of these sectors, thus really straddling the divide and rendering it methodologically problematic. Whichever side of the debate one chooses, it is apparent that the nineteenth and twentieth centuries witnessed anything but a unidirectional shift from artisanal to factory production due to advances in technology.

A further implication of proto-industrialization was that the industrial revolution was not a revolution at all. If industrialization had its roots in the cottage manufacturing of the seventeenth century, and if the advent of mechanization and especially steam power was not responsible for its "kick-start," then the changes to the structure of the European economy had been a long time in happening and the revolution was not so revolutionary or abrupt after all. This debate was heightened by Crafts (1976) and Wrigley and Schofield (1981), among others, when they reworked the statistical information used by Deane and Cole (1962) to show that there was a marked "kink in the curve" of national production after mechanization. Their conclusion was that overall growth was slower than had been thought and that the story was one of continuity and stability, not dramatic upheaval (Berg 1994; Landes 1991). So, the debate continues between those who argue that the numbers deny that anything revolutionary occurred and those, like Landes (1991) and Berg (1994), who argue that, whether the numbers reveal it or not, "there was a break

[which] was indeed revolutionary in its import. It consisted in new ways of doing things, supported by new ways of thinking about the problems and tasks of productions" (Landes 1991, p. 13).

One conclusion that may be drawn from this brief survey of a complex body of literature is this: If we wish to understand the changes in the workplace of yesteryear or the changes in today's workplace, we must consider not only the impact of technology. We must also consider the roots and enablers of the changes, those social, political, legal, economic, and cultural factors that help to explain why things have changed as they have in the past and are changing in the manner in which they are changing today.

The Emerging Popular Interpretation of Post-Industrialization

Because the causal role of technology has been widely accepted in Western popular culture (Smith and Marx 1994), it is not surprising to find that computers are often identified as powerful agents of social and economic change ushering in the new "post-industrial" form of organization (Bell 1989; Bolter 1984; *Business Week* 1993; Davidow and Malone 1992; *Monthly Labor Review* 1992; Sussman 1973). This new story is similar to the industrialization myth in that it emphasizes technology as the causal agent and considers the new flexible, dynamic form of organization the next step in a natural and ever-improving evolution in the organization of work and one that mirrors the evolution of technology and is partly caused by it.

Indeed, many authors, when arguing for a deterministic model of social and cultural change, explicitly draw an analogy between IT and the causal nature of previous technological innovations. For example, Bolter (1984) claims that IT is a defining technology of our time because it changes our relationship to nature just as the clock and the steam engine were defining technologies in their time. His technologically deterministic view of both current and historical changes is clearly shown by his statements that "once the new technology [the clock] was called forth, it proceeded with its own relentless logic and eventually helped to reorder the values of the whole culture" (Bolter 1984, p. 100) and that "the computer is the contemporary analog of the clocks and steam engines of the previous six centuries. . . . We will be different people because we live with [computers]" (Bolter 1984, p. 10).

Though the causal agents and mechanisms of change are still debatable, overall, the description of the new post-industrial organization of work presented in the media is fairly consistent. While the early and mid-twentieth century appeared to be marked by considerable growth in the size of firms and by the gradual integration and aggregation of business functions, the late twentieth century seem[ed] marked by a trend in the opposite direction. Recently, the large proportion of nonproduction (mostly white-collar, middle management, or professional) workers have come to be seen as a drain on competitiveness in both Western and Japanese companies (*Economist* 1995d; Thurow 1986; Tomasko 1987). (However, see *Economist* 1995a for the opposing view arguing that companies that have dismissed many middle managers are now coming to realize the value of the knowledge and perspective they have lost.) Many top management teams have been trying to create organizations that are leaner, meaner, and more flexible in order to meet the challenges of rapidly changing technologies and the vagaries of an apparently more dynamic economy (Best 1990; Labib and Appelbaum 1994).

Thus, in many firms, the traditional organizational structure is now changing in ways that have purportedly been caused by new advances in computerized information systems and new information technologies, which have reduced the demand for labor and lowered the costs of managing information. As stated in the *Monthly Labor Review* (1992),

> Vital to the new economy are flexible and information-based technologies, the most important being the computer. Such technologies permit higher productivity and quality and the tailoring of products and services to smaller markets and even to individual customers. (*Monthly Labor Review* 1992, p. 44)

Many who study IT believe that improved telecommunications has reduced the advantages of intrafirm management and performance of professional staff activities (e.g., MIS [management information systems], personnel, marketing, research) and reduced the need for middle managers as conduits for information (Gurbaxani and Whang 1991; Malone and Rockart 1991; Miles and Snow 1986; Reddy 1990; Rockart and Short 1989). The advantages of the large firm, which were seen as rooted in the low costs of intrafirm communications, are seen as eroded by the rapid decline in the costs of interfirm communication (Malone et al. 1987; Miles and Snow 1986; Mills 1991; Nilles et al. 1976; Olson 1983; Reddy 1990). According to this school of thought, because of advances in IT and the move to an information-based economy, it is no longer necessary to perform all aspects of the production, commerce, and distribution processes in-house or to locate them all in one geographic place (Brynjolfsson et al. 1994). Malone and Rockart (1991) explicitly reported that, based on their research on the effect of IT on the cost of information, "information technology should lead to an overall shift from internal decisions within firms to the use of markets to coordinate economic activity" (p. 131).

Thus firms in some industries have come to rely on external sources for a larger number of components and for administrative and support services, which often results in the disaggregation or "spinning off" of portions of these activities to other organizations. Some of the production functions and many of the staff functions performed by professionals in large organizations are now being contracted out to smaller, more specialized firms. Increasingly, organizations are dispersing geographically and disaggregating; entire administrative functions and production of components that were previously performed in-house are now contracted out or performed by temporary workers on a contract basis. Now, it is argued, organizations should limit their own operations to a few core areas of competence and engage in partnerships with other firms that have different areas of competence in order to produce a product or provide a service. The new structure has been called the dynamic network organizational form and has been associated with the widespread downsizing of organizations and the firing of many nonproduction, white-collar workers (Best 1990; Malone and Rockart 1991; Miles and Snow 1986; Piore and Sabel 1984; Reddy 1990; Rockart and Short 1989).

Concurrently, much of the work control function formerly performed by supervisors and middle managers is now seen as superfluous; increasingly, these activities are seen as embedded in the ubiquitous computer hardware and software. As Jackson and Humble (1994) write, "Information technology is increasingly making information easier to access and share, replacing the middle manager's traditional role as a key link in the communication chain" (p. 16). The number of managerial employees in large firms is shrinking, and scholars have associated this with the use of IT. Downsizing has become widespread over the last five years (Cameron et al. 1991; Freeman and Cameron 1993; Labib and Appelbaum 1994) and has become an accepted, almost routine way of managing; many believe it will remain common during the foreseeable future.

Simultaneously, growth in the geographic dispersion of work, in self-employment, in the business services sector generally, and in the temporary worker industry in particular has been very rapid (Carey and Hazelbaker 1986; Howe 1986; Pearson 1986). It is difficult to get accurate data on the size of the "contingent" workforce including part-timers, freelancers, subcontractors, independent professionals, and temporary workers. However, in his widely read book, *The Age of Unreason,* Charles Handy (1989) stated that "less than half of the workforce in the industrial world will be in 'proper' full-time jobs in organizations by the beginning of the twenty-first century" (p. 31), and one recent estimate is that the contingent workforce has already exceeded 28 percent of U.S. workers (Greenbaum 1994). Many of the workers who have been fired have started their own small businesses or consulting firms, competing for contracts in the marketplace. Others have filled a series of temporary positions either through temporary agencies or independently. Concurrently, we have seen a rise in home-based work and telecommuting through the use of IT. Martino and Wirth (1990) explicitly attribute this growth to the lower cost of IT. They state that "technological innovation is a leading factor in the development of telework" (p. 534). Future growth of employment in large organizations may well be nonexistent. A large and growing sector of the workforce that would previously have entered a stable long-term employment relationship with a large, hierarchical organization will, instead, likely engage in a series of temporary contractual arrangements to provide a service or product for a limited period of time, much as workers did before the industrial revolution.

It appears, then, that we may be in the midst of yet another industrial revolution or at another "industrial divide" (Piore and Sabel 1984), precipitated by the use of the computer and the shift to a knowledge-based economy and with profound changes being made to the workplace and concomitant changes to society as a whole. IT seems to be restructuring the economy into a more flexible, dynamic network of organizations, with many smaller, leaner firms narrowly focused on their areas of competence and engaged in temporary partnerships with other firms in order to produce a product or provide a service in response to fluctuating demand. Interestingly, this scenario shares many characteristics of the flexible specialization form of industrial organization found in some manufacturing districts of the nineteenth century and currently seen in such areas as the textile district of Prato [in Italy] and the computer industry in the Silicon Valley of California (Sabel and Zeitlin 1985; Scranton 1991). Some authors (Best 1990; Piore and Sabel 1984) have argued that IT has forced more firms to adopt this form of industrial organization, and so the social, cultural, and economic conditions that arose to support these districts in the past must be established today to support flexible specialization, prevent disastrous competition, and promote innovation.

Challenges to This Popular Version

While the changes currently being made in the organization of work are profound, management researchers are not generally investigating their causes in a comprehensive and systematic fashion. Consequently, an oversimplified and often misleading story is being told about the causes of the shift to the post-industrial form of organization. This new myth is similar to the industrialization myth in that it emphasizes technology as the causal agent and considers the flexible, dynamic form of organization a natural and ever-improving evolution in the organization of work, one that mirrors the evolution of technology and is primarily caused by it. However, as we have shown in our historical analysis, this flexible form is not new. It was historically common in many industries, in the forms of flexible specialization and the putting-out system of manufacturing, and has persisted into contemporary times in some (Best 1990; Piore and Sabel 1984; Sabel and Zeitlin 1985; Williams et al. 1987).

Similarly, the myth of technological determinism has been exploded for industrialization (Smith and Marx 1994), and there is no proof of its truth for post-industrialization. Though advances in IT may be affecting the organization of work, other factors may be equally important in explaining the shift away from the typical industrial form (Best 1990; Scranton 1991). Without careful and detailed research, causation is impossible to determine. Several theories have been suggested to explain the changes observed, but none has adequately addressed the questions: Why have these particular changes occurred? Why have these changes occurred now and not earlier or later? Without theories that are sufficiently well developed to address these issues, testable hypotheses cannot be derived, and so the theories are no more useful than tautologies. Several of the causal agents widely accepted in the literature are described below with a critique of the evidence for their relationship to IT and to the organization of work. These agents include flexibility in the location of work, disintegration of the mass market, compression of time and space, the increasing pace of change, increasing levels of risk, increased flexibility, and global competition.

It has been suggested that the availability of IT has now rendered the location of work more flexible and that this has caused the decentralization of work (using satellite offices or working from home) (Martino and Wirth 1990). The popular view of the industrial revolution posits that the location of work became centralized primarily because the new technology required access to a centralized power source (e.g., water power, the steam engine). However, electricity has provided an opportunity for decentralization of the power supply and, therefore, decentralization of the place of work since the early 1890s, but it has not appreciably affected the geographic dispersion of workers. No explanation is provided in the literature for why IT has countered this long-standing tradition of a centralized workplace, but electricity did not. Therefore, there is no consistent evidence of the technology as the main driving force for decentralization. There may be other factors associated with IT that were not associated with electricity (such as the ability to closely supervise workers), but these must be illuminated by theory before they can be tested.

Similarly, another reason cited for the change to a flexible work organization is the decline of the mass market and the demand for customized products (Piore and Sabel 1984). One of the critical limits to mass production is the development of a mass market for consumption of standard products (Sabel and Zeitlin 1985; Scranton 1991). However, during industrialization, the mass market was specifically created by mass producers, often through advertising and marketing (Sabel and Zeitlin 1985; Sussman 1973). The literature on IT and the organization of work has not shown that the mass market is substantially disintegrating, explained why it is breaking down now, or explained why producers cannot develop additional mass markets (particularly with the increasingly global marketplace) in Eastern Europe, Africa, and the Far East (Williams et al. 1987). Without evidence of a disintegration of the market and an explanation of why manufacturers were once able to create a mass market to support industrialization but are no longer able to do so, this claim becomes a tautology, not a testable theory.

Another reason cited for the change to a flexible work organization is the capability of IT to compress time and space. However, IT has been doing so for the last 150 years in the form of the telegraph and the telephone (Yates and Benjamin 1991). So, why are we seeing the change in organizational forms now? Perhaps we have crossed a crucial cost threshold. Only carefully performed studies will be able to answer this question and illuminate where this threshold lies.

The increased pace of change and the increased level of risk experienced by owners of businesses have also been cited as causes of the change to a flexible work organization. However, there has been no objective, quantitative, empirical, economic evidence presented of changes in environmental turbulence over the last 30 years (the period of post-industrialization) (Holbein 1993). Furthermore, there is considerable evidence that perceptions of environmental dynamism (upon which changes in organizational structure are based) are not generally related to objective measures of turbulence (Boyd et al. 1993; Holbein 1993; Milliken 1987). Finally, historical analysis shows other economically risky periods (including wars, depressions, and massive unemployment) that did not result in an appreciable increase in the flexible organization form.

Two additional reasons cited for the change are that the technology has become more flexible (i.e., computer-aided design, computer-integrated manufacturing) and multifunctional and that the marketplace has become increasingly global; therefore, the level of competition has increased (Piore and Sabel 1984). However, Williams and his colleagues (1987) strongly argued that potential flexibility is quite different from flexibility in use and that most "flexible manufacturing systems" in the United States are not used very flexibly and that, indeed, most advanced computer capabilities are not used. Furthermore, they argued that computerized manufacturing technology (with its high capital expense and development costs) does not fundamentally change the scale economies of manufacturers and so does not generally disadvantage mass producers relative to batch producers. Firms selling to a larger market would still be at an advantage because they could spread their fixed costs over more customers (*Economist* 1995c; Williams et al. 1987). Furthermore, historical evidence has not been presented showing a sharp increase in the level of competition experienced by firms and industries in which changes in the organization of work are occurring. There is, however, some evidence that globalization provides some additional distinct advantages to multinational firms (e.g., global reach, decreasing risk, knowledge management, economies of time) over smaller firms (*Economist* 1995c) by opening even larger mass markets. Globalization has been associated with increases in average firm size when other variables were controlled (Brynjolfsson et al. 1994).

Interestingly, these two characteristics (flexibility and globalization) were shared with the artisanal and putting-out manufacturing systems of proto-industrialization and with flexible specialization. The simple hand tools and machine tools used in such systems were more multifunctional, requiring more skill on the part of the worker. In the period of proto-industrialization, strong trading ties existed among the Western European nations and among the colonial powers and their colonies, and many of the manufactured goods (particularly those involved in manufacturing cloth) were traded throughout Europe, Asia, and the Americas. Perhaps the change in the organization of work is due more to the potential flexibility of the technology, to the renewed globalization of trade, or to the combination of flexibility and globalization than to the presence of IT per se. However, so far, there has been insufficient research into this area to draw firm conclusions. Furthermore, what evidence has accumulated casts doubt on the adequacy of these explanations alone (Brynjolfsson et al. 1994; Williams et al. 1987). Future research is needed to understand the roles of flexibility and globalization in the organization of work. In summary, there is insufficient evidence to support the conclusion that IT has caused widespread changes in the organization of work due to its flexibility, compression of time and space, the disintegration of the mass market, or increasing levels of risk or global competition.

Of course, not all researchers investigating the changing nature of work have taken a hard-line, technologically determinist position; some have taken more social constructionist positions (Best 1990; Lloyd-Jones and Lewis 1994; Piore and Sabel 1984; Scranton 1991). Social constructionists believe that social and cultural forces give different social meanings to artifacts and so strongly affect technological changes. These groups are seen to influence the selection of those designs that solve the problems of powerful interest groups and that fill their needs (Hughes 1994). An in-depth treatment of the various arguments surrounding technological determinism versus social construction is not possible here (interested readers may want to investigate Smith and Marx 1994). However, the social construction literature on industrialization and on post-industrialization can illuminate likely nontechnical agents affecting the current changes in the organization of work. The importance of these factors is argued below, and a suggestive list of likely agents is reviewed as the first step in developing a theory about the relationship between IT and the organization of work.

The first step in building a more complete and accurate model of the forces affecting the changing organization of work is to determine which types of organizations are changing and which are not. Currently, it is not clear which sectors of the economy in various countries are organized in the industrial form, which have been organized in the flexible form, and how the mix of organizational forms has changed historically. Though some evidence is available regarding the factors associated with changes in the organization of work for specific industries in specific geographic areas during specific periods of time (see, e.g., Lloyd-Jones and Lewis 1994; Scranton 1991), much more work will be needed to illuminate the interaction between technology, society, and the organization of work. Future research should focus on additional detailed descriptions of the mix of structures for various industries and markets, both now and in the past, in order to further develop the search for correlates that may be causally linked to the structure of work. Without such careful, descriptive work, it is too easy to be influenced by a few rare and recent, but memorable, examples of flexible organizations and to overestimate the extent of the changes taking place.

Likely conditions affecting the shift to smaller organizations, outsourcing, and downsizing seen in post-industrialization are new configurations of the social, political, and economic factors that affected industrialization. Though this does not represent an exhaustive list, some likely inhibiting or encouraging factors include the following: changing cultural norms, macroeconomic forces, demographics and labor relations, and legal conditions. Each of these is briefly discussed below.

One possibility is that the societal norms about how efficient and productive organizations should be structured have changed over the last 30 years. In explaining the recent interest in entrepreneurship, Bruce Kirchhoff (1994) suggests that after exposure to the Depression and World War II, American society came to respect and admire large corporations and the public sector because of their demonstrated ability to meet these national challenges and to see them as the preferred source of employment, as the primary source of wealth creation, and as the best means of wealth distribution. However, this respect and admiration has been greatly eroded recently and replaced by a view of large corporations and government as wasteful and inefficient.

According to the theory of institutionalization, organizations whose structures respond to the pressures of institutions in their environment (regardless of their operational advantages) and, therefore, reflect the norms of society, gain legitimacy and the resources they require for survival. Thus they are more likely to prosper (DiMaggio and Powell 1983; King et al. 1994; Meyer and Rowan 1977). Consequently, organizations within an institutional environment will become similar to each other. Institutionalization is most likely to be seen in situations where criteria for organizational performance and the best means to achieve these are unclear, companies are highly regulated, and interorganizational relationships are common (DiMaggio and Powell 1983). There is some evidence of the propagation of the factory form of manufacturing throughout the economy due to institutionalization, particularly just after World War I. Some national governments (powerful institutions) actively encouraged the conversion to mass production after World War II (Sabel and Zeitlin 1985) as a form of "modernization." It is equally likely that organizations of today would be strongly influenced by their culture's norms regarding appropriate structure and levels of efficiency.

Previous researchers illuminated the impact of macroeconomic forces on the organization of work in much more detail than can be covered here. However, we briefly touch on a couple of fundamental issues. One is the use or abandonment of the gold standard with the shift to floating exchange rates (Lloyd-Jones and Lewis 1994; Piore and Sabel 1984) and the relative strength and volatility of various currencies as a determinant of the cost and location of production (*Economist* 1995d). Another is the rate of inflation, the pursuit of deflationary or inflationary monetary policies, the stability and levels of interest rates, the availability of capital for investment and expansion, and the ability to move capital internationally (Best 1990; *Economist* 1995b; Scranton 1991). All of these forces affect a firm's strategy and tactics as it pursues profits and are likely to influence choices about the organization of work through their effects on the costs and availability of capital, labor, and other resources. Many of these effects are simple and immediate, but some may require a specific configuration of influences or may take years to develop.

A related issue is the amount and type of legal regulations and their enforcement. These can include tariff protection and agreements, free-trade treaties, antitrust laws, product and owner liability laws, international commerce and contract law, labor laws, and taxation rates. Japan's relatively closed markets are often cited as a major cause of Japanese companies' economic success (Best 1990). In rejecting the computer as a cause of the current economic restructuring, public policy professor David Howell (1995) suggests that legal restrictions may be a more powerful influence. He explains that in the United States, institutions designed to protect low-skilled workers from wage competition have recently been dismantled, labor law monitoring has declined, and the real value of the minimum wage has diminished.

This change in the legal environment, not IT, has led U.S. firms to attempt to gain competitive advantage by reducing labor costs through increased use of temporary, part-time, contract, and off-site workers in the United States and abroad. Indeed, lax standards for labor and environmental protection and reduced owner liability are often cited as powerful forces drawing many organizations to move their facilities out of the industrialized countries altogether.

Other issues likely to affect the changing organization of work include demographics and labor relations. Some researchers see computer technology and the new organization of work as an opportunity to reduce the power of labor by replacing it with capital or fragmenting workers into various categories with divergent interests (i.e., full-time vs. part-time, contractual vs. permanent, home based vs. office based) (Greenbaum 1994). Increases in the unemployment rate certainly improve the bargaining position of employers relative to employees. The current shift in the United States and Canada to an older population may result in a demand for more services and fewer new durable goods, thus shrinking the mass market for these goods.

In summary, IT has been widely accepted as the driving force behind the changing organization of work, which in turn has been credited with increasing efficiency, effectiveness, and quality while providing faster time to market, lower overhead costs, increased customization, and, therefore, improved competitiveness (see, e.g., Magnet 1992; Malone and Rockart 1991). However, empirical evidence of these benefits has been inconsistent at best (*Business Week* 1993; *Economist* 1995a) and often nonexistent (Cascio 1993; Labib and Appelbaum 1994). A flattened hierarchy, disaggregation of functions, decentralization of work location, and increased use of partnerships are expected to lead to a renewed reliance on temporary subcontracting and self-employment. Interestingly, this "new" organizational structure of the workplace is strikingly similar to past models, such as proto-industrialization and flexible specialization (Mendels 1972; Mendels and Deyon 1982; Sabel and Zeitlin 1985), which arose without the presence of IT. The current literature on causes of these recent changes in the organization of work has proven inadequate to account for the shift away from industrialization. To illuminate what is happening to the world of work and to explain why it is happening, we need to concentrate on three areas: (1) producing better, more detailed, descriptive research on the changes occurring; (2) developing clearer, more complete, less simplistic theories on the causes of the changes from which testable hypotheses can be developed; and (3) performing systematic theory-testing research to illuminate the causes of the organization of work during modern times, recent history, and pre-industrial history.

CONCLUSIONS

The similarities between the "new" organizational structure being touted today as industry's salvation and other, older models such as the putting-out system, artisanal production, and flexible specialization are striking. They also warn us against quickly assuming that the "new" organizational structure is simply the result of recent changes in technology. Instead, we need to consider the possibility of social, economic, political, and cultural causes of this organizational change while clarifying the role of technology.

It is possible that the similarities between the proto-industrial and post-industrial eras are due to common goals. In each case, the central decision makers sought and seek to reduce their risk as well as to obtain more flexibility. Such flexibility would, and did, permit a firm to respond more quickly to changing technologies and markets while minimizing the cost to the firm of adapting to those changing technologies. The flexibility also permits a firm to protect itself from the vagaries of an increasingly unstable economy. Another possibility is that the organizational changes, past and present, came as the result of social movements, macroeconomics, and forces of institutionalization rather than technology. Though there is considerable evidence of social and economic influence in determining the trajectory of industrialization (Goodman and Honeyman 1988; Jones 1987, 1992; Piore and Sabel 1984; Sabel and Zeitlin 1985; Scranton 1991), little research on post-industrialization has focused on social and economic influences and on how they are affecting this transformation of work. It is also likely that institutions are affecting the decisions made by managers to make the changes associated with this "new" form of organization.

It seems that if the challenge is to try to understand the nature of the changes rocking the workplace today and, secondly, to understand and manage the possible consequences of those changes, the historical literature could be useful in helping us identify the questions that need to be asked. It gives us a useful place to start by identifying factors that shaped the workplace in the past and which may be shaping it today.[1]

NOTE

1. This research was partially supported by a grant from the Social Sciences and Humanities Research Council. An earlier version was presented at the National Academy of Management Meetings in 1995 in Vancouver, BC.

REFERENCES

Applegate, L., "Managing in an Information Age: Transforming the Organization for the 1990s," in *Transforming Organizations With Information Technology,* S. Smithson, R. Baskerville, O. Ngwenyama, and J. DeGross (Eds.), Elsevier, North-Holland, Amsterdam, 1994, 15-95.

Bell, D., "The Third Technological Revolution and Its Possible Socioeconomic Consequences," *Dissent,* Spring (1989), 165-176.

Berg, M., "Small Producer Capitalism in Eighteenth-Century England," *Business History,* 35, 1 (1993), 17-39.

——, *The Age of Manufactures 1700-1820: Industry, Innovation, and Work in Britain,* 2nd ed., Routledge, New York, 1994.

——, P. Hudson, and M. Sonenscher (Eds.), *Manufacture in Town and Country Before the Factory,* Cambridge University Press, Cambridge, UK, 1983.

Best, M. H., *The New Competition: Institutions of Industrial Restructuring,* Polity Press, Cambridge, UK, 1990.

Blau, P. M., "A Formal Theory of Differentiation in Organizations," *American Sociological Rev.,* 35 (1970), 201-218.

—— and R. A. Schoenherr, *The Structure of Organizations,* Basic Books, New York, 1971.

Bolter, J. D., *Turing's Man: Western Culture in the Computer Age,* University of North Carolina Press, Chapel Hill, NC, 1984.

Boyd, B. K., G. G. Dess, and A. M. A. Rasheed, "Divergence Between Archival and Perceptual Measures of the Environment: Causes and Consequences," *Acad. Management Rev.,* 18, 3 (1993), 204-226.

Brynjolfsson, E., T. W. Malone, V. Gurbaxani, and A. Kambil, "Does Information Technology Lead to Smaller Firms?" *Management Sci.,* 40, 12 (1994), 1628-1644.

Business Week, "The Virtual Corporation: The Company of the Future Will Be the Ultimate in Adaptability," February 8, 1993, 98-103.

Cameron, K., S. J. Freeman, and A. K. Mishra, "Best Practices in White-Collar Downsizing: Managing Contradictions," *Acad. Management Executive,* 5, 3 (1991), 57-73.

Carey, M. L. and K. L. Hazelbaker, "Employment Growth in the Temporary Help Industry," *Monthly Labor Rev.,* 109, 4 (1986), 37-44.

Cascio, W. F., "Downsizing: What Do We Know? What Have We Learned?" *Acad. Management Executive,* 7, 1 (1993), 95-104.

Chandler, A. D., Jr., *The Visible Hand,* Harvard University Press, Cambridge, MA, 1976.

Child, J., "Predicting and Understanding Organization Structure," *Admin. Sci. Quarterly,* 18 (1973), 168-185.

Crafts, N. F. R., "English Economic Growth in the Eighteenth Century: A Re-examination of Deane and Cole's Estimates," *Economic History Rev.,* 29 (1976), 226-235.

Davidow, W. H. and M. S. Malone, *The Virtual Corporation,* HarperCollins, New York, 1992.

Deane, P. and W. A. Cole, *British Economic Growth, 1688-1959: Trends and Structure,* Cambridge University Press, Cambridge, UK, 1962.

DiMaggio, P. J. and W. W. Powell, "The Iron Cage Revisited: Institutional Isomorphism and Collective Rationality in Organizational Fields," *American Sociological Rev.,* 48, April (1983), 147-160.

Economist, "The Salaryman Rides Again," February 4, 1995a, 64-66.

——, "The Puzzling Infirmity of America's Small Firms," February 18, 1995b, 63-65.

——, "Alive and Kicking: The Death of the Multinational Has Been Much Exaggerated," U.S. edition, June 24, 1995c, S20-S25.

————, "Japan Looks West: Time for a Little Corporate Role Reversal," U.S. edition, June 24, 1995d, S16-S19.

Edwards, R., *Contested Terrain: The Transformation of the Workplace in the Twentieth Century,* Basic Books, New York, 1979.

Freeman, S. J. and K. S. Cameron, "Organizational Downsizing: A Convergence and Reorientation Framework," *Organization Sci.,* 4, 1 (1993), 10-29.

Goodman, J. and K. Honeyman, *Gainful Pursuits: The Making of Industrial Europe 1600-1914,* Edward Arnold, London, 1988.

Greenbaum, J., "The Forest and the Trees: Defining Labor Skills," *Monthly Rev.,* 46, 6 (1994), 60-66.

Gurbaxani, V. and S. Whang, "The Impact of Information Systems on Organizations and Markets," *Comm. ACM,* 34, 1 (1991), 59-73.

Hamerow, T. S., *The Birth of a New Europe: State and Society in the Nineteenth Century,* University of North Carolina Press, Chapel Hill, NC, 1983.

Handy, C., *The Age of Unreason,* Harvard Business School Press, Boston, 1989.

Holbein, G. F., "A Longitudinal Assessment of Environmental Dynamism," presented at the National Academy of Management meeting, Atlanta, GA, 1993.

Houston, R. and K. Snell, "Proto-Industrialisation? Cottage Industry, Social Change, and the Industrial Revolution," *Historical J.,* 27, 2 (1984), 473-492.

Howe, W. J., "The Business Services Industry Sets Pace in Employment Growth," *Monthly Labor Rev.,* 109, 4 (1986), 29-36.

Howell, D. R., "Collapsing Wages and Rising Inequality: Has Computerization Shifted the Demand for Skills?" *Challenge,* 38, 1 (1995), 27-35.

Huey, J., "The New Post-Heroic Leadership," *Fortune,* February 21, 1994, 42-50.

Hughes, T. P., "Technological Momentum," in *Does Technology Drive History? The Dilemma of Technological Determinism,* M. R. Smith and L. Marx (Eds.), MIT Press, Cambridge, MA, 1994, 101-113.

Jackson, D. and J. Humble, "Middle Managers: New Purpose, New Directions," *J. Management Development,* 13, 3 (1994), 15-21.

Jones, S. R. H., "Technology, Transaction Costs, and the Transition to Factory Production in the British Silk Industry, 1700-1870," *J. Economic History,* 17 (1987), 71-96.

————, "The Emergence of the Factory System in 18th Century England: Did Transportation Improvement Really Matter?" *J. Economic Behavior and Organizations,* 19 (1992), 389-394.

Kemp, T., *Industrialization in Nineteenth-Century Europe,* 2nd ed., Longman, New York, 1985.

Kieser, A., "Crossroads: Why Organization Theory Needs Historical Analyses—and How This Should Be Performed," *Organization Sci.,* 5, 4 (1994), 608-620.

King, J. L., V. Gurbaxani, K. L. Kraemer, F. W. McFarlan, K. S. Raman, and C. S. Yap, "Institutional Factors in Information Technology Innovation," *Information Systems Res.,* 5, 2 (1994), 139-169.

Kirchhoff, B. A., "Entrepreneurship Economics," in *The Portable MBA in Entrepreneurship,* W. D. Bygrave (Ed.), John Wiley, New York, 1994, 410-439.

Kling, R. and S. Iacono, "The Control of Information Systems Developments After Implementation," *Comm. ACM,* 27 (1984), 1218-1226.

Labib, N. and S. H. Appelbaum, "The Impact of Downsizing Practices on Corporate Success," *J. Management Development,* 13, 7 (1994), 59-84.

Landes, D., *The Unbound Prometheus: Technological Change and Industrial Development in Western Europe from 1750 to the Present,* Cambridge University Press, Cambridge, UK, 1969, 1-29.

————, "Introduction," in *Favorites of Fortune: Technology, Growth, and Economic Development Since the Industrial Revolution,* P. Higgonet, D. Landes, and H. Rosovsky (Eds.), Harvard University Press, Cambridge, MA, 1991, 1-29.

Lloyd-Jones, R. and M. J. Lewis, "Personal Capitalism and British Industrial Decline: The Personally Managed Firm and Business Strategy in Sheffield, 1880-1920," *Business History Rev.,* 68, Autumn (1994), 364-411.

Magnet, M., "Who's Winning the Information Revolution?" *Fortune,* November 30, 1992, 110-117.

Malone, T. W. and J. F. Rockart, "Computers, Networks, and the Corporation," *Scientific American,* 265, 3 (1991), 128-136.

————, J. Yates, and R. I. Benjamin, "Electronic Markets and Electronic Hierarchies: Effects of New Information Technologies on Market Structures and Corporate Strategies," *Comm. ACM,* 30, June (1987), 484-497.

Martino, V. D. and L. Wirth, "Telework: A New Way of Working and Living," *International Labor Rev.,* 129, 5 (1990), 529-554.

Mendels, F., "Proto-Industrialization: The First Phase of the Process of Industrialization," *J. Economic History,* 12 (1972), 241-261.

———— and P. Deyon, "Proto-Industrialization: Theory and Reality," Eighth International Congress of Economic History, Section A-2: Proto-Industrialization, Budapest, Hungary, 1982.

Meyer, J. W. and B. Rowan, "Institutionalized Organizations: Formal Structure as Myth and Ceremony," *American J. Sociology,* 83, September (1977), 340-363.

Miles, R. E. and C. C. Snow, "Organizations: New Concepts for New Forms," *California Management Rev.,* 28, 3 (1986), 62-73.

Milliken, F. J., "Three Types of Perceived Uncertainty About the Environment: State, Effect, and Response Uncertainty," *Acad. Management Rev.,* 12, 1 (1987), 133-143.

Mills, D. Q., *Rebirth of the Corporation,* John Wiley, New York, 1991.

Mills, D. R., "Proto-Industrialization and Social Structure: The Case of the Hosiery Industry in Leicestershire, England," Eighth International Congress of Economic History, Section A-2: Proto-Industrialization, Budapest, Hungary, 1982.

Monthly Labor Review, "The Advent of the New Economy," February 1992, 44-46.

Nilles, J. M., F. R. Carlson, P. Gray, and G. J. Hanneman, *The Telecommunications-Transportation Tradeoff,* Wiley, Chichester, UK, 1976.

Nolan, R., A. Pollock, and J. Ware, "Creating the 21st Century Organization," *Stage by Stage,* 8, 4 (1988), 1-11.

Olson, M. H., "Remote Office Work: Changing Work Patterns in Space and Time," *Comm. ACM,* 26, 3 (1983), 182-187.

Pearson, R., "Occupational Trends in Britain to 1990," *Nature,* 323 (1986), 94.

Perrow, C., *Complex Organizations: A Critical Essay,* 3rd ed., Random House, New York, 1986.

Piore, M., "Dualism as a Response to Flux and Uncertainty," in *Dualism and Discontinuity in Industrial Societies,* S. Berger and M. J. Piore (Eds.), Cambridge University Press, Cambridge, UK, 1980, 13-81.

———— and C. F. Sabel, *The Second Industrial Divide,* Basic Books, New York, 1984.

Quinn, J., *The Intelligent Enterprise,* Free Press, New York, 1992.

Reddy, R., "A Technological Perspective on New Forms of Organizations," in *Technology and Organization,* P. Goodman, L. Sproull, and Associates, Jossey-Bass, San Francisco, 1990, 232-253.

Reich, R., *The Work of Nations,* Vintage Books, New York, 1991.

Rockart, J. and J. Short, "IT in the 1990s: Managing Organizational Interdependence," *Sloan Management Rev.,* Winter (1989), 7-16.

————— and —————, "The Networked Organization and the Management of Interdependence," in *The Corporation of the 1990s: Information Technology and Organizational Transformation,* M. S. Scott Morton (Ed.), Oxford University Press, New York, 1991, 189-219.

Sabel, C. and J. Zeitlin, "Historical Alternative to Mass Production: Politics, Markets, and Technology in Nineteenth-Century Industrialization," *Past and Present,* 108 (1985), 133-176.

Samuel, R., "Workshop of the World: Steam Power and Hand Technology in Mid-Victorian Britain," *History Workshop J.,* 3 (1977), 6-72.

Scranton, P., "Diversity in Diversity: Flexible Production and American Industrialization, 1880-1930," *Business History Rev.,* 65, Spring (1991), 27-90.

Smith, M. R. and L. Marx (Eds.), *Does Technology Drive History? The Dilemma of Technological Determinism,* MIT Press, Cambridge, MA, 1994.

Sussman, C., *Understanding Technology,* Johns Hopkins University Press, Baltimore, MD, 1973.

Thurow, L. C., "White-Collar Overhead," *Across the Board,* 23, 11 (1986), 24-32.

Tilly, C., "Protoindustrialization, Deindustrialization, and Just Plain Industrialization in European Capitalism," CRSO Working Paper No. 235, University of Michigan, Ann Arbor, 1981.

Tomasko, R. M., *Downsizing: Reshaping the Corporation for the Future,* AMACOM, New York, 1987.

Webber, A. M., "What's So New About the New Economy?" *Harvard Business Rev.,* January-February (1993), 24-42.

Williams, K., T. Cutler, J. Williams, and C. Haslam, "The End of Mass Production?" *Economy and Society,* 16, 3 (1987), 405-439.

Wrigley, E. A. and R. S. Schofield, *The Population History of England, 1541-1871: A Reconstruction,* Cambridge University Press, Cambridge, UK, 1981.

Yates, J. and R. I. Benjamin, "The Past and Present as a Window on the Future," in *The Corporation of the 1990's: Information Technology and Organizational Transformation,* M. S. Scott Morton (Ed.), Oxford University Press, New York, 1991, 61-92.

2

Information Technology and Organizational Change in the British Census, 1801-1911

MARTIN CAMPBELL-KELLY

This chapter describes the historical development of data processing in the British census and the related organizational changes from 1801 to 1911.

During this period of a little more than a century, the processing of the British census evolved from a decentralized manual operation, to a centralized manual activity, and finally to a fully mechanized system, as traced in the following sections. This study in Victorian data processing illuminates a number of contemporary issues concerning the influence of information technology on organizations.

First, an examination of Victorian data processing methods forces us to question what we mean by an information technology (IT). Most modern IT specialists would not think of the humble business form as being a technology at all, but this study shows that it was an extraordinarily powerful aid to data processing in the nineteenth century.

Second, very few organizations have a history of data processing extending back to the beginning of the nineteenth century. The history of the adoption of IT within a single organization over an extended period of time enables us to explore the resulting influences on the workforce, independent of short-term external economic factors.

Third, the study sheds light on the nature and location of organizational memory, providing one answer to the question posed by Nelson and Winter (1982, p. 99): "Where does the memory reside?" Because the data processing operation following each decennial census lasted for just two to three years—and had to be rebuilt for each subsequent census—the preservation of the organizational memory was an operational requirement.

Finally, the British census proved very resistant to the adoption of advanced information technologies. A comparison with the contemporary U.S. census—which embraced new technology with enthusiasm—affords an opportunity to examine the economic, cultural, and organizational factors responsible for these contrasting responses to a technological opportunity.

DECENTRALIZED DATA PROCESSING:
THE 1801-1831 CENSUSES

The U.S. census owes its existence to the American Constitution of 1787, which required a decennial enumeration of the population so that the taxes on the different states of the Union, and their representation in Congress, could be made in proportion to their populations (Anderson 1988).

In Britain, however, the first census was taken not out of a constitutional requirement but rather as a way of resolving the Malthusian population controversy. In his *Essay on the Principles of Population* in 1798, Thomas Malthus argued that any population would grow geometrically until it was inevitably checked by famine and disease (Glass 1973). The 1800 Census Act was designed principally to determine whether or not the population was actually increasing and therefore leading to a Malthusian crisis. Of course, since the 1801 census would merely establish a base, only the 1811 and subsequent decennial censuses would determine the trend; but there was no requirement other than precedent to undertake them. Until the establishment of a permanent census by the Census Act of 1920, each census was enacted by a special act of Parliament, and the funds voted to it were grudgingly given. Thus, although the British census was at the leading edge of information processing in terms of scale, the operation itself was generally underfunded and penny-pinching—particularly in comparison with the later censuses of the United States, which by the 1880s had become the leading census-taking nation in the world.

The four censuses of 1801, 1811, 1821, and 1831 were organized by John Rickman (*Dictionary of National Bibliography,* 1771-1840). Rickman had been actively involved in promoting the census and drafted the legislation for the 1800 Census Act (Williams 1911, pp. 40-43). The concept of a centralized information processing organization or statistical office was unknown in Rickman's time, so that the processing of the census was almost completely decentralized.

For the 1801 census, enumeration took place on March 10, 1801, and was conducted mainly by "overseers of the poor or, failing them, substantial householders assisted by church officials and, if need be, 'constables, tithing men, headboroughs, or other peace officers.' " (Nissel 1987, p. 52). An enumerator for each district was required to make door-to-door inquiries, to consolidate the responses, and to return an abstract to the Census Office in London. The abstract consisted of 10 numbers—giving the number of families and dwellings in the enumeration district, the number of males and females, and a crude occupational classification. The enumerator's abstract was returned on a preprinted standard form, which elicited the exact information required and presented it in a form which was easy for the Census Office clerks to process; this is one of the earliest examples of the use of a standard form on a large scale (Figure 2.1).

It is not known how the clerical operation of processing the 1801 census was organized under Rickman, nor the amount of clerical labor involved, but there were probably only a handful of clerks employed to produce the two-volume census report. Rickman was allocated a tiny office in Birdcage Walk, London, and given the "authority to choose his clerks" under the patronage system (Williams 1911, p. 40). The final population count of 9 million persons was announced on December 21, 1801, some eight months after the enumeration.

The pattern of the 1801 census was repeated under Rickman's supervision for the 1811, 1821, and 1831 censuses, although with a modest increase in the scope of the questions. For example, the 1821 census included questions on the age structure of the population (which was needed for the use of friendly societies and the computation of government annuities). The 1831 census included a more detailed occupational breakdown. This census also saw the introduction of a mirror data processing innovation by supplying the enumerators with "formula papers," preprinted forms on which to capture the original data (Figure 2.2), and instructions for their use: "In proceeding from House to House, be careful to carry the printed *Formula* papers in a Pasteboard or other convenient Cover, and if Ink is used by the inquirer, let him also use Blotting Paper" (Census 1831, p. vii). As in the three previous censuses, the enumerator returned only an abstract of the

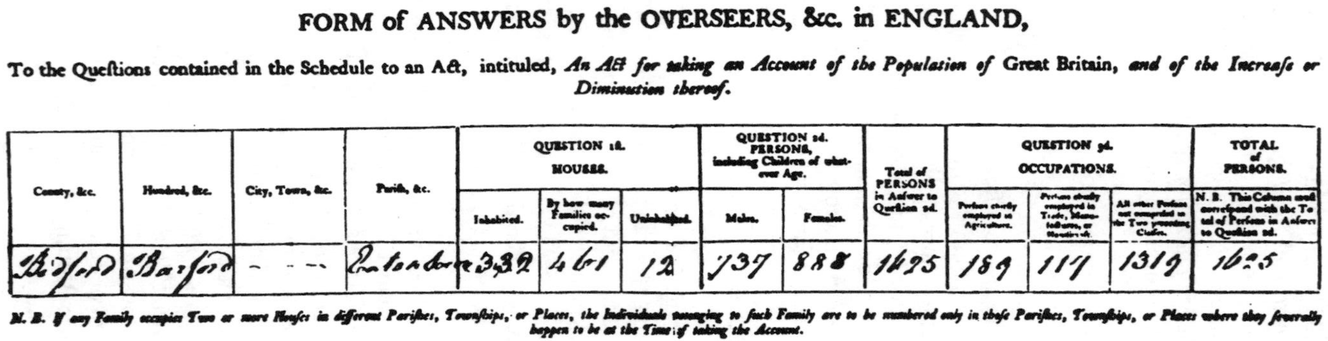

FORM of ANSWERS by the OVERSEERS, &c. in ENGLAND,

To the Questions contained in the Schedule to an Act, intituled, *An Act for taking an Account of the Population of Great Britain, and of the Increase or Diminution thereof.*

County, &c.	Hundred, &c.	City, Town, &c.	Parish, &c.	QUESTION 1st. HOUSES			QUESTION 2d. PERSONS, including Children of whatever Age.		Total of PERSONS in Answer to Question 2d.	QUESTION 3d. OCCUPATIONS			TOTAL of PERSONS.
				Inhabited.	By how many Families occupied	Uninhabited.	Males.	Females.		Persons chiefly employed in Agriculture.	Persons chiefly employed in Trade, Manufactures, or Handicraft.	All other Persons not comprised in the Two preceding Classes.	N. B. This Column is not designed, which taken the Total of Persons in Answer to Question 2d.
Bedford	- -	*Barford*	*Renhold*	339	461	12	737	888	1625	189	117	1319	1625

N. B. If any Family occupies Two or more Houses in different Parishes, Townships, or Places, the Individuals occupying to such Family are to be numbered only in single Parishes, Townships, or Places where they severally happen to be at the Time of taking the Account.

Figure 2.1. Standard Form for the Census Return, 1801

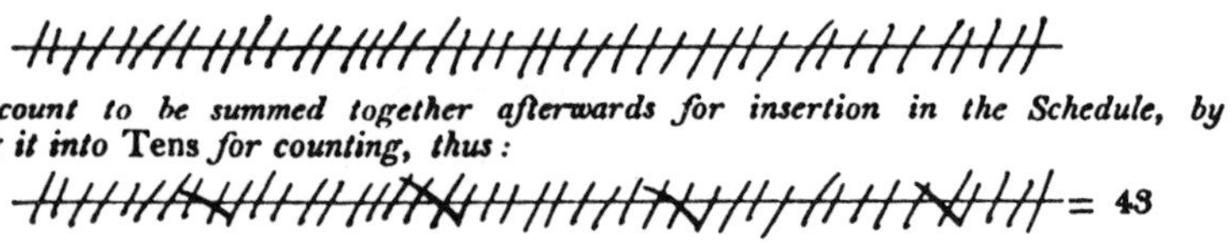

Figure 2.2. Instructions for Enumerators' Formula Sheets, 1831
SOURCE: Census 1831, p. vii.

household responses, unsupported by names and addresses or formula papers.

VICTORIAN DATA PROCESSING:
THE GENERAL REGISTER OFFICE

From 1841, in the wake of the General Registration Act of 1836, the British census became the large centralized activity we now recognize in the modern census.

The General Registration Act was the outcome of two forces in England in the 1830s: the statistical movement and political reform (Cullen 1975). The first British statistical societies were established in 1833-1834 as a response to the growing scientific interest in statistics of all kinds, particularly in continental Europe. The leading British organization was the London Statistical Society formed in 1834 (later renamed the Royal Statistical Society). There was a strong linkage between the statistical movement and political reform because of the use of statistical evidence for the factory acts, legislation for sanitary improvements, and criminal reform.

The General Register Office was established in July 1837 to maintain a national register of births, marriages, and deaths—"hatches, matches, and dispatches," to revive the old saw—and to conduct a decennial population census. The General Register Office was regarded as a modern wonder and was well reported in the popular press. The *Illustrated Times* reported in 1861,

> In arched chambers of immense strength and extent are in many volumes the genuine certificates of upwards of 28,000,000 persons who have either been born into life, married, or passed into the grave. . . . From time to time, an attendant glides into the place in search of some volume . . . for the purpose of being copied or inspected. In these numerous books, there are the names of paupers and

patricians, those of soldiers in ranks, and officers of all grades up to Arthur Duke of Wellington. Here are to be found the records of nonentities, side by side with those once learned in the law or distinguished in literature, art, or science. (Anon. 1861, p. 240)

The first Registrar General was the novelist Thomas Henry Lister (*Dictionary of National Bibliography*, 1800-1842), who was appointed in a typical act of patronage of the period. The registration of births, marriages, and deaths was a heavily decentralized operation, the actual registration being devolved into 626 registration districts with approximately 2,000 local registrars. The General Register Office itself was located in Somerset House in London; it was run initially by a small workforce of about five clerks and essentially acted as a centralized records repository. As the number of records (which was cumulative) built up, the clerical workforce grew in proportion so that after a few years it had become a major clerical operation, with a workforce of 80 to 90 persons under the sole authority of the Registrar General, who complained of "a responsibility in point of number which I believe does not attach to any other single person serving under the Crown" (Graham 1846).

The workforce included "four officers, 17 first and senior clerks, 30 juniors, and eight messengers on the establishment plus . . . ten temporaries, six sorters of transcripts, one labourer, four transcribers, and seven indexers not on the establishment" (Cullen 1975, p. 30). We do not know how the office organization was devised, but Lister probably took as precedents the handful of London-based, large-scale offices then in existence—the Bank of England, the East India Company, the post office, the Admiralty, and so on. Although Lister was said to have been a better novelist than statistician (Finer 1952, p. 143) and was appointed under the patronage system, he was a capable office administrator and had the foresight to appoint the pioneer of social statistics, William Farr (*Dictionary of National Bibliography*, 1807-1883), as "Abstractor of Statistics" in July 1839—a position he was to hold for 40 years (Eyler 1979).

Meticulous plans were laid for the 1841 census, some details of which are preserved in the fine prose of Lister's autograph *History of the Census of 1841*. Lister was explicit about the need to centralize the census tabulation for accuracy and control:

I will mention here that I would have no Abstracts made but at the Central Office. The duties of the Local Authorities should be confined to the preparation and transmission of simple facts. The abstraction, condensation, classification, and arrangement of those facts should be done upon one uniform system, and upon the responsibility of one person or Board. To have Abstracts made in the country to be afterwards sent up and used as the materials for other Abstracts to be made in London is only to divide and weaken responsibility, to make uniformity of system impossible, to increase the chance of error, and to lessen the means of correction." (quoted in Glass 1973, pp. 115-116)

The 1841 British census was the first "modern" census in which separate schedules were distributed to each household and institution in the land for self-completion. The census was organized through the administrative structure of 2,193 local registration districts. Each of the registration districts was divided into a number of enumeration districts containing "not more than 200 and not less than 25 inhabited houses." There were approximately 35,000 enumeration districts (and enumerators) altogether.

So far as is known, there was no continuity between the 1841 census and the previous censuses. Like the General Register Office, the Census Office was an entirely new organization, unfettered by prior working practices or other institutional rigidities. Given this freedom, Lister and Farr were able to adopt an hierarchical and specialized workforce, an organizational innovation already made in the General Register Office. Not only did this form of organization give Farr close control over the accuracy of census data processing, it also enabled him to make economies in the cost of the workforce by employing casual clerks and copyists. These low-grade clerks occupied the lower rungs of the social ladder, above common laborers but no higher than artisans (Lockwood 1958).

For the first time, to avoid double counting, a census night was instituted so that each household was required to complete the census schedule—delivered the previous week—on Sunday, June 6, 1841. As soon as possible the following week, the household schedules were collected by the enumerators, who then transcribed them into an "enumeration book." All the data on the household schedule was copied across to the enumeration book, which retained all the information content but reduced the physical volume; this made it more convenient to process at the Census Office by reducing the amount of page turning. At the same time, the enumerator was required to count up the number of people in his district and produce a summary similar to the previous censuses. Finally, the local registrar received the enumeration books from his enumerators, made his own checks and totals, and then dispatched all the material to the Census Office.

Thus, notwithstanding Lister's progress toward centralization, there was a significant amount of preprocessing of the census data before they arrived at the Census Office; this enabled the rough population counts to be calculated on similar lines to the earlier censuses. The 1841 census was a halfway stage between the decentralization of the early censuses and complete centralization following mechanization in the 1911 census.

TABLE 2.1 Census Statistics, 1841-1901

Census Year	Total Cost (£)	Census Office Expenses (£)	Census Office Expenses as a Percentage of Total Cost	Maximum Number of Census Office Clerks		Population (millions)	Cost per 1,000 Population (£)
				Total	Female		
1841	66,727	24,400	37			15.9	—
1851	93,132	33,062	36	106	0	17.9	5.20
1861	95,719	28,605	30			20.1	4.77
1871	119,977	39,730	33	111	0	22.7	5.28
1881	122,876	35,906	29	151	not stated	26.0	4.73
1891	120,599					29.0	4.16
1901	148,921			185	75	32.5	4.58

SOURCE: Census *General Reports.*

The census tabulation was directed by Farr. The census report included many more detailed tabulations than [it had] previously—notably tables of the age structure of the population and occupational classifications. The tabulation took one year and eight months to complete, although no details have survived other than a brief passage in the *Enumeration Abstract:*

> On the arrival of the enumerators' schedules in London, each individual of whichever sex was presented to us with five distinct propositions attached to each name, making upwards of one hundred million separate facts to be reduced into tabular statements by copying, and the results to be formed into geographical districts by means of three hundred and thirty thousand separate calculations, all of which were to be tested by a system of checks in order to prevent error. This was to be accomplished by the aid of an establishment which was to be collected together for this express purpose, remunerated with the lowest salaries, and without prospect of employment from the Government beyond the continuance of the office. (Census 1841, p. 38)

The printed census reports appeared in five volumes during 1843-1844. The total cost of the census was £66,727, of which the central Census Office expenses were £24,400 (Table 2.1).

Subsequent censuses, until mechanization in 1911, were conducted along similar lines. The cost of the census (which averaged about £5 per 1,000 population) varied little over the period, although the number of questions on the census schedule, the sophistication of the tabulations, and the page counts of the census reports all increased, indicating a gradually improving efficiency.[1] For example, the 1851 census tabulated the age structure by year instead of in five-year groups as in the previous census; this was done at the suggestion of Farr and was aimed at improving mortality statistics. Also in 1851—as befitted the year of the first International Exhibition of Science and Industry—a much more sophisticated occupational census was undertaken, again at the instigation of Farr. The 1851 census schedule was the first over which Farr exercised a major influence, and in addition to the improved age structure and occupational tabulations, he included questions on handicaps and physical disabilities, which reflected his preoccupation with social and medical statistics.

For the 1851 census, 106 temporary clerks were appointed, who were supervised by three or four principal clerks transferred from their normal duties in the General Register Office (Figure 2.3). The tabulation was completely unmechanized, all the information processing being achieved by transferring handwritten data from one standard form to another. The principal standard forms were "abstract sheets" and "tabling sheets," which were both large preprinted forms measuring 19 inches by 26 inches (or, in some cases, twice as large).

The tabulation was a three-stage process, which was mechanical in principle if not in practice. The production of the age-structure tables was typical. The abstract sheet—or "ticking sheet"—for the age-structure tabulation was ready-ruled into a grid, each cell of which corresponded to one of the age groups in the tabulation for males and females. First, an abstracting clerk transferred the age data from a set of enumeration books for a registration district by placing a tick (i.e., a check mark) for each person in the corresponding age cell. When this had been done, a second clerk—the casting clerk—totaled up the number of ticks in each of the cells on the abstract sheet and recorded the result alongside as a decimal number. As a check, subtotals were computed, and these could be verified against the corresponding totals in the original enumeration books. Finally, in the third and last stage of the tabulation, the contents of all the abstract sheets for a county or metropolitan area were consolidated onto a tabling sheet. This sheet was laid out in exactly the form of a table in the final census report, and the typesetting was done directly from it. This eliminated a further copying process and the possibility of transcription errors.

In the system established by Farr—which was used for the censuses from 1841 until mechanization in 1911—the clerks each performed a very limited range of tasks and were paid as little as the labor market would bear. Specialization of clerical function using the lowest cost clerical labor possible was

INDEXING DEPARTMENT (GALLERY) OF THE CENSUS OFFICE.

Figure 2.3. Indexing Department of the Census Office, 1861

SOURCE: Anon., "The Census," *Illustrated Times*, April 13, 1861, p. 235.

used in all Victorian data processing organizations (Campbell-Kelly 1992, 1993). Such work organization embodied the Babbage Principle, originally expressed in a manufacturing context:

> that the master manufacturer, by dividing the work to be executed into different processes, each requiring different degrees of skill or of force, can purchase exactly that precise quantity of both which is necessary for each process; whereas, if the whole work were executed by one workman, that person must possess sufficient skill to perform the most difficult, and sufficient strength to execute the most laborious, of the operations into which the art is divided. (Babbage [1835] 1989, p. 125)

Although there is no direct link between the Census Office and the Babbage Principle, the idea of the "division of mental labour" was well known in Britain through Babbage's ([1835] 1989) influential *Economy of Manufactures*. Babbage was knowledgeable about data processing organizations such as the Banker's Clearing House and had been an unsuccessful candidate for the position of Registrar General and director of the census in 1837 (Campbell-Kelly 1994).

The Babbage Principle was used to the fullest, so that for every task, clerks with just sufficient skill were employed. Thus, as Registrar General Graham later reported to a commission on the civil service in 1875,

> As to class I and II [grades of clerk], I wish only for class II. in this office, preferring experienced hands . . . well able to teach and superintend the junior clerks and writers and boys and piece-workers, rather than see the better educated class I intruded into the higher grades of this department. I do not want them here; they would be thought to be interlopers. (Graham 1875, p. 388)

Graham made heavy use of child and low-grade labor to reduce costs: "There is very great economy in . . . employing boys at 4d. [old English pence] an hour and writers at 10d. an hour compared with clerks" (p. 388).

With the civil service reforms of 1854, which ended the patronage system, Graham was given still closer control over the supply of labor and used the civil service examination to filter applicants for the Census Office. Female clerks, who were cheaper to employ for the same grade of work, were used in the 1881 census when this became socially acceptable. Outside the Census Office, the enumerators were the salaried assistants to the district registrars. The work of these minor civil servants was tightly prescribed by the enumeration books, which specified precisely the format in which data were to be prepared.

Although much of the census processing was mindless drudgery, where there was some advantage in using a higher order of clerical skill, this was done. This occurred, for example, in the coding of occupations. For the 1851 census, Farr devised a classification scheme consisting of 431 different occupational groups, which he subsequently used for relating mortality to occupation (and which was to have a major impact on social medicine). A dictionary was compiled of some 7,000 job titles including hundreds of evocative but obscure occupations such as (to cite only a few of the entries under the letter B) "Barker, Bat-printer, Baubler, Bear breaker, Beatster, Blabber, Black picker, Block minder, Bomb setter, Branner, Brazil maker, Budget trimmer, Bull-dog burner, Bullet pitcher, Busheller, Butt woman, Buttoner-up" (Census 1881, p. 26). The higher grade abstracting clerks tended to specialize in occupational abstraction, as it made considerable demands on the memory, in order not to spend too much time leafing through the dictionary of occupations.

The Farr occupational classification scheme remained in force until 1921, and the dictionary of occupations—revised for each upcoming census—constituted an important component of the organizational memory. Other physical realizations of the organizational memory included the ticking sheets, tabling sheets, and enumeration books, all of which were carried forward from one census to the next, evolving slightly at each census as minor revisions were incorporated. The human component of the organizational memory was mainly carried forward by Farr, his assistant, and a handful of clerks.

RESISTANCE TO MECHANIZATION:
THE 1881-1901 CENSUSES

Farr retired from his post as statistical superintendent of the General Register Office in January 1880, at the age of 73, and died three years later. He had been a force for innovation in the General Register Office and had been responsible for most of the improvements in mortality statistics and census tabulation.

Farr had also been very receptive to mechanization. His most notable experiment was the production of the definitive *English Life Table* in the late 1850s using the Scheutz Difference Engine, the most advanced (and temperamental) calculating machine of its day (Farr 1864; Lindgren 1990, p. 285). Although this was a table-making exercise quite unconnected with census data processing (and the technology could not have been used in this connection), it is illustrative of Farr's enthusiasm for new information technologies. By 1872, he had also acquired several Arithmometers for statistical calculation when they were at the leading edge of calculating technology (indeed, almost the only calculating technology). During the 1880s and 1890s, after Farr's retirement, a vast array of reliable office appliances came onto the market, particularly adder-listers and comptometers, which would have been useful in producing census totals. But under Farr's successor, the opportunity was never taken.

While Farr had been a promoter of census taking, his successor as statistical superintendent, William Ogle, who held office from 1880 to 1894, was more concerned [with limiting] the scope of the census than [with promoting] it. He resisted efforts from the Royal Statistical Society and the Institute of Actuaries to expand the scope of the census inquiries, and the office machine revolution swept past, leaving the Census Office virtually untouched. Under Farr, Britain and the United States had spent comparable sums on their censuses (as measured by the cost per capita). But by 1900, the United States was spending several times more per capita than was Britain.

However, the key innovation in census processing in the 1890s was not the use of ordinary office machines but rather punched-card tabulation. The punched-card method had been pioneered in the mid-1880s for the 1890 U.S. population census by Herman Hollerith (*Dictionary of American Biography,* 1860-1929). The tabulation of the 1890 U.S. census was a mechanical data processing phenomenon whose magnitude was unprecedented. It was processed using a battery of about 100 census machines to tabulate 63 million cards prepared using about 700 card punches; the result was a monumental census report of 10,220 pages. Altogether, a peak workforce of 3,143 clerks was employed punching cards, operating the tabulating machines, and preparing the census reports (Anderson 1988, p. 242).

Even before the 1890 census was under way, Hollerith had begun to actively market his machines to the census offices of other countries (Austrian 1982). The system was adopted by Austria, Norway, and Canada for their 1890 censuses, and by 1895, Russia and France had also decided to use the system. Britain would not succumb until the 1911 census.

In December 1894, Hollerith, together with Robert P. Porter, the superintendent of the 1890 U.S. census, gave an invited address to the Royal Statistical Society. Hollerith, in the afterglow of the success of the American census, gave a long, detailed account of his census-tabulating system in which he paid homage to Farr's pioneering census work: "I am glad to be able to say here today that in my struggle to secure the adoption of this system in the United States, I often had recourse, with great advantages, to references to and quotations from the works of your Dr. Farr" (Hollerith 1894, p. 678). So far as is known, Hollerith never met Farr. But if he was hoping to curry favor with the British census authorities by this tribute, he was mistaken. In the discussions that followed Porter and Hollerith's presentations, Ogle poured cold water over what he considered to be the excesses of the American population census:

> The American census differed enormously from the English census in its scope. Our own was limited to the enumeration of the people and houses, with some simple particulars concerning them such as their age, sex, and occupation. But this was a comparatively insignificant part of the American census, which branched out into multitudinous inquiries, doubtlessly of high interest, but scarcely, as it seemed to him, coming properly under the designation of census work. For example, in the census report of 1881 there was, if he remembered rightly, a whole volume devoted to the habits and natural history of fishes, the modes of capturing them, and other piscicultural matter. It appeared to him that it was a mistake to combine such inquiries as this with the census proper, that is, with the enumeration of the people. This latter could be carried out in a single day by ordinary enumerators at a comparatively cheap rate, while the special inquiries required a huge staff of highly trained experts, a long period of time, and a fund which, it appeared from Mr. Porter's paper, ran into millions sterling. (Hollerith 1894, pp. 682-683)

Indeed, the 1890 U.S. census had cost a total of $11.5 million compared with the cost of the British census of £120,599 (the equivalent of about $600,000). Even allowing for the larger population of the United States, the cost per 1,000 citizens was $183 (£36) in the United States compared with £4 in the United Kingdom. But Ogle was wrong to discount the punched-card system solely because of the greater scale and apparent excess of the American census; a few census machines would have transformed the tabulation of the relatively small British census. Noel Humphreys—Farr's assistant in the General Register Office and memorialist after his death—was much more enthusiastic, stating "that his experience of the last census almost made him long for another census in order to be able to try the effect of the electric tabulating machine" (Hollerith 1894, p. 683). However, Ogle and bureaucratic inertia had determined otherwise. Despite mounting criticism from the Royal Statistical Society and the Institute of Actuaries of the need to use a card system and to have a permanent census office, the 1901 census was conducted along the old lines.

In fact, the sole mechanical aid used for the 1901 census was a single Tates Arithmometer purchased for 50 guineas, the expenditure of which was sanctioned by Her Majesty's Treasury with characteristic penny-pinching ceremony "to be charged to the grant for the Census of England and Wales, 1901, subhead G Incidental Expenses" (Registrar General 1901). Eighteen months into the tabulation, the Arithmometer broke down and had to be sent away for repair. Seeking an urgent replacement, [it was] found that the five machines in the General Register Office (bought in Farr's time) were "worn out and practically useless." Only the personal intervention of the Registrar General finally coaxed another 50 guineas from the Treasury for a replacement Arithmometer.

A single Arithmometer shared between a peak clerical labor force of 185 has to be compared with the 13th U.S. census of 1900—in which 311 tabulating machines, 20 sorting machines, and 1,021 card punches were in use by the peak workforce of 3,143 people.

MECHANIZATION:
THE PUNCHED-CARD CENSUS OF 1911

The push to mechanize the British census came from outside rather than inside the General Register Office. In 1896, Hollerith had incorporated the Tabulating Machine Company in the United States to market his census machines and to develop punched-card machines for commercial users. In 1904, a British subsidiary (The Tabulator, renamed the British Tabulating Machine Company [BTM] in 1907) was formed in London to import and lease the American-made machines (Campbell-Kelly 1989). The chairman of the British company was Porter, the British-born former superintendent of the U.S. census. For the next several years, the company's general manager unsuccessfully canvassed the General Register Office to use the company's machines for the 1911 census.

In 1908, in the run-up to the 1911 census, the Census Office undertook a major review of its census processing methods (apparently for the first time since 1888!). This review was intended to both draw on the experience of the 1901 census and respond to the external criticism of the Census Office's failure to adopt the Hollerith system for the 1901 census (Registrar General 1908). The review was also stimulated in part by the Treasury, which had begun to take an interest in office mechanization with a view to reducing administrative costs in the civil service generally.

The following year, the Census Office decided to conduct a trial of the Hollerith machines and approached BTM. However, by this time the American company had given up census work altogether in favor of commercial punched-card applications and could no longer supply the census machines. The British company, which was anxious to obtain the census contract for both publicity and revenue reasons, made a crash development of a counting-sorting machine especially for the British Census Office. This machine had to be abandoned because of unreliability in the summer of 1910 after several months' trial, but in any case, the Census Office had by then decided on a modified version of a standard commercial tabulator. In December 1910, only four months before enumeration day and after the usual haggling over terms, BTM secured a contract to supply machines and cards for the 1911 census eventually amounting to 15 sorters, 6 census machines, 2 tabulators, and 68 keypunches (Anon. 1911).

The introduction of punched-card methods in the Census Office had the effect of centralizing and further deskilling much of the work. It also introduced significant additional expenditure on data processing equipment amounting to about a third of the salary bill (Table 2.2). In the field, the main change over the previous censuses was that enumerators were no longer required to transcribe the household schedules into enumeration books or to make abstracts since punched cards were now to be prepared directly from the household schedules. The enumerator's role was thus reduced largely to that of distributing and collecting forms and ensuring that they had been fully and legibly completed.

Within the Census Office, the clerical workforce was effectively split into two tiers—an elite of high-grade clerks and a large corps of machine workers. For data preparation, a relatively small number of experienced coding clerks encoded the non-numeric occupational and place-of-birth data into numerical form on the household schedules, which were then punched by a very much larger number of unskilled keypunch operators and checkers. There was a peak staff of 170 keypunch operators "recruited from young girls just leaving the elementary schools," working in two shifts of six hours each. When the cards had been punched, they were visually verified against the original schedules by a peak force of 81 female checkers who were aged 18 to 21 and marginally better qualified than the punchers. Altogether, 45 million cards were punched (Figure 2.4), and during the 12 months in which they were produced, the initially untrained operators built up their punching skills from 127 cards per hour at the outset to 417 cards per hour by the end (Census 1911, p. 262).

In the census tabulation, in place of the ticking system and abstract sheets, the punched-card machines were used to automatically accumulate totals by reading cards at the rate of 150 cards per minute. In place of the old tabling sheets, there were large preprinted "machine results sheets", into which the totals recorded on the census machine counters were transcribed. (Punched-card machines did not print their results at this time.) The census reports were then typeset directly from the machine results sheets. Like the card preparation, machine tabulation was performed by a two-tier workforce (Figure 2.5):

> An experienced clerk was in charge of each Counting or Tabulating Machine. He was responsible for seeing that the correct cards were put into the machine in the right order and for recording the results. A boy assistant was also allotted to each

TABLE 2.2 Census Statistics, 1911-1931

				Maximum Number of Census Office Clerks				
Census Year	Total Cost (£)	Census Office Expenses (£)	Census Office Expenses as a Percentage of Total Cost	Total	Female	Data Processing Equipment (£)	Population (millions)	Cost per 1,000 Population (£)
1911	161,481	35,987	22	350	221	13,805	36.1	4.48
1921	351,334	118,432	34	550	285	not stated	37.9	9.28
1931	299,733	106,414	36	447	277	22,560	40.0	7.50

SOURCE: Census *General Reports.*
NOTE: The fluctuation in cost per 1,000 population in 1921 and 1931 is due to postwar inflation and deflation (Census 1921, p. 9; Census 1931, p. 20).

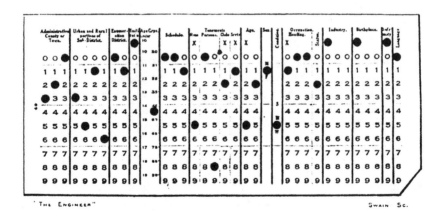

Figure 2.4. Personal Card, 1911 Census
SOURCE: Anon., "The Tabulator," *The Engineer,* March 17, 1911.
The 15 fields between the bold vertical rules on the card recorded: enumeration district (Fields 1-3), whether the place of residence is an institution (Field 4), the age group (Field 5), schedule number within the enumeration district (Field 6), details of residence (Field 7), actual age (Field 8), sex (Field 9), marital condition (Field 10), occupation code and employer-employee status (Field 11), industry code (Field 12), place-of-birth code (Field 13), physical infirmity (Field 14), and nationality (Field 15).

Figure 2.5. Punched-Card Tabulation, 1911 Census
SOURCE: Manchester University, National Archive for the History of Computing.
The photograph shows the census machine developed by BTM [the British Tabulating Machine Company] from a standard punched-card tabulator. The operator at the front of the picture is "needling" a batch of cards to check the sequence before replacing them in the storage trays in the foreground. The machine boy (seated) is attending to the automatic card feed, which read cards at a rate of 150 cards per minute. Note the large machine-results sheet on the work surface in front of the census machine; readings from the census machine counters were copied onto the sheet by the supervising clerk.

machine, and it was his duty to fetch the boxes of sorted cards from the filing racks, assist in proving the cards, feed and operate the machine, and return the cards to the racks. On the completion of a counting process for an administrative area, the result sheets were scrutinised, and any apparent discrepancy [was] investigated before the cards were re-sorted for the next counting process. (Census 1911, p. 262)

At the peak of the census operation, there were approximately 350 people employed, "comprising 90 male clerks and their superintendents, 81 female checkers and their superintendents, 32 machine boys, 140 punch operators, and a small staff of porters and messengers."

The great attraction of mechanization—which had always been appreciated—was that once the cards had been punched, it was possible to extract many more useful tabulations out of them at a comparatively low cost. In the

1911 census, the 36 million personal cards averaged 13.6 card passages through the machines—9.5 through the sorting machines and 4.1 through the census machines. Once all the cards had been punched, the actual census reports were prepared by a staff of "36 second-class clerks and 19 machine boys."

CONCLUSIONS

In the introduction to this chapter, I suggested that an historical study of the British census over a long period of time could shed light on a number of issues concerning the impact of IT on organizations.

The first issue was: What constitutes an IT? In the late twentieth century, we tend to think of IT in terms of sophisticated artifacts embodying computer, communications, and software technologies. This study, however, suggests that much simpler constructs can constitute an effective information processing technology. Thus the standard form used by enumerators in the 1801 census (Figure 2.1) was a significant data processing innovation that simplified data extraction in the Census Office. It was also nonobvious, and the U.S. census did not adopt this idea until its fourth census:

> The assistants were free to collect the information as they chose. Neither
> Congress nor the president thought to print and mail out special census forms,
> nor did they specify any size or type of paper. (Not until 1830 would the fed-
> eral government print the census forms and mail them to the enumerators.)
> (Anderson 1988, p. 14)

An equally significant innovation was the ticking system used for totaling census data used in the 1841 to 1901 censuses. An almost identical method, known as the tally system, was used for the 1850 to 1880 U.S. censuses (Truesdell 1965, pp. 1-4). There is no evidence to connect these two innovations; they were probably both spontaneous responses to processing an increasing volume of information.

Another aim of this chapter was to examine the influence of IT on the workforce over an extended period of time. In short, the adoption of IT was accompanied by the creation of a hierarchy based on levels of skill, and the more sophisticated the technology, the more pronounced this became. Thus, in the decentralized censuses of 1801 to 1831, the small number of clerks in the Census Office worked under a system of patronage and performed relatively unstructured nonroutine tasks, while in the field the enumerators— who were respected citizens such as poor-law officials, police officers, and clergymen—operated with considerable autonomy.

With the introduction of the centralized census operation in 1841, the workforce became specialized and hierarchical both inside and outside the Census Office. Inside the office, at the apex of the hierarchy, senior clerks were responsible for preparing the individual tables for the census report, beneath them were supervising clerks responsible for the smooth running of the abstraction process, and so on down to the lowest grade of ticking clerk.

This form of labor organization improved data processing accuracy and costs in a number of ways. First, specialization of function enabled work measuring; both the General Register Office and the Census Office measured the output of clerks from the 1860s and even employed piece-rates for some classes of work. Second, close supervision improved accuracy and quality control; clerks had so little latitude in their work that slow or inaccurate workers could be quickly weeded out or assigned to less demanding duties. Costs were further reduced by using the Babbage Principle to employ the lowest grade labor capable of an individual task; thus a few well-qualified (but expensive) clerks were used in supervisory roles, while much greater numbers of male, female, and boy clerks were used for data abstraction.

In the punched-card census of 1911, the division of labor became still more pronounced. Inside the Census Office, a high-grade male elite supervised the work of low-grade men and boy machine workers. The high-grade clerks were responsible for monitoring the progress of tabulations, preparing tables, and seeing them through the press, while the machine workers were responsible for feeding cards into the tabulating machines, clearing card jams, and carrying boxes of cards between the storage racks and the machines. Likewise, female clerks of an intermediate grade monitored the work of hundreds of girl keypunch operators. In the field, the role of the enumerator was now reduced to that of the delivery and collection of forms and ensuring their correct completion; no processing of the data was required at all.

The census operation was torn down and rebuilt every 10 years, with only a tiny nucleus of permanent staff retained between censuses; in the 1911 census, for example, there were just three permanent officials. The fact that the organization could be so quickly reestablished every 10 years begs the question: Where does the memory reside? In a permanent, evolving organization, the organizational memory is located in the acquired know-how of individuals and is codified in manuals of procedure (Nelson and Winter 1982, pp. 96-136; Yates 1990).

The continuity from one census to the next was achieved by both mechanisms, but mainly the latter. A significant amount of clerical labor (of the order of 20 percent of the staff) was re-employed from previous censuses, bringing with them prior knowledge, and they could quickly train newcomers. But much more important, the printed materials—census forms, enumeration books, tabling sheets, and the dictionary of occupations—which were maintained between censuses took the memory forward. After 1911, the machine-tabulation procedures (such as tabulator plugging diagrams) were carried forward from one census to the next. In effect, the printed materials and machine-tabulation procedures constituted the "software" of the information processing system. After computerization in 1961, this became software in the real sense, but its secondary function was still to carry forward the organizational memory to the next decennial census.

Thus the human component of the census operation increasingly served merely as an interface between the census information processing system, on the one hand, and the suppliers and consumers of census information, on the other. In a sense, the census was a precursor of some modern organizations in which the organizational memory is increasingly encoded in software and located less and less in individuals.

Finally, this study sheds some light on the nature of resistance to innovations in IT. While there can be no question that the British census suffered from severe bureaucratic inertia, the adoption of new technology was not a black and white issue but rather one which has to be related to crises in information processing, the goals of the organization, and external pressures.

Punched-card machines were used in the U.S. census of 1890 primarily as a response to a crisis in information processing; the 1880 census had taken seven years to process by manual methods, and something had to be done. The superintendent of the census was a political appointment, and the appointee had considerable latitude in determining his organizational goals. Punched-card machines were adopted not least because Superintendent Porter was a technological enthusiast and a booster of the Hollerith system. Beyond the census, there was intense interest in the outcome of the census. It was a moment for the nation to "feel its muscle," and the popular press, such as *The New York Times,* eagerly anticipated the results:

> Our males of arms-bearing age will make every civilized nation bear to us a pigmy relation, and our wealth will have grown by millions to more millions than purse-proud Britain can boast. These are faint foreshadowings of what the eleventh census will disclose during the coming months. (quoted in Austrian 1982, pp. 58-59)

Thus a key organizational goal for Porter was to satisfy the desire of a democratic nation for facts about itself.

The press was also caught up by the romance of Hollerith's census machines. The rhetoric of office systemization and IT was very strong in the United States compared with Britain (Yates 1989). Thomas Martin, a popular science writer, wrote lyrically in an article, "Counting a Nation by Electricity": "After a scrutiny as close and careful as it could be made, it seems only possible to say one thing, namely, that the apparatus works as unerringly as the mills of the Gods but beats them hollow as to speed" (Martin 1891, p. 522). What few, if any, writers pointed out was that—apart from speed— the Hollerith machines produced little real productivity gain. According to a popular article in *Century Magazine,* written by the then Director of the Census William Merriam (1903, p. 838), the 1880 census reports cost $3,873 per published page, while the 1890 reports cost $3,674 per page.[2]

By contrast, in Britain none of these favorable conditions prevailed. First, there was no crisis in information processing; the 1891 and 1901 censuses both took the normal two to three years to complete. Second, the director of the British census was an apolitical civil servant with little freedom for negotiating his goals or budget; the scope of the census and its budget were determined by parliamentary vote—and Parliament's primary concern was to contain costs. Finally, there was no great popular appetite for census statistics. Although there had been some press interest in the General Register Office and the census in the mid-nineteenth century, there was little popular interest in the 1890s. (And even had there been, there was no democratic precedent for British governments responding to popular demand.) Given these strong motives to maintain the status quo, it is understandable that the director of the census was risk averse and clung to the old manual traditions. When the British census was finally mechanized in 1911, the machines had been used in the United States for three censuses and in several European countries for two. This significantly lessened the risk of adopting the new technology. The final push toward mechanization was provided by external pressure from the Royal Statistical Society and the Institute of Actuaries—professional, rather than popular, pressure groups (Ackland 1903, p. v).

To characterize the U.S. census as innovative and go-ahead while the British census was conservative and fossilized is too simplistic. In each case, the response to a technological opportunity was determined by the organization's cultural heritage, its organizational goals, and the need to react to external pressure groups.

NOTES

1. It is difficult to produce objective measures of census data processing efficiency. In the United States, the only published efficiency measures were the total cost, the cost per capita, and the total number of pages of census reports. The total cost of the British census and the cost per 1,000 citizens were published, but not the number of pages of the census reports.

2. Anderson (1988, p. 242) gives much less favorable figures, working out at $2,698 and $4,373 per page for the 1880 and 1890 censuses, respectively. This might be taken as an attempt on Merriam's part to exaggerate the productivity gain by using the Hollerith system, but because

the cost per page of census reports was such a crude and even arbitrary metric, this seems unlikely.

REFERENCES

Ackland, T. G., *A Digest of the Results of the Census of England and Wales in 1901*, C. and E. Layton, London, 1903.

Anderson, M., *The American Census*, Yale University Press, New Haven, CT, 1988.

Anon., "The Census," *Illustrated Times*, 13 April (1861), 235, 239-241; 20 April (1861), 259.

Anon., "The Tabulator," *The Engineer*, March 17 (1911), 96-97, 146-148, 179-180, 196-197.

Austrian, G., *Herman Hollerith: Forgotten Giant of Data Processing*, Columbia University Press, New York, 1982.

Babbage, C., *Economy of Manufactures, 1835," Vol. 8 of Works of Babbage* (M. Campbell-Kelly, Ed.), Pickering & Chatto, London, 1989.

Campbell-Kelly, M., *ICL: A Business and Technical History*, Oxford University Press, Oxford, UK, 1989.

———, "Large-Scale Data Processing in the Prudential, 1850-1930," *Accounting, Business, and Financial History*, 2 (1992), 117-139.

———, "The Railway Clearing House and Victorian Data Processing," in L. Bud-Frierman (Ed.), *Information Acumen*, Routledge, London, 1993.

———, "Charles Babbage and the Assurance of Lives," *Ann. History of Computing*, 16, 3 (1994), 5-14.

Census 1831 [1841, 1881, 1911], etc., *Enumeration Abstracts* and *General Reports*. (See Office of Population Censuses and Surveys 1970 for listing of individual volumes)

Cullen, M. J., *The Statistical Movement in Early Victorian Britain*, Methuen, London, 1975.

Eyler, J. M., *Victorian Social Medicine: The Ideas and Methods of William Farr*, Johns Hopkins University Press, Baltimore, MD, 1979.

Farr, W., *English Life Table*, Her Majesty's Stationery Office, London, 1864.

Finer, S. E., *The Life and Times of Sir Edwin Chadwick*, Methuen, London, 1952.

Glass, D. V., *Numbering the People*, Famborough, UK, 1973.

Graham, G., Letter to Robert Peel, PRO Registrar General 29/17, May 1 (1846).

———, Evidence in *Report of the Civil Service Inquiry Commission*, Her Majesty's Stationery Office, London, 1875.

Hollerith, H., "The Electrical Tabulating Machine," followed by a discussion, *J. Royal Statistical Society*, 57 (1894), 678-689.

Lindgren, M., *Glory and Failure: The Difference Engines of Johann Müller, Charles Babbage, and Georg and Edvard Scheutz*, MIT Press, Cambridge, MA, 1990.

Lockwood, D., *The Blackcoated Worker*, Allen and Unwin, London, 1958.

Martin, T. C., "Counting a Nation by Electricity," *Electrical Engineer*, 12 (1891), 521-530.

Merriam, W., "The Evolution of Modern Census Taking," *Century Magazine*, April (1903), 831-842.

Nelson, R. R. and S. G. Winter, *An Evolutionary Theory of Economic Change*, Harvard University Press, Cambridge, MA, 1982.

Nissel, M., *People Count: A History of the General Register Office*, Her Majesty's Stationery Office, London, 1987.

Office of Population Censuses and Surveys, *Guide to Census Reports: Great Britain 1801-1966*, Her Majesty's Stationery Office, London, 1970.

Registrar General, "Purchase of Tates Arithmometer," *Census Returns: Correspondence and Papers,* Public Record Office, London, Registrar General 19/15 (1901).

————, "Memorandum re: Census of 1901," *Census Returns: Correspondence and Papers,* Public Record Office, London, Registrar General 19/45 (1908).

Truesdell, L. E., *The Development of Punch Card Tabulation in the Bureau of the Census, 1890-1940,* Department of Commerce, Washington, DC, 1965.

Williams, O., *Life and Letters of John Rickman,* Constable, London, 1911.

Yates, J., *Control Through Communication,* Johns Hopkins University Press, Baltimore, MD, 1989.

————, "For the Record: The Embodiment of Organizational Memory, 1850-1920," *Business and Economic History,* 19 (1990), 172-182.

3

Texas Politics and the Fax Revolution

JONATHAN COOPERSMITH

In politics, the timely acquisition and diffusion of information can be a matter of electoral life or death. Since the early 1990s, the spread of modern information technologies has greatly altered the face of politics in Texas. By focusing on the adoption and use of the fax machine, this chapter illustrates how this technology has changed the organizing process and conduct of electoral and legislative politics in Texas.

Faxing is one of many information technologies employed by campaigns and political organizations in the last decade. Others include satellite and cable TV, VCRs, direct mail, telephone banks, cellular telephones, optical scanners, electronic mail, and even pagers. Underlying all these forms of communication is the computer. Contemporary political action is inconceivable without computers to organize information and link technologies together, as computer-based faxing will demonstrate.

The mixing of politics and information technologies has attracted a great deal of academic and commercial interest, producing results ranging from uninhibited excitement at the prospect of teledemocracy to more grounded analyses of the increasing professionalization, specialization, and financial costs of campaigns (Armstrong 1988; Benjamin 1982; Meadow

1985; Selnow 1994; Swerdlow 1988). Researchers have also studied information technologies and their consequences for communication and societies (Compaine 1988; Pool 1990; Rice 1984). While their approaches, assumptions, and conclusions vary widely, a common denominator in these studies is the argument that new technologies are triggering a significant reshaping, possibly fundamental, of society.

The flood of data generated, analyzed, and transmitted by the new information technologies has increased pressure on political organizations to utilize them effectively. This rapid technological evolution is part of a larger, ongoing professionalization of politics, which has shifted much of the expertise necessary to run a political campaign from party organizations to consultants and businesses (McCurry 1989; Sabato 1981).

Unlike television, the incorporation of faxing into politics has added only slightly to the cost of a campaign. The equipment has become so inexpensive and well packaged that fax broadcasting capabilities are easily affordable and accessible to anyone willing to read a manual. Operating costs are paper and telephone charges. Furthermore, faxing has already been incorporated into the services offered by consultants such as daily polling reports.

Faxing does not do what has not been done previously. But it does allow campaigns to do more, stay more informed, and disseminate information far more quickly and accurately than before. There are three major consequences. First, the political process has accelerated significantly compared with 5 or 10 years ago. Most obviously, the cycle for political news has shrunk from days to hours or minutes. Campaigns need to be very well organized to act and react coherently and quickly. Faxing both demands better organization and assists it.

Second, faxing enables organizations to generate a unified political theme statewide easily and quickly, creating the semblance, if not the reality, of a grassroots movement. Local members can express that message to their local media and representatives within hours. The contemporary grassroots campaign is as likely to be organized from a capital as from the heartland (Brinkley 1993). Faxing gives centralized organizations the ability to appear decentralized and gives decentralized organizations the ability to act in a coordinated manner.

Third, faxing has increased the "technology gap" in politics. Republicans and conservative groups have proven more adept than Democrats at integrating fax machines into their operations, displaying greater strategic and tactical imagination. This divide extends into other information technologies and reflects larger cultural and historical differences between the parties. As many organizations have discovered, mere possession of a technology does not guarantee its effective use. Users can realize a technology's potential only through organization and application.

To understand the effects of faxing, this study looks at campaign organizations in Texas, the two major political parties, the legislature, lobbyists, interest groups, and the press. The methodology is an exercise in recent history; the sources are open-ended interviews with members and observers of certain types of Texas political organizations, published news stories, and secondary studies of campaign information technologies.

The focus is Texas, but national politics is not neglected. The reason is simple: Presidential races often pioneer, refine, publicize, and diffuse the political use of new technologies as campaign managers try to promote their candidates and messages by all possible means. The high visibility and large resources of presidential races allow them to set the standard of what is considered a normal campaign technology. Conversely, the enormous number of state and local races represents thousands of petri dishes for experiments which, if successful, may diffuse horizontally and upward (Berke 1992; Luntz 1988). For faxing, the innovative experiments occurred outside Texas.

THE FAX MACHINE

The excitement about the fax machine lies in its rapid, accurate dissemination of printed and graphic information. Couriers, regular mail, and express mail also carry hard copy, but only the fax machine transmits this material almost instantaneously. Telephones convey information orally, but faxing can convey larger amounts of factual information (such as addresses and numbers) and imagery to many people. By combining the speed of a telephone call and the visual presence and accuracy of paper, faxing greatly accelerates the process of communication. In a profession where time and accuracy are crucial, this combination provides major benefits.

To understand the diffusion of faxing, a brief technical history is in order (summarized from Coopersmith 1993). A facsimile machine transmits an image electrically over a distance. This concept has not changed since the first facsimile patent, based on the telegraph, in 1843 and the first commercial service in 1865. What has changed greatly are the underlying technologies and resultant improvements in quality, operations, and speed.

A market for fax technology did not develop until the 1920s when newspapers, eager to print the latest photographs in their competitive battles for circulation, invested the necessary financial and human resources. This wirephoto service demanded specially trained employees and dedicated equipment including high-quality telephone lines. Together with the military and Western Union, newspapers provided niche markets for special-purpose fax equipment until the advent of general-purpose machines in the mid-1960s for business use.

The slow speed (three to six minutes a page), high cost of the equipment and of long-distance telephone rates, and the incompatibility among different manufacturers restricted the attraction of fax machines to potential users. Unlike a photocopier, faxing is a network technology where all components of a system must work before it can function. For fax machines, this meant the widespread availability and compatibility of other machines to transmit and receive. Incompatibility among different manufacturers' equipment limited the value of early machines, consequently lowering interest in obtaining a fax machine. Many fax machines were used in internal networks established within large corporations and the federal government.

The introduction of digital fax machines in the early 1980s changed that situation. Compared with their analog predecessors, these stand-alone machines had much greater speeds (20 seconds a page), far lower cost, and compatibility with other fax machines. Externally, reduced long-distance telephone tariffs, higher quality telephone circuits, and the growing pressure for faster communications made faxing more attractive to businesses. By 1988, the explosion of sales created the necessary critical mass to make faxing an accepted business medium in the United States. In an example of positive feedback, as more people purchased machines, the number of people who could be faxed grew, further increasing faxing's utility. Rising expectations accelerated adoption too; how could you be taken seriously if you did not have a fax machine? (Cowan 1984). Faxing benefited from—and contributed to—the growing "just-in-time" enthusiasm. A faxed letter connoted a premium communication, symbolically more important and urgent than a regular letter or even overnight express delivery.

Faxing also benefited from the minimum adaptation required by managers and organizations to integrate a fax machine into an office. Good design meant a user only needed to know the basic office skills of dialing a telephone and operating a photocopier. The decreasing cost of plain-paper machines significantly improved the readability, feel, and longevity of faxed messages, further increasing the fax's fit into the office. This minimum adaptation, combined with decreasing costs, pushed the adoption of fax machines from large firms to smaller businesses and outside the business world.

Fax machines grew in capability too, further expanding their attractiveness. Consumers could choose among an increasing variety of options ranging from basic, low-cost machines to more expensive, multifunctional equipment. Like General Motors, fax manufacturers offered something for nearly every market niche with increasing capabilities for more money.

At the bottom end of the spectrum was the basic stand-alone machine, which required the user to dial the number and then feed pages in individually. More advanced equipment offered stored lists of numbers, automatic page feeding, and broadcasting. These options allowed a person to send multiple copies—to broadcast—by simply pressing a few buttons, greatly decreasing the time and labor to send the same document to many recipients. Broadcasting was a major attraction for political users. For example, in 1990 the Texas Democratic party needed two days for someone to stand over its basic stand-alone fax machine and transmit a press release to all state media. Consequently, for urgent releases, the party faxed only its top priorities, the largest daily newspapers and major TV stations. After introducing a fax broadcasting system in 1992, the time to fax the Texas media dropped sharply to half a day (McDonald 1995).

Fax modems, introduced in 1985 but entering widespread use only in the early 1990s, enabled a person to send a fax directly from a computer without printing. The original document existed only in computer memory. Unlike stand-alone fax machines, fax modems required a manual to understand how to operate a particular system. Fax modems allowed faster broadcasting with less labor than a stand-alone machine because the computer stored the message and the numbers. Such systems ranged from an individual computer, to networks of PCs connected with a fax server, to dedicated computer-fax systems with multiple telephone lines.

These last systems are primarily owned and operated by independent fax transmission and delivery services. Although existing since the 1960s, only with the widespread diffusion of fax machines have these services found a large market. Instead of using its own equipment to send large numbers of faxes, a business can hire a firm like New Jersey-based Xpedite Systems, which employs thousands of telephone lines to "blast fax" thousands of faxes nationwide in a few minutes (Keiser 1995).

In an excellent example of a range of technologies evolving to fit different environments and needs, four types of fax equipment existed by 1992: basic and stand-alone machines; advanced stand-alone equipment, which can broadcast; computer-based fax modems; and very high-volume equipment for blast faxing. These machines differ greatly in capability and the resources needed to fax a message. All, however, can transmit and receive with each other due to the universal G3 standard, created in 1980 by the International Telecommunications Union from Japanese and British proposals. The G3 protocol meant that, for the first time in the history of fax technology, fax machines could communicate with every G3 machine, regardless of manufacturer.

This compatibility means that the faxed message received by a newspaper or representative may originate from a local citizen's group operating from someone's kitchen in the evening, a political party, or a professionally orchestrated public relations campaign. In this sense, faxing is a decentralized, universal technology equally accessible to the neophyte and the professional. Superior resources and tactics, however, can provide greater saturation and more effective deployment of fax technology. Faxing's political potential was realized best by those whose tighter organization and greater sophistication enabled them to utilize the fax machine as much more than simply a faster mail service. The history of technology and military history provide a rich tapestry of the challenges encountered in reshaping internal organization to maximize effectiveness of new technologies (Bijker and Law 1992; Morison 1974).

The market evolution of a new technology often occurs in two basic stages. At first, users employ the new product as a better version of an old technology (e.g., Krueger 1989). As the potential of the new technology is better understood and it diffuses among a wider population, new uses evolve as people experiment. For example, in World War II, the navy developed the proximity fuse to destroy enemy aircraft, but the army soon employed the fuse to attack soldiers on the ground (Baldwin 1980). This evolution is neither fixed nor inevitable. Much depends upon the receptivity of the audience. As Johnson and Rice (1984) demonstrated in their study of word processing, institutions differed widely in how they utilized the same information technology.

Technologies do not diffuse automatically; people promote, adopt, and adapt them. A key role is played by Aitken's (1976) "translators," people "who moved information from one system to another, interpreting it and changing it in creative ways as they did so." In faxing, translators existed throughout the political culture. Directed adoption was promoted by salespeople and consultants offering their advice and services. Informal adoption occurred through the widespread movement of people from one campaign to another, political parties, information in political newsletters and journals, and casual exchanges of information.

CAMPAIGNS

The fax machine has established deep roots in elections, where time is always at a premium. In a perfect world, everyone is well informed and sufficient time exists for every activity. Campaigns, however, are exercises in semicontrolled chaos, with never enough resources or time to do everything. Anything that can increase the effectiveness of campaign staff is utilized. Faster communication by fax is one such tool. Faxing has another advantage: The technology is so well packaged that almost any volunteer or staffer can operate a stand-alone fax machine.

From the perspective of campaigns, a major difference between faxing and many other new information technologies is their audience. Campaigns employ television and radio for direct access to voters, bypassing the interpretive filter of reporters. Faxing, however, communicates with voters only indirectly through reporters, campaign staff, and supporters.

Faxing multiplies enormously the communicative ability of a campaign, increasing its effectiveness by hastening internal and external communications. Internally, for example, field agents now send their nightly reports to headquarters in written rather than oral form, the coordination of schedules that demanded a week now lasts only a day, the numbers erroneously scribbled down from a telephone conversation now are correctly received, and pollsters transmit the latest data and their analyses to the candidate on the road. Such operations can be greatly strengthened by faster and more thorough coordination, as the 1988 George Bush presidential campaign demonstrated (Gillette 1992). Externally, ad copy can reach newspapers at the last minute so that the advertisements are more timely, statements reach journalists in minutes instead of hours or days, and campaigns coordinate their activities and messages easier and faster with the national party headquarters.

The fax machine is an important communications tool in itself, but its true contribution occurs when used with other technologies to increase their effectiveness. For example, faxing has reduced the time needed to coordinate satellite interviews and feeds of candidates, a staple of elections since Walter Mondale's 1984 presidential campaign, from days to hours (Sabato and Beiler 1988).

In a demonstration of the synergy of linking communication technologies together, faxing enabled the 1994 Texas gubernatorial candidates, Republican George W. Bush and Democrat Ann Richards, to arrange interviews with TV stations statewide quickly and efficiently. After renting satellite time and a ground station (in Austin, the Channel 24 station), a press agent faxed TV stations the necessary coordinates and information to capture the satellite feed. The campaign offered each station the opportunity to interview the candidate at a certain time. Consequently, the candidate could appear on 30 different stations in a few hours without leaving the studio. Not only do candidates receive coverage on local news programs, but the questions from local reporters and anchors are often friendlier and less searching than from the better informed (and more critical) state or national press. As important, the entire process consumes far less time and money than traveling to 30 different studios (Cryer 1995).

In another example of internal and external campaign coordination, advance work has integrated faxing into its operations. Faxing allows easier coordination among campaign agents, local organizers, and the media. State-

wide campaigns can fax schedules, speeches, press releases, and other information to local offices, the state committee, and other participants. Previously, this material was disseminated by telephone, mail, or courier. Faxing
demands less lead time, labor, and cost (Cryer 1995).

Storing lists of telephone numbers on a fax machine enables a campaign to
easily fax many people for only the cost of the telephone calls. As the later
discussion of "talking points" illustrates, this is a low-cost way of keeping
party and elected officials, donors, activists, and other supporters involved in
the campaign. Faxing can replace or augment regular and express mailings,
giving campaigns more flexibility at less expense. Bulk rate mail shares the
low cost of faxing but takes several days to reach its targets. Express mail provides next-day delivery but is significantly more expensive than faxing a few
pages of campaign literature.

One key component of any campaign is good communications with the
press. This is a major challenge in Texas, which has 534 newspapers, 703 radio stations, and 136 TV stations scattered over 266,807 square miles (Texas
Press Association and Texas Broadcasting Association 1995). Most have a
fax machine. The exceptions tend to be small, rural weeklies which use a local commercial service down the street, such as Mailbox, and resent paying
for unwanted faxes, as the Bush gubernatorial campaign inadvertently discovered (Beshear 1995).

Much political faxing consists of press releases, long one of the main
media weapons of a campaign. Since 1992, faxing has become the standard
means of distributing press releases, replacing the old approach of either
mailing or hand-delivering releases to the press corps in Austin. Faxing saves
considerable time but also is less expensive and demanding of staff who no
longer have to print releases and then stuff and deliver envelopes (Sturzl
1995).

Faxing makes it easier for a press spokesperson to send information to the
media, strengthen the candidate's statements with supporting documents,
and reply quickly to questions and charges. Underlying this flow of paper is
the essential role played by the press in carrying information back and forth
between opposing campaigns. This role is accomplished directly by reporters
asking questions and indirectly by stories published and transmitted over
press association wires.

Campaigns' ability to respond to each other almost instantly by fax has
changed the temporal dynamics of campaigning. Instead of a day between
charge and countercharge, the tempo of campaigns has accelerated so much
that instant response is not only possible but required. Campaigns can no longer be confident that their statements will dominate the news; conversely,
they can prevent their opponents from defining the news that day.

One result is a compressed news cycle. Until 1990, the news cycle was two days, starting with publication of a candidate's position on an issue or reaction to an event (Cryer 1995). An opponent's reply would not appear until the next day's newspaper or evening news show. This two-day cycle reflected the time for the opponent's campaign to learn about the initial statement and then formulate and transmit its reply to the press. By 1992, rare was the story that did not carry the original statement along with the opponent's reply. By 1994, articles sometimes included the reply to the reply (e.g., Hamilton 1994).

Laptop computers and cellular phones, in addition to fax machines, contributed to this accelerated media pace. Reporters covering Texas candidates began carrying laptops in 1988 and cellular phones in 1990. Reporters can file stories more quickly and, aided by electronic databases, more comprehensively, from anywhere the cellular phone works. Instead of a reporter scribbling notes and scrambling to find a Western Union office or fighting with colleagues for the only public phone in a small town, the modern reporter types the story into a laptop and transmits it by cellular phone.

Advanced communications also allow reporters to call their office or colleague covering the other candidate to ask for a reaction. The other candidate's press office, if at all competent, promptly responds with a faxed release to the press as well as answering a specific reporter's questions (Attelesey 1995). Faxing thus allows campaigns to respond closer to reporters' deadlines with more accuracy than a telephone conversation and ideally to reach other journalists in time to affect their stories.

Faxing presents a visible indicator of a campaign's or an organization's competency. Slow or incomplete responses, especially those that arrive after a story deadline has passed, reflect poorly on the sender. While rarely written about, such competency shapes reporters' perceptions of the people they cover.

Fax broadcasting is a large reason why faxing is so completely accepted in politics. Broadcasting means that one person with a fax machine can contact literally hundreds of people in a few hours. By skilled targeting (e.g., key legislators and staff members, radio talk show hosts, journalists), one person can greatly affect the evolution of an issue. An excellent example is Frank J. Gaffney, Jr., "director of what is essentially a one-man think tank called the Center for Security Policy" and known for his "fax bursts—his tactical forte" (Blumenthal 1995).

On a larger scale, a barrage of faxes, sent to members of a group urging them to call or write letters (usually of protest), can create a seemingly spontaneous "Astroturf" grassroots movement literally overnight. The results can be quite effective, as the Clinton administration discovered during its abortive 1993 efforts at imposing an energy tax (Brinkley 1993). One activist has claimed that with eight faxes, he can quickly reach 1 million people (Russakoff 1995).

If fax broadcasting was a gigantic leap from the basic stand-alone fax, blast faxing went a step further to make large-scale faxing nearly instantaneous. Blast faxing exemplifies both how campaigns often adopt similar tactics and the increase of outsourcing functions to specialists. The analogy is an arms race; as one campaign adopts a new technology, others follow out of fear, opportunity, and availability (Evangelista 1988).

The appeal of a blast fax service like Xpedite Systems is its almost simultaneous delivery of faxes. The firm likens itself to AT&T, providing a service with no control over or knowledge of the messages it transmits. In February 1995, Xpedite had 3,000 telephone lines and a theoretical maximum output of 80,000 pages per hour. Although more costly than broadcasting from a campaign office, fax blasting provides quicker delivery because of its wealth of telephone lines and frees the campaign machines for other use. Furthermore, the difference between delivery in minutes and delivery in hours can be very important in meeting press deadlines and responding quickly.

In 1992, both the Clinton and Bush campaigns used Xpedite Systems. The company entered Texas politics the next year through Kay Bailey Hutchinson's successful campaign to fill the U.S. Senate seat vacated by Lloyd Bentsen. The initial interest came from a campaign staffer who had used Xpedite Systems in the Bush campaign. Hutchinson's victory and the diffusion of her staffers into other races provided the word-of-mouth referrals vital for a political service. In 1994, with the exception of the unsuccessful Richards gubernatorial campaign, every statewide candidate used Xpedite Systems (Keiser 1995).

This greater usage also resulted from the firm's decision to pursue the political market. The revenue from the Hutchinson race convinced executives that the political arena could be profitable. From 1993 to 1994, the firm's income from political faxing grew fivefold to approximately $800,000, a significant increase but still less than 2 percent of the firm's total revenue and a minuscule amount of the 1994 $200 million fax broadcasting market ("Messaging Carriers" 1995). To achieve that growth in political business, Xpedite Systems hired a market development manager, produced sales literature targeted at campaigns, and dispatched sales agents.

The firm's success was not automatic. "A lot of sales support and hand-holding" were required to overcome two major difficulties. The first was generic to this niche market: convincing campaigns that the service was worth the cost. In addition to speed, Xpedite Systems emphasized that its price brought the assurance, in the form of a delivery report, that all of the requested numbers had been contacted. The second difficulty was specific:

convincing prospects to use Xpedite Systems over smaller firms, despite its higher costs (Donohue 1995; Keiser 1995).

In an example of creating new applications, campaigns have molded the fax into an offensive weapon, building on techniques pioneered in the 1992 presidential election where the fax machine emerged as a weapon for media spin control. The Bush and Clinton campaigns transmitted attack faxes, "a daily, red-meat press release," to reporters. For the beleaguered Bush campaign, this was one of its few successful offensive operations. The primary goal was negative press coverage of the Clinton campaign, but improving the morale of campaign workers was an important secondary consideration (Matalin and Carville 1994).

Clinton strategist Jeff Eller took another approach by faxing daily "talking points" to over 2,000 politicians and contributors, transmitting at night to obtain the lowest telephone rates (Eller 1993; Weisberg 1993). Talking points, also known as the message of the day, are a few concisely stated ideas that a campaign headquarters wants to emphasize (Matalin and Carville 1994; Rosenstiel 1993). The campaign can promote its own theme or respond to events and even to articles not yet printed. A campaign can follow the stories coming over the newswire and then fax talking points to its supporters, who contact their local media in time to incorporate their comments into the story. Sometimes covering the press can go too far; *The New York Times* cut off the Clinton campaign's subscription to its wire service after the campaign critiqued a story several hours *before* it was published (Black 1994; Kurtz 1993).

In an ironic example of the adoption of campaign techniques, the Texas Republican party used talking points as part of its 1994 strategy. The central office faxed its daily message to the 80 members of the State Republican Executive Committee, county chairs, and other political activists. The recipients were asked to promote the message among party members and to their local media. This aided in the statewide creation and dissemination of one coherent party theme, yet with a local viewpoint that increased its value to the local press.

Broadcasting is not essential for attack faxing. In the hands of a good tactician, faxing can turn almost any information into a weapon. Wire services provide advance schedules of candidates, such as the AP Daybook, so the media can arrange to cover events. But a campaign can also use this information to fax local media with hostile questions to ask its opponent, a tactic the Richards campaign used successfully (Beshear 1995; Cryer 1995).

Exploring and (mis)interpreting the history of your opponents is a long established tool of political campaigns (Felknor 1992; Sabato 1994). Modern technologies, including the fax, have greatly accelerated the process while providing much more information (Bodisch 1995; Cooper 1991). The fax machine is Janus-faced with regard to the time-honored traditional activities of leaking documents and denouncing opponents. Faxing can widely disseminate a negative report with far more effectiveness than ever before. Unsolicited documents can appear on a journalist's or campaign's fax machine, raising questions about their authenticity and the possibility of disinformation or a sting (Matalin and Carville 1994). Often the originating machine can be traced, however, revealing the sender. While not decreasing the value of anonymously sent information, this can shift a story from the attack to the attacker. For example, presidential candidate Bob Kerry was forced to fire his main media adviser in 1992 after reporters traced a fax disparaging other Democrats back to him (Kowet 1992).

Rare is the technology whose use is without drawbacks. Faxing incurs problems of information overload, missent memos, and the less obvious but severe problem of less time to think. None of these problems is unique to the political realm. Information overload holds for faxes as well as printed material. Faxed press releases have suffered the same fate as their traditional counterparts: being ignored. The flood of information into a press office, particularly a major newspaper or TV station, can overwhelm even the most hardened political junkie (Ingley 1992; Kuempel 1995).

A nightmare for any campaign or lobbyist is the missent memo or other confidential communication that reaches the press or opposition (Barbash 1995; Stein 1988). Faxing allows the rapid transmission of information; it also allows bigger errors. By pushing the wrong button, a memo can reach hundreds of people the sender never intended [to reach] such as journalists. Perhaps the prime example is the bulletin faxed by the Republican National Committee before the last Bush-Clinton presidential debate. Mistakenly sent to the press instead of Republican state chairs, it told them how to characterize the yet-to-occur debate as a brilliant Republican victory. The spin attempt became the story (Kurtz 1992). Missent faxes may also provide the opposition with information or provide the impression of a disorganized organization (Kamen 1995; Matalin and Carville 1994). Similar cases occasionally surface in Texas but rarely reach the public attention (Cryer 1995; Ratcliffe 1994).

As a preventive measure, the state committees and campaigns instituted strict procedures to ensure that different lists are kept separate in the computer or fax machine to avoid such mishaps. Nonetheless, many campaigns have come within a pushed button of a major missent fax mishap (Cryer 1995; Gower 1995; Shipley 1995).

Fax's very advantage of speed can be a disadvantage, encouraging people to act before they can really think. Harder to quantify because it is less visible, the expectation—which soon becomes the need—to respond instantly may generate the dreaded "shooting yourself in the foot" statement, especially in a campaign's closing days when the pressure is intense and time for thoughtful judgment is rare. Even here, a fax sent in haste presents a less publicly damaging picture than an outburst captured on videotape (Matalin and Carville 1994; von Wupperfeld 1995).

PARTIES AND RELATED ORGANIZATION

In accordance with Will Rogers' dictum, "I'm a member of no organized party, I'm a Democrat," a gap exists between Republicans, including some independent conservative groups, and Democrats, including some independent liberal groups, in institutionalizing the application of new information technologies. Nearly every person interviewed noted a difference in the Democratic-Republican usage.

This is a relative, not absolute, gap. Both parties employ fax machines and other information technologies. During the 1994 governor's race, the Richards Democratic campaign was probably more innovative in its offensive uses of faxing and satellite TV than was the Bush Republican campaign. Some Democratic consultants are as technically sophisticated and innovative as their Republican counterparts. Both parties have officials who understand the potential of these technologies.

Overall, however, Republicans have more thoroughly diffused the new communication technologies into their organizations and campaigns, and the Republican party has been more innovative and far-reaching in its fax applications than has its Democratic counterpart. The newer Republican party leadership has devoted more attention to internal and external communications than have the Democrats. While Texas, like the rest of the South, has been shifting toward the Republican party, the greater GOP application of information technologies has hastened that evolution (Swansbrough and Brodsky 1988). As one indicator, the number of Republicans in the 181-member Texas legislature grew from 10 in 1969, to 21 in 1977, to 58 in 1985, to 71 in 1993 ("Expanding From the Top Down" 1993).

The state Republican headquarters acquired a fax machine in the mid-1980s initially for regular office operations such as communicating with its direct mail vendor. Although some press releases were faxed, its staff still reproduced and delivered most releases to the press by hand or mail. Party priorities shifted in 1991 with the arrival of Karen Hughes as executive director. A former Dallas television reporter, Hughes dramatically improved the party's communications with the media to increase press understanding—and coverage—of the Republican party of Texas. She directed the installation of the first fax broadcasting system in 1991 as part of a larger effort to improve press relations. Reporters soon noticed that the party answered faxes more quickly and faxed news releases that addressed their needs better (Gower 1995; Lewis 1995; Slater 1995).

The Democratic party acquired its first fax machine in 1989 also for office work. Both state parties acquired a computer-based fax broadcasting capacity in time for the 1992 election. In 1995, the Democratic party operated two stand-alone fax machines and two computer-based fax broadcasting systems with 3 of 10 telephone lines dedicated to faxing. The Republican party of Texas has two stand-alone fax machines with broadcasting capabilities, which created queues of party workers waiting to fax until the office installed a network linking all its computers to the fax machines in the summer of 1995.

Both parties use the fax primarily to send press releases, sometimes replying to an earlier attack fax (Diehl 1994). Both parties also send more faxes than they receive. Much of the incoming correspondence is in response to party requests or from party members requesting specific information. County chairs often fax local news such as the resignation and replacement of a chair. After the 1994 general election, the Republican party contacted each chair for information on the local elections. Faxed replies saved the central office a few days waiting for the mail or calling each of the 254 county clerks.

A significant difference between the two state parties is how they employ faxing to strengthen their internal coherence and external image. The Republican party has been more aggressive than the Democrats and has a greater percentage of party officials linked by fax. At the level of the state executive committees, approximately 75 percent of the 62 Democratic members [were] reachable by fax in early 1995, a threefold increase since 1992. Approximately 88 percent of the 80 Republican members [were] reachable [in 1995]. At the level of county chairs, 73 percent of the 254 Democrats [had] faxes in 1995, compared with approximately 20 percent in 1992. Approximately 80 to 90 percent of their Republican counterparts [had] access to a fax [in 1995] (Gower 1995; McDonald 1995).

The Republican party uses its higher level of access to transmit its chair's report and other regular correspondence to the State Republican Executive Committee. In 1995, the party established a fax network, asking activists with fax machines to assume responsibility for a specific number of local and long-distance faxes. The advantages to the headquarters are threefold: reduced long-distance charges, greater member participation, and better contacts with local media (Gower 1995).

One fax network administrator is Barnie Henderson, Jr., a Republican executive committee member for Senate District 5, who exemplifies how faxing can be used to establish and strengthen local, state, and national links. Henderson uses his fax machine to receive and transmit news within the party and distribute press releases to the 70 media outlets in the district's 19 counties. In addition to Texas politics, he subscribes to *Scoop: Your Inside View to the Strategies and Activities of the Conservative Movement in Washington,* an occasional newsletter faxed by the National Center for Public Policy Research. Much of the information Henderson gathers is further disseminated by a bulk mail newsletter he distributes to over 200 people (Henderson 1995).

His Democratic counterparts are not quite as active (Day 1995). The Austin Democratic headquarters does receive daily faxed briefings from the White House and Democratic National Committee, enabling the Texas party to better follow Washington activities and to shape its activities accordingly. What the Democratic party does not do, however, is disseminate that information and state news widely within Texas.

The Republican party's better performance in this arena has increased the amount and timeliness of information about the party available to the press and party activists. Better utilization and application of communications technologies are not the primary reasons for the party's ascension, but they have clearly contributed significantly.

THE LEGISLATURE, LOBBYISTS, INTEREST GROUPS, AND REPORTERS

Just as faxing has become an integral part of campaigns, so too has it become embedded in the world of the Texas legislature, the 1,628 registered lobbyists and more than 4,500 interest groups trying to influence it, and the 512 reporters who cover it (Bryce 1995; Olsen 1995; Traxler 1995). As is often the case when a new technology enters an established institution, formal rules have lagged behind the possibilities of the technology, and questions of access are still unclear. Campaigns and parties were quicker to adopt faxing than was the legislature because their structures were less formalized, fewer rules restricted their operations, and they had easier access to funds.

In 1990, when the authoritative *Texas State Directory* first listed fax numbers for the governor's office and the legislature, public faxing of the legislature became an open option. Since then, public access has increased greatly; of the 181 legislators, the number listing fax numbers for their district offices grew from 40 in 1990 to 108 in 1995 (*Texas State Directory* 1990-1995). Indicative of their party's greater application of information technology, Republicans were more likely than Democrats to publish their numbers. A majority of House and Senate Republicans listed their numbers by 1993; in 1995, most Democratic representatives still did not publish their numbers. Reflecting their larger districts, the 31 senators were more likely to list their numbers than were the 150 representatives. A majority of senators have listed fax numbers since 1991; this did not occur in the House until 1995.

The public list of numbers, however, is incomplete; Xpedite Systems sells a list of the fax numbers of every legislator's Austin, district, and private offices. The gap between publicly accessible numbers and the complete set indicates that the rules of use are still under negotiation as legislators, like newspapers, wonder whether too much communication with the citizenry is a totally positive phenomenon.

Is the fax machine a technology for the representative or the public? This is the question of access. By restricting knowledge of their fax numbers, representatives have the advantage of communicating only with people and groups they choose. Those not so privileged must resort to other means of communicating, which, from their perspective, denies them the opportunity to transmit their opinions instantly. This could be seen as a form of electronic censorship (Marin and Johnson 1995; Mersop 1995).

A strong argument against publishing fax numbers is the very real potential of incoming messages overwhelming an office's fax machine. Indeed, some groups have jammed offices with faxes and phone calls as a protest (Brown 1995; Pytte 1989). U.S. Representative Charles E. Schumer's spirited defense of the Clinton administration during the July 1995 congressional hearings on Waco earned him hundreds of hate faxes (Clines 1995b; Kovalski 1995).

The Texas legislature has slowly but wholeheartedly embraced the fax machine. Faxing has greatly facilitated the flow of information between the district and main Austin offices of legislators, allowing them to remain in closer contact with "the folks back home." Distance is no longer a barrier. For example, before fax, the only way for Senator Jim Turner in College Station to receive a speech written in Austin that day was for a courier to drive the 100 miles (Wells 1995).

Representatives have particularly benefited from faster receipt of local newspaper stories in Austin. Instead of listening to a telephoned description of an article or waiting several days for the local newspapers to arrive by post, the district office can fax the article to the legislator's Austin office the day of publication. This greater speed allows representatives to gauge local thinking more quickly and react more promptly with less effort. A representative can reply to the story the same day it appeared.

Much of faxing's value to representatives stems from its ability to transmit graphic information, so amendments and bills can be quickly, widely, and accurately transmitted for analysis and consideration. Faxing has become the easiest and fastest way to send a position paper or amendment around the capital.

The experience of the Texas House of Representatives illustrates the importance of organization in adopting a new technology (Avila 1995; Welsh 1995). For the 1993-1994 session, internal rules allowed the purchase or rental of a fax machine for a district office from a member's operating account. For the 1995-1996 session, this account could pay for a fax machine in the capital office. Before this change, a representative had to use campaign or personal funds to acquire a fax machine for Austin.

Starting in 1991, a central fax number for each chamber received messages for members with actual delivery by messenger (Geltmeier 1995). This service has evolved greatly as lawmakers and staff struggled to organize a service to help, not hinder, them. The number of fax machines employed by the House central fax office grew from 2 in 1991 to 10 in 1995. This growth was accompanied by a major organizational shift in the use of fax after incoming faxes overwhelmed the service during the 1993 session.

Initially, all machines could transmit and receive. The machines were distributed around the House area and in a central office near the post office. Demand was cyclical, corresponding to when the legislature was meeting. Volume grew in the last weeks of the session, when most bills are passed and the pace is frenetic. Incoming messages peaked in 1993 at approximately 5,500 in one month and in 1995 at approximately 7,000. Outgoing messages equaled less than one third of the incoming volume, although including faxing from members' offices would increase this percentage.

In 1993, the internal messenger service would not convey outgoing messages to the fax machines on grounds of confidentiality, so staffers had to go. But the flood of incoming faxes often resulted in people waiting for an available machine. Lines would form, defeating the purpose of fast transmission. As important, waiting meant that a staffer was away from the office, a serious consideration in the House, where members usually have only two or three staffers.

Even though the peak 1995 incoming traffic was 30 percent above the 1993 level, a similar gridlock did not occur due to more machines and a restructured operation. The office of the sergeant at arms dedicated three machines in a central location to receive all incoming faxes. Seven other machines, which could only transmit, were distributed around the House offices for easy access. This separation of transmission from reception allowed staffers to send faxes without waiting for a free outside line. In addition, more members had their own fax machines, diverting some traffic from the House-wide system.

The image of the shady lobbyist prowling the halls of the state capitol and corrupting legislators is a staple of Texas politics.[1] Today, the lobbyist still graces the capitol, but instead of cash-stuffed envelopes, the accoutrements are a pager, a cellular telephone, a laptop computer, and a portable fax machine. The lobbyist's office still receives a morning delivery from a legislative reporting service but now obtains updates of legislation by fax or electronic mail. Faxing and these other technologies enable a lobbyist to amass information more quickly, operate effectively away from the office, keep clients informed, and organize collective action (Clayton 1995; Sturzl 1995; Valles 1995). Organizing by faxing is far easier than organizing by telephone. Not only is time saved trying to reach people, but because information is sent in written form, excuses about misconstrued messages are no longer possible. Nor do postdated letters and claims of lost mail constitute believable excuses ("Raising the Specter" 1995).

For interest groups and lobbyists, faxing has improved communication with their members, the legislature, and other lobbyists. The nature, structure, and goals of interest groups vary greatly, and their use of faxing reflects these differences. Statewide organizations, such as Mothers Against Drunk Driving (MADD), may have an Austin headquarters but officers and branches scattered throughout the state. For activities requiring the consent of several people, such as writing policy statements, the fax greatly accelerates communication and at far less cost than an overnight delivery service or bringing people together for a meeting (Brown 1995).

Fax polling enables an organization to quickly ascertain its members' views. The most advanced application of this technique is the Fiscal Impact Assessment Team (FIAT) created by the Texas Municipal League (TML), a nonpartisan association of city governments, in 1993. The Austin headquarters will fax the 45 FIAT members a proposed bill and ask them to estimate its cost on a form and fax the form back within 30 minutes. The league can then provide key legislators with its findings later that day, thus providing well-grounded information to argue its case (Sturzl 1995). This rapid reaction is very important during the biennial legislative session, which lasts only 140 days. A similar exercise by express mail would demand 3 days and cost much more.

One of the most impressive organizational uses of the fax machine is the fax tree used to mobilize people. Its prefax equivalent is a mailing or the telephone tree, where the main office would call a list of people, who then called their own lists. Compared with faxed talking points or "membership alerts," telephone trees convey far less information. Telephone trees additionally suffer the disadvantages of their verbal messages being misunderstood or unanswered telephones. As important, dialing and speaking demand more people and time than does broadcast faxing. These drawbacks can be overcome by an automated calling machine for short messages, such as the one recently installed by the Republican party of Brazos County for routine notification of events (Lewis 1995).

Perhaps the most skillful operator of a fax tree has been the Texas branch of the American Family Association (AFA), a conservative organization, which uses a fax network to reach its most active members. Its Austin office will fax approximately 100 members, who then retransmit the message by their own faxes or photocopying and mailing. Within a few hours, several hundred people can be notified and respond by contacting their legislators and local press with faxes, telephone calls, and letters. During the peak of the 1994 election, the association faxed over 500 pages a week (Gower 1995; Roberts 1995). In contrast, the liberal Texas Abortion Rights Action League (TARAL) does not have a fax notification network; instead, it uses a non-computerized telephone tree and postcards to reach its members with urgent notices (Johnson 1995). This difference of fax use by ideological position mirrors the two political parties' different applications of fax. This similarity is not coincidental.

Before the fax, the TML's Austin office used to overnight express material, a costly operation, or activate a telephone tree, a time-consuming process. Since he added fax broadcasting in 1993, Executive Director Frank Sturzl can fax 400 people in a very short time. The AFA takes a shotgun approach to lobbying, relying on large numbers of citizens calling and writing their representatives. The TML employs a rifle strategy, a more directed, targeted approach based on fax and computer databases. Its Grass Roots Involvement Program (GRIP) was created from post-election surveys asking members who they knew in the new legislature. The result was a database that provides at least five contacts for every legislator. This is targeting to a degree previously unattainable. When activated, GRIP allows Sturzl to fax his members with information about who to contact and the topic to discuss (Rosenthal 1993; Sturzl 1995).

The difference between the two groups reflects their different nature. The AFA claims to be a broad-based, grassroots movement; its power derives from its ability to mobilize people. The TML's more limited membership moves in the same circles as representatives and their staffs. Contacts are more effective than numbers.

CONCLUSION

By focusing on Texas politics, this chapter has illustrated the adoption of an information technology by the political world and its adaptation to the specific needs of the electoral and legislative processes. In a few cases, such as blast faxing, the transfer came directly from businesses trying to expand their markets. Mostly, the adoption of faxing followed a "trickle-down" approach from the 1992 presidential campaign, which saw the first large-scale applications of faxing and other information technologies (Kolbert 1992; Kowet 1992). Although commercially available since the mid-1960s, fax machines did not play a significant role in Texas politics until 1992. Full incorporation into the political process appeared in the 1993 and 1994 races, the same time faxing began to play a major role in the legislature.

The essentials of campaigning, political parties, legislative sessions, and lobbying have not changed. Nor is concern about the importance of technology to the political process new (Herring 1929). What has changed are the enabling technologies, their uneven institutional use, and the temporal dynamics of political processes. Texas politics in 1995, in comparison with that of 1985, demands more organizational competence, is more expensive and more democratic, and is paced much faster. Faxing has played a major role in these changes, particularly in allowing small groups to emerge as big players in the ever-shifting worlds of politics.

All statewide and many local campaigns have adopted faxing to various degrees. Its ability to hasten internal and external communications is perhaps faxing's most important attribute. This acceleration has significantly aided the increased temporal pace of political organizing.

Faxing's attributes of low cost and easy integration into office operations meant low barriers to entry. The wide range of capabilities in fax machines permitted different levels of commitment and exploitation. Faxing's near-universal adoption in the business and political world increased its value as well as raising the level below which a candidate will not be viewed seriously. Faxing is an excellent example of organizational integration and adaptation.

Faxing also illustrates the technology gap between the Republican and Democratic parties. To some degree, this gap is national and historical; Democrats and liberal groups have lagged in applying new technologies. For example, the Republican party opened a media center on Capitol Hill in 1978; the Democrats did not do so until 1984 (Bonafede 1984). Republicans and conservative groups have employed these information technologies more effectively (Armstrong 1988; Meadow 1985; Porteous 1994; Seib 1994).

Greater financial resources permit these applications, but the real explanation is commitment. Two contributing factors are the background of its members and the minority status of the Republican party. Sabato (1981) has noted that Republicans tend to be drawn from the managerial class and thus have more awareness of information technologies and more hands-on experience in how to use them.

As important is the party's minority status in Texas. Only in the last decade have Republicans emerged from generations of Democratic domination (Bauer 1990; Dyer 1988; Murchison 1985; "Republicans Rising" 1993). The

Democratic leadership may be less accustomed to innovative thinking about organization and technologies because, until recently, there was no need to stray from the tried-and-true.

Because they are going against the grain, Republican leaders may invest more attention and importance to organization and thus to technologies to strengthen them internally. Minority parties, with less to lose and more to gain by innovating, have often pioneered new communication technologies in the U.S. Congress, according to Senate historian Don Richie (Clines 1995a).

By increasing central control of information, faxing and other information technologies can strengthen the top-down structure of large campaigns and parties, as the Clinton campaign demonstrated in 1992. Yet these same technologies also allow small but well-organized groups to exert a disproportionate influence on a political party or legislature. The phenomenon is not new, as Lenin demonstrated with his mastery of Russian Social Democratic politics, but the ability for such groups to act on a large scale is unprecedented. In 1994, the "Religious Right" out-organized mainstream Republicans and took over the Texas party convention by democratically seizing control of county conventions and nominating its own candidates, making Texas one of 18 states where its forces control the party on some issues (Berke 1994; Persinos 1994; Merida and Dewar 1993; Saberi 1993; Weisskopf 1993).

Conservative political groups have greatly expanded their use of fax networks since 1994 (Russakoff 1995). Their far greater utilization of this information technology has already reshaped the dynamics of politics in Texas and the United States as a whole. Whether other political groups will follow is an open question.

CODA

Since the 1994 elections, modern communications technologies have further accelerated the pace of politics while increasing outsiders' access to campaigns and causes. Four technologies—faxing, e-mail, the Internet, and cellular phones—have become even more integrated into the political process than they were a few years ago.

The fax machine still plays an essential role in campaigns: to communicate both inside an organization and with outsiders, usually party and issue activists, the media, and other opinion makers. The technology and its applications have matured, however, and they have moved into the background and are now taken for granted.

By contrast, e-mail and the Internet now play far greater roles than they did a few years ago, reflecting the greater diffusion of these technologies into American society. E-mail is increasingly finding application as a supplement to, or even a substitute for, faxing. The same virtues of faxing—rapid communication, easy operations from a computer, transmission of the printed word—also account for the spread of e-mail. Faxing, however, still holds an edge for transmitting graphic or other complex material.

Jimmy Carter's 1976 presidential campaign was the first to use e-mail. Two decades of technological improvement (including much greater ease of use) and dropping costs were required before e-mail became an essential campaign tool (Selnow 1998). As in the commercial world, e-mail is almost essential for communications within a statewide campaign.

E-mail is not without its shortcomings. One problem is geographic. The quality of telephone lines in smaller communities is not always up to the demands of e-mail. A low-quality line will degrade a fax, but it will still be readable. By contrast, an e-mail message will be completely garbled. E-mail service is also less likely if a long-distance charge is needed to reach an Internet service provider (Sturzl 1998; Young 1998). Whether telephone deregulation will overcome these difficulties is unclear.

Nor is e-mail suited for direct contact with voters. The demographic data so vital for effective application of direct mail do not exist yet for e-mail addresses. A sender would essentially be firing his or her message blindly into the electronic void. Equally important, that message would probably be regarded as unsolicited "spam" and either promptly erased or used to justify voting against that candidate (Young 1998).

In contrast, the World Wide Web has become an excellent way to provide information. In Texas in 1998, the major candidates for state offices all had their own Web pages, as did the two parties. Organizations like the TML also have Web sites to publicize their activities and keep their members informed. Campaigns have great incentives to create Web sites. They can provide the public and journalists with a cornucopia of easily accessible information, yet in a controlled format. Like fax, Web sites have the advantages of fairly low cost and compatibility with the modern, computerized office. Once set up, a Web site is easy to maintain. Furthermore, a campaign without a Web site is demonstrating its lack of technological ability (Selnow 1998; Slater 1998).

The simple act of having a Web page, however, does not signify anything about its content or lack thereof. While some sites may be updated daily, a random sample of political Web sites found far more sites unchanged for months, if not years (e.g., in July 1998, the Texas A&M College Republicans' site still prominently displayed links from the 1996 presidential campaign as well as the April 1998 election ballot).

While the new interactive electronic media of e-mail and the Internet have attracted most of the attention, cellular phones have probably had more immediate effect on campaigns. Mobile phones are not new; politicians have used them for decades, but the drastic drops in cost to acquire and use them, the added privacy provided by digital instead of analog transmission, and the geographic extension of coverage have made the cellular phone an essential item for the high-level staffer as well as the candidate, replacing pagers as the mark of importance.

Not only do cellular phones permit much greater voice communications within a campaign, they enable reporters to reach staff and candidates anywhere at anytime and vice versa. This greater accessibility means that it is rare for an efficient campaign to let an opponent's statements go unchallenged.

The consequences of this continuing diffusion of communications technologies are far-reaching. First, the compression of the news cycle has continued unabated since the 1996 election. For example, the Democratic National Committee aggressively tracked the 1997 congressional hearings on campaign financing, inundating reporters with its rapid responses (Bennet 1996; Bennet and Van Natta 1997). The Internet should further continue this acceleration.

Second, just as the American military is aggressively promoting information superiority as a way to merge the different components of the armed forces into a coherent, tactically superior tool of state policy, so too is the political world trying to adapt communications technologies for tactical and strategic advantage.

At the national and state levels—the "big leagues"—differences between the parties are increasingly shrinking. Democratic and more liberal groups have reduced the technology gap with Republican and more conservative groups. The AFA now sends out press releases by e-mail as well as fax. TARAL, however, also employs e-mail to reach its members as well as the media. At lower levels in Texas, Republicans are still more likely than Democrats to use faxing, e-mail, and Web pages, reflecting the different societal composition of the parties and the concomitant access to and familiarity with those technologies.

Modern information technologies will continue to alter the face of politics. Perhaps the largest uncertainty is what role the Internet, still in the formative stages, will play. Will its ability for anyone to create his or her own Web site destroy the "iron lock of the mainstream media" on creating and reporting news? (Selnow 1998). Or, will we see even more focus on symbols and presentation at the cost of thoughtful deliberation?[2]

NOTES

1. As the unsavory and legendary saying goes, "If you can't take their money, drink their whiskey, screw their women, and vote against' em anyway, you don't belong in Texas politics," (Ivins 1992, p. 58).

2. A National Science Foundation, Technology, and Society Program grant supported this research.

REFERENCES

Aitken, Hugh G. J., *Syntony and Spark: The Origins of Radio,* Princeton University Press, Princeton, NJ, 1976.

Armstrong, Richard, *The Next Hurrah: The Communications Revolution in American Politics,* Beech Tree Books, New York, 1988.

Attelesey, Sam, *Dallas Morning News* correspondent, interview, February 7, 1995.

Avila, Lisa, administrative aide to Representative Steve Ogden, interview, March 3, 1995.

Baldwin, Ralph B., *The Deadly Fuze: The Secret Weapon of World War II,* Presidio Press, San Rafael, CA, 1980.

Barbash, Fred, "Arms Deal Scandal Roils London Politics," *The Washington Post,* June 20, 1995.

Bauer, John R., "Partisan Realignment and the Changing Political Geography of Texas," *Texas J. Political Studies,* 12, 2 (1990), 41-66.

Benjamin, Gerald (Ed.), *The Communications Revolution in Politics,* Academy of Political Science, New York, 1982.

Bennet, James, "Candidates Respond Rapidly, Picking 'Gotcha' Over Debate," *The New York Times,* May 28, 1996.

——— and Don Van Natta, Jr., "So Far, Democrats Feel Like Early Winners," *The New York Times,* July 13, 1997.

Berke, Richard L., "Satellite Technology Allows Campaigns to Deliver Their Messages Unfiltered," *The New York Times,* October 23, 1992.

———, "Religious Conservatives Conquer G.O.P. in Texas," *The New York Times,* June 12, 1994.

Beshear, David, press assistant in George Bush gubernatorial campaign, interview, February 16, 1995.

Bijker, Wiebe E. and John Law (Eds.), *Shaping Technology/Building Society: Studies in Sociotechnical Change,* MIT Press, Cambridge, MA, 1992.

Black, Christine M., *The Pursuit of the Presidency: '92 and Beyond,* Oryx Press, Phoenix, AZ, 1994.

Blumenthal, Sidney, "The Western Front," *The New Yorker,* June 5, 1995, p. 40.

Bodisch, Duke, opposition research specialist, interview, February 22, 1995.

Bonafede, Dom, "Strides in Technology Are Changing the Face of Political Campaigning," *National J.,* April 7 (1984), 657-661.

Brinkley, Joel, "Cultivating the Grass Roots to Reap Legislative Benefits," *The New York Times,* November 1, 1993.

Brown, Kirk, former Mothers Against Drunk Driving president, interview, February 13, 1995.

Bryce, Robert, "Access Through the Lobby," *Texas Observer,* February 24, 1995, pp. 14-17.

Clayton, Bill, Capital Consultants, letter, February 17, 1995.

Clines, Francis X., "In Appeal to Internet Surfers, Democrats Hope to Catch a Wave," *The New York Times,* June 30, 1995a.

————, "An End to Hearings, None to Hateful Faxes," *The New York Times,* August 2, 1995b.

Compaine, Benjamin M. (Ed.), *Issues in New Information Technology,* Ablex, Norwood, NJ, 1988.

Cooper, Terry, "Negative Image," *Campaigns & Elections,* September (1991), 18-25.

Coopersmith, Jonathan, "Facsimile's False Starts," *IEEE Spectrum,* February (1993), 46-49.

Cowan, Ruth Schwartz, *More Work for Mother,* Basic Books, New York, 1984.

Cryer, Bill, press secretary to Governor Ann Richards, interview, February 2, 1995.

Day, Annie Laura, Democratic Executive Committee member, Senate District 5, interview, August 8, 1995.

Diehl, Kemper, "Fax Wars Help Candidates Keep Battle Going Over Long Summer," *San Antonio Express News,* June 5, 1994.

Donohue, Michael, market development manager of Xpedite Systems, interview, March 1, 1995.

Dyer, James A., Arnold Vedlitz, and David B. Hill, "New Voters, Switchers, and Political Party Realignment in Texas," *Western Political Quarterly,* March (1988), 155-167.

Eller, Jeff, strategist in Clinton presidential campaign, interview, July 29, 1993.

Evangelista, Matthew, *Innovation and the Arms Race,* Cornell University Press, Ithaca, NY, 1988.

"Expanding From the Top Down," *Congressional Quarterly Weekly Review,* May 22, 1993, p. 1316.

Felknor, Bruce L., *Political Mischief: Smear, Sabotage, and Reform in U.S. Elections,* Praeger, Greenwich, CT, 1992.

Geltmeier, Deena, assistant editor of *Texas State Directory,* interview, March 2, 1995.

Gillette, Michael L., "Interview With James Shearer," in *Snapshots of the 1988 Presidential Campaign,* Vol. 1: *The Bush Campaign,* Lyndon B. Johnson School of Public Affairs, Austin, TX, 1992, pp. 81-136.

Gower, Angelina, database support and production coordinator of Republican party of Texas, interview, February 14, 1995.

Hamilton, Arnold, "Richards, Bush Both Vow: No New Taxes," *Dallas Morning News,* October 30, 1994.

Henderson, Barnie, Jr., Republican Executive Committee member, Senate District 5, letter, February 9, 1995.

Herring, Pendleton, *Group Representation Before Congress,* Brookings Institution, Washington, DC, 1929.

Ingley, Caroline, fax consultant, interview, March 5, 1992.

Ivins, Molly, *Molly Ivins Can't Say That, Can She?* Vintage Books, New York, 1992.

Johnson, Becky, Texas Abortion Rights Action League communications director, letter, February 20, 1995.

Johnson, Bonnie McDaniel and Ronald E. Rice, "Reinvention in the Innovation Process: The Case of Word Processing," in Ronald E. Rice (Ed.), *The New Media: Communication, Research, and Technology,* Sage, Beverly Hills, 1984, pp. 157-184.

Kamen, Al, "Boy, Did They Get a Wrong Number," *The Washington Post,* August 14, 1995.

Keiser, John, account manager of Xpedite Systems, interview, February 22, 1995.

Kolbert, Elisabeth, "Technology Brought In to Add Personal Touch," *The New York Times,* June 9, 1992.

Kovalski, Serge F., "Congressmen Discover Defense of ATF Is Risky," *The Washington Post,* July 28, 1995.

Kowet, Don, "High-Flown Stump Oratory," *Washington Times,* March 9, 1992.

Krueger, Rick, Will Kitchen, and Karen Kitchen, "Using Information Technology," *J. State Government,* November-December (1989), 207-209.

Kuempel, George, *Dallas Morning News* correspondent, interview, January 31, 1995.

Kurtz, Howard, " 'Talking Points' Spin Out of Control in Fax Fiasco," *The Washington Post,* October 17, 1992.

————, "White House Monitors TV News Feeds," *The Washington Post,* April 6, 1993.

Lewis, Rodger, chairman of the Brazos County Republican party, interview, February 2, 1995.

Luntz, Frank I., *Candidates, Consultants, and Campaigns: The Style and Substance of American Electioneering,* Basil Blackwell, Oxford, UK, 1988.

Marin, Jonathan K. and Wendy Johnson, "Pennsylvania Tunes Out," *The New York Times,* Letters to the Editor, August 11, 1995.

Matalin, Mary and James Carville with Peter Knobler, *All's Fair: Love, War, and Running for President,* Random House, New York, 1994.

McCurry, Michael, "The New Electronic Politics," *Campaigns & Elections,* March-April (1989), 23-32.

McDonald, Steve, technical director of Texas Democratic party, interview, February 9, 1995.

Meadow, Robert G. (Ed.), *New Communication Technologies in Politics,* Annenberg School of Communications, Washington, DC, 1985.

Merida, Kevin and Helen Dewar, "The People Find Their Voice," *The Washington Post National Weekly,* February 8-14, 1993.

Mersop, Alida, "Subcommittee Has Unlisted Fax Number," *The New York Times,* Letters to the Editor, July 15, 1995.

"Messaging Carriers Have an Excellent Year," *EMMS,* December 12, 1994. (Electronic Mailing and Messaging Services)

Morison, Elting E., *From Know-How to Nowhere: The Development of American Technology,* Basic Books, New York, 1974.

Murchison, William, "The Republican Roundup," *Policy Review,* Summer (1985), 81-82.

Olsen, Claudia, House of Representatives communications, interview, August 3, 1995.

Persinos, John F., "Has the Christian Right Taken Over the Republican Party?" *Campaigns & Elections,* September (1994), 20-24.

Pool, Ithiel de Sola, *Technologies Without Boundaries: On Telecommunications in a Global Age,* Harvard University Press, Cambridge, MA, 1990.

Porteous, Skipp, "The Techno-Religious Right," *Free Inquiry,* Fall (1994), 7-8.

Pytte, Alyson, "Avalanche of Fax Messages Lands Close to Home," *Congressional Quarterly,* September 30, 1989, pp. 2553-2554.

"Raising the Specter," *The Hill,* September 13, 1995.

Ratcliffe, R. G., "Just the Fax, Ma'am: Trip May Be for Political Hay," *Houston Chronicle,* July 16, 1994.

"Republicans Rising in Texas," *Congressional Quarterly Weekly Review,* May 22, 1993, pp. 1309-1316.

Rice, Ronald E. (Ed.), *The New Media: Communication, Research, and Technology,* Sage, Beverly Hills, CA, 1984.

Roberts, Wyatt, executive director of American Family Association of Texas, interview, February 13, 1995.

Rosenstiel, Tom, *Strange Bedfellows: How Television and the Presidential Candidates Changed American Politics, 1992,* Hyperion, New York, 1993.

Rosenthal, Alan, *The Third House: Lobbyists and Lobbying in the States,* Congressional Quarterly Press, Washington, DC, 1993.

Russakoff, Dale, "No-Name Movement Fed by Fax Expands," *The Washington Post,* August 20, 1995.

Sabato, Larry J., *The Rise of Political Consultants: New Ways of Winning Elections,* Basic Books, New York, 1981.

———, *Feeding Frenzy: How Attack Journalism Has Transformed American Politics,* Free Press, New York, 1994.

——— and David Beiler, "Reflections on New Technologies and Trends in the Political Consultant Trade," in Joel Swerdlow (Ed.), *Media Technology and the Vote: A Source Book,* Annenberg School of Communications, Washington, DC, 1988.

Saberi, Erin, "From Moral Majority to Organized Minority: Tactics of the Religious Right," *Christian Century,* August 11 (1993), 781-784.

Seib, Gerald F., "As Politics Go Digital, Info Highway Traffic Is Heavy in Right Lane," *The Wall Street Journal,* March 16, 1994.

Selnow, Gary W., *High-Tech Campaigns: Computer Technology in Political Communication,* Praeger, New York, 1994.

———, *Electronic Whistle-Stops: The Impact of the Internet on American Politics,* Praeger, Westport, CT, 1998.

Shipley, George, Shipley & Associates, interview, February 14, 1995.

Slater, Wayne, *Dallas Morning News* correspondent, interview, February 17, 1995.

———, *Dallas Morning News* correspondent, interview, July 2, 1998.

Stein, M. L., "Fax Fluke Puts Pol's Poll in Hands of Press," *Editor & Publisher,* August 6, 1988.

Sturzl, Frank, executive director of Texas Municipal League, interview, February 7, 1995.

———, executive director of Texas Municipal League, interview, July 9, 1998.

Swansbrough, Robert H. and David M. Brodsky, *The South's New Politics: Realignment and Dealignment,* University of South Carolina Press, Columbia, 1988.

Swerdlow, Joel L. (Ed.), *Media Technology and the Vote: A Source Book,* Annenberg School of Communications, Washington, DC, 1988.

Texas Press Association and Texas Broadcasting Association, conversations, February 28, 1995.

Texas State Directory, Austin, TX, 1990-1995.

Traxler, Janet, Texas Ethics Commission, interview, August 3, 1995.

Valles, Bob, Valles & Associates, interview, February 14, 1995.

von Wupperfeld, Paul, president of Log Cabin Republicans, correspondence, January 6, 1995.

Weisberg, Jacob, "True Fax," *The New Republic,* July 5 (1993), 11-12.

Weisskopf, Michael, "How the Gospel Grapevine Mobilizes Its Troops," *The Washington Post National Weekly,* February 8-14, 1993.

Wells, Diane, district office staff for Senator Jim Turner, interview, February 7, 1995.

Welsh, Rod, sergeant at arms, Texas House of Representatives, interview, August 4, 1995.

Young, Peck, political consultant, interview, July 2, 1998.

PART II

THE RHETORIC OF INFORMATION TECHNOLOGY AND
ORGANIZATIONAL TRANSFORMATION

Part II looks at information technology (IT) and organizational transformation from the rhetorical perspective. Rhetorical tools and perspectives have become increasingly popular in organizational analysis. They are suitable for examining both the societal rhetoric around IT-based transformation and individual cases of IT adoption. Because the data used by many IT researchers consist of interview transcripts and ethnographical notes, examining these data through rhetorical lenses is particularly appropriate. Too often, researchers take literally statements and terminology that need to be examined more closely. Moreover, the rhetorical lens highlights the interpretive role of the researcher too often suppressed in the search for "objectivity," encouraging the embrace rather than the denial of this role. The first chapter in this part of the volume examines the rhetoric of IT and organizational transformation at a societal level, the second looks at a particular aspect of the rhetoric around one organization's use of IT, and the third uses rhetorical tools to examine transformation around a specific application of IT.

This part of the volume begins with "Computerization Movements: The Rise of the Internet and Distant Forms of Work" by Suzanne Iacono and Rob

87

Kling. This chapter challenges the common tendency to assume that we can study IT and organizational transformation without looking beyond the organization to broader social movements. The authors take as their starting point the importance of public discourse around computerization in shaping how individuals in organizations interpret the technology and in persuading and mobilizing people to act. They argue that "a socially constructed process of societal mobilization that we call *computerization movements*" (p. 97) is a major factor in the rapid growth of the Internet. They hasten to assure readers that this assumption "does not mean that these technologies are not useful or valuable for the organizations that adopt them"; rather, they say, "it does mean . . . that there are important macrosocial and cultural dimensions that are often neglected in discussions of the rise of these technologies and their implied consequences for organizational change" (p. 97). In analyzing both the general computerization movement and the specific computerization movement around distant forms of work, they adopt a three-part analytic framework. *Technological action frames,* which are built up and exist in interaction and discourse, provide individuals with core beliefs about the technology and its role in the future. *Public discourses* around new technologies shape particular understandings and interpretations of the technologies. Finally, it is only through *organizational practices* that transformation may actually occur. These *practices* are shaped by the *public discourses,* which in turn are shaped by the *technological action frames.* All of these relationships are recursive (e.g., practices also shape public discourses) and nondeterministic.

In this dense and rich chapter, Iacono and Kling use the first two elements of this framework to examine the framing of the Internet and of internetworking, showing the emergence of the dominant technological action frame for the general computerization movement—the death of distance. Then, they look at the public discourse that spreads the computerization movement including government, scientific, media, and organizational, and professional discourses. Finally, they turn to a specific computerization movement—distant forms of work—to demonstrate how frames, discourses, and practices interact. This chapter provides a broad overview of social movements around computerization and shows how advocates of these computerization movements have aided in the expansion of the computer industry and the spread of internetworking in the face of uncertainty around the economic and social gains associated with computerization in related discourses. It reminds the researcher to retain some skepticism toward the rhetoric of computerization.

The second chapter in this part of the volume, "Politically Wired: The Changing Places of Political Participation in the Age of the Internet" by Charles Bazerman, is a nice companion to Coopersmith's piece on the use of the fax in Texas politics (Chapter 3 in this volume). Bazerman uses a rhetorical perspective in thinking about the how the more recent Internet (especially Web-based) technology may influence national-level political participation. The author sees the eventual influence of the Internet on political participation as just beginning to unfold and, therefore, not predictable by any means. Still, he notes that the "character of the local activity space is extremely important for what happens, what people think and learn, and what social consequences emerge" (p. 138). Bazerman notes that written genres (a rhetorical term referring to recognizable types of writing or speaking such as the inaugural address), unlike spoken ones, must "announce and assemble the context" for the reader (p. 139). Both the construction of the rhetorical space and the interaction within it are likely to "start by emulating and extending the interactions made possible in prior media," but over time they are likely to "become transformed to take advantage of the new mediational opportunities" (p. 140). Having established this starting point, the author then examines how much earlier mediational technologies, literacy and printing, transformed and extended pre-literate forms of political life in their use over time, ultimately helping to create today's field of public participation in politics.

Turning to politics on the World Wide Web, Bazerman briefly examines the many ways in which politics is occurring in this new locale—including the Web sites of established media, political organizations, and technologically adept amateur producers of political commentary—and is adding to the complexity of political organizing. The author focuses more closely on the opportunities and new directions being taken on the Web by examining the Democratic National Committee's (DNC) site at two points in time separated by a year (June 1997 and June 1998). He never lets us forget, however, that these two times are arbitrary and that "there is no reason to think that the current DNC site will stabilize as the form by which major party participation will be enacted in the cyber-age" (p. 151). He takes a long view in moving forward, as in looking back, pointing out that we too are players in the continuing evolution of political participation in this new medium and that much is at stake:

> The ancient issue of democratic politics—how democracy becomes more than rabble-rousing—is being posed fresh in the cyber-age under new conditions and dynamics of communication. The solutions that we will develop in the long run are as yet unsettled, but the future of our political culture depends on them. (p. 152)

The third chapter in this part of the volume, "Information Technology in a Culture of Complaint: Derogation, Deprecation, and the Appropriation of Organizational Transformation" by John R. Weeks, turns to the use of IT in a particular organization, providing an engaging and witty analysis of the role of complaints around IT in a British bank. Based on his ethnographic study of this bank (designated BritArm), the author notes the high frequency of complaints about technology in general at BritArm and specifically about the TecSec system that has been introduced to aid in the work of the newly established back office processing center for "perfecting security," that is, for ensuring the security of loans for the bank's branch offices. In the strong and negative culture of BritArm, he argues that complaints have two different functions: *derogation* and *deprecation*. Derogations "signaled a passive resigned acceptance" of something rather than attempting to secure change (p. 162). The purpose of such derogations in this culture was to establish common ground with others, and their result typically was empathy and comradeship rather than a solution to the complaint. Unlike derogations that accepted the status quo, deprecations genuinely solicited redress or change. Direct deprecations were rare in the BritArm culture because of their potential for creating an embarrassing situation; rather, complaints that started as deprecations of individuals often were shifted to derogations of TecSec, a safer and less embarrassing stance. As Weeks tells us, "Rather than be separated by complaints and accusations, all parties come together in shared suffering of the bank's inadequacies in the area of IT" (p. 172).

What does the rhetoric of complaints around the technology tell Weeks about IT and transformation in this bank? It suggests "that the ritual functions of complaint are institutionalized in the bank in such a way that even if current problems with the IT were solved, other problems likely would be found to complain about in their stead" (p. 175). More generally, the author advises that "when analyzing attitudes toward IT, we need to examine not only the *causes* of complaint . . . but also the *consequences* of complaint" (pp. 174-175). In this case, the rhetoric of complaint has provided a window into the organizational culture and a pointed illustration of how important an understanding of that culture is to those studying or implementing IT.

From focusing on the societal rhetoric around computers to using rhetorical tools and frameworks in analyzing particular organizational uses of IT, the chapters in this part of the volume demonstrate the value of rhetorical perspectives in illuminating IT and organizational transformation. Informed by these perspectives, managers, technologists, and researchers all can better situate IT implementations within the broad societal rhetoric, within a rhetorical field that extends over time and across rhetorical space, and within the culture of a particular organization. Seeing how IT is configured technically never is enough; researchers in this area already have illuminated the importance of situating IT temporally and spatially. These chapters suggest that IT also must be seen as it is situated rhetorically, just as the chapters in Part I emphasized the need to situate them historically. Although every study cannot look closely at everything, researchers—as well as those in the "real world" who design, implement, and manage them—must be sensitive to rhetorical concerns. If they ignore them, they do so at the cost of grave misunderstanding.

4

Computerization Movements

The Rise of the Internet and Distant Forms of Work

SUZANNE IACONO

ROB KLING

Recent surveys suggest that about 122 million people worldwide and 70 million people in North America currently use the Internet at home, work, school, libraries, or community centers (Nua Ltd. 1998). Since the Internet's inception in 1969 as the ARPANET, its growth has been explosive. When restrictions against commercial use were lifted during the late 1980s, Internet traffic, defined as data flow on the U.S. Internet backbone, doubled in size roughly each year (Guice 1998). Whereas numerous surveys have proliferated a wide range of user estimates and considerable controversy about how exactly to measure use, no one disputes the upward curve and fast growth. Public discourse has largely interpreted this phenomenon as the dawning of a new social epoch variously called the information age, the digital age, or the age of cyberspace and cybermedia (Berghel 1995). It is argued that, in this age, nearly all forms of social life will be mediated by digital communications, distance will be overcome, a new social order will emerge, and lives will be transformed. The Clinton administration (White House 1993) has mobilized wide-scale support for this view by promising to further develop the Internet into a national information infrastructure (NII) that will "unleash an information revolution that will change forever the way people live, work, and interact with each other."

What is most critical about these assertions of social transformation is not their fidelity (or lack of fidelity) to truth but rather that they selectively "frame" or provide an "interpretive schema" by which disparate social groups and organizations can understand and interpret the meaning of the Internet for their own social contexts and practices. Such frames are built up in many public debates, not just those about new technologies. For example, public debate about gender and sexuality issues in U.S. and U.K. military establishments has developed contending frames such as "some institutions/ tasks are not for everyone" and "everyone deserves an equal chance" (Fisher 1997). These frames offer commonsense notions about why things are the way they are or why they should be changed. In practice, they also can be persuasive and can mobilize various constituencies to support one side or another.

In public discourse about the Internet, frames have been built up to suggest that organizations will have "faster communications" or "closer relationships with consumers" if they connect to the Internet. Many organizations (e.g., Fortune 1000 firms, government agencies, educational institutions, health organizations) have resonated with these frames and been mobilized to get connected. But what it means to "be on the Internet" is an ambiguous concept. Although numerous organizations today have Web sites, some might lack the capability for two-way or multi-way interactions, others might have both Web sites and interactivity, and still others might have e-mail but no Web sites. Increasingly, however, having some sort of "Internet presence" became an obligatory part of doing certain types of business during the late 1990s.

In this chapter, we argue that the meaning of the Internet is being built up or "framed" in macro-level discourses such as those of the government, the media, and scientific disciplines. The spread of these frames across many layers of public discourse mobilizes large-scale support and suggests specific lines of action within micro-social contexts such as organizations restructuring themselves so as to implement and effectively use internetworking technologies in their routine activities. We call these processes *computerization movements* and suggest that they are similar to other social movements such as the labor movement and the women's movement in the ways in which they reject dominant cultural codes and package alternative beliefs, values, and language for new preferred forms of social life.

In the next section, we present the traditional conceptions of the social processes that have driven the rapid growth of the Internet over the past 30 years and suggest an alternative social process based on computerization movements. Then, we describe the ways in which these movements draw on existing ideational materials to frame the key meanings of new technologies and mobilize societal support for them. Framing is a critical part of these processes because it allows ordinary people to gain deeper understandings about how new technologies are used in situations that might be foreign to them. Next, we illustrate computerization movements by focusing on historical shifts in the meaning of a specific movement—computer-based work—and the current set of discourses that have emerged around "new" distant forms of work. Because computerization movements advocate systematic changes in existing organizational arrangements, we should expect that some discourses and activists would emerge to oppose certain modes of computerization, forming a counter-computerization movement. We discuss counter-computerization discourses that have played key roles in defining and altering the meaning of internetworking and computer-based work. Finally, we conclude and suggest ways in which to incorporate a computerization movement perspective into further study.

WHY ARE ORGANIZATIONS
RAPIDLY CONNECTING TO THE INTERNET?

The Internet typically is defined as a network of networks or an internetwork. Internetworking means using special-purpose computers or hosts to connect a variety of autonomous networks for transmitting data, files, and messages in text, audio, video, or graphic formats over distances. In 1995, the National Science Foundation (NSF) backbone consisted of nearly 51,000 networks (NSF 1995). According to recent estimates, more than 72 million hosts now are connected to those networks (Internet Software Consortium 2000), with 90 million hosts projected by the end of the year 2000 (Matrix Information and Directory Services 2000). Although any number of individuals and organizations routinely track Internet traffic, and numerous national surveys have been administered by researchers and media organizations, there are no available statistics on the number of organizations connected to the Internet. Making such an estimate might be difficult given that choices about what counts as an organization would have to be made. For example, Internal Revenue Service tax filings might be used, but then subsidiaries might be overlooked, as might clubs and other nonprofit organizations. We can only surmise from our reading about the Internet that, today, nearly all Fortune 1000 firms, major federal and state public agencies, universities and colleges, other nonprofits, and any number of small entrepreneurial firms currently are connected.

Why are these organizations rapidly connecting to the Internet? One common answer argues that organizations connect to the Internet because of the assumed economic or strategic advantages resulting from changed buyer-supplier relationships. It is suggested that the Internet is a more efficient and effective marketing channel than are traditional delivery mechanisms. With the advent of the World Wide Web during 1993-1994, user-friendly browsers available on many desktops, the tremendous growth in the Internet, and the low marginal costs associated with offering products and services to customers, there has been a stampede of businesses to the Internet (Rao et al. 1998). Electronic markets also should benefit consumers. By lowering the costs of searching for alternative products, such markets are expected to encourage greater price competition and lower prices (Elofson and Robinson 1998). Furthermore, use of the Internet opens up new markets by moving organizations closer to their customers (Palmer and Griffith 1998). For example, in education, as the competition for students increases, universities and colleges with small local markets have expanded their programs to include those who are distant from their campuses. Students who are distant from centers of higher education also will benefit by obtaining degrees from home and by learning from distant experts. From this point of view, the trend for autonomous organizations to get connected is simply a byproduct of the availability of cost-effective telecommunications technologies coupled with benefits assumed through the interconnections. Decisions regarding these connections are based on the resource needs of the organization and the expectations of reduced costs and improved capability.

A variant of this answer focuses less on immediate economic gains and more on issues of long-term survival. In this view, connections to the Internet are seen as an essential part of the learning organization. Organizations no longer can learn all that they need to know internally (Powell 1996). New ways of gaining information are essential. For example, marketing information can be gained from electronic communities and online focus groups (Kannan et al. 1998). Commercial firms develop partnerships and maintain continuing communication with external parties such as research centers, laboratories, and even former competitors. Educational institutions and households also can take advantage of the information and services available on the Web. These linkages are both a means of gaining access to new knowledge and a way of exploiting those capabilities for innovation and experimentation. The outcome is long-term economic viability.

A second type of answer focuses on major epochal social transformations and argues that the United States is shifting from a society in which industrial activity and modernist systems and infrastructures dominate to one in which information, knowledge, and postmodern systems and infrastructures will dominate (Bell 1979; Lyotard 1984). Toffler (1980), a popular writer about these ideas, argues that the "Third Wave" economy is based on information and that the central event of the past century has been the death of matter (Dyson et al. 1996). Toffler and colleagues argue for the inexorability of progress, asserting that the Third Wave economy will arrive. As a consequence, everyone should join the "growing millions" in cyberspace. According to this view, Internet connections are nothing less than the first step in the creation of a new civilization.

The first answer depends on *organizational or managerial rationalism* and has a strong grounding both in conventional economic analysis of information flows along value chains (cf. Porter and Millar 1985) and in the resource dependence view of organizations in American sociology (cf. Pfeffer 1987). Connections to the Internet are conceptualized as organizational tools or prosthetic devices that enhance the performativity of an organization in its environment (Poster 1990). From this point of view, organizations adopt the technologies that are best for them, and they generally are able to implement and use them to their advantage. The second answer depends on technological determinism and an assumed causal relationship between the technological artifacts and methods of an era (e.g., farm implements, factories, computers) and the economies and societies that emerge. Although each of these responses offers insight into internetworking processes, we believe that they ignore some of the broadly noneconomic dimensions of sociotechnical change in industrialized countries.

In this chapter, we argue for an alternative conception of the rapid growth of the Internet based in a socially constructed process of societal mobilization that we call *computerization movements* (Iacono and Kling 1996; Kling and Iacono 1988). The mobilization of support for the Internet and other internetworking technologies does not mean that these technologies are not useful or valuable for the organizations that adopt them. It does mean, however, that there are important macrosocial and cultural dimensions that often are neglected in discussions of the rise of these technologies and their implied consequences for organizational change. (For a similar discussion of the neglect of macrosocial forces in understanding the relationship between new technologies and changes in work life, see Winter and Taylor [Chapter 1] in this volume.)

Our main thesis is that participants in computerization movements build up frames in their public discourses that indicate favorable links between internetworking and a new preferred social order. These frames help to legitimate relatively high levels of investment for many potential adopters and package expectations about how they should use internetworking in their daily routines and about how they should envision a future based on internetworking. Within organizations, meaning-making processes are ongoing as members attempt to restructure themselves around these new technologies. The symbolic struggle over these new technologies socially constructs the organizations that adopt them. Organizational change, then, is determined neither by the imperatives of the technology nor by the planned changes of organizational management (see Orlikowski [Chapter 9] in this volume). Instead, changes in work life are shaped (but not determined) by the prevalent discourses informing new technologies and the practices that emerge around them in actual workplaces.

COMPUTERIZATION MOVEMENTS

Sociologists have used the concept *movement* to refer to many different types of collective action. The most common term found in this literature is *social movement,* often used in a generic way to refer to movements in general. Lofland (1995) defines social movements as "amorphous, sprawling, and far-flung *conglomerations* of organizations, activists, campaigns, and the like that are construed to share social or personal change goals" (p. 194, italics in original). But sociologists also have written about *professional movements* (Bucher and Strauss 1961), *artistic movements,* and *scientific movements* (Aronson 1984; Star 1989). What analyses of these movements share is a focus on the rise of loosely organized, insurgent action to displace or overcome the status quo.

Today, the dominant theoretical perspectives for explaining the emergence, recruitment processes, and eventual success or failure of social movements are undergoing a paradigm shift. Structural explanations based in resource mobilization (McCarthy and Zald 1977) and political process (McAdam 1982) have been criticized as too mechanistic and limited by their natural science framework (Mueller 1992). Early social movement theories took seriously the presumed dualism between words and deeds, and they excluded ideas, beliefs, values, and identity as critical explanators of collective action.

But recently, social movement theory has become more sensitive to the semiotic meaning sciences and has placed culture at the center of its concerns (cf. Johnston and Klandermans 1995; Morris and Mueller 1992). For example, Snow and colleagues (1986) focus on the struggle over the production and counter-production of ideas and meanings associated with collective action. From their point of view, social movements are deeply involved—along with the media, local governments, and the state—in the "politics of signification." Within such social intercourse, attributions of blame and transformational goals do not emerge from a void, nor are they developed anew each time participants talk to each other, a politician gives a speech, or a journalist writes about the movement. Instead, "collective action frames" serve as relatively stable interpretive media by which new members are recruited, the collective meanings of social movements are maintained, and oppositional discourses are developed (Snow and Benford 1992).

Similarly, Swidler's (1995) conceptualization of "culture as tool kit" of rituals, symbols, stories, and worldviews demonstrates how activists borrow concepts, understandings, language, and values from existing cultural repertoires to construct new understandings, attribute blame for current problems, and prescribe the actions that should be taken to ameliorate them. She argues that during periods of change, old cultural models are rejected and new ones are articulated and constructed from existing ideational materials. Taken together, these views suggest that social movements are socially constructed through the ideational and cultural materials currently available to societal members.

A separate stream of research—on sociotechnical change (Bijker 1997; Bijker and Law 1992)—also has focused on the social construction of meaning but around the development of new technologies. Similar to Snow and Benford's (1992) attempts in social movement theory to use collective action frames to explain how meanings can be collectively shared and acted on, Bijker (1997) uses the concept of "technological frames" to describe the ways in which social meaning is attributed to technical artifacts, tying together relevant social actors and the particular ways in which they understand a technology as "working." A critical insight in Bijker's (1997) conceptualization of frames is that they are built up and "exist" only in discourse. Technological frames are not just cognitive elements (in people's heads), nor do they attain some sort of superstructure status (above people's heads). Instead, technological frames are constituted when interactions among relevant actors begin about a particular artifact.

We base our understanding of computerization movements in these larger debates about the role of culture, and specifically discourse and frames, in the mobilization of collective action and the development of meaning around a focal technology. Most research on information technology (IT) and organizational change has focused on adoption and change within single organizations. Macrosocial and cultural elements are assumed to be unproblematic constants, and the issue of why so many organizations at similar points in time attempt to implement the same technologies with varying levels of success is left unexplained (for some notable exceptions, see Orlikowski 1993; Orlikowski and Gash 1994; Yates 1994). The opposite problem can be found in the literature on social and cultural movements. Although it focuses on the wide-scale recruitment of constituents for broad social change, it typically fails to examine how organizations are sites for social action and change. Our research brings these bodies of study together.

Our analysis focuses on a process of societal mobilization with three primary elements. The first element is *technological action frames.* These are multidimensional composite understandings—constituted and circulated in language—that legitimate high levels of investment for potential users and that form the core ideas about how a technology works and how a future based on its use should be envisioned. The second element is *public discourses*. These are the discursive practices—the written and spoken public communications—that develop around a new technology. Public discourse is necessary for particular understandings about new technologies to widely circulate. The third element is *organizational practices*. These are the ways in which individuals and organizations put technological action frames and discourses into practice as they implement and use technologies in their microsocial contexts.

These three elements—technological action frames, public discourse, and organizational practices—are related. Technological action frames shape and structure public discourse whereas public discourse shapes and structures organizational practices. For example, Foucault (1972) demonstrates how a shift in medical discourse during the early 1800s in the midst of a cholera epidemic

> put into operation such a body of rules that a whole domain of medical objects could then be reorganized, that a whole group of methods of recording and notation could be used, that the concept of inflammation could be abandoned and the old theoretical problem of fevers could be resolved definitively. (p. 168)

He argues that during this period, medical organizations restructured themselves based on these new scientific discourses, altering their traditional practice of medicine and the outcomes for patients (e.g., their chances of actual survival).

But these relationships are nondeterministic. People's technology practices usually are much more complex than the more restricted public discourses about practices. For many practitioners, there often is a gap between their own discourse and practice. For example, in a recent conversation with a university professor about her class of online students spread across multiple time zones, the professor enthused about how the class eliminated time and space. But then she went on to say that she had to be available on Saturdays because many students worked during the week and she had a rule against e-mail on Sundays to give herself a break. Her course did not eliminate time and space, although it did restructure her time and practices. But she did not know how to talk analytically about these shifts. As a consequence, there was a gap between her discourse about online classrooms and her actual practice.

Relationships among the three elements also can be recursive. People may enrich their discourses and even modify their frames as they struggle to discuss the actual complexity of their practices. As a consequence, practices can generate new discourses, and new discourses can build up new technological frames. In addition, various social groups can attribute differential meaning to new technologies, developing contending discourses as they implement and use new technologies in their own organizations. However, it is difficult for changes in local practices to cause changes in the public discourse about the benefits of a technology. As with the university professor, private talk about use of a new technology often reflects the dominant public framing despite the material reality of divergent practices. Much of local practice with new technologies is tacit, at least until users are prompted by an outsider to explain their actions. But even when new understandings become part of local discourse, they often remain local rather than being widely or rapidly circulated across other organizations and social settings. It is for this reason that public discourse about new technologies and the technological frames embedded in them can remain relatively stable and misrepresent actual practice for long periods of time.

But not all technological frames or the discourses in which they are embedded are equally persuasive or mobilizing. Computerization movements rise and fall in their influence, and some seem to be much livelier at particular times. Furthermore, computerization movements are not monolithic. Blumer (1969) distinguishes between specific and general social movements. Specific movements are the various wings or submovements of broader general movements. Many movements—such as those that advance feminism, civil rights, systematic management, quantification in the sciences, and computerization—are heterogeneous. These distinctions help us to characterize the relationship between a general computerization movement around internetworking and a specific or distinct wing around its intersection with computer-based work. In what follows, we discuss in some detail two elements—technological action frames and public discourses—and their role in the emergence of a general computerization movement around the Internet. In a later section on computer-based work, we focus on the third element—practices—as they are informed by technological frames and discourses and carried out by organizational members.

Technological Action Frames

Theoretical Background

Bijker (1997) suggests that new technologies are interpretively flexible. Different social groups do not see different aspects of a single technology. Instead, they attribute different meanings and constitute different artifacts. For example, the field of cryptography traditionally has received little public attention. Recently, however, debate over a hardware encryption device, the Clipper Chip (now called Skipjack because of a trademark conflict), has become national news. In this debate, the government argues for the wide-spread use of this device because it would allow the government to unencrypt the coded messages of people or organizations that use the Internet for illegal purposes. On the other hand, computing activists, such as John Perry Barlow and Mitch Kapor of the Electronic Frontier Foundation, argue that use of this device would increase the government's electronic surveillance capabilities on ordinary citizens and the commercial enterprises that also use the Internet. These activists have framed the device as one that endangers citizen privacy and gives the government a back door for electronic eavesdropping (Barlow 1993). For them, the Clipper Chip is yet another instantiation of "Big Brother," whereas for the government, it is a criminal catcher.

The opposing meanings about encryption in the preceding example can be conceptualized as "interpretive schemata" or "technological frames" developed by different social groups—in this case, the U.S. government and computer activists—to pinpoint the technology's potential significance to them and to mobilize others to see things their way (Bijker 1997; Orlikowski and Gash 1994). Technological frames are useful because they simplify and condense elements of complex technologies and their potential use and, therefore, enable groups of people to interact about what they might mean. Technological frames are conceptual or analytic lenses that are built up within and between social groups as they struggle over the meaning of a technology and constitute it in their discourses. Bijker (1997) lists the major dimensions of technological frames as goals, key problems, problem-solving strategies, requirements to be met by problem solutions, current theories, tacit knowledge, perceived substitution function, user practices, and exemplary artifacts. Taken together, these dimensions constitute the meaning of a particular technology and frame it in specific ways.

Similarly, social movement theorists have articulated dimensions of their related concept, collective action frames. Snow and Benford (1992) suggest that collective action frames serve to punctuate and attribute meaning. Punctuation singles out some existing social condition as intolerable or focuses attention on certain values, such as equality and freedom, that might be at risk. Attributions have two parts: diagnostic (i.e., focusing the blame for current wrongs or problems) and prognostic (i.e., developing beliefs about what should be done to ameliorate a situation and assigning the responsibility for those actions). In our analyses of technological action frames, we focus primarily on goals, diagnostic and prognostic attributions (including beliefs), current theories, expected user practices, and exemplary artifacts.

Both streams of research—social movements and sociotechnical change—argue that at specific points in time, a particular frame can become dominant. In the development and diffusion of new technologies, dominant frames can stabilize the meaning of technologies for indefinite periods until they are contested. Social movement theorists suggest that many narrow collective action frames encouraging certain lines of action can surface and coexist early in a movement's cycle. But at certain points and within specific social movements, master frames develop in their discourses. For example, Snow and Benford (1992) report that the proposal for a freeze on the development and deployment of nuclear weapons in 1980 energized and renewed peace movement activity that had been dormant for several decades. The idea of a nuclear freeze constituted a new master frame that mobilized previously passive citizens to organize and protest the development of new nuclear weapons. Although this new framing might seem to narrow the more expansive peace movement frame, Goffman (1986) suggests that the act of framing does not so much introduce restrictions as it does open up new possibilities. In other words, framing allows for more people and social groups to explicitly target current social problems and understand more clearly what they should do about them. Framing serves to enhance action, not dampen it.

When master frames develop in movement discourse, large-scale social action and mobilizations are more likely. But dominant or master frames also can wither as their meaning becomes less potent to social groups because of the rise of competing new frames or as cultural conditions change (Snow and Bedford 1992). In our own conceptualization of technological action frames, we use the terms *dominant* and *master frames* to mean the same thing, that is, the rise and relative stabilization of a set of key meanings for a focal technology.

Framing the Internet

A short history. Guice (1998) points out that the common view of the development of the Internet is based in an engineering perspective and straight path between the ARPANET of the late 1960s and today's Internet. He quotes Vinton Cerf, the "father of the Internet" and coauthor of the TCP/IP protocol (the Internet's data communication standard), as saying that the Internet is "the direct descendant of strategically motivated fundamental research begun in the 1960s with federal sponsorship" (Cerf 1995, quoted in Guice 1998, p. 202). Guice argues that this account glosses over the many conflicts, twists, and turns that actually have taken place during the development of the Internet. For example, the ARPANET depended on other protocols for a decade before TCP/IP emerged as an innovation and alternative. Other alternatives still exist. IBM's Systems Network Architecture and OSI (Open Systems Interconnections) both were developed during the 1970s, and the latter emerged during the 1990s as a European alternative to TCP/IP. Pfaffenberger (1996) makes a similar argument about the development of Usenet, "the poor man's ARPANET," by focusing on its lengthy and often traumatic history as designers and administrators struggled to conceptualize and control the growing network.

But it is not only the artifacts that have changed over the years. The meaning of internetworking has had similar shifts. Initially, the objective of the ARPANET was to allow for resource sharing. Grand scientific challenges could not be resolved by one government agency, university, or research laboratory alone. The goal was to harness distributed resources (e.g., knowledgeable people, computers) to solve complex problems faster. Much of the discourse surrounding this frame focused on the power of computation to displace human muscle power from work tasks and to extend the reach of the human brain (cf. Ginzberg 1982).

But there was a gap between the dominant frame of the technology and its actual use. In practice, e-mail among distributed colleagues emerged as the key use of the ARPANET. Being on the Internet primarily meant having access to e-mail for long-distance communication and collaboration. Many IT- and science-oriented firms were the first private organizations to get connected, primarily so that their scientist and engineering staffs (e.g., in research and development departments) could have access to e-mail. By the early 1990s, many universities, large public agencies, civic organizations, and for-profit technology firms had connected to the Internet. Aside from e-mail, they began to use Gopher (an Internet service) to publish documents such as catalogs, white papers, and reports. Being on the Internet began to take on other dimensions such as information sharing with external organizations, customers, and the general public.

At about this time, the U.S. government began debating the development of a more extensive, higher bandwidth NII and the various goals and purposes it would serve. Two opposing goals emerged in these policy debates: universal public access and grand scientific computing (Guice 1998). With the announcement of the National Research and Engineering Network (NREN) in 1991, it appeared that public spending would support the building of an infrastructure for scientists and engineers—continuing the traditional focus of internetworking—rather than give access to the general public. Between 1991 and 1993, however, the proponents of universal access pushed for their goals as a greater common good, and the central idea behind the NII shifted away from the solution of scientific problems toward societal and economic transformations that potentially could benefit everyone.

A number of alternative technological infrastructures were considered for the NII. Proponents and vendors of cable television and wireless telephony, for example, struggled unsuccessfully to have their infrastructures selected as the model for the NII. Whereas differences between the histories and cultures of these industries and internetworking (e.g., differences in scope, access ethics, economic orientation, and extent of technological development) can partially explain the selection of internetworking (cf. Press 1994), Bijker (1997) argues that the stabilization of an artifact is a political process subject to interests and values.

In 1992, the World Wide Web was released by CERN, the European Laboratory for Particle Physics. During the subsequent few years, Internet browsers were developed and the Web became the easiest part of the Internet for ordinary people to use. By 1995-1996, many private organizations had created Web sites to advertise their products and, hopefully, sell them to a larger audience. By the late 1990s, for most organizations, being on the Internet meant having a Web site.

The death of distance. This shift in the goals of internetworking toward universal access not only mobilized more people and organizations to get connected but also generated a discourse that assumes that societal and global transformation will follow. In particular, geographic distance is said to no longer be relevant. A new dominant technological action frame has emerged—the death of distance:

> The world has become a smaller place in the 20th century. . . . Telecommunications technology made terrestrial distances insignificant. The transformation of the world into a global village caused revolutionary changes in the physical and social infrastructure, rivaling those of the industrial revolution. (Adam et al. 1997, p. 115)

In this frame, the key problem to achieving full-scale, worldwide integration is distance, and internetworking provides the solution; distance will be "obliterated" (Dyson 1997). The major scientific theories used to explain these transformations are based in technological determinism. For example, because new information and communications technologies are available at low cost to many people and institutions, Bell (1979) has argued for a shift to a postindustrial society, whereas Toffler (1980) has argued for the emergence of a Third Wave economy. The targeted users of internetworking technologies include everyone—governments; civil societies; commercial, health, and education institutions; and consumers in general. In practice, these users are expected to get connected to the Internet and use it extensively to communicate and share information. The Internet was envisioned as the major integrating architecture of the world at the end of the 20th century.

But this framing of distantiation as central to the meaning of new technologies is not new. It has a history that goes back well into the late 18th century. We are not cultural historians and can only indicate a few of the more interesting ways in which this frame has been culturally robust over that period. The discourses that embed the death of distance frame typically focus on those technologies that have so vastly increased the speed of travel or communications that the lives and work of people who use them have changed fundamentally. For example, a non-stop jet that allows one to have breakfast in London and dinner in New York on the same day illustrates this idea in a contemporary and prosaic way.

During the late 18th century, the "first victory over time and space," according to Mattelart (1994), was the semaphore telegraph developed in France to establish communication among its armies. Over a period of about 50 years, a network was developed that connected Paris to its provincial cities and consisted of 534 semaphore stations covering 5,000 kilometers. In the United States, from the late 18th century to the 19th century, a number of systems were developed—postal, railroad, canal, electricity, and telegraph. With the arrival of each new system, communication was progressively touted as eliminating space and time through increased reach and speed. For example, a journalist writing in the *Madison Daily Tribune*[1] in 1851 heralded the arrival of the railroad to local hog farmers:

> Before the railroad era, it required two weeks and oftener three to drive hogs from Hendricks County to Madison. A drove of hogs loaded on the cars at Bellville on Thursday was landed at North Madison the same afternoon. This is annihilating space and time. (quoted in Windle and Taylor 1986, p. 12)

With the arrival of the railroad, distances no longer would be a significant obstacle in the distribution of products to their markets, and the East Coast of the United States could be united with its western boundaries. The mobilization of support for the development of the telegraph was framed in a similar way. Davis (1997) reports how a U.S. congressman tried to convince colleagues to give start-up money to Morse for the telegraph circa 1847:

> The influence of this invention on the political, social, and commercial relations of the people of this widely extended country will of itself amount to a revolution unsurpassed in world range by any discovery that has been made in the arts and sciences. Space will be, to all practical purposes of information, annihilated between the states of the Union and also between the individual citizens thereof. (p. 10)

More recently, Marshall McLuhan (cf. McLuhan and Powers 1989) envisioned the growth of broadcasting systems and the ubiquitousness of the television set in households around the globe as a mechanism for the attainment of a "global village." His argument centered on the significance of the medium as an interconnecting mechanism over whatever value specific broadcast content might have for certain groups of people.

Over the past several hundred years, then, enthusiasts and analysts of various new technologies have proclaimed the death of distance and have employed it in their rhetoric about the expected social transformations. Mattelart (1994) argues that a concern about rapid communications and transportation systems grew out of Enlightenment philosophies. Before the Enlightenment, space simply evoked the idea of an empty area. But after Descartes, mathematicians began to appropriate space. They made it part of their domain and invented a variety of different types of spaces (e.g., curved spaces, non-Euclidean space) (Lefebvre 1991). Some historians argue that this working out of space through various transportation and communication systems was heightened in North America as part of the westward expansion of the United States, enabling the creation of one national democratic government in a vast continent. Others, including Mattelart (1994), also observe that annihilating distance was not simply a matter of realizing democracy on a grand scale but also was a product of readily identifiable economic and military interests. In short, the ability to reach across space and time with new technologies has had a strong cultural resonance in many industrial societies.

For the Internet, the significance of the death of distance typically is theorized in two ways. First, space will be structurally transformed and consolidated so that geography, borders, and time zones will become irrelevant (Cairncross 1997). Rather than pockets of civilization, such as industrialized cities and regions, being separated or even isolated by vast distance, new spatial forms and practices based on a near frictionless information economy will prevail. A new technological infrastructure based loosely on the current Internet will define this space, open up new markets and information flows, and civilize it into a global networked society (Castells 1996).

Second, social relationships will be culturally transformed and democratized. Those on the periphery of society (e.g., those in rural areas, night shift workers, home workers and schoolers, retired people) can become more involved and receive the same types of education, medical services, and work opportunities as other centrally located actors currently enjoy. Furthermore, people and organizations can directly connect with other people, places, organizations, and real-time world events without the mediating influence of government agents or media organizations. New transnational communities will be forged, and institutional power based in geographic centrality and control will be reduced; decentralized social action and perfect information sharing will prevail.

From our research and reading of the discourses associated with internetworking, we have found five recurring beliefs that inform this master frame around internetworking (Table 4.1). They circulate in many discourses and engender the taking of certain lines of action in microsocial contexts (e.g., individuals subscribing to online services or signing up for online courses, organizations adopting the newest internetworking equipment). These beliefs are a foundation for social transformations that include the extensive use of internetworking. Technological progress is emphasized, and competing beliefs are deflected. In this moral order, the users of the most advanced technologies are the most virtuous. And, as in melodramas where good triumphs in the end, only developers and users of advanced internetworking technologies will conquer the unknown and achieve the good life.

Beyond the rhetoric. Although increased access to information, more inclusionary practices, and dis-intermediated relationships certainly might be laudable goals for an internetworking movement, their actual attainment in a purely positive form is hardly certain. In contradiction to the utopian image of a peaceful and inclusive global village, at the end of the 20th century, various ethnic identities all over the world were fighting for their independence and exclusion from national societies. The rhetoric of time and space elimination is totalizing. It assumes that because internetworking is technically feasible, people everywhere will want to get connected and be able to benefit similarly. But in practice, actual improvements from new technologies are more narrow (e.g., time savings on airplane flights, access to the latest stock transactions) and might benefit only a small elite segment of society. And as Poster (1990) notes, "ruling powers, hegemonic cultural patterns, and individual fear" (p. 72) can make it difficult for members of specific groups to interact with each other, let alone with outsiders, regardless of the technology in use. Women in Saudi Arabia and students in the People's Republic of China, for example, have been the foci of their governments' attempts to control their communications.

Furthermore, if global electronic connections displace local interactions and relationships, then some geographic regions might suffer. In Bangalore, India, the influx of multinational software development firms has created regional disparities between the highly skilled people who work for those firms and others who still are mired in poverty and substandard living conditions (Madon 1997). As entire segments in the region identify with a cosmopolitan global society, their attention to and identification with local civic issues and needs diminishes and the region suffers. Those in the region who are not connected risk being seen as irrelevant (Castells 1996).

Social transformations from global internetworking may have similar disruptive effects on local relationships throughout the world. But even if universal access were available and everyone was connected to this more cosmopolitan network, more comprehensive electronic surveillance becomes

TABLE 4.1 Five Beliefs About Internetworking

1. *Internetworking is central to a new world order.* Computerization movement activists argue that internetworking is the dominant mechanism for creating and structuring the world that they prefer. Visions of a future perfect world supplant the imperfect world in which we currently live. The new world will be more participative and democratic, more open and accessible, more diverse and information intensive because of the central role of internetworking. Use of the Internet will revolutionize the way in which we do business, educate our young, and conduct our lives. This belief gives proposals for change a peculiarly technocentric character; internetworking is central to all socially valuable behavior and is the panacea for many social problems. Everyone will be closer to everyone else, and no one will be excluded.

2. *Improved internetworking can further revolutionize the world order.* This argument is tied to the notion that the continuous cavalcade of new technologies and the inevitable march toward the future are inextricably linked to the achievement of social progress. Like people who purchase new cars or stereos with every model change, the heroes of this vision invest heavily and endlessly in new computer technologies. When the current social arrangements fail to produce the promised results, rather than be disillusioned or try other alternatives, they place their investment hopes in the next generation of technology. Computerization movement activists push hard on two fronts. First, people and organizations ought to use state-of-the-art internetworking equipment. Second, state-of-the-art internetworking technologies should be universally available. Beliefs about the importance of state-of-the art technologies have become so widespread that people invariably are embarrassed by the presence of older equipment or by less than universal access to machines and networks in their own workplaces, schools, and homes. When organizations perceive themselves to be less networked than other similar organizations, they institute planning committees and point to their plans and the progress they have made in achieving more extensive internetworking.

3. *Internetworking pushes the conceptual limits of time, space, and the known world.* Whereas the first two beliefs focus on the legitimation of aggressive acquisition of internetworking technologies and their central place in a more ideal social world, this belief focuses on the purpose of that investment and what it is good for. Time and space, our own human frailties, and the often-unmanageable aspects of bureaucratic institutions currently limit us. Communications networks and related technologies are said to embody transcendent qualities that will push the limits of the known world. We no longer will be bothered by distance and time differences, all needed information will be available online, and our organizations will become more flexible and nimble and less hierarchical. Computerization movement activists imply that there are no limits to meaningful internetworking by downplaying the actual limits of new technologies and the continuing benefits of current technologies. In addition, they fail to balance internetworking activities against competing social values. The Internet mediates the most meaningful activities—the only real learning, the most important communications, or the most meaningful work. Other media for learning, communicating, or working are treated as less important. The most important aspects of life occur when online. The physical world is relegated to IRL (in real life) or life offline (Rheingold 1993).

(Continued)

TABLE 4.1 Continued

4. *No one loses from internetworking.* The implementation and use of internetworking technologies are portrayed as inherently apolitical activities. Computerization movement activists rarely acknowledge that systematic conflicts might follow from the restructuring of major social institutions. Many activists ignore social conflict in their discussions of internetworking, or they imply that it will reduce conflict if it already exists. Some authors explicitly claim that connected organizations will be less authoritarian and more cooperative than their less connected counterparts. The belief that internetworking fosters cooperation and collaboration allows computerization movement advocates to gloss over deep social and value conflicts that social change can precipitate. In practice, organizational participants can have major battles about what type of equipment to acquire, how to organize access to it, and what standards should regulate its use. At the societal level, internetworking is portrayed as consistent with all major societal goals. Conflicts among social groups such as labor, government, and higher education; between workers and their managers; or between teachers and administrators are ignored. Any short-term sacrifices that might accompany the attainment of these goals, such as displaced workers, are portrayed as minor unavoidable consequences.

5. *Irrational resistance is the only obstacle to success.* The only obstacles to achieving these visions are obsolete regulatory laws and people who "cling irrationally to their old ways" (Lewis 1998). Examples of stereotypical beliefs about resistant or naive users are not difficult to find in the literature on internetworking. In organizations, management information systems staff routinely report that resistant users undermine the implementation of new technologies (Kling and Iacono 1984). Even when computerization movement activists are advocating increasingly complex technologies, the major impediments to success are technophobic uncooperative people, not problems in the computerization strategy or the extent to which activities or organizations must be reorganized to accommodate large-scale changes.

increasingly possible. The "gridding of space" (de Certeau 1984) through global networks makes its occupants and their actions and interactions increasingly available for observation, surveillance, and information gathering. The vision of a global networked society—where everyone knows what everyone else is doing—also can be fearsome. But today, most people are enthralled with the idea that space and time may be eliminated through internetworking.

Public Discourses

Theoretical Background

Public discourse is essential to the spread of computerization movements. Technological action frames circulate in public discourses and act as a form of currency whose structure and meaning remain relatively constant across a variety of discursive practices. Social agents borrow the technological action frames that they find in public discourse, use them in their own contexts and discourses, and (in so doing) often embellish or extend them. As a consequence, the widespread circulation of dominant frames in discourse at macro levels of analysis (e.g., in that of the government, the media, or professional associations) can influence and shape micro-level discourse and practices across similarly situated organizations. For example, Foucault (1977), in his research on prisons, discovered connections among macro-level discourse in relevant scientific disciplines, micro-level discourse within the prisons themselves, and the practices of prisons (i.e., the ways in which they restructured themselves). Poster (1990, p. 90) points out that Foucault depended on at least three "layers" of discourse to develop his history of prisons and the motivations for their restructuring: (1) the texts generated in the science of criminology, (2) the tracts of reformers, and (3) the paperwork required for the operation of prisons. Organizational restructuring often is related to the discourses to which that organization pays attention.

Four Layers of Public Discourse

We have uncovered four layers of public discourse that are critical to the campaigns of computerization movement activists: (1) government discourses (Poster 1990), (2) the discourses of scientific disciplines (Poster 1990), (3) media discourses (Gamson 1995), and (4) organizational and professional discourses (Yates 1999). Although we have distinguished these discourses for analytic reasons, they should not be construed as separate in practice. For example, the discourses of governments are widely covered by the media. But media discourse often amplifies and popularizes government discourse, as in the case of the U.S. government's NII becoming more widely known in the mass media as the "information superhighway." The media also can build up contending discourses, for example, by pointing out the "speed bumps" on the information superhighway or by covering stories about downsizing and the impacts of new technologies on work organizations. Some combinations of discourse can be powerful. Poster (1990) notes, "When government acts 'technically,' on a 'scientific' basis, to solve a problem, its action is automatically legitimate" (p. 39). The combination of government and scientific discourses lends authority, legitimacy, and a rational basis for organizations to take action. To the extent that a master technological action frame about internetworking technologies—the death of distance—is widely circulating, we would expect to find its pervasive use in a variety of public discourses.

Government discourse. By 1993, internetworking had moved into national discourse and the Clinton White House had published the pivotal text for the internetworking movement, *The National Information Infrastructure: Agenda for Action* (White House 1993). Since that time, government discourse has been essential in the development of its meaning. From State of the Union and commencement speeches; to the formation of new agencies, task forces, and programs; to the production of reports by the Department of Commerce, the National Council, and the White House, all incorporate the master technological frame of this computerization movement. Distance is the problem; electronic integration, connections, and internetworking are the solutions; better education, health services, and work environments, as well as transformed lives, are the goals; and everyone should be a user in many of the domains of life (e.g., work, learning, leisure, shopping) and over the course of a life from childhood to old age. With this document, President Clinton and Vice President Gore promised to link innovation and growth in internetworking with a transformed and reinvigorated society. If developed, the NII "can ameliorate the constraints of geography and economic status and give all Americans a fair opportunity to go as far as their talents and ambitions will take them." This document established funding for research and development for an NII modeled on the current Internet. By stabilizing the meaning of the NII around a particular set of focal technologies, devices, and transmission protocols (those used in internetworking), and by encouraging the further development of these technologies, the government has, in part, contributed to a major upheaval in the nation's telecommunications infrastructures and industries.

In addition, *The National Information Infrastructure* (White House 1993) was a strategic reformulation of the meaning of the Internet. With this text and the associated discourses that have since emanated from it, nearly all societal organizations are encouraged to connect to the Internet. The potential benefits of such connections are consistently articulated, whereas the fact that most U.S. organizations might have to painfully restructure themselves to actually use and benefit from those connections rarely is mentioned. But government discourse has legitimized this new approach to the organization of businesses, educational institutions, and households throughout the United States, and many organizations are actively seeking to reorganize themselves around distant forms of social life.

Discourses in scientific disciplines. Contrary to the ivy tower stereotype of much academic research and writing, the ideas and findings of many scientific disciplines today are instituted in practice in industry and government agencies (Poster 1990). Most current discourse about internetworking, even within the hard sciences of engineering and computer science, borrows heavily from sociological conceptualizations of large-scale epochal transformations to explain what these new technologies might mean to the people who use them. Although few would label themselves technological determinists, most analyses focus on the accelerated pace of technological innovation as the driving force for societal change (e.g., as costs go down and standards emerge, borders and barriers are broken down) (cf. Cairncross 1997).

But the rhetorical strategy of most of these analyses is to stigmatize current infrastructures and systems in terms of the industrial or modern ideas they embed (Dyson et al. 1996) while casting new internetworking infrastructures and systems in utopian terms (Table 4.1). Mass media communications systems, such as broadcasting and newspaper distribution, are characterized by their limitations, and current physical infrastructures are vilified. Cities, as centralized hubs of social life, are characterized as decaying systems. Although there no doubt are many problems in existing systems, this stigmatization process actually might turn public attention away from finding solutions and then funding them or from carefully reflecting on important social values that might be cast aside (e.g., cities as melting pots, broadcast journalism as a means to synthesize information and frame current events).

Conversely, new communications systems and infrastructures based on internetworking are characterized in utopian terms. They are more direct, participative, democratic, socially engaging, and community oriented. These discourses invite public participation in the rejection of the past and uncritical identification with and acceptance of the ideological packaging of internetworking. Although some research on electronic communications advances these notions, a growing body of research contends that social interactions over the Internet are not always so utopian. For example, research has found that gender biases can be perpetuated in many electronic groups (cf. Herring 1996) and that powerful participants can dominate a discussion and use it for their own strategic purposes (cf. Hert 1996).

Mass media discourses. The symbolic struggle over the meaning of the Internet is carried out daily in general audience media discourses. In *Business Week, Fortune,* and *Wired* magazines, as well as on *The News Hour, Nightline, Frontline,* and CNN, legions of computer scientists, social scientists, entrepreneurs, journalists, and participant observers outline the course of events that is expected to propel U.S. society from its current form into the new millennium. Gamson (1995) suggests that movement activists are media junkies. Internet activists are no different. Many have become mass media stars (e.g., Esther Dyson, Howard Rheingold, Katie Hafner) with their popular books widely read and cited in many circles. These activists package an ideology about what the Internet means and frame relevant events, beliefs, and actions in ways that make the unfamiliar technology more familiar. Their discourses often are indistinguishable from those of their scientific brethren (and sisters) as they, too, largely borrow from social science theory to attribute blame for current social problems and suggest positive guides based on internetworking to correct them. But their stories about new technologies and what they are good for are not socially neutral; they organize in advance how ordinary people and organizations should think about and perform work, engage in learning, and spend their leisure time (de Certeau 1984).

The media discourses of computerization movement activists are extremely rich. Mainstream magazines, as well as cyber-zines, portray new social heroes and articulate new models for success. Whereas few today might know the names of the heads of the world's largest banks, everyone knows the names of computer industry luminaries and the places that are the current centers of action (e.g., Silicon Valley, the MIT Media Lab, CERN). Stories and characters from influential chat rooms, discussion groups, and online communities (e.g., the Well, LambdaMOO) have become part of popular lore and the foci of much discussion in bars and classrooms alike (cf. Dibbell 1996; Hafner 1997). The passageway to these new cultural and social practices requires the possession of new objects (e.g., Pentium-chip computers, lightweight laptops, 56K-bps modems, Internet browsers, computer accounts, passwords, local phone numbers of Internet service providers). Everyday language and activities are transformed as people "surf the Web," "log in," "post" messages, "click on links," and recite "dot com" Web addresses.

Media discourse is a cultural resource from which the general public can borrow to understand the significance of new technologies and the actions the public should take to participate. These discourses are not just "out there"; they embed themselves in people's everyday discourses as they repeat common beliefs about these new technologies and struggle over their meanings at work, school, and home or in their informal social networks (Gamson 1995). One need only examine the extent to which these new words, phrases, people, places, and ideas have seeped into one's own daily conversations with co-workers, friends, and family to understand how these discourses have become embedded in everyday life.

Institutional and professional discourses. The final layer of discourse is that which emerges within individual organizational settings and specific professional associations. These discourses add operational specificity to the technological action frames set up by the government, scientific disciplines, and media. The proponents, champions, and enthusiasts of internetworking within specific organizations and professional associations establish committees to study the new opportunities and their associated costs, deliberate on the meaning of new technologies for their own organizations and professional members, develop and circulate white papers, invite knowledgeable experts to company or professional advancement forums and seminars, and generally educate their members about what these technologies might do for them. They identify current organizational or professional problems and suggest how these new technologies can alleviate those problems while simultaneously transforming them (e.g., allowing them to survive or expand as they enter the new century). In practice, various social groups may develop contending discourses about what these new technologies mean to their organizations or professions. For example, Noble (1998) outlines the struggles at York University in Toronto, where faculty went on strike when university administrators forced many untenured faculty to put their courses on video, CD-ROM, or the Internet or lose their jobs. In the end, the faculty retained unambiguous control over all decisions relating to the use of technology as a supplement to their classroom instruction or as a means of instructional delivery.

Within these microsocial contexts, social groups struggle over the meanings of these new technologies as they amplify or contend with the dominant technological action frame to fit their own preferences and goals. In the course of these struggles, organizations are reorganized and professions are redefined. Sometimes, best practices and other testimonials to effective restructuring become public knowledge through stories in trade journals and business publications. But more frequently, discourses about actual practices remain relatively obscure. Organizations might be embarrassed when their adoption of a new technology turns political or their intended results are not quickly obtained. Some of the best accounts of these struggles come from careful historical analyses, enthnographic studies, and case analyses that highlight actual practice and the various sense-making struggles and upheaval that may be associated with organizational restructuring. When these accounts become public, contending discourses can emerge and new technological action frames can be developed.

COMPUTER-BASED WORK:
ON THE ROAD TO DISTANT FORMS OF WORK

Many specific computerization movements already have been spawned by the more general internetworking movement (e.g., electronic commerce, distant learning, telemedicine). What these specific computerization movements share is a similar approach for how to organize business, education, and medical practices when geographic distances no longer are considered to be relevant. In this section, we illustrate our computerization movement perspective by focusing on the rise of distant forms of work. This specific computerization movement intersects and gives new life to a computerization movement that has been influential for some time—computer-based work. We first discuss the technological frames, discourses, and practices related to the earlier computer-based work movement. Then, we discuss its intersection with internetworking and the current discourses around distant forms of work.

Work Automation

Automating the Firm

The use of machines to automate various aspects of office work began during the second half of the 19th century. By the end of the 19th century, typewriters were widely available in many offices (Giuliano 1982). Fully functional digital computers were developed during World War II. Whereas debates still circulate about whether the first digital computer was the British Colussus or the American ENIAC (Edwards 1996), by the mid-1950s the Univac, the first commercial computer, was being used for billing and accounting in insurance firms (Yates 1999). From the 1950s to the mid-1980s, the computerization of work was framed as a work automation activity.

Technological action frames were built up around many work automation technologies—from the earliest organizational accounting systems, to computer-based numerical control systems on shop floors, to expert systems in professional offices. Managers in many large hierarchical organizations at the time perceived a number of major problems—lack of control over work processes, uncertainty in decision making, and increasing demand for clerical workers to handle the growing volume of business transactions. Their solution was the implementation of work automation systems—formal, closed-loop, information processing and feedback systems that enabled system-level self-correction and the automation of many work processes and activities through step-by-step procedures. The dominant scientific theories employed to understand how and why organizations should restructure themselves to incorporate work automation systems were cybernetics (Weiner 1948), systems theory (Churchman 1971; Dertouzos 1972; Rapaport 1986), and theories of organizational information processing (Galbraith 1974). The primary goals of many organizations that implemented these new systems were those of increased productivity (including cost reductions) and reduced uncertainty.

Scientific discourses about work process automation emerged during the pre-World War II era. At Harvard University, Howard Aiken and Wassily

Leontif, inspired by Babbage's work in Britain a century earlier, developed the science of mathematical economy, a formal theory of input-output analysis, and a design for an early electromechanical computer (Beniger 1991). Independently, George Stibitz at Bell Laboratories and John Atanasoff at Iowa State University were developing prototypes of electronic and electromechanical automatic digital calculators. Alan Turing, a British mathematician, discovered that machines could carry out mental operations and published an article titled "On Computable Numbers" during the mid-1930s (Turing 1936). Later, during the war, Turing worked with a team of scientists at the British Government Code and Cypher School to develop computational devices that could automate and speed up the decryption of encoded German messages (Edwards 1996).

Yates (1999) reports that in the United States during World War II, many mathematically trained actuaries also worked on military projects involving statistics and cryptology and came to learn about new electronic computers through these government discourses and practices. As the war ended and these actuaries went back to work, they were eager to examine the potential of computers for the insurance industry. At the 1947 meeting of the Society of Actuaries, a committee was formed to study their potential use. The committee worked closely with IBM and Remington Rand's Univac division to develop technologies that would be explicitly useful to their firms and profession. Their report was distributed to their members in 1952 and helped to spread ideas about how computing could enhance productivity. Although initially the committee had wanted to see the development of applications that would specifically help its profession (e.g., in automating mortality studies and financial analyses), these computations represented insufficient volumes of work to justify the expense of the machines. As a consequence, they concluded that the most effective use of new computers would be for routine billing and accounting processes. The efforts of this committee and other similar committees at the Life Office Management Association and Insurance Accounting and Statistical Association initiated sales to a number of insurance companies. These innovations provided models for the evolution of computing in other insurance companies and large firms that routinely handled large volumes of billing and accounting transactions.

During the 1960s, a variety of work automation systems continued to be developed and implemented for use in banks, government agencies, and manufacturing firms. In its most extreme form, organizations expected to be able to increase their productivity through investments in technology and the substitution of machines for labor. In a less extreme form, organizations expected to hire less skilled, lower paid workers who could perform more work with the aid of a machine. In one set of estimates, each word processing machine was thought to be equal to between one and five typists (Reinicke

1984), whereas every robot introduced into an automobile plant could replace two workers (Shaiken 1985).

Management theorists within academia (cf. Leavitt and Whistler 1958; Simon 1977) saw computerization as a mechanism for enhanced control over decision making in hierarchical organizations. If information from frontline workers could be quickly pushed up the hierarchy and integrated into top-level decision making, then managers could recentralize decision authorities, reassert control over work processes, and increase organizational productivity and competitiveness. Top managers in large organizations informed by these new theories and technologies advocated the computerization of their firms. Information became privileged, and many management information systems were developed and implemented for use by mid-level managers. An entire new field, management information systems, emerged in academia to develop theories and research programs centered on technological improvements in organizational decision making. Most of these theories and many new technologies such as decision support systems were aimed at enhancing the work of individuals in organizations (e.g., supervisors, mid-level managers). In practice, many organizations had problems developing and implementing these new systems. Gladden (1982) estimates that nearly 75 percent of all systems development projects either never were completed or, if completed, never were used.

Many contending discourses emerged in academia and labor. The early work automation frame reignited the age-old fear that workers have of being replaced by machines (Castells 1996). During the 1950s, Weiner (1954) predicted that automation would result in a depression within 25 years that would make the 1930s depression seem trivial. A discourse emerged around this idea and maintained this pessimistic position throughout the next several decades (cf. Jenkins and Sherman's [1979] *The Collapse of Work* and Hines and Searle's [1979] *Automatic Unemployment*). From the 1970s through the 1990s, researchers in the field of industrial and labor relations developed a discourse that articulated for a wider audience the process of automation within manufacturing organizations, focusing on deskilling and computer-mediated work (Adler 1992; Braverman 1974; Hirschhorn 1984; Shaiken 1985; Zuboff 1988). Others focused on the impacts of new technologies on clerical and other white-collar workers (Feldberg and Glenn 1983; Gregory and Nussbaum 1982; Iacono and Kling 1987; Mumford 1983) and on general reductions in the quality of work life in extensively computerized settings (Attewell and Rule 1984; Kling and Iacono 1989). Debates emerged in the discourses of sociology, computer science, and information systems about all of these topics. Many argued, however, that the apparent negative employment effects were overstated because of simplistic notions about the substitution of machines for labor (Hunt and Hunt 1983). Although some occupations, such as telephone operators, clearly have seen reductions in their numbers through the automation of their jobs (Denny and Fuss 1983), the more or less continuous growth of jobs in the United States contradicted the idea that machines could substitute for labor. Moreover, empirical studies on deskilling, monitoring, and quality of work life did not find that negative outcomes were necessarily determined by the new technologies, as predicted by the framing of the technology and its associated discourses. Instead, outcomes were nondeterministic and depended on a variety of factors including type of organization, general economic conditions, and the predominant management philosophy.

Automating the Professions and Jobs

By the mid-1980s, the types of computers and applications available in the marketplace had increased significantly. Many professionals and semi-professionals in the workplace were eager to have increased access to these new machines and their related applications to develop their own local systems and manipulate organizational information for their own needs. This type of computer use often is referred to as "end-user computing" (Rockart and Flannery 1983). However, it was not the ready availability of new machines in the workplace that engendered these changes; rather, it was extra-organizational discourse in professional societies promoting the computerization of their members' work. Similar to the Society of Actuaries during the earlier period, national and regional accounting and finance associations advocated the use of personal computers (PCs) and spreadsheets during the early 1980s as part of the professionalization of their members. From the 1970s through the 1980s, material control and production associations pushed for material requirements planning systems and, subsequently, manufacturing resource planning systems as ways in which to rationalize and increase the productivity of manufacturing organizations (Kling and Iacono 1984). During this same period, several associations, such as the Data Processing Managers Association and the Association of Computing Machinery (ACM), emerged to serve computer specialists and the managers of data processing and management information systems departments.

In each administrative sector, some related groups have taken on the mantle of computerization as a subject of professional reform. These professionals do not work for computer vendors; they identify themselves as accountants, production planners, or information systems specialists, for example, with an interest in using certain computer applications in the course of their work in insurance firms, manufacturing companies, or the public sector. In practice, many had to struggle within their organizations to acquire new machines and applications (e.g., PCs, spreadsheet software) (cf. George et al.

1995; Kling and Iacono 1984, 1989). Many professionals and their managers developed strategies to acquire new machines for their personal use over periods of time by hiding their purchases in departmental budgets or by reconstituting cast-off machines (e.g., old test equipment used on the manufacturing floor) for use in their own offices. Because these struggles to gain access to machines and applications constituted grassroots efforts on the part of various professionals and semiprofessionals, there was little discourse that rose to counter the idea of more ubiquitous computing for many types of workers.

Automating the Office and the Distant Worker

By the mid-1980s, most large organizations already were using their own wide-area networks or value-added networks (telecommunications services purchased from outside vendors) to communicate across their distant divisions and workplaces. Many also were implementing local-area networks (within buildings and offices) to enhance work group computing. Giuliano (1982) suggests that in such an "information-age office," people could communicate with one another and with their home offices through "one of a half dozen 'electronic mail' networks now available throughout the U.S." (p. 150). He argues that people would increasingly conduct their work not only in the office but also while traveling, while on the shop floor, and while at home. Not only would they have access to their personal files, but they could access information from their companies' mainframes. The buildup of these technologies during the mid-1980s was the fuel for a number of highly exaggerated and short-lived claims for an "office of the future" in which workers could "compute" from home while having real-time access to the critical events and information of a more virtual and paperless workplace (Miles 1987; Toffler 1980).

With the decreasing costs of computers and modems, telecommuting (i.e., remote supervision with a reduction in commuting) as a form of distant work became a viable option (Mokhtarian 1991). During the mid-1980s, many departments of transportation concerned with increasing traffic jams and air pollution attempted to mobilize many large organizations to experiment with and implement telecommuting programs. They argued that organizations concerned about a shortage of workers or space could expand their workforces while still maintaining communications and control through computer networks. For example, workers could respond to customers' telephone calls by using PCs and special telephone lines at home or at satellite offices. Although some companies did implement experimental programs—often to comply with government requirements—most did not move toward telecommuting as a major new form of work.

Much of the empirical research on telecommuting has found that manage-ment issues are a factor in preventing its widespread adoption (Staples et al. 1998). Managers report difficulties in managing their workers, and managers dislike their lack of control over work processes. The Technology and Telecommuting: Issues and Impacts Committee of the National Science Counsel (1994) (hereafter the Technology and Telecommuting Committee) developed a report on the status of telecommuting in the United States and found telecommuting to be quite narrow in its traditional conceptualization. We agree and suggest that telecommuting has largely been framed as a work automation technology. It typically is aimed at individual workers who use computers all day and for whom control over work productivity is paramount. The key management strategies employed to ensure control are either piece-work or management by objective. In practice, these workers can be cut off from the discourses of their workplaces and subjected to extensive work monitoring. In *The National Information Infrastructure* (White House 1993), it is argued that people can live anywhere and telecommute to their offices if they are connected to the NII. It is assumed that, simply because internet-working technologies are available, people will move to less populated areas and that land use patterns will change. But most workers are not going to move simply because it is feasible to telecommute.

There are many factors that may cause people to move. Work may be one of them. But job security is a key worry in U.S. workplaces today, and people tend to live where they will have many job opportunities. The U.S. Depart-ment of Transportation estimated that there were about 2 million tele-commuters in 1993 and expected those numbers to grow over the 1990s decade. We suggest, however, that overreliance on the technological frame of work automation and the way in which it has informed the managerial prac-tices for telecommuting are primary reasons why telecommuting has not been the vast success that was expected despite its assumed benefits for the public good and the availability of new internetworking technologies.

Work Collaboration

During the late 1980s and early 1990s, disillusionment set in over the lack of productivity gains from the widespread individual use of computers and information systems. Computing and telecommunications systems ac-counted for half of the capital investments made by private firms, while annual rates of productivity growth remained low, especially in the service sector. The wide-scale recognition of this problem was termed the "pro-ductivity paradox" (Dunlop and Kling 1991). A new technological action frame—work collaboration—emerged. Its development depended largely on the earlier counter-discourses about work automation. It was widely argued that workers should be recognized as organizational assets; they should be empowered, not replaced. Environments should be created so that workers can fully contribute to the limits of their ability instead of being monitored eight hours a day (Creed and Miles 1996). Because work is a social endeavor, it was argued, technologies should support social communication and collaboration rather than individual work done in seclusion from the ongoing activities of the firm.

Technological frames were built up around many work collaboration technologies (e.g., screen-sharing software, group schedulers, group authoring tools, group support systems, shared databases). A major problem for management at the time was the lack of evidence of productivity gains from heavy investments in work automation technologies. The major solution was the use of technologies that would facilitate information sharing and collaboration. Potential users included everyone in an organization. A key belief was that productivity from the new technologies that supported group work had the potential to exceed what had been achieved with PCs used by individuals (Bullen and Bennett 1991). Furthermore, it was expected that the use of these technologies would transform organizations into more collaborative places to work. Nearly everyone in an organization would have access to organizational information, and nearly everyone would be empowered to make decisions and innovate as necessary in their jobs. Since the 1950s, the framing of work computerization had come full circle. Computing originally was believed to enable a shift in control and decision authorities to centralized and top management. By the late 1980s and early 1990s, new technologies were expected to decentralize authority and empower lower level employees and professionals.

Discourses about work collaboration initially were embedded in the software engineering and computer science research laboratories of commercial firms (e.g., XeroxPARC, MCC, SRI) and universities (e.g., MIT Laboratory for Computer Science and University of Arizona GroupSystems research projects). Participants called the technologies they were developing, and the forms of work they were espousing, computer-supported cooperative (and, later, collaborative) work (CSCW). CSCW was coined as a galvanizing catchphrase and later was given more substance through a lively stream of research and the emergence of a community of interest. Conferences identified with the term, and participants advanced prototype systems, studies of their use, and key theories about their development and potential impacts. The media promoted this stream of research. But unlike the general internetworking movement that is highly visible in mainstream media, CSCW was discussed primarily in business publications (e.g., *The Wall Street Journal, Business Week*), the business sections of daily newspapers, and computer and information science publications (e.g., *Communications of the ACM*). In these discourses, pundits and consultants predicted organizational transformations (e.g., the flattening of organizational hierarchies, the empowering of lower level workers) through use of these new technologies (cf. Wilke 1993).

Researchers examining the early use of CSCW applications in organizational settings, however, found little evidence of transformation. Within these sites, there was little discourse about the new technologies (e.g., how to use them, their expected benefits, their role in the firm). As a consequence, many potential users perceived the new technology in the old work automation frame. Researchers found that they were mainly used as devices for extending the capabilities of individuals (Bullen and Bennett 1991) or that they were not used as originally intended (i.e., for information sharing or collaboration) or were not used at all (Orlikowski 1993). Furthermore, these researchers argued that the expectation that groupware or CSCW technologies can transform organizations to be more collaborative is based in technological determinism. In practice, many working relationships can be multivalent and mix elements of cooperation, conflict, conviviality, competition, collaboration, commitment, caution, control, coercion, coordination, and combat (Kling 1991). But the frames that were built up around collaborative work technologies had come largely from technologists wishing to push their products. Like others before them, they were rejecting the old cultural models of work and were attempting to mobilize support for new ways of doing work. But managers were slow to buy these technologies.

Distant Forms of Work

During the early 1990s, the themes of many popular management consultants shifted toward more socially rich conceptions of work practices, focusing on cross-functional teams, partnerships, and strategic alliances, and the like. Whole literatures emerged heralding new forms of organization—flexible, networked, learning, trust-based governance forms, cluster, and virtual. These conceptualizations argued for the importance of lateral forms of communication within and across organizations enabled by new internetworking technologies. The idea of collaborative work was given new life through the intersection of the internetworking computerization movement.

One vision of this new organization argues that large hierarchical organizations will vertically disintegrate to become small lean organizations joined in networks and alliances. The apostles of these virtual corporations, like the earlier disciples of other forms of computer-based work, are not shy about pushing their ideas. Davidow and Malone (1992), who wrote *The Virtual Corporation,* argue that unless the United States becomes a leader in forming virtual organizations by the year 2015, it will lose its competitive edge.

Whereas many organizations already had a variety of internal and external networks in place using proprietary protocols and standards, the rise of internetworking stabilized the exemplary artifacts of an emerging and contending technological frame for computer-based work around the Internet and open protocols and standards. Government discourses, which supported the research and development of internetworking technologies, legitimized distant forms of work based on the Internet, the World Wide Web, and other internetworking technologies despite the narrow conceptualization in the NII of distant work as telecommuting.

Today, the merging of new organizational forms, collaborative work technologies, and the broad internetworking movement has resulted in a new technological action frame with the dominant ideational element of distributed or distant forms of work. Distributed work is defined as "work that is done in a location different from that of the supervisor, subordinate, or fellow team member" (Technology and Telecommuting Committee 1994, p. 8). Technological frames have built up around many new technologies and concepts related to distributed work such as intra- and extranets, electronic communities, Web-based conferencing tools, and desktop videoconferencing. Some technologies have been reconstituted from their earlier framing as work collaboration tools. For example, Lotus Notes, a primary work collaboration technology, initially was assumed to enhance work collaboration for anyone and everyone in an organization. Today, it is given to team members and managers who are distributed and who must use electronic communications to accomplish their work. A major problem identified by organizations is that people must work together (e.g., on cross-functional or global teams) while they often are distributed in time and space. For example, many people work on multiple teams, travel to see customers, or are not co-located with their colleagues and teammates. The major solution is internetworking to enable their distributed work. The primary goals of many organizations that choose to adopt distant forms of work are increased communications at all levels within and across relevant social groups of organizations (e.g., sales force, product repair people, customers, suppliers, buyers, team members, partners) for real-time or near real-time information sharing and the integration of distributed knowledge.

Not surprisingly, the theoretical basis for this technological frame is forming around the ideas of networks, social networks, and knowledge networks (cf. Sproull and Kiesler 1991). But the idea of a network is less a theoretical model than a rhetorical tool for researchers to easily discuss the variety of complex and not well-understood relationships found in organizations today (Guice 1998). A number of different streams of research have developed around these core ideas. Some studies of virtual organizations, for example, have taken an economic perspective and focused primarily on buyer-supplier networks rather than on work life (Kraut et al. 1998). Another stream has focused on the technologies used in internetworking and the choices that managers and professionals make about how to communicate with coworkers, not on the work itself or on the ways in which organizations restructure around these new technologies (cf. Fulk et al. 1990; Zack and McKenney 1995). Studies of computer-mediated communication (cf. Sproull and Kiesler 1991) have investigated the use of e-mail and distribution lists in organizations and assert that these technologies can make organizations become networked as users begin to communicate and form relationships with people with whom they never would have communicated otherwise. One study (Hesse et al. 1993), for example, found that oceanographers who were on the periphery of their scientific community benefited more from their use of electronic networks than did those who were more centrally located. In sociology, Powell's (1996) work on trust-based forms of work and Meyerson and colleagues' (1996) work on swift trust have engendered studies of trust in temporary virtual teams (Iacono and Weisband 1997; Jarvenpaa and Leidner 1998). One thread that runs throughout these various streams of research is that geographic barriers are no longer relevant. Little attention is paid, however, to the possible social or cultural barriers that still might be present.

But today, there is a dearth of studies that focus on the practices of distributed work (e.g., how distributed work is accomplished, how people communicate, how monitoring is carried out [or not], how leadership works, how people learn or innovate, what the impacts of these types of work are on the people who engage in them). One study of distributed work focuses on the long-term communicative practices of the computer scientists and researchers who used the early Internet to develop the Common Lisp programming language (cf. Orlikowski and Yates 1995). Other studies currently are being conducted on the use of videoconferencing across distant work sites (Ruhleder and Jordan 1997) and continuous video integration of work sites (Graham 1996). Some discourse about distant forms of work has emerged in reports commissioned by the government (cf. Technology and Telecommuting Committee 1994). But this research stream still is very new, and few conclusions can be drawn about what the actual practices of distributed workers will be.

Although some counter-discourse emerged around the early telecommuting technologies (e.g., by pointing out the isolation of telecommuters, their extensive monitoring, and loss of a social office), by and large, distributed workers do not have those problems. Rather than working at home most of the time, they travel with their laptops to see clients or other colleagues. But new problems have arisen. A white paper on "High-Performance Computing and Communications, Information Technology, and the Next-Generation Internet" reports that there are many logistical and maintenance problems related to internetworking (Kling 1997). This report expects that these issues will become more salient as the technologies become more sophisticated, the users become less sophisticated, and technical support is less available.

Media discourses also have pointed out some of the problems that distributed workers might have such as the blurring of home and work, work that encompasses more hours of the day or week, and the extensive learning that has to go on before these technologies can be used effectively. But one of the more ironic twists is the idea that the new "borderless economy," instead of allowing people to live and work anywhere they desire, has created an "elite class of nomads" or the "business homeless" who live nowhere or, perhaps even worse, live in "mind-numbing" airports much of the time (Iyer 1998; Rayner 1998). One unanticipated outcome of distributed work might be that, rather than distance becoming irrelevant through new technologies, distance may become increasingly relevant as people travel more frequently to accomplish their work. Castells (1996) argues that worldwide networking will exclude entire segments of society—those that are not networked—and result in a highly segmented global society. But given the indeterminacy of the meaning of new and complex technologies, a future based on internetworking can only be discerned at this point with some difficulty.

Summary

In this analysis, we have examined the framing, discourses, and practices of three historical shifts in the computer-based work computerization movement—from work automation (including telecommuting), to work collaboration, to distant forms of work. We have seen that with these shifts, new technological action frames were constituted in the discourses of the government (especially for telecommuting), professional associations (especially for work automation), scientific discourses (work automation, work collaboration, and distant forms of work), and the mass media (work collaboration and distant forms of work). These discourses have mobilized various types of organizations to adopt these technologies, but in practice, the goals related to these frames have remained elusive. Productivity gains, especially in the service sector, remained low while work automation was prevalent. Across a variety of work settings with groupware or CSCW applications, collaboration was difficult to achieve. And distant forms of work, rather than integrating distributed people and resources, actually might cause more workers to travel distances. As a consequence, there are continuing gaps between the discourses about these work technologies and actual practices in microsocial contexts. We also have seen that careful scientific studies of the use of these technologies in work life play a critical role in the development of contending discourses and the further development of new technological action frames. For the most part, the dominant critiques of various modes of computerization have come from the discourses produced by careful scientific research on work practices. These discourses are essential in correcting the many misrepresentations and misunderstandings about the nature of organizational restructuring and how new technologies influence work practices.

CONCLUSIONS

We have argued that the rise of the Internet and other internetworking technologies in U.S. organizations has been stimulated by a set of loosely linked computerization movements. We analyzed these movements by investigating how societal mobilization is socially constructed through the interplay of three elements: technological action frames, public discourses, and practices. Technological action frames are built up in public discourses and can be persuasive to broad audiences. They can mobilize similarly situated organizations to reject old cultural models and to identify with new ones, for example, by getting connected to the Internet and restructuring work around these new technologies. Our analysis of organizational change differs from most organizational analyses by considering computerization movements that cut across society as important sources of interpretations and beliefs about what internetworking is good for and what social actions people should take to secure the future they envision.

Today, a dominant technological frame is being built up around the Internet. A major ideational element is the death of distance. This idea simultaneously attributes blame for societal problems to the distances among distributed people and social institutions and suggests ways in which to ameliorate the situation—use internetworking to obliterate distance and to integrate, connect, or network distributed people and organizations. The media, the government, and scientific disciplines embed these beliefs, goals, and attributions into their own discourses about how internetworking might apply to various sectors of society. Theories derived from scientific disciplines provide organizing rationales (e.g., transition to a networked world, participation in an information society) for unbounded internetworking. Computerization movements play a role in persuading organizations to accept an ideology that favors everybody adopting state-of-the-art internetworking technologies. Their discourses, however, rarely explain the values, resource commitments, and extensive restructuring that accompany their visions. Although computerization movements can generate a *rhetoric* of transformation, evidence thus far does not point to widespread *actual* transformations as intended. Actual transformations (or failures to transform) work themselves out in situated practices. To date, there is little research on these socio-technical practices.

Contending discourses often arise in the mass media or in scientific discourse as actual practices unfold. For example, organizations might find it difficult to achieve high levels of productivity. Or, telecommuters might not perform as well as expected because of the loss of the social office. Such findings may contradict the hypothesized benefits and current framing of new technologies, resulting in contradictions about their meanings. Contending discourses, by framing technologies in alternative ways, can have powerful effects on the development of new meaning about a set of technologies and can constitute new technological frames. For example, criticisms about the work automation frame developed into discourses about more collaborative ways of working. New technologies were developed to support such work (e.g., electronic calendaring systems, meeting technologies, e-mail, Web-based conferences and discussions). Today, there are few contending discourses about distant forms of work. But we have no reason to doubt that as studies of actual practice emerge, the gaps between discourses and practices will be uncovered.

We believe that when one studies the sites where internetworking is being adopted, traces of discourses that have been imported into the adopting organization from other sources will be easy to spot. Members of adopting organizations consult with specialists, belong to professional associations, read professional journals and mass media publications, take courses, are affiliated with government committees, and visit other organizations to examine their practices. To the extent that the framing of a new technology has become dominant, we would expect to find its widespread use in the discourses within and across many organizational sites. And we also would expect to find many gaps between the discourses and the practices as people struggle to understand what a particular technology means and how to apply it in their own work lives. These ideas open up rich lines of empirical research. Much more work needs to be done to examine particular computerization movements. We need to learn more about the situational and interactional elements of computerization movement activists and the ways in which cultural templates such as master frames are developed and translated into practice. We hope that our analysis of the Internet and computer-based work will encourage scholars to examine computerization movements in other social settings and to analyze their own discourses and practices.

During the past 50 years, computerization movements have helped set the stage on which the computer industry expanded. As this industry expands, vendor organizations (e.g., Microsoft) also become powerful participants in persuading people to computerize and internetwork. Some computer vendors and their trade associations can be powerful participants in specific decisions about equipment purchased by a particular company or a powerful force behind weakening legislation that could protect consumers from trade abuses related to computing. But their actions alone cannot account for the widespread mobilization of internetworking in the United States. They feed and participate in it; they have not driven it. Despite the lack of evidence for increased productivity in organizations, investment in new computing and telecommunications systems continues to grow at a staggering rate. Part of the drive to internetwork is economic, but part also is driven by the efforts of computerization movement advocates in the government, various scientific disciplines, and mass media who mobilize constituencies. Moreover, the social changes that one can attribute to internetworking sometimes can be disruptive and socially conservative (e.g., loss of attention to regional needs, · increased disparity between the "haves" and the "have-nots," more opportunities for government surveillance), contrary to the positive change portrayed by the internetworking computerization movement. But we suspect that the pervasiveness of internetworking and the new energy infused into the movement through the NII will have a significant cumulative effect on American life.

There is no well-organized opposition or broad-based alternative to the internetworking computerization movement. Even countries such as China that traditionally have feared and controlled citizen contact with foreigners have started to develop their own NIIs. In the name of "economic informatization," China now allows people to use the Internet but requires registration with the police. It also blocks certain Web sites and monitors the content accessed by its citizens. A general counter-computerization movement in most countries might well be stigmatized and marginalized as "Luddite." Because computerization movement activists portray internetworking as a means to transform society, a general counter-computerization movement would have to oppose internetworking in all sectors of society and all institutions (e.g., education, work, home). A successful ideological base for such opposition probably would have to be anchored in an alternative conception of society and the place of technology in it. Although there is no active movement to counter internetworking in general, many have joined Senator Exon and others in proclaiming the Internet to be a danger and support the ideas behind his legislation to regulate speech on the Internet (Cannon 1996). At the same time, organizations such as the Electronic Frontier Foundation and the American Civil Liberties Union continue to struggle to support individual rights to free speech and other civil liberties for Internet users. But these discourses and counter discourses are highly legalistic and bound up with governmental ideals rather than deeper understandings of actual practices. In their most likely form, the computerization movements of this new century will constitute a conservative transformation reinforcing patterns of an elite-dominated, stratified society.

NOTE

1. Madison, Indiana, was a major hog processing and shipping town on the Ohio River.

REFERENCES

Adam, N., A. Awerbuch, J. Slonim, P. Wegner, and Y. Yesha (1997), "Globalizing Business, Education, Culture Through the Internet," *Communications of the ACM,* 40 (2), 115-121.

Adler, P. S. (1992), *Technology and the Future of Work.* New York: Oxford University Press.

Aronson, N. (1984), "Science as a Claims-Making Activity: Implications for Social Problems Research," in Joseph Schneider and John I. Kitsuse (Eds.), *Studies in the Sociology of Social Problems.* Norwood, NJ: Ablex, 1-30.

Attewell, P. and J. Rule (1984), "Computing and Organizations: What We Know and What We Don't Know," *Communications of the ACM,* 27 (12), 1184-1192.

Barlow, J. P. (1993), "A Plain Text on Crypto Policy," *Communications of the ACM,* 36(11), 21-26.

Bell, D. (1979), "The Social Framework of the Information Society," in M. Dertouzos and J. Moses (Eds.), *The Computer Age: A Twenty-Year View.* Cambridge: MIT Press, 163-211.

Beniger, J. R. (1991), "Information Society and Global Science," in C. Dunlop and R. Kling (Eds.), *Computerization and Controversy: Value Conflicts and Social Choices.* San Diego: Academic Press, 383-397.

Berghel, H. (1995), "Digital Village: Maiden Voyage," *Communications of the ACM,* 38 (11), 25-145.

Bijker, W. E. (1997), *Of Bicycles, Bakelites, and Bulbs: Toward a Theory of Sociotechnical Change.* Cambridge, MA: MIT Press.

——— and J. Law (Eds.) (1992), *Shaping Technology/Building Society: Studies in Sociotechnical Change.* Cambridge, MA: MIT Press.

Blumer, H. (1969), "Social Movements," in B. McLaughlin (Ed.), *Studies in Social Movements: A Social Psychological Perspective.* New York: Free Press, 8-29.

Braverman, H. (1974), *Labor and Monopoly Capital: The Degradation of Work in the 20th Century.* New York: Monthly Review Press.

Bucher, R. and A. Strauss (1961), "Professions in Process," *American Journal of Sociology,* 66, 325-334.

Bullen, C. and J. L. Bennett (1991), "Groupware in Practice: An Interpretation of Work Experiences," in C. Dunlop and R. Kling (Eds.), *Computerization and Controversy: Value Conflicts and Social Choices.* San Diego: Academic Press, 257-287.

Cairncross, F. (1997), *The Death of Distance.* Boston: Harvard Business School Press.

Cannon, R. (1996), *The Legislative History of Senator Exon's Communications Decency Act: Regulating Barbarians on the Information Superhighway.* Available: www.cybertelecom. org

Castells, M. (1996), *The Rise of the Network Society.* Cambridge, MA: Blackwell.

Cerf, V. (1995), *Computer Networking: Global Infrastructure for the 21st Century.* Available: www.cs.washington.edu/homes/lazowska/cra/networks.html

Churchman, C. W. (1971), *The Design of Inquiring Systems: Basic Concepts of Systems and Organizations.* New York: Basic Books.

Creed, W. E. D. and R. E. Miles. (1996), "Trust in Organizations: A Conceptual Framework Linking Organizational Forms, Managerial Philosophies, and the Opportunity Costs of Controls," in R. M. Kramer and T. R. Tyler (Eds.), *Trust in Organizations.* Thousand Oaks, CA: Sage, 16-38.

Davidow, W. H. and M. S. Malone (1992), *The Virtual Corporation.* New York: HarperCollins.

Davis, E. (1997), "Spiritual Telegraphs and the Technology of Communications: Turning Into the Electromagnetic Imagination," series on *Watch Your Language* at Public Netbase Media-Space, April 10. Available: www.t0.or.at/davis/davislec1.html

de Certeau, M. (1984), *The Practice of Everyday Life.* Berkeley: University of California Press.

Denny, M. and M. Fuss (1983), "The Effects of Factor Prices and Technological Change on the Occupational Demand for Labor: Evidence From Canadian Telecommunications," *Journal of Human Resources,* 18 (Spring), 161-176.

Dertouzos, M. (1972), *Systems, Networks, and Computation: Basic Concepts.* Huntington, NY: R. E. Krieger.

Dibbell, J. (1996), "Taboo, Consensus, and the Challenge of Democracy," in R. Kling (Ed.), *Computerization and Controversy: Value Conflicts and Social Choices* (2nd ed.). San Diego: Academic Press, 552-568.

Dunlop, C. and R. Kling (Eds.) (1991), *Computerization and Controversy: Value Conflicts and Social Choices.* San Diego: Academic Press.

Dyson, E. (1997), "Education and Jobs in the Digital World," *Communications of the ACM,* 40 (2), 35-36.

———, G. Gilder, G. Keyworth, and A. Toffler (1996), "Cyberspace and the American Dream, *The Information Society,* 12, 295-308.

Edwards, P. (1996), *The Closed World: Computers and the Politics of Discourse.* Cambridge: MIT Press.

Elofson, G. and W. N. Robinson (1998), "Creating a "Custom Mass-Production Channel on the Internet," *Communications of the ACM,* 41 (3), 56-62.

Feldberg, R. L. and E. N. Glenn (1983), "New Technology and Its Implications in U.S. Clerical Work," in *Office Automation: Jekyll or Hyde?* Cleveland, OH: Working Women Educational Fund.

Fisher, K. (1997), "Locating Frames in the Discursive Universe," *Sociological Research Online,* 2 (3). Available: www.socresonline.org.uk/socresonline/2/3/4.html

Foucault, M. (1972), *The Archaeology of Knowledge and the Discourse on Language* (A. Sheridan, Trans.). New York: Pantheon Books.

——— (1977), *Discipline and Punishment* (A. Sheridan, Trans.). New York: Pantheon Books.

Fulk, J., J. A. Schmitz, and C. W. Steinfield (1990), "A Social Influence Model of Technology Use," in J. Fulk and C. Steinfield (Eds.), *Organization and Communication Technology.* Newbury Park, CA: Sage, 117-142.

Galbraith, J. R. (1974), "Organization Design," *Interfaces,* 4 (3), 28-36.

Gamson, W. A. (1995), "Constructing Social Protest," in H. Johnston and B. Klandermans (Eds.), *Social Movements and Culture.* Minneapolis: University of Minnesota Press, 85-106.

George, J., S. Iacono, and R. Kling (1995), "Learning in Context: Extensively Computerized Work Groups as Communities of Practice," *Accounting, Management, and Information Technology,* 5 (3/4), 185-202.

Ginzberg, E. (1982), "The Mechanization of Work," *Scientific American,* 247 (3), 67-75.

Giuliano, V. E. (1982), "The Mechanization of Office Work," *Scientific American,* 247 (3), 148-165.

Gladden, G. (1982), "Stop the Life-Cycle, I Want to Get Off," *Software Engineering Notes,* 7 (2), 35-39.

Goffman, E. (1986), *Frame Analysis.* Boston: Northeastern University Press.

Graham, M. (1996), "Changes in Information Technology, Changes in Work," *Technology in Society,* 18, 373-385.

Gregory, J. and K. Nussbaum (1982), "Race Against Time: Automation of the Office," *Office: Technology and People,* 1, 197-236.

Guice, J. (1998), "Looking Backward and Forward at the Internet," *The Information Society,* 14 (3), 201-211.

Hafner, K. (1997), "The World's Most Influential Online Community (and it's not AOL)," *Wired,* May 5, pp. 98-104, 106-114, 118-122, 124-126, 128, 130, 132, 134, 136, 138, 140, 142.

Herring, S. (1996), "Two Variants of an Electronic Message Schema," in S. C. Herring (Ed.), *Computer-Mediated Communication: Linguistic, Social, and Cross-Cultural Perspectives.* Philadelphia: John Benjamins, 81-106.

Hert, P. (1996), "Social Dynamics of an On-line Scholarly Debate," *The Information Society,* 13, 329-360.

Hesse, B. W., L. Sproull, S. Kiesler, and J. P. Walsh (1993), "Returns to Science: Computer Networks in Oceanography," *Communications of the ACM,* 36 (8), 90-101.

Hines, C. and G. Searle (1979), *Automatic Unemployment.* London: Earth Resources Research.

Hirschhorn, L. (1984), *Beyond Mechanization: Work and Technology in a Postindustrial Age.* Cambridge, MA: MIT Press.

Hunt, H. A. and T. L. Hunt (1983), *Human Resource Implications for Michigan: Research Summary.* Kalamazoo, MI: W. E. Upjohn Institute for Employment Research.

Iacono, S. and R. Kling (1987), "Office Technologies and Changes in Clerical Work: A Historical Perspective," in R. Kraut (Ed.), *Technology and the Transformation of White-Collar Work.* Hillsdale, NJ: Lawrence Erlbaum, 53-75.

———— and ———— (1996), "Computerization Movements and Tales of Technological Utopianism," in R. Kling (Ed.), *Computerization and Controversy: Value Conflicts and Social Choices* (2nd ed.). San Diego: Academic Press, 85-105.

———— and S. Weisband (1997), "Developing Trust in Virtual Teams," in *Proceedings of the 30th Hawaii International Conference on System Sciences* (Vol. 2). IEEE Computer Society, Maui, HI, 412-420.

Internet Software Consortium (2000), *Internet Domain Survey, January 2000.* Available: www.isc.org/ds/www-200001/report.html

Iyer, P. (1998), "The New Business Class," *The New York Times Magazine,* March 8, pp. 37-40.

Jarvenpaa, S. and D. Leidner (1998), "Communication and Trust in Global Virtual Teams," *Journal of Computer-Mediacted Communications,* 3 (4). Available: www.ascusc.org/jcmc/vol3/issue4/jarvenpaa.html

Jenkins, C. and B. Sherman (1979), *The Collapse of Work.* London: Eyre Methuen.

Johnston, H. and B. Klandermans (1995), *Social Movements and Culture.* Minneapolis: University of Minnesota Press.

Kannan, P. K., A-M. Chang, and A. B. Whinston (1998), "Marketing Information on the I-Way," *Communications of the ACM,* 41 (3), 35-43.

Kling, R. (1991), "Cooperation, Coordination, and Control in Computer-Supported Work," *Communications of the ACM,* 34 (12), 83-88.

———— (1997), *The NGI as an Effective Support for Professional Work and Social Life,* white paper for Presidential Advisory Committee on High-Performance Computing and Communications, Information Technology and the Next-Generation Internet, December 4. Available: php.ucs.indiana.edu/~ekling

——— and S. Iacono (1984), "The Control of Information Systems Development After Implementation," *Communications of the ACM,* 27 (12), 1218-1226.

——— and ——— (1988), "The Mobilization of Support for Computerization: The Role of Computerization Movements," *Social Problems,* 35 (3), 226-243.

——— and ——— (1989), "Desktop Computerization and the Organization of Work," in T. Forester (Ed.), *Computers in the Human Context: Information, Technology, Productivity, and People.* Cambridge, MA: MIT Press.

Kraut, R., C. Steinfield, A. Chan, B. Butler, and A. Hoag (1998), "Coordination and Virtualization: The Role of Electronic Networks and Personal Relationships," *Journal of Computer-Mediated Communications,* 3 (4). Available: www.ascusc.org/jcmc/vol3/issue4/kraut.html

Leavitt, H. J. and T. L. Whistler (1958), "Management in the 1980s," *Harvard Business Review,* November-December, pp. 41-48.

Lefebvre, Henri (1991), *The Production of Space* (D. N. Smith, Trans.). Cambridge, MA: Blackwell.

Lewis, M. (1998), "The Little Creepy Crawlers Who Will Eat You in the Night," *The New York Times Magazine,* March 1, pp. 40-46.

Lofland, J. (1995), "Charting Degrees of Movement Culture: Tasks of the Cultural Cartographer," in H. Johnston and B. Klandermans (Eds.), *Social Movements and Culture.* Minneapolis: University of Minnesota Press, 188-216.

Lyotard, J-F. (1984), *The Postmodern Condition* (G. Bennington and B. Massumi, Trans.). Minneapolis: University of Minnesota Press.

Madon, S. (1997), "Globalization and Development in Bangalore," *The Information Society,* 13, 227-243.

Matrix Information and Directory Services (2000), *Internet Growth.* Available: www.mids.org

Mattelart, A. (1994), *Mapping World Communication* (S. Emanuel, Trans.). Minneapolis: University of Minnesota Press.

McAdam, D. (1982), *Political Process and the Development of Black Insurgency 1930-1970.* Chicago: University of Chicago Press.

McCarthy, J. D. and M. N. Zald (1977), "Resource Mobilization and Social Movements: A Partial Theory," *American Journal of Sociology,* 82, 1212-1241.

McLuhan, M. and B. R. Powers (1989), *The Global Village.* New York: Oxford University Press.

Meyerson, D., K. E. Weick, and R. M. Kramer (1996), "Swift Trust and Temporary Groups," in R. M. Kramer and T. R. Tyler (Eds.), *Trust in Organizations: Frontiers of Theory and Research.* Thousand Oaks, CA: Sage, 166-195.

Miles, A. (1987), *Home Informatics: A Report to the Six Countries Programme on Aspects of Government Policies Toward Technical Innovation in Industry.* Delft, Netherlands: Six Countries Programme Secretariat.

Mokhtarian, P. (1991), "Defining Telecommuting," *Transportation Research Record,* 1305, 273-281.

Morris, A. D. and C. M. Mueller (Eds.) (1992), *Frontiers in Social Movement Theory.* New Haven, CT: Yale University Press.

Mueller, C. M. (1992), "Building Social Movement Theory," in A. D. Morris and C. M. Mueller (Eds.), *Frontiers in Social Movement Theory.* New Haven, CT: Yale University Press, 3-26.

Mumford, E. (1983), *Designing Secretaries.* Manchester, UK: Manchester Business School.

National Science Foundation (1995), *History of NSFNET Growth by Networks.* Available: nic.merit.edu/nsfnet/statistics/history.netcount

Noble, D. F. (1998), *Digital Diploma Mills: The Automation of Higher Education.* Available: firstmonday.dk/issues/issue3_1/noble/index.html

Nua Ltd. (1998), *How Many Online?* June 28. Available: www.nua.survey.net/surveys/about/index.html

Orlikowski, W. J. (1993), "Learning From Notes: Organizational Issues in Groupware Implementation," *The Information Society,* 9, 237-250.

———— and D. Gash (1994), "Technological Frames: Making Sense of Information Technology in Organizations," *ACM Transactions on Information Systems,* 12 (2), 174-207.

———— and J. Yates (1995), "Genre Repertoire: The Structuring of Communicative Practices in Organizations," *Administrative Science Quarterly,* 39, 541-574.

Palmer, J. W. and D. A. Griffith (1998), "An Emerging Model of Web Site Design for Marketing," *Communications of the ACM,* 41 (3), 44-51.

Pfaffenberger, B. (1996), "If I Want It, It's OK: Usenet and the (outer) Limits of Free Speech," *The Information Society,* 12, 365-386.

Pfeffer, J. (1987), "A Resource Dependence Perspective on Intercorporate Relations," in M. Mizruchi and M. Schwartz (Eds.), *Intercorporate Relations: The Structural Analysis of Business.* New York: Cambridge University Press, 25-55.

Porter, M. E. and V. E. Millar (1985), "How Information Gives You Competitive Advantage," *Harvard Business Review,* July-August, pp. 149-160.

Poster, M. (1990), *The Mode of Information.* Chicago: University of Chicago Press.

Powell, W. W. (1996), "Trust-Based Forms of Governance," in R. M. Kramer and T. R. Tyler (Eds.), *Trust in Organizations.* Thousand Oaks, CA: Sage, 51-67.

Press, L. (1994), "National Information Infrastructures: The Internet and Interactive Television," in *Conference on the Electronic Highway,* University of Montreal, May. Available: som.csudh.edu/fac/lpress/2cult.htm

Rao, H. R., A. F. Salam, and B. DosSantos (1998), "Introduction (Marketing and the Internet)," *Communications of the ACM,* 41 (3), 32-34.

Rapaport, A. (1986), *General Systems Theory: Essential Concepts and Applications.* Kent, UK: Abacus Press.

Rayner, R. (1998), "Nowhere, USA," *The New York Times Magazine,* March 8, pp. 42-46.

Reinicke, I. (1984), *Electronic Illusions: A Skeptic's View of Our High Tech Future.* New York: Penguin.

Rheingold, H. (1993), *The Virtual Community.* Reading, MA: Addison-Wesley.

Rockart, J. F. and L. S. Flannery (1983), "The Management of End-User Computing," *Communications of the ACM,* 26 (10), 776-784.

Ruhleder, K. and B. Jordan (1997), "Capturing Complex, Distributed Activities: Video-Based Interaction Analysis as a Component of Workplace Ethnography," in Allen S. Lee, Jonathan Liebenau, and Janice I. De Gross (Eds.), *Information Systems and Qualitative Research.* London: Chapman and Hall, 246-275.

Shaiken, H. (1985), *Work Transformed: Automation and Labor in the Computer Age.* New York: Holt, Rinehart & Winston.

Simon, H. A. (1977), *The New Science of Management Decision-Making.* Englewood Cliffs, NJ: Prentice Hall.

Snow, D. A. and R. D. Benford (1992), "Master Frames and Cycles of Protest," in A. D. Morris and C. M. Mueller (Eds.), *Frontiers in Social Movement Theory.* New Haven, CT: Yale University Press, 133-155.

————, B. E. Rochford, Jr., S. K. Worden, and R. D. Benford (1986), "Frame Alignment Processes, Micromobilization, and Movement Participation," *American Sociological Review,* 51, 464-481.

Sproull, L. and S. Kiesler (1991), *Connections: New Ways of Working in the Networked Organization.* Cambridge, MA: MIT Press.

Staples, D. S., J. S. Hulland, and C. A. Higgins (1998), "A Self-Efficacy Theory Explanation for the Management of Remote Workers in Virtual Organizations," *Journal of Computer-Mediated Communications,* 3 (4). Available: www.ascusc.org/jcmc/vol3/issue4/ staples. html

Star, L. (1989), *Regions of the Mind: Brain Research and the Quest for Scientific Certainty.* Stanford, CA: Stanford University Press.

Swidler, A. (1995), "Cultural Power and Social Movements," in H. Johnston and B. Klandermans (Eds.), *Social Movements and Culture.* Minneapolis: University of Minnesota Press, 25-40.

Technology and Telecommuting Committee (1994), *Research Recommendations: To Facilitate Distributed Work.* Washington, DC: National Academy of Sciences.

Toffler, A. (1980), *The Third Wave.* New York: William Morrow.

Turing, A. (1936), "On Computable Numbers, With an Application to the Entscheidungsproblem," *Proc. London Math. Society,* 42 (2), 230-265. (Correction in Vol. 43, pp. 544-546 [1937])

Weiner, N. (1948), *Cybernetics.* Cambridge, MA: MIT Press.

———(1954), *The Human Use of Human Beings: Cybernetics and Society.* Boston: Houghton Mifflin.

White House (1993), *The National Information Infrastructure: Agenda for Action.* Available: metalab.unc.edu/nii/nii-table-of-contents.html

Wilke, J. (1993), "Computer Links Erode Hierarchical Nature of Workplace Culture," *The Wall Street Journal,* December 9, pp. A1, A7.

Windle, J. T. and R. M. Taylor (1986), *The Early Architecture of Madison, Indiana.* Madison: Indiana Historical Society.

Yates, J. (1994), "Evolving Information Use in Firms, 1850-1920," in L. Bud-Frierman (Ed.), *Information Acumen: The Understanding and Use of Knowledge in Modern Business.* New York: Routledge, 26-50.

———(1999), "The Structuring of Early Computer Use in Life Insurance," *Journal of Design History,* 12 (1), 5-24.

Zack, M. and J. McKenney (1995), "Social Context and Interaction in Ongoing Computer-Supported Management Groups," *Organization Science,* 6, 394-422.

Zuboff, S. (1988), *In the Age of the Smart Machine: The Future of Work and Power.* New York: Basic Books.

5

Politically Wired

The Changing Places of Political Participation in the Age of the Internet

CHARLES BAZERMAN

Literacy, print, and journalism have during recent centuries become associated with an informed citizenry, political participation, and democratic forms of government. Freedom of the press—the First Amendment with its implied ability to question orthodoxy and entrenched interests, expose the deeds and misdeeds of the powerful and those entrusted with the powers of the state, and present alternative views of life and belief—has regularly been viewed as the cornerstone of U.S. democracy. To this we have added, over the past century and a half, a strong belief in public education to provide all citizens the means to participate in the free exchange of information as part of their political rights and responsibilities as citizens. Most recently, radio, television, and the Internet have extended the promise of public information, a more informed citizenry, and greater citizen participation in democratic processes.

Our public commitments to a free press, public education, universal literacy, and accessible communications media have combined in an ideology of rational public discourse that thrived in America long before Habermas reminded justifiably suspicious 20th-century intellectuals of the 18th-century formation of the public sphere. The realities, of course, have been more complicated than either our political ideologies or the Habermasian project have articulated, for both offer a broad sweep of hopes that obscure the particularities of actual historical formations. Only by continual struggle with the many forces that meet together in our communications forums do we manage to produce a political discussion that both engages significant parts of the population and occasionally rises to the seriousness of issues before us. The Internet, while changing the dynamics and opportunities of communication, nonetheless continues a complex system of political communication forged in previous media and still contains means to degrade or elevate our politics. It remains up to us as citizens and political actors to struggle with the rhetorical opportunities and dynamics of this new medium and make choices about the type of politics in which we wish to engage.

Among the many complexities of power, economics, interests, personality, passions, social interaction, ideology, culture, and religion that keep politics both more and less than rational deliberation are those that arise from the dynamics of literate interchange, the historical formation of forums, and the generic shaping of utterances within those forums. Recent research on genre and discursive systems, along with situated cognition and action, suggests that the character of the local activity space is extremely important for what happens, what people think and learn, and what social consequences emerge (Bazerman 1988, 1994a, 1994b, 1997a, 1997b, 1999; Berkenkotter and Huckin 1995; Devitt 1991; Freedman and Medway 1994a, 1994b; Russell 1997a, 1997b). While the shape of politics to emerge in the cyberworld still is somewhat obscure, by considering the forums of political interchange that are emerging on the Internet, how they draw on previous forums and genres of political interchange, and the pressures that seem to be encouraging the heightening of certain elements within those genres, we may gain a first reading of some choices in front of us.

CONTEXT IN SPEECH, WRITING, AND CYBERSPACE

To consider the impact of electronic genres on our political life, I now make some gross distinctions between genres in the two major previous media of communication: speech and writing. The idealized distinctions I make are in full awareness of the many overlaps, fuzzy middles, and particular cases that complicate the picture; nonetheless, the ideal types will help us to identify the affordances of the media and potential tendencies in their use.

With face-to-face spoken genres, where major aspects of the interpersonal and material context may be immediately visible or directly sensible, everything from the physical gestures of participants to the chairs people sit on and the birds that fly overhead may become salient aspects of context (e.g., greeting genres focus one on interpersonal markers of particular interlocutors— smiles and waves and physical signs of well-being). In face-to-face encounters, distant events and situations also may be called on as relevant context (e.g., the prior meeting last week in another city that perhaps was mentioned in discussion, the actions of legislators that frame every encounter of citizen and government official). However, these distant events generally are brought to bear on a situation in the here and now.

In more distantly mediated print genres (or even some phone conversations), however, the genre itself typically must announce and assemble the context. That is, when we receive a personal letter from the Internal Revenue Service (IRS), we all know that we are likely to be drawn up into its bureaucratic machinery, and the type of letter more specifically lets us know where—whether in the simple accounting of wrong addition or the inspectable world of substantiating deductions. Moreover, although we might have to pass through a number of specifiable physical places with observable humans (e.g., an IRS office with an IRS examiner, a U.S. district court with lawyers and judges), the place we are caught up in is a place of symbolic interaction lodged deep within documents; it is not a physical space. So, whereas spoken face-to-face genres may change the footing (Goffman 1981) or perception of a situation, genres at a distance have to call forth a total recognition of the cultural symbolic space. We may think of this in terms of a stage, which in face-to-face interaction may undergo changes of lighting and perspective as genre, footing, or contextualization clues change the saliences of interaction. But genres of distant communication must call forth an imagined world of which they are part, a world not only of co-participants but also of all the objects and utterances that are indexically and intertextually linked to the utterance of the moment.

The Internet, and particularly the World Wide Web, provides another configuration as the virtual contexts take on more concrete immediacy in embedding utterances within networks of other utterances that occur in visible proximate virtual locales through links. We explore this later through our examples.

But locating the scene—the relevant contexts and indexical relations—is only part of the work of genre, the quieter part. Genre puts the scene into action and identifies activities expectably to be completed by the time the genre runs its course. In fact, we might say that the virtual scene is built for action, assembled specifically around the activity to be discursively carried forth. The IRS letter assembles a place and relevancies and intertextualities all brought to mind not for our idle amusement or terror but rather because the IRS wishes to conduct some particular business with us and we, in reading, begin to assemble where we stand and what actions are available to us.

In face-to-face encounters, we may at times be in repose, sitting on a lounge chair and staring idly at the clouds in the company of intimates, but the moment we make a comment, we start to give shape to the discursive moment. More forcefully, the moment we notice a more distant correspondence, or the moment we look at print materials or answer the phone, we are drawn into different times and places with specific types of transactions afoot. It is the active purposiveness of the discursive locales that brings to mind and imagination all the contextual relevancies and socially localizing elements attached to the type of communication into which we enter.

As more and more of our interactions are mediated electronically, the activities may start by emulating and extending the interactions made possible in prior media, but the interactions and attendant relations and structures realized through the activities are likely to become transformed to take advantage of the new mediational opportunities, to move away from the practices that were conformable to prior media but awkward on the new medium, and to respond to the new communicative dynamics brought into being by the new medium. Those interactions that still seem important and still are best done in the prior media likely will remain in the prior media, but those activities that flourish in the new medium will create major new definitions of social activity, providing new means of carrying out our social needs and desires within new types of places.

RHETORIC, GENRE, AND
THE HISTORY OF PRINT CULTURE

Political communication, in the European tradition, gave rise to the study of rhetoric as a way in which to increase the force and power of individuals' public participation in the agora of the Greek polis. Rhetoric's genres of forensic, deliberative, and epideictic discourses (i.e., roughly courtroom argument, parliamentary debate, and public oratory of praise and blame) were built around face-to-face forums that emerged and were regularized around the activities of those genres—courts, legislatures, and public speeches or sermons by leaders to mobilize communal values (often executive but sometimes legislative and sometimes spiritual, particularly after the introduction of Christianity). The continuity of these institutional forums, the intertextual or discursive contexts they provide for each new utterance, and the activities enacted through the associated discursive genres have in fact formed the basic structures of our core political institutions, particularly with the 18th-century revival of the republic as the preferred political form, although with radically different notions of individuality, citizen rights and equality, and social negotiation.

However, literacy and literate genres from the earliest historical periods began transforming and extending forms of political life (Goody 1986). Written codes of law added a solemnity and consequentiality to legislative considerations because they were not just arguing for a single war or instance but rather were producing a consistent and enduring set of regulations for daily life. Written law and court records provided the means to increasingly turn judicial discourse into a matter of textual interpretation, comparison of current matters to prior texts, and the production of an inspectable court record to justify decisions, so that the law as a system rose above the direct sentiments of individual revenge and justice enacted on immediate participants.

The regularity of law meant that citizenship could be defined in terms of commitment to and obedience toward abstract rules—law abidingness, responsibilities, rights, and privileges—instead of personal commitment to individual, personally familiar leaders. Decision making and power were removed from public forums to clerics, bureaucrats, and scribes who controlled the written records of an increasingly organized, regularized, extended, and distant state that knew its citizens through the organized record keeping. The forums became associated with the records of their previous judgments, laws, and rulings, and these records provided specific intertextual context for each new instance of judgment and decision making.

However, printing provided public forums for attack and critique of the state and for the formulation of alternative programs. Polemics and manifestos could be distributed in various levels of secrecy or openness, especially as printing technology became less expensive and widely available (Eisenstein 1983). Governments concerned themselves with identifying subversive material and controlling its circulation, resulting in regulation of printing including copyright (Rose 1993).

Availability of alternative views and the organization of heterodox opinion through circulation of common texts found common cause with the new economic power of commercial classes aggregated outside the state but supported by accounting and literate practices. Print culture fed the associated desires for commercial and political information through pamphlets, journals, and newspapers concurrently with the times of political revolutions and reforms of the past four centuries.

Newspapers, written ballots, literate practices of expanding commerce, and calls for informed citizenry were associated with the expansion of schooling beyond the training of clerics, bureaucrats, and (to a lesser extent) the aristocracy who monitored, with some negligence, the work of clerics and bureaucrats. Newspapers were particularly associated with the expanding educated urban commercial classes in Britain and the United States during the 18th and 19th centuries along with the rise of political parties. Newspapers became forums for people to imagine themselves into wider political arenas and more distant events than they might have contact with daily, and they provided opportunities for people to identify themselves as partisans and members of communities (Habermas 1989). In the United States during the latter half of the 19th century, the formation of an independent press also became associated with investigative journalism, public accountability, and the development of professional journalistic standards (Schudson 1995). That is, the press developed a somewhat independent perspective, to some extent outside government, party, or particular economic interest (although always within limits and viewed with some skepticism), from which to view government and political processes. By reading the newspapers (or multiple newspapers and journals of opinions), citizens could become observers and evaluators (actively or passively) of public officials and political actors, entering into a continuing, if vicarious, relationship with government and politics. News then supported a political culture of critique, celebrity, spectator rooting, and competition. Citizens also could enter into marginal amateur production of political opinion through letters to the editor, but the production of news, critique, and opinion became largely a professional matter. These professional productions, in turn, provided the information that supported local civic activity, activist group participation, and individual and group communication with legislators. Community and activist group newsletters and other communications came to rely on the news, as did citizen participation in campaigning and elections. Thus, newspapers became a major forum that mediated political participation of ordinary citizens, and the intertextual record of the news (both as remembered by individuals and as a research file for continually unfolding events to be placed in retrospective contexts) became the context for further news items.

The political culture informed by the news also got played out secondarily in personal social gatherings where people exchanged opinions as a type of identity play (Billig 1988) as well as exchange of thoughts. This political culture was given further, if somewhat restrictive and ritualizing, shape through surveys by which public opinion was expressed and aggregated, thereby becoming news and having a continuing influence on government as politicians kept closer and closer tabs on the moods of the voters as well as the news representation of the voters. Radio and television talk shows gave individuals an expanded opportunity to take this private exchange and turn it into public assertion and larger group affiliation processes, with consequences for public representations of public opinion as mediated through the print and electronic press.

In this evolving climate of public opinion, political parties developed their own internal cultures and media of communication and participation, in part enacted through traditional patronage and ward politics but also in part enacted through other forms of more conceptualized partisan commitment involving speeches, humor, demonizing characterizations of the opposition, newsletters, serious program papers, and forms of public hoopla and celebration. These activities, in turn, become re-presented in the general news media, over which partisan groups attempt to exert control through media events, spin-doctoring, sound bites, and other means of shaping political messages for the news media.

The characterizations I have just provided are broad and sweeping, but beyond the particulars I point to, I want to suggest the range and complexity of political culture mediated through face-to-face, print media, and radio and television genres. This then provides a rich but finely shaped field of public participation that new forms of electronic communication may extend and transform at the same time as the existing modes of participation provide models of communication that may at first be fairly directly translated onto the Internet.

POLITICS ON THE WORLD WIDE WEB

The Web became a clearly recognized presence as early as the 1994 election, with candidates already creating Web sites to set out their positions and elicit support (Fund 1994; Harmon 1994; Lewis 1994; Powers 1994; Seib 1995). In the 1996 election, parties and candidates had extensive and elaborate Web sites as well as many private, independent, commentary, journalistic, and humor sites, and the number of sites continues to grow with each public controversy and each political season (Allen 1996; Mossberg 1996; Seib 1997).[1]

Quite visibly, the Web has provided fertile soil for many politically related sites that provide forums and contexts for specific forms of participation. Major news and political commentary organizations have established their own sites re-presenting material presented in other media—many newspapers (e.g., *The New York Times, The Wall Street Journal, Boston Globe, Los Angeles Times, Chicago Tribune, Houston Chronicle, The Washington Post*), political magazines (e.g., *Congressional Quarterly, American Prospect, Washington Weekly, Tikkun*), public and private television and radio news shows (NPR's *All Things Considered*, PBS's *Evening Newshour*, MSNBC, CNN). Some are exclusively devoted to political news, such as CNN's *AllPolitics*. Further new electronic journals have appeared (e.g., *Slate, HotWired*).

Many of these sites are linked with each other and with other reputable sources of political and governmental information, giving some shape to a recognizable universe of legitimated professional public political information and commentary. This makes "What Washington is talking about" more public and accessible and virtually concrete, no longer requiring citizens to be at the right combination of cocktail parties, listen to many interview shows, and keep up subscriptions to a wide range of journals. By following links around the Web, one can have some access to the political buzz in a fairly short time. However, although all of these sites provide news and commentary for various publics to contemplate, and although this news and commentary may provide the basis for later actions such as voting, community participation, and political involvement, immediately in themselves, these electronic journals afford no active form of participation except letter writing in response (typically, e-mail response is facilitated).

More technologically adept individuals can elevate themselves from consumers to producers of political chat by setting up amateur political home pages, and there are many such home pages pursuing political commentary and humor. Pages are built in fan support of political heroes and in attack of political enemies as well as in support and attack of parties and programs. Individuals assert their identities, share their visions, and aggregate resources for like-minded people. Humor usually is pointed, aimed at political enemies. The activities on such pages clearly are derivative of, on the one side, the public media culture of political celebrity and partisanship and, on the other, local community political argument; both extremes feed off of each other. It is not surprising that the talk show hosts, themselves mediating between national news and local discussion, become Web celebrities at the center of fascination and discussion—heroes of political talk on the Internet. On June 17, 1997, a search using the Excite search engine revealed 998,146 matches on the name Rush Limbaugh, 898,241 on the name Ollie North, 172,574 on the name Pat Buchanan, and 12,339 on the name Geraldine Ferraro. Whereas this clearly indicates the political direction of this phenomenon, it also suggests that even a Democrat new to the talk scene gets some attention. This amateur commentary is outspoken and aggressive, expressing both strongly positive and strongly negative comments, as symbolized by the Punch Rush Limbaugh home page (www.indirect.com/www/beetle87/rush/index.html).

Like the talk shows, the amateur Web political pages give non-politicians and non-journalists access to a media stage on which to perform political and journalistic activities, elevating their local talk into public performances and identities that extend out beyond their geographically immediate groups and allowing them to affiliate with geographically separated people of common interests. By participating in talk shows, and even more by creating Web sites, individuals can imagine themselves as politically engaged without too much monitoring of the concrete consequences, if any, of such participation. The locale of such talk clearly is outside more official political talk—outside the beltway, so to speak—but it also clearly is contextually and intertextually related to the public circulation of news and commentary.

One of the consequences of the multiplicity of amateur political sites, many of which are hotlinked to each other and to the more official sites (some amateur pages consist only of index pages of annotated links), is that producers and consumers can immerse themselves more fully and immediately in critical, independent, and partisan information and commentary. We might call this an intensification and a greater availability of the long-standing culture of political talk. The intensification, however, seems to bring about a qualitative change in that people can produce more extended turns for a more extended audience.

The amateur political talk sometimes aggregates within more organized sites of controversialism, often around minor political parties, cult followings, and activist groups—sometimes mediated through the identity of celebrity talk figures. For example, the Rush Limbaugh Featured Site (www2.southwind.net/vic/rush/rush.html) contains links to the Berkeley College Republicans, Newt Gingrich sites, the Republican National Convention site, the Massachusetts Republican Party, and other conservative groups.

Controversialism, always an aspect of advocacy journalism, has found new journalistic opportunities on the Internet as individuals set themselves up as public sources of news, rumors, or editorial opinions that immediately become widely accessible both to political activists and to more mainstream and professional journalists. The amateur production of "news" outside the standard practices, institutions, and self-regulation of print journalism (as loose as those procedures are), and outside the scope of libel laws written for a print age, has led to the elevation of unconfirmed reports and gossip into apparent journalistic credibility. For example, Matt Drudge, with his daily *Drudge Report,* has been a primary means of breaking unreliable reports, particularly aimed against President Clinton (Felsenthal 1998; Harmon 1998; Kaplan 1997; Kurtz 1997; Shaw 1998). The spread of less reliable unconfirmed stories into mainline Internet journalism sites is fostered by the immediacy of discussion, which makes traditional time pressures of "being scooped" more intense.

Organized political argument and activism also aggregates around a variety of movements, interests, and organizations, with more or less programmatic coherence such as libertarianism, objectivism, and many varieties and sites of environmentalism. The activities afforded by these sites are complex and multiple, and I do not begin to examine them here, but I should note that the sites often are affiliated with non-cyber-political organizations. The pages of political organizations, in turn, typically present information, platforms, candidate biographies and positions, speeches, news, resources, and links to candidate pages and affiliated organizations.

Furthermore, there are a variety of national, state, and local government sites, some of which are aimed at presenting the accomplishments of the agencies and the incumbent administrations along with agency-relevant information, query access, forms, and form-filing opportunities. Individual office holders have their pages affording a variety of activities and providing a variety of governmental, political, and constituent service information. Legislative caucuses and other political groups of office holders also have their sites.

In addition, there are public service independent organizations that provide nonpartisan information on office holders, candidates, and elections such as the Vote Smart project.

Thus, the political landscape on the Web is becoming increasingly complex and, to some extent, is taking on its own novel character, building on prior forms of political activity but transforming them. Political culture is finding far more public forums and is being spread more easily. It is easier to immerse oneself into an array of opinions, surround oneself with networks of like-minded individuals, and assert a place in public political culture by establishing a Web page and links. A local person, even without affiliation with political groups or some institution that harbors political activity (e.g., a university campus), can form a public political presence and establish an identity within a political group, even a fringe group.

Although the increased opportunities for participation and affiliation seem to foster the ideals of democracy, there also are fewer filters on the partisanship, controversialism, and unreliability of reports that can become widely visible and seem to have some spillover effects on more traditional media. Individuals with Internet access are finding much larger soapboxes, megaphones, and opportunities for affiliations over much wider areas than in the past; at the same time, they are able to bypass traditional systems of responsibility, regulation, and accountability. The attempt by the courts to apply libel laws to the Internet in the *Drudge Report* case is only the beginning of a struggle to develop new systems of accountability for electronically mediated political speech. Similarly, there is no doubt that we will see a struggle to organize the fragmenting trends of Internet political controversy and to mobilize the aggregating possibilities of electronic linking and networking so as to influence issues played out on the mass scale of the nation.

THE DEMOCRATIC NATIONAL COMMITTEE WEB SITE

The traditional means of fostering, aggregating, and developing some coherence to political participation has been the official party organizations. Of the two major parties in the United States, it has been the Democratic party to this point that has made the greatest effort to establish a strong Internet presence through its Web site, first established in June 1995.[2] The remainder of this chapter examines the Web site of the Democratic National Committee (DNC) to see the institutional party response to the dynamics of Internet political communication.[3]

The first impression that the DNC site (www.democrats.org) presents, as examined on various days in June 1997, is that it is embedded in the culture of news. The upper right of the home page has a publicity photo of President Clinton signing legislation and the left, just below a bold title "Democratic Party Online," has the day's date, suggesting the daily updating of news. Just below is a ticker-tape banner announcing the latest news bulletins. Below that, the hot button table of contents is headed by "DNC News." (The news ticker itself also is directly related to that news page, both in the content of the headlines and as a hotlink.) Over the next three years (last viewed in August 2000), the appearance of the front page changed to follow the evolving design used by major Internet news organizations, but the visual analogy to news remained constant.

Thus, the DNC site is immediately set within a context of breaking news, defining political participation as a form of involvement with unfolding news stories. The news, as might be expected, is partisan. "The Daily News" from the DNC on June 10, for example, includes the headlines "Unemployment Drops Again While Wages Continue to Rise," "Republicans Force President to Veto Disaster Relief—It's 1995-1996 All Over Again," "Barbour Sold Business Deals in China to Foreign Contributor," and "Gingrich Admits Fundraising Hearings Targeted at President, Vice-President; Wacko GOP Investigator Reportedly Stalks Witnesses."

Each of these headlines is followed by a few sentences of elaboration, emulating the lead paragraph of a news story, followed by a citation to a professional news organization (where it possibly is hotlinked to the full story at the news agency's home site) or by reference (and hotlink) to a DNC news release that elaborates the story and provides references to the independent press. There also is an archive of previous stories going back to the initiation of this news page feature on March 26, 1997.

The reference to the independent press (and, as often as possible, to right-leaning news sources) is important to maintain credibility for the reported news, even as it has a partisan edge and implications, because the larger part of the rhetorical impulse seems to be over trustworthiness and credibility—which party and which individuals can be relied on to deliver and who is misleading the American public. The approximately dozen stories on any day going back about a week divide up pretty evenly into tales of Clinton's and congressional Democrats' accomplishments and Republican leaders' embarrassments. In the middle usually is placed a quotation of the day, again highlighting a Democratic accomplishment or a Republican betrayal. The news, as reported here, is really a trafficking in celebrity, credit, and potential support.

This partisan retelling of the news, traced back to independent news sources, relies on news media already heavily engaged in reporting political warfare, partisan events and leaks created for the media, and pre-spun news releases. That is, the news already is filled with stories of partisan import with consequences for evaluation of the opposing parties and consequent support. Part of the political struggle is for each party to gain an upper hand in this struggle over appearances of credibility. The DNC page presents itself as embedded within this partisan struggle for control of news impressions; thus, it places its readers in the role of consumers of political opinion or as purveyors of it insofar as they use the news reports as a resource for their own political discourse.

To draw the visitors more fully into a realm of partisan representation of the news, the page offers direct subscription to the news site through e-mail, and this service is offered through several postings on the main page, the news page, the Get Active page, and several other spots. The subscription page appeals to subscribers as party activists who will help to purvey the information to others:

> Think about the potential. . . . For the first time in our Party's history, we have
> the ability to arm you with up-to-the minute news and information direct from
> Party Headquarters!
> . . . When the DNC launched Democratic News, our goal was very simple—
> to help equip supporters with the information they need to deliver the Demo-
> cratic Party's message. DEMOCRATIC NEWS enables the Party to get the
> same information to thousands of Democrats across the country instantaneously.

Whether these updates provide grist for dinner table talk, talk show retorts, or editorial writing, they increase the circulation of partisan news, with a particular orientation to celebrity hero and villain politicians—most notably the president and vice president and the congressional leaders of both parties as well as whoever might be the target of the latest Republican embarrassment. (As of August 2000, this service still was active, periodically providing the same partisan news that appears on the Web site but with increasing activist information about meetings and volunteer and job opportunities. Hotlinks from the e-mail messages to related Web sites also were added, taking advantage of new technology.)

This sense of partisan celebrity is further enacted through the DNC's version of the Punch Rush Limbaugh page—an opportunity to vote on whether Gingrich should pay his fines from his own funds. Each 99-cent call to the 900 "Stop Newt Hotline" profits the Democratic Congressional Campaign Committee. This is accessed through the What's Hot page along with a more sedate survey (also prominently displayed on the main home page) that collects Internet use information rather than political opinions. This page also links to sites of three rather high-minded, nominally nonpolitical causes: the

Franklin Delano Roosevelt Memorial project, the Net Day initiative (aimed at gaining volunteers to wire up schools), and the Kids Campaign (an extensive set of resources on children's issues). So, "what's hot" apparently again consists of representations of high-road activities and accomplishments of the Democratic office holders, with which one can become affiliated, and low-road attacks on the deviousness of the opposition party, which one can enjoy and become incensed over.

Other opportunities for user participation are presented on the Get Active page. Here, one can join the DNC, volunteer to work for local candidates, find out about internship positions, get voter registration information and download a registration form, sign the guest book (also linked on the main home page), and subscribe to the DNC News (described earlier). Except for the latter, all of these are traditional and soberly respectable activities carried out by the political party. Interestingly, beyond the DNC membership fee (choices of $20 up to $100) and the Stop Newt Hotline, there is no fund-raising carried out on the site, presenting the Democratic party as a source of information and a site for identification and involvement without any pressure or cost. The suppression of the strong fund-raising motive that pervades much of modern political life suggests a conscious strategy of engagement by the designers of the page. The only thing visitors are pressured to give up is their names. The Guest Book, the volunteer registration, the subscription to the DNC News, and the User Survey all are means of gathering names. As anyone who has worked in politics knows, the only thing more valuable than money in politics is mailing lists of supporters; these provide access to both money and votes.

The DNC site also supports access to more in-depth information on policies, positions, and government actions as well as access to local Democratic parties and related information through two pages: the DNC FAQ (frequently asked questions) page (which embeds links in its prose responses to questions such as "How does the DNC work with local and state candidates?" and "Where can I find the Party's platform?") and the Democratic Party Headquarters page (which is an extensive index of related links). These extensive links largely keep one within the orbit of Democratic party organizations and affiliates, but one page, Linking With America, leads the user outward to a wide array of amateur political sites, campaign professionals, local groups, activist abortion rights and environmental groups, and to the entire complex of left/liberal political culture.

The structuring of the site to keep the user in the orbit of the DNC pages and affiliated organizations is one of the major changes that had occurred in the site since the 1996 election—when the site was more irreverent, playful, and cyber-culture oriented—and also quickly led the user outside the narrow world of Democratic party representations of the world, Democratic party activities, and Democratic party sentiments into a general, young, ironic, and multivalent left political culture. Now, the DNC pages try to keep the users engaged for a longer period in a more official, controlled, organized, and institutional world of political practice and with a more coherent viewpoint whereby the world is divided between workers for good and abusers of the public trust.

By June 1998, the site had moved further toward institutional sobriety and providing more extensive access to policy statements and concrete policy accomplishments. Although the basic format of the site remained the same, a new set of pages, accessed through a new entry-page title, "Where We Stand," gives extensive details of "Economic Progress Under President Clinton," "Democratic Platform," "Democratic Position Papers," "Democratic Accomplishments Overview," and "State by State Presidential Accomplishments" (actually kept at the whitehouse.gov Web address). The information presented here is concrete and extensive. There are, for example, more than 40 detailed position papers available on topics such as "Clean Air," "Permanent Replacements for Lawful Economic Strikers," "Violence Against Women," and "National Endowment for the Arts." Although some of this information was accessible in earlier versions of the site, gathering these pieces of information together here and supplementing them foregrounds the party as an instrument of policy rather than a vehicle of partisan interests. The site also distanced itself from raucous partisanship by dropping the outdated Stop Newt Hotline and not replacing it with any similar amusement. Nonetheless, the partisan "Democratic News" remains. By August 2000, in anticipation of the presidential campaign, the Democratic site had incorporated further new technology such as multimedia links and live video from the party convention. The attack pages on opponents were moved to separate Web addresses but remained hotlinked to the main party front page. A moderated bulletin board posting statements on "Why I am a Democrat" was added.

The changes that have occurred on the DNC site, as a professional strategy of party presentation and supporter enlistment that seems to have taken over from a type of exuberant overflow of the youthful political culture of cyber-savvy 20-something staffers, suggest not only that a great deal of thought and energy is going into the creation of institutionally significant Web sites but also that some thought and energy is going into thinking about what types of engagement and participation are being offered to the nonprofessional participant in political culture. No doubt, the Web and participant design are in dialectic with the responses and opinions of users (it would be interesting to note how that information is gathered and used), probably in a way that parallels any marketing, entertainment, or political venture.

At the moment, the result appears to be a backing away from the type of partisan brawling that seems to pervade amateur politics on the Web and a movement toward providing more solid and extensive information and policy thought (although, of course, still partisan). If such a trend continues and is matched by similar developments on the Web sites of other political institutions such as advocacy groups, citizen information organizations, and political parties and campaigns, then some of the hopes for access to increased political information may be realized.

It might be that on more serious policy issues, beyond the visceral controversial issues that are manipulated in marketing strategies for parties and candidates and that evoke the type of controversialist amateur participation that seems so pervasive on the Web, the discussion is so professionalized and dependent on substantial informational and intellectual resources that citizen participation already requires a large investment in becoming informed and much work in finding a place in the conversation. Yet, on particular issues such as the environment and health care, large numbers of citizens have shown the commitment both to understand the issues and to assert their presence in the policy discussions. It is perhaps around special issues that depth of information and discussion might develop most forcefully on the Internet.

POLITICS AND
SOCIALITY IN THE CYBER-AGE

The example of the DNC site, for the moment, still seems to draw on our culture of news, now spun and pre-spun into a partisan frame, heavily weighted with emotions of benefaction and trust set against suspicion and repulsion and then projected onto celebrity heroic and villain figures. These emotions of political culture are being muted from their most virulent forms of political entertainment and are given the somberness of institutional authority, yet they pervade the selection and organization of the information. Nonetheless, this morality drama is providing entryways into increasingly more substantive information and deliberation.

There is no reason to think that the current DNC site will stabilize as the form by which major party participation will be enacted in the cyber-age. Perhaps the major parties will find other strategies for enlisting partisans and support. Perhaps the opportunities of cyberspace will support other political organizations or forms of action. But what does seem clear already is that long-standing issues of political and journalistic responsibility are only written fresh and more compellingly on the Web. On the Web, the time immediacy, wide geographic spread, democratic access, and ability to make large amounts of information available do not in themselves protect us from the narrowest forms of partisanship, rumor, scurrilous attacks, and crude appeals; indeed, the Web has shown itself to be an inviting place for the baser forms of politics. The Web can serve equally as an instrument of

further centralization, advancing the causes of the most legitimated institutions, as quality information with institutional approval may become a distinctive and valued commodity against an unregulated open market of unreliable information and as institutional voices delegitimate the voices of
amateur citizens. Even if we find the right mix of legitimated information
from multiple sources and perspectives with opportunities for citizens to
develop and express their positions and form political identities, we still need
to establish vehicles for political opinion to aggregate in ways that become
effective within mass society.

The ancient issue of democratic politics—how democracy becomes more
than rabble-rousing—is being posed fresh in the cyber-age under new conditions and dynamics of communication. The solutions that we will develop in
the long run are as yet unsettled, but the future of our political culture depends
on them.

NOTES

1. An early study of the Internet on politics, using a general communication flow model, pre-
dicts that the two-way communication afforded by the Internet "should have a positive influence
on political participation" (Bonchek 1996). But the optimistic predictions, in treating information as an abstracted commodity conveyed in any communication, take no account of the particular forums, contexts, and activities within which the information is deployed, nor does it examine
the types of participation and roles enacted by individuals in the communicating of the information. Another set of studies in progress (Bimber 1998) is tracking the demographics of political
use of the Internet. The preliminary data released from this project are starting to identify who
uses the Internet for what political purposes, but they do not examine the specific content or communicative form of the interactions. Until we have a more finely grained examination of exactly
what occurs within the communications, in what types of forums and contexts, within what genres they are organized and deployed, and what forms of social activity occur within these genres,
any predictions that we might make about increasing democracy would have to be tempered by
awareness of our own ignorance. To use a not inappropriate analogy, just because more people
might gather in more venues to watch sports on more channels and media; trade opinions about
sports in person and electronically; gather and communicate sports information in magazines,
trading cards, and Web sites; and deal in memorabilia does not necessarily make a nation more
athletic, fit, skilled in team interactions, or communally bonded in sportsmanship. It is the nature
of the participation carried out through structured, socially organized activities in recognizable
forums and contexts that shapes the social results.

2. This followed the Clinton administration setting up public bulletin boards and e-mail
access as soon as the administration arrived in office (Mossberg 1993).

3. By the middle of 1997, the Republican National Committee (RNC) had set up a similar
site (www.rnc.org). As of June 1998, it had many features similar to those of the DNC site including news and a news subscription service, party information and platform, announcement of
party training and events, and membership sign-up. In addition, it has a gift shop, an RNC
Weekly Trivia Contest, and a chat room. Even more than the DNC site, the RNC site seems to be
pervaded by accounts of the misdeeds of the leaders of the opposition party, not only on the news

page but also on an "Interactive Clinton Calendar" that puts scandals on a time line, a set of links devoted to "The Selling of America's House," and a "Clinton/Gore/DNC Chinagate Chart." The links page, besides linking party and government sites (as does the DNC site), also links to conservative organizations, such as the Cato Institute and the Heritage Foundation, and to "Fun and Games," which includes an electronic futures market and two parody sites: the moderately right Capital Steps and the more extreme right Paul Silhan's PARO-DISE (Silhan is a regular on Rush Limbaugh's radio program).

REFERENCES

Allen, M. (1996), "Eat, Sleep, and Breathe Politics on the Internet," *The New York Times,* January 29, p. C4.

Bazerman, C. (1988), *Shaping Written Knowledge: The Genre and Activity of the Experimental Article in Science.* Madison: University of Wisconsin Press.

———— (1994a), *Constructing Experience.* Carbondale: Southern Illinois University Press.

———— (1994b), "Systems of Genre and the Enactment of Social Intentions," in A. Freedman and P. Medway (Eds.), *Genre in the New Rhetoric.* London: Taylor & Francis, 79-101.

———— (1997a), "Discursively Structured Activities," *Mind, Culture, and Activity,* 4, 296-308.

———— (1997b), "The Life of Genre, the Life in the Classroom," in W. Bishop and H. Ostrom (Eds.), *Genre and the Teaching of Writing.* Portsmouth, NH: Boynton Cook, 19-26.

———— (1999), *The Languages of Edison's Light: Rhetorical Agency in the Material Production of Technology.* Cambridge, MA: MIT Press.

Berkenkotter, C. and T. Huckin (1995), *Genre Knowledge in Disciplinary Communication.* Hillsdale, NJ: Lawrence Erlbaum.

Billig, M. (1988), *Ideological Dilemmas: A Social Psychology of Everyday Thinking.* London: Sage.

Bimber, B. (1998), *Government and Politics on the Net Project.* Available: www.sscf.ucsb.edu/survey1/main.html

Bonchek, M. (1996), *From Broadcast to Netcast: The Internet and the Flow of Political Information,* Ph.D. dissertation, Harvard University.

Devitt, A. (1991), "Intertextuality in Tax Accounting," in C. Bazerman and J. Paradis (Eds.), *Textual Dynamics of the Professions.* Madison: University of Wisconsin Press, 336-357.

Eisenstein, E. (1983), *The Printing Revolution in Early Modern Europe.* Cambridge, UK: Cambridge University Press.

Felsenthal, E. (1998), "Drudge Match," *The Wall Street Journal,* March 11, p. A1.

Freedman, A. and P. Medway (Eds.) (1994a), *Genre in the New Rhetoric.* London: Taylor & Francis.

———— and ———— (Eds.) (1994b), *Learning and Teaching Genre.* Portsmouth, NH: Heinemann.

Fund, J. (1994), "We Are All Pundits Now," *The Wall Street Journal,* November 8, p. A22.

Goffman, E. (1981), "Footing," in E. Goffman (Ed.), *Forms of Talk.* Philadelphia: University of Pennsylvania Press, 124-159.

Goody, J. (1986), *The Logic of Writing and the Organization of Society.* Cambridge, UK: Cambridge University Press.

Habermas, J. (1989), *The Structural Transformation of the Public Sphere: An Inquiry Into a Category of Bourgeois Society.* Cambridge: MIT Press.

Harmon, A. (1994), "The Digital Soapbox," *The New York Times,* November 2, p. D1.

————(1998), "Gossip on the Web Gives News a Novel Spin," *The New York Times*, February 2, p. A12.

Kaplan, K. (1997), "A Question of Ethics," *Los Angeles Times*, November 17, p. D3.

Kurtz, H. (1997), "Cyber-libel and the Web Gossip-Monger," *The Washington Post*, August 15, p. G1.

Lewis, P. (1994), "Electronic Tie for Citizens and Seekers of Office," *The New York Times*, November 6, p. A15.

Mossberg, W. (1993), "White House Lets You Turn On Your PC, Tune Into Politics," *The Wall Street Journal*, March 18, p. B1.

————(1996), "The Web Makes Even This Election Seem Interesting," *The Wall Street Journal*, October 3, p. B1.

Powers, W. (1994), "Virtual Politics," *The Washington Post*, November 8, p. E1.

Rose, M. (1993), *Authors and Owners*. Cambridge, MA: Harvard University Press.

Russell, D. R. (1997a), "Rethinking Genre in School and Society: An Activity Theory Analysis," *Written Communication*, 14, 504-554.

————(1997b), "Writing and Genre in Higher Education and Workplaces," *Mind, Culture, and Activity*, 4, 224-237.

Schudson, M. (1995), *The Power of News*. Cambridge, MA: Harvard University Press.

Seib, G. (1995), "Cyberpoliticking: Presidential Races Are Being Changed by Latest Technology," *The Wall Street Journal*, August 4, p. A1.

————(1997), "Digital America," *The Wall Street Journal*, November 12, p. A24.

Shaw, D. (1998), "Speed of Reporting Via the Web Tests Accuracy and Ethics," *Los Angeles Times*, March 31, p. A20.

6

Information Technology in a Culture of Complaint

Derogation, Deprecation, and the
Appropriation of Organizational Transformation

JOHN R. WEEKS

Why do people complain about information technology (IT)? This might sound like a pedestrian question, one whose answer could be expected to hold about as much interest as a scholarly treatment of why the chicken crossed the road. It seems obvious that people complain about a technology because they want it to be improved or removed. But the old joke about the jaywalking chicken may be instructive in shaking our certainty about this. The joke is funny (albeit only once) because the answer, "to get to the other side," is self-evidently correct and yet unexpected. We do not expect it because we take it for granted; we skip past it in our search for explanations based on deeper poultry urges. A first introduction to tautology for most children, the joke points to the fact that we cannot answer its question in a more satisfying way without more information about the chicken and its situation. Returning to my original question, the analogous answer is that people complain about a piece of IT to voice dissatisfaction with it. This is by definition[1] and, I claim, is the only thing we can say in general. All more satisfying answers will be context specific.

This chapter draws from the specific context of an ethnographic study of an ongoing organizational transformation in a large British retail bank to argue that complaint about IT does not always express a desire for change or a return to the status quo ante. Sometimes it performs these expressive functions, but complaint is best understood, to use Goffman's (1971, p. 63) terminology, as an *interaction ritual* that also may perform certain social functions. In this chapter, I distinguish between two rituals of complaint about IT in the bank—*derogation* and *deprecation*—and describe the uses of each in the organization. Derogation, "a lowering of honor or esteem"[2] of IT, serves as what Goffman (1971, pp. 62-69) terms a *supportive ritual*—bringing people together, building relationships, and strengthening bonds of community. Deprecation of IT, "an expression of an earnest desire that something be averted or removed," fulfills the standard expressive function of complaint but also can be—again with a nod to Goffman (pp. 108-118)—a *remedial ritual*—repairing relationships threatened by more personal complaints. In these guises, the situated rhetoric of complaint plays a role not only in the provocation of organizational transformation and its resistance but also in the acceptance and appropriation of the transformed organization. Specifically, these rituals of complaint were available to people in the bank to help them cope with the dislocation and changes implied by the centralization and partial automation of back-office clerical work. This is so because of the particular stage set by the bank's culture and the details of this transformation it was undergoing. I describe these before returning to the discussion of derogation and deprecation.

UNPOPULAR CULTURE

Let us start modestly, however, with an example of a complaint about an organization's technology that is not a call for redress or, indeed, action of any sort. Toward the end of my eight months of participant observation with the bank, which I refer to as the British Armstrong Bank (or BritArm),[3] I first met Ben. Ben is a pseudonymous senior manager in BritArm's London head office. As he led me into the stuffy conference room where we were to have our discussion, he walked over to open the window. It promptly fell shut. He fiddled with the mechanism, but he could not get the window to stay open. "BritArm technology," he said with a smile as he gave up and sat down. "Now, let me tell you a little bit about myself."

He went on to give a résumé of his career with the bank, but with his little derogation he already had told something about himself—not about his aggravation with the bank's technology but rather about his affinity and agility with its culture. Small jokes at the expense of the bank, and especially its IT, are common conversational icebreakers at BritArm. BritArm employees complain about the bank in the same way as the British public complains about the weather—incessantly and with good humor. And, as with gripes about the weather, these jibes at the bank prompt quick agreement but do not by themselves signal antagonism. When expressed by the culturally competent, they draw people together with their allusion to shared experience. They put people at ease with one another through the comforting routine of their recital. Ben's quip about the bank's technology was no more a call for something to be done than his earlier greeting, "How do you do?" was a request for a medical report.

Instead, it was an artifact of what I describe as BritArm's "unpopular culture" (Weeks 1997). At BritArm, self-deprecation is taken to extremes, even by British standards. Never once did I hear a positive word about the culture or the technology, and seldom did I hear anything positive about any other aspect of the organization. Complaints, on the other hand, were common. I was told repeatedly that the bank is too bureaucratic, too rules driven, not customer focused enough, not entrepreneurial enough, too inflexible, too prone to navel gazing, too centralized—and, it was added, too negative. Its technology, I was told, is outdated on installation, poorly maintained, and plagued by delays and a shortage of funds that too often are misspent. An often-heard story about how the bank came to have its much-derided branch banking computer system has it that the company that wrote the software marketed it to all of the major banks in Britain. All of the other banks had the sense to reject it, but BritArm was the exception. People familiar with the project deny that account, claiming it to be a bank myth. "Typical of people in the bank to believe the worst," one technology manager told me. Indeed. This is an organization in which speaking notes were sent out to managers to help them explain to employees why the £1.5 billion operating profits posted that year by BritArm—an increase of roughly one third over the year before—was, in fact, bad news.[4] And, what is more, managers and clerks may come and go, assets may be acquired and disposed of, the organization may be restructured periodically, new systems may be introduced, jobs may be redefined, and processes may be redesigned, but the common wisdom holds that "the bank hasn't really changed in 300 years."

The bank is an example of a negative but strong culture that nobody admits to liking and everybody feels helpless to change. Complaints within the bank about its IT must be understood in this context. And despite the nearly exclusive attention paid in the literature to cultures that are, in the words of Whyte (1955, p. 299), "interesting and pleasant" for members, there is no reason to believe that BritArm is unique in the unpopularity of its culture.

It is important here to be clear about what is meant by *culture*.[5] Hannerz (1992) offers a conceptual framework that is particularly apt when trying to understand BritArm and its culture of complaint. This is because Hannerz concerns himself with what he calls the "complex cultures" of, for example, contemporary Americans and Brits rather than the simpler cultures of the historical Trobriand Islanders and Nuer. To use the adjective *simple* is not to say that such cultures are easy to understand or lacking in richness and subtlety; rather, it is to say that, whether or not Evans-Pritchard (1940) and Malinowski (1922) were prudent to treat the cultures they studied as self-contained and homogeneous, ethnographers studying in the United States and United Kingdom today would not be prudent to do so. The classic "small-society" model of organizations, decreasingly applicable even to small societies during these days of global communication and commerce, is particularly inappropriate for the study of organizations whose members received their primary socialization[6] in a large, porous, and variegated society (Baba 1989, p. 7). It is impossible to understand culture at BritArm U.K. without referring to the broader British culture in which the bank is set and that it reflects to some extent.

Hannerz (1992, p. 7) conceives of culture as having three dimensions. The first dimension, labeled *ideas and modes of thought,* corresponds to the two levels of *espoused values* and *basic underlying assumptions* in Schein's (1992, p. 17) model familiar to students of organizations. The second dimension, labeled *forms of externalization* (Hannerz 1992), corresponds to the level of *artifacts* in Schein's (1992) model. They are "the different ways in which meaning is made accessible to the senses, made public" (Hannerz 1992, p. 7). Hannerz (1992) labels the third dimension *social distribution,* which comprises "the ways in which the collective cultural inventory of meanings and meaningful external forms—that is, [the first and second dimensions] together—is spread over a population and its social relationships" (p. 7). It is in the attention Hannerz pays to this third dimension, the social distribution of culture, that he differs from other anthropological and organizational theorists. It is primarily along this dimension that complex cultures differ from simple ones, and it is this aspect of his framework that makes it appealing for the current study.

Rejecting the customary commitment, in anthropology and other disciplines, to "the idea of culture as something shared, in the sense of homogeneously distributed in society," Hannerz (1992) finds it more useful to start from the premise that "culture is distributed and includes understandings of distributions" (p. 15).

> The major implication of a distributive understanding of culture, of culture as an organization of diversity, is not just the somewhat nit-picking reminder that individuals are not all alike but that people must deal with other people's meanings; that is, there are meanings, and meaningful forms, on which other individuals, categories, or groups in one's environment somehow have a prior claim but to which one is somehow yet called to make a response. (p. 14)

In other words, people within a complex culture recognize that they have a perspective that is different from the perspectives of certain other people in the organization, they have some idea (correct or not) of these differences, and they try to take them into account in their contacts with others.

There are two other implications of this model of culture that are equally important for the present work. Both have to do with asymmetries. First, the culture being imperfectly shared means that there are differences among individuals in the gap between the entire cultural inventory and their personal share in it (Hannerz 1992, p. 32). Some individuals in the bank have more cultural knowledge and agility than do others. Second, some individuals have more influence over the culture than do others. Borrowing the term from Mills (1963, p. 406), Hannerz (1992) refers to these people collectively as the "cultural apparatus" (p. 82). In organizations, the cultural apparatus includes leaders (Schein 1992, p. xv), "boot camp" trainers (Kunda 1992, pp. 5-6), designers of organizational rites (Trice and Beyer 1985, pp. 371-372), and generally "all those specializations within the division of labor which somehow aim at affecting minds, temporarily or in an enduring fashion; the people and institutions whose main purpose it is to meddle with our consciousness" (Hannerz 1992, p. 83). The influence of the cultural apparatus is potent but always imperfect. Its message is filtered and reinterpreted by its audience.

> From the point of view of the population . . ., the cultural apparatus and its messages become a part of that situation which has to be defined and for which an adaptation (perhaps moral and intellectual as well as practical) has to be created. (pp. 91-92)

To be concrete, the cultural meaning of a new IT in the bank is provided to users to some extent by the designers of the technology but primarily by the executives who mandate its implementation. This meaning arrives with the technology into the branch or back office and, in a process well described by authors such as Orlikowski (1992), colors but does not determine the reception, use, and eventual impact of the IT.

THE TRANSFORMATION

The setting of the current study is a BritArm back-office processing center called a *securities center* (ASC)[7] that opened in July 1993, one year before I began my fieldwork there. ASC was created as a pilot test for the bank's broader "delivery strategy" for moving back-office work out of the branches and into centralized paper factories. The manufacturing analogy is explicit in the bank (encoded even in new job titles such as "Doer 1" and "Doer 2"); it is part of the provided meaning of the change. The idea, not unique to BritArm, is to centralize processing so as to generate sufficient economies of scale to make partial automation practical. In the case of ASC, this processing involves collecting and reviewing the paperwork necessary to perfect guarantees, mortgages, and mortgage debentures taken by the bank to secure lending. A job formerly done by senior clerks under the supervision of the lending manager now was being done at ASC by junior clerks, and even by temporary agency staff, assisted by a computer system called *TecSec*.

One of 16 such securities centers across the bank, ASC perfected the security for 248 branches. Its 124 employees handled approximately 1,100 new items of security each month and worked to complete approximately 8,000 leftover items of security that were partially completed by branches when ASC opened and securities work was transferred to it. Besides the manager, there were three senior assistant managers and eight assistant mangers, one leading each team of Doers 1 and 2. For part of my time studying ASC, I became a Doer 1; that is, I checked to make sure that charge forms and title documents were in order, that insurance and ground rent payments were up to date, that property valuations had been obtained, and so on. Doers 2 handled the exceptional (and exceptionally important) cases. In turn, the assistant managers laboriously checked every aspect of our work; *perfection* is the operative word when perfecting securities. In the unlikely event that the bank had to rely on a piece of security in court, I was told repeatedly, every *i* must be dotted and every *t* must be crossed.

The original plan had been to make TecSec a true "expert system," but that had been deemed to be too expensive by senior executives. The compromise, a heuristic system, was essentially an online version of the progress sheets that clerks previously used to track their work. An internal report on ASC found fault with this approach: "The software requires more securities expertise to operate than was expected, and its inflexibility frustrates knowledgeable users and makes it difficult for them to use their judgment to take shortcuts and expedite things." Experienced Doers 2 learned that one sometimes had to "lie to the system"—when, for example, documents arrived from customers in an unexpected order—to force it to produce needed forms. Meanwhile, assistant managers learned that they had to check 100 percent of the work done by their Doers 1, who often trusted the system more than their own common sense.

By 1994, ASC was producing quality security; a bank inspection found that "the standard of completion of security by the securities center is particularly good," but it was over budget by £425,000 per annum.[8] In addition, lending managers complained that security was taking too long to be completed, so that their ability to deliver customer service was being impaired. Lending managers also said that they preferred having securities done in their branch or corporate business group where they could have control over the process and could be sure that their senior clerks would get some, but not too much, securities experience. This points to the fact that not only were new premises created, but people were moved—ASC's staff were drawn from branches all over two regions of the bank—and jobs were redesigned as a result of the new structure and technology. In addition, career paths were changed as the bank looked to provide "horses for courses," as the commonly heard cliché has it. As explained to me, the idea was to find the paper pushers and create places like the securities centers to allow them to push paper exclusively. Find the salesmen and put them in front of the customers. Find the leaders and groom them for top jobs. Recognize that most bank hires are incapable of performing in multiple roles and subdivide the work accordingly.

Although *pilot test* is the bank's own terminology, it is perhaps misleading here. There was no question of a reversal or dramatic revisal of the delivery strategy; indeed, it was being rolled out to other areas of the back office even as the securities centers still were cutting their teeth. What is more, the creation of the securities centers and the introduction of TecSec themselves represented a sizable, if localized, transformation of the organization in their own right. A major effort, the change was coordinated by a team in the misleadingly named Network Strategy and Development (NS&D) department in the head office. It produced a 400-page implementation handbook that was given to each regional operations manager who would oversee a securities center. The dispute over the value of this handbook falls along predictable lines. Doug Thomas, one of the NS&D managers responsible for the implementation design, opined,

The trouble with securities centers is that people don't follow the recipe. It is like baking a fruitcake—and you can take this metaphor as far as you like. You don't want crap fruit, but you don't need the best fruit either—that is like the staff. If the recipe says cook it for two hours at 100 degrees, that is what you should do. You can't—like some regions wanted to—cook it for one hour at 200 degrees. The centers that have done best are those that have followed the recipe closest. Of course, you can't follow it blindly, but you can follow it. The trouble was, I didn't have any power to force them to follow it. Very frustrating.

Compare his comments to the equally strong view of a member of the management team at ASC:

Literally, the only parts of this center that are working well are those parts where we ignored the implementation handbook. It isn't realistic, it assumes a best-case world, and we would have been better off starting from scratch on our own without it.

All things considered, the situation offered an ideal vantage point from which to observe the culture of complaint and its intersection with organizational transformation. There certainly was no shortage of subject matter.

DEROGATION

Returning to the episode with Ben and his window, we saw that it revealed both the depth and shallowness of the unpopular culture at BritArm. It runs deep enough to shape patterns even of casual greeting in the bank and to lead to a BritArm reading of elements of British culture. And yet, it can be superficial in that it does not always correspond to feelings of deep discontent or a desire for redress. To use Hannerz's (1992) terminology, the distinction within the form of complaint is between modes of thought antagonistic toward some aspect of the current situation and those acquiescent in the status quo. This is the difference between a complaint considered to be a deprecation and one considered to be a derogation. The question "Considered so by whom?" is relevant because, as we shall see, there are interesting cases of disagreement on this point between speakers and various members of their audience. There is no unequivocal partition between the two categories; the distinction is in play at the bank. Nevertheless, derogation and deprecation of IT are conceptually distinct, and it is worth exploring the role that each plays in the ongoing efforts of ASC managers, staff, and internal customers to cope with the transformation implied by the bank's delivery strategy.

Ben's joke about BritArm technology was a derogation. This is because it was a complaint; it put the bank down, but it did not express a deprecation's "earnest desire" for change. Instead, it signaled a passive resigned acceptance of the window's closing and the state of the bank's technology as things that, for the time being, we were going to have to live with. It is in this sense that we can say Ben was expressing acquiescence in the status quo. This is not to say that he did not possess a desire that the bank's IT and window fittings improve, but merely that he did not express that desire here. His remark was not a solicitation of redress; rather, it was a way in which to make me laugh, to put me at ease, and to warm up our conversation. It was a supportive ritual meant to strengthen (even if only slightly) our relationship by identifying himself as a culturally competent insider and by including me to some degree, granting me some rights as an insider.[9]

This might sound obvious, and it almost certainly would be obvious to BritArm employees for whom the use of derogatory remarks to produce these sorts of desirable social outcomes is well established. It would be counterintuitive to employees of Uedagin, the Japanese retail bank studied by

Rohlen (1974) where "love Uedagin" is considered the proper attitude toward the company.

> Because it is their community and the source of a good life for them, and because it is made up of their fellow workers, people should naturally feel emotional attachment for the bank and express it through pride, dedication, and enthusiastic participation. (p. 50)

In such a context, derogation can be expected to lead to frowns, unease, and coolness. Brought up under a different realm of primary socialization, the British employees of BritArm are more comfortable than Rohlen's Japanese with self-mockery and are rather less comfortable with displays of pride or enthusiastic participation.[10] The secondary socialization they receive at BritArm reinforces, if it does not create, the idea that derogation can strengthen the bonds of community.

As one example of how this plays out at BritArm, consider the following example drawn from my fieldnotes.[11]

> After I had been sitting alongside Cutler, my Doer 2 mentor, for two weeks learning the intricacies of his role at the securities center, he asked if I would like to be a "huge help" to him and his colleagues on Team 2. I was put on my guard by the sly grin on his face and the conspiratorial glances he shared with those sitting nearby. But I was enthusiastic about the prospect of ingratiating myself to a useful informant and of shifting my fieldwork to participant observation. I readily agreed.
>
> The task Cutler had in mind for me was the revaluation of a portfolio of shares lodged with the bank by a customer to secure a line of credit. It wasn't urgent; the job had been left undone for over a month. But it was required by the bank's internal auditors, and Cutler didn't know when he would be able to find time to do it. The job was tedious. Cutler retrieved for me the customer's file, which contained hundreds of share certificates from over 120 different companies.[12] Figuring out what was what was made difficult by companies that had merged, been acquired, gone bankrupt, or changed names over the years. It took me the rest of the day merely to produce a list of which current share prices I needed to obtain. Normally, when shares are taken by the bank as security, they are held in a central department which takes care of revaluations. This customer was an exception for reasons no one at the securities center knew.
>
> I had to write the list out in longhand since the computers on our desks had no facility for doing word processing or spreadsheet work. There were 2 computers in the center, out of 80, with Microsoft Word and Excel on them, but I was advised that it was best just to do the job by hand. This was frustrating since the customer's file contained a computer printout of the previous valuation from two

years ago. It would have saved time and effort had I been able to start with that and make additions and modifications to it. There was in any case, though, no soft copy of the previous valuation, so I would have had to retype it all anyway even with a computer at my disposal.

Members of the team paid me a lot of attention while I worked away on this. Nick, the team leader, came by a number of times to see how I was getting on and to show his appreciation. After a couple of hours, Cutler apparently started to feel guilty about having given it to me to do. "You've gone awfully quiet over there," he said. Our desks were head to head in a line with other desks in the open-plan office. "You know, you don't have to do it," he added. "Just leave it, and I can finish it later." I assured him that I didn't mind. "But it's very boring. You must be bored out of your mind over there." Not wanting to complain, I said that I was all right with it, that it was good to have a little job to do. "Yeah, but it's pretty tedious, isn't it?" I demurred, but after several people stopped by over the course of the afternoon to sympathize and tell me how boring was the work that I was doing, I confessed [that] yes, it was fairly tedious. "Oh, I know," I was told.

The floor under the desk I was sitting at had a slight tilt to it, not uncommon in old English buildings. It meant that my chair kept slowly sliding away from the desk, and I had to keep scooting myself in all the time. It was uncomfortable, and Cutler noticed me fiddling around with the chair adjustments to see if I could stop from rolling back. "Uncomfortable, isn't it?" he said. I agreed, complaining [that] my back was starting to hurt from all this scooting and sliding. He and Joan, the Doer 1 sitting next to him, laughed and said that they [both had] used to sit over on that side but [had] moved desks for precisely that reason. We complained convivially about the conditions under which we were forced to work, and I said I didn't know how Tom—the man whose desk I was borrowing—put up with it. It transpired that Tom had previously been a coal miner, so this deprivation was likely pretty mild by his standards.[13]

Encouraged by this friendly banter, I went on to make derogatory remarks about how ridiculous it was to do this by hand, about the state of the brush in my bottle of correcting fluid, and about the customer who, I hypothesized aloud, didn't actually need the line of credit but just opened it so that we would be the custodian of his shares. Joan and Cutler seemed to find my exasperation hilarious, and Joan told me, "Now you know what it is like to be a BritArm securities clerk." This struck me. If she was right, then being a securities clerk at BritArm feels like basking in the warm glow of adversity with sympathizers all around. I felt more like a part of the team than I ever had before, and the event marked a turning point in my relationship with Team 2. They treated me with less suspicion and more inclusion afterward. To have suffered enough to be able to complain about the bank was to be part of the group, and to have made these mild derogations was evidence of my bona fides as "all right."

As I was being socialized to understand, derogation is an important element of the culture at BritArm. The ritual of making derogatory remarks about some aspect of the bank—often its IT—and in return receiving empathy, and perhaps sympathy as well, is a glue that strengthens the bonds between the individual and the group. The dull routine of the back office was punctuated with exclamations such as "I hate this machine," "How can we get any work done with phones always ringing?" and "The branches still aren't filling in requisitions correctly." If the complaint was valid (more on validity in a moment), then the response would take the form of laughter, a comment along the lines of "Oh, I know" or "Terrible, isn't it?" or a rejoinder of another complaint. If not, then sympathy would be withheld and the response would be a mocking "Awwww" and laughter, a comment such as "Oh, come on," or (worse) silence.

The phenomenon is not unique to back-office departments. In the public space of the banking hall, exclamations are kept to a minimum, but people whisper across desks and form into small huddles to exchange complaints and condolences (and myths such as the story of how the bank came to have its current branch banking computer system). In the bank vault or file room, over beers in the pub at lunch, behind the closed door of a manager's office, in the car on the way to see a customer, in conference rooms before meetings, in staff rooms while the kettle is boiling—all across the bank, as regularly as peach, fish, and banana time in Roy's (1960) Clicking Department, time out from work is taken up with this ritual exchange.

The ritual takes on a particular importance, however, in a newly established office such as ASC. Few of the managers or clerks had worked together, or even known one another, before the creation of the securities center. Now, they were to work in teams as the pioneers of a new way of perfecting security. They are self-described (for the most part) as members of a particularly retiring and risk-averse segment of a generally retiring and risk-averse occupation. (The more extroverted and aggressive bankers typically chose to remain at the branches where they now would be expected to actively sell the bank's products to customers.) The comforting ritual of derogation provided a commonly available means of building rapport and work relationships, of coming together as a group, and even of building an identity as members of the securities center. Complaint can build identity at the bank because, although *everyone* complaints, not everyone complaints about the same things. Derogation's allusion to shared experience presumes a reference group. Ironically, then, the complaining ad nauseam about TecSec and its many imperfections, about the failure of the bank to provide the promised facility for security requisitions to be electronically transmitted from the branches to the securities centers, or about the inability of the hardware to handle extra doers in cases of cyclical peaks in security requisitions might have helped to alleviate what could have been much more serious organizational impediments to the success of the delivery strategy such as dysfunctional teams, employee anxiety, staff turnover, and perhaps even work-to-rule or other forms of passive resistance.

The ritual of derogation is structured by two notions: what counts as a valid complaint and what constitutes an appropriate response. Validity hinges on audience perceptions of the complainant and the opinion expressed in the complaint itself. As I have argued, derogations (as distinct from deprecations) are not solicitations of redress. One does not make fun of TecSec in the expectation that someone will hear and make things better. Indeed, the sense that staff have of the isolation and distance of the IT department might help to account for the popularity of the bank's IT systems as targets of derogation.[14] One derogates to get a laugh, some understanding, or sympathy. But to work in this way, the audience must agree with the opinion expressed by the complainant. Complaints about the weather do not work as conversation starters unless there is agreement that the weather is bad. Otherwise, the complaints are unwarranted and, therefore, invalid. Throughout Britain, there is widespread agreement that the weather is bad and that nobody ever does anything about it; throughout BritArm, there is widespread agreement that the case of IT is little different. Therefore, both always are valid targets of complaint. Furthermore, however, the audience has to agree that the complainant deserves redress, even though the complainant expresses neither desire for nor expectation of redress. My complaint about office ergonomics would not have worked to bolster my insider status if the others had not agreed that my desk was uncomfortable and that, all else equal, I deserved to be more comfortable. If redress is seen to be undeserved, then the complaint is a *whinge* and, therefore, invalid.[15]

Evaluations of validity and appropriateness are contingent on the relationship between complainant and audience. The same joke about the bank's technology that provokes feelings of bonhomie when voiced by an insider is an insult when voiced by others, as I found to my discomfort on several occasions. With every new group at BritArm that I studied, I had to earn anew my derogation privileges. Derogation acts to reproduce and reinforce bonds between the individual and the group, but it cannot produce them where they do not exist. An outsider cannot expect to make friends at the bank by insulting BritArm. Nor does merely working for BritArm give one carte blanche to be derogatory about the bank.

It would be misleading to suggest that there were rules as to when sympathy would be given rather than offense taken; there was much individual variation. Some people seemed to be so unpopular that they could not complain about the weather without being contradicted, whereas others had the savoir faire of the court jester and could get away with almost any remark. There were, however, two important overarching patterns. The first is that derogatory remarks were more likely to elicit positive responses when the target of the comment was an aspect equally close to or equally distant from the salient contexts of the complainant and audience. So, for example, the manager of the securities center and an IT manager could joke together over lunch about the ineptitude of the head office budgeting process or the quirks of the demands sent down by the Legal, Technical, and Securities Department (LT&S). But a derogatory remark about the absurdity of a recent consultant's review of TecSec commissioned by the bank that reported, "TecSec is perceived by its users to be a 'good' useful system," was not found to be so funny or endearing by the IT manager.

The second pattern is that derogatory remarks were more likely to elicit sympathy and understanding when the hierarchical distance between the complainant and the audience was low. Derogations among peers or between a subordinate and a superior were not problematic, but if two or more layers of the hierarchy between the complainant and the audience were introduced, then misunderstanding was more likely. I was told by senior managers that it was inappropriate for them to share any negative feelings they might have about the bank or its IT with junior managers or staff, and I seldom saw this norm violated, although those negative feelings often did travel down by cascade as senior managers would share derogations with direct reports, who in turn might share them with their direct reports, and so on.

Equally seldom was derogation by someone low in the hierarchy eliciting empathy or sympathy from someone higher up. The problem in this case is that signals break down and derogations are confused for deprecations. The desire for change that distinguishes a deprecation from a derogation is not always (or even often) stated explicitly. Sometimes, the complainant only hints at a desire for change. So long as the audience members know that they cannot be expected to provide redress for the complaint, there is no confusion.[16] But ambiguity can creep in if the complainant is uncertain whether his or her audience can offer redress or if the audience members do not know whether they can reasonably be expected to do so. Of course, this can happen even when there is no hierarchical distance between the complainant and the audience. A team leader who complains in a managers' meeting about the computer illiteracy among Doers 1 likely will receive sympathy from his or her peers but perhaps also advice on how to deal with the situation. At times, when people complained to me about the bank, I was unsure whether they wanted my opinion, wanted my sympathy, or perhaps thought that my computing background could be of some use to them. This caused me considerable anxiety. To offer an opinion of advice when sympathy was requested was to risk insulting the person by implying that I thought I knew better than he or she did what to do; to offer sympathy when redress was requested was to risk frustrating the person by appearing to be unwilling to help. Perhaps feeling that it always is best to assume that anyone complaining up the hierarchy expected redress, and restricted by their norm of stoicism from appearing sympathetic to less senior personnel expressing negative views about the bank, managers treated as deprecations virtually all of the complaints directed to them from lower in the hierarchy. It is to the ritual of deprecation that I next turn.

DEPRECATION

Unlike derogations, deprecations are complaints expressing an "earnest desire that something be averted or removed." Deprecations are antagonistic to the status quo; they are solicitations of redress. But clear direct deprecation is relatively rare at BritArm. This is because deprecation can provoke embarrassment. It can cause a loss of face by pointing out inadequacy or by forcing a public statement of unwillingness or inability to provide redress. Aversion to embarrassment is a powerful force at the bank, and it leads to distinct patterns of deprecation that are examined in this section. It is worth pointing out first, however, that BritArm is once again reflecting broader British culture in its antipathy to embarrassment. The ready and delicate sense of what is fitting and proper in dealing with others so as to avoid giving offense or causing embarrassment is summarized in the word *tact*.[17] Although by no means is it the case that every Brit possesses the gift of tact, it is undeniable that the British understand themselves to be a tactful people—tactful, indeed, to a fault, as British humorists such as Douglas Adams are want to note:

"Tell me the story," said Fenchurch firmly. "You arrived at the station."

"I was about twenty minutes early," Arthur said. "So I bought a newspaper to do the crossword, and [I] went to the buffet to get a cup of coffee . . . [and] some biscuits. . . . Laden with all these new possessions, I go and sit at a table. . . . So, let me give you the layout. Me sitting at the table. On my left, the newspaper. On my right, the cup of coffee. In the middle of the table, the packet of biscuits."

"I see it perfectly."

"What you don't see," said Arthur, "because I haven't mentioned him yet, is the guy sitting at the table already. He is sitting there opposite me. . . . Perfectly ordinary. Briefcase, business suit. He didn't look," said Arthur, "as if he was about to do anything weird."

"Ah, I know the type. What did he do?"

"He did this. He leaned across the table, picked up the packet of biscuits, tore it open, took one out, and . . ."

"What?"

"Ate it."

"*What?*"

"He ate it."

Fenchurch looked at him in astonishment. "What on earth did you do?"

"Well, in the circumstances, I did what any red-blooded Englishman would do. I was compelled," said Arthur, "to ignore it."

"What? Why?"

"Well, it's not the sort of thing you're trained for, is it? I searched my soul and discovered that there was nothing anywhere in my upbringing, experience, or even primal instincts to tell me how to react to someone who has quite simply, calmly, sitting right there in front of me, stolen one of my biscuits."

Fenchurch thought about it. "I must say I'm not sure what I would have done either." (Adams 1985, pp. 547-549)

What is lacking is not so much training in how to respond as it is training in how to respond given the tact that "any red-blooded Englishman" knows is required in the situation. Deprecation is harder in some situations than in others, however, as comedian Victoria Wood jokes. She tells a story about taking British Rail and finding a couple having sex on a crowded commuter train to London. Nobody says a word, studiously ignoring the two until they finish and light up cigarettes. Then someone says, "Excuse me, this is a 'no smoking' compartment" (Wood 1991).

It is interesting to note that Wood's apocryphal commuter does not say "I would like you to put out those cigarettes." By recounting the "no smoking" status of the compartment rather than expressing a desire that the cigarettes be put out, the speaker has effectively depersonalized the complaint and is able to use British Rail rules as an intermediary to the deprecation. These two tactics of tactful deprecation—the use of depersonalization and intermediation—make the remark about smoking possible where a remark to the couple about sex would not be possible. Both of these tactics are common at the bank, and IT is commonly a component of them.

This is in contrast to what Argyris (1954) found in his ethnography of an American bank. He did find a strong aversion to embarrassment among the employees of the bank, and he reports, "Fifty-five percent of the employees spontaneously list 'tact and diplomacy' as the most often required ability in their formal work. The next most often listed ability, 'accuracy,' has two thirds less votes" (p. 74). At that bank, however, this led not to tactful deprecation but rather to an absence of deprecation. Noting that "interviews emphasize that many of the employees would much rather accept relatively unhappy circumstances than complain," Argyris quotes one "somewhat dissatisfied" employee as saying,

7RHETORIC

I'll tell you what I think of it. It's not always a pleasant thought to me. If you are an ass kisser, you will get along all right. I think if you speak the way you feel, you will get nowhere, not here. The only thing that's good, you know, is to bow down, to knuckle down to the guys, but that would be my feeling. I don't think people think this is a friendly bank. (p. 74)

The suggestion here is that the requirements of secondary socialization in this bank are working contrary to those of the employees' primary socialization. It would be too strong to say that Argyris's bank is "un-American," but the need for "ass kissing" and repression of complaint are not seen as characteristically American by employees of that bank as the use of tactful depersonalization and intermediation are seen as characteristically British by employees of BritArm.

In part, the use of intermediaries in deprecation is due to a bureaucratic protocol of complaint at the bank whereby one is supposed to direct a complaint to one's manager, who starts it on its way up and down the hierarchy through the proper channels on its way to the appropriate party. A complaint about TecSec from a user might be heard and repeated by a half dozen people, then, before it is heard by someone who can do more about it than just pass it along. Even in cases where that protocol does not apply or is being ignored, however, deprecations at the bank very often are made through intermediaries to spare the complainant and recipient the embarrassment of having to face each other and cope with the reactions provoked.

Fears of deprecation creating embarrassing scenes seem well-founded. Perhaps because of the rarity of direct deprecation, even mild rebukes can provoke passionate reactions.

One day while I was working as a Doer 1 under the watchful eye of Cutler, Joan, another Doer 1 on the team, took a call from a corporate account executive (CAE) about a planning report on some land he was proposing the bank take to secure a loan. The CAE told Joan that Cutler had promised last week that he would look into prices for the report and order it; now, the manager is calling to check what progress has been made. None. Cutler says that he remembers talking to the guy but that he never promised to get a report and would never have said he would check around about prices. That is just not something he does; the price of reports is not something that the center worries about, he argues. Joan tells the CAE that nothing has been done yet but that they will send for the planning report right away. She tells Cutler that [the CAE] didn't sound happy as he hung up, and she goes to fax the request off to a firm to do the report. Cutler is flushed and clearly upset. He repeats to Joan that he would never promise something like that—to check the prices. He tells me that complaints such as these are "really not on. We're all one company!"

A little while later, Nick, the team leader, comes over having just received a call of complaint from the CAE. Cutler says that he honestly doesn't remember what he said to the CAE but that he doesn't think he promised to price and obtain the report. Nick tells him not to worry, that they are all under a lot of pressure and they have so many things going on at once that it is no wonder they might forget one or two things. He quickly adds that he's not saying Cutler did forget to send the report. Cutler explains to me that it seems he screwed up. He repeats that he can't recall exactly what happened. They just get too many calls. These people in the branches, he says, think that the center is here working only for them. But they have dozens of branches to serve.

Nick gets off the phone and asks to speak to Cutler. He says that he told the CAE essentially not to worry about the planning report because TecSec reports that it is a post-reliability formality. This means that it is bank policy to release the loan funds to the customer before this formality is completed. The CAE, Nick says, gave him grief about this, saying that if that was true, it shouldn't be. After all, if we find out afterward that there is a motorway about to be built through the land, we would really be stuck. Cutler goes to the small bookcase of loose-leaf binders called the action sheets and selects the appropriate volume. These are the bank's standard operating procedures; they are updated regularly via circular, and each branch and office would have a set. It is not clear from the action sheets, though, whether checking the planning report is a pre- or post-reliability formality. Cutler goes back to the progress sheets they used before the process was semi-automated. To his relief, it confirms the post-reliability status of planning reports. TecSec is vindicated.

Cutler and Nick talk about it some more, though, and Nick says that the CAE has a point with his motorway example and suggests that Cutler call LT&S in London to clarify the issue and find out why this formality is post-reliability. Also, he suggests that Cutler call the firm handling the report to see if it can be handled as a rush job. While on hold with LT&S, Cutler asks Ken, a Doer 2 on another team, what he thinks. Ken says that planning reports almost never turn up anything and that they can take months to get. LT&S confirms this analysis and notes that if the manager is concerned, he has the discretion to hold the money back until the report is obtained. Cutler reports this to Nick to report back to the CAE and goes back to work, having spent over an hour on this issue.

There is no telling how this episode would have gone differently if the complaint had been made directly to Cutler and not to Joan and then Nick. The interesting thing is that putting the two parties directly concerned on the phone together never was suggested. Furthermore, even without having to confront Cutler, the CAE still quickly seized the opportunity to switch the target of his deprecation from Cutler to the impersonal TecSec.

It is much less embarrassing to face someone as an intermediary to a deprecation than as its instigator. The least embarrassing deprecations of all are those that are not instigated by any person, those in which everyone involved is merely an intermediary. This is the case when the deprecation is depersonalized. The deprecation's solicitation of redress is expressed as stemming not from any personal desire of the complainant but rather from the impersonal requirements of bank IT or policy. This is why, for example, performance problems involving even minor violations of policy are deprecated, whereas more serious problems that do not violate the letter of any rule often are not directly deprecated. Managers rely on the much derogated black-and-white bureaucratic inflexibility of the reams of policy action sheets—and now of the TecSec system—to ease the deprecation that is part of their job. Note that this is exactly the same finding made by Smith (1990, p. 74) in her study of an American bank. There, middle managers protested the removal of bureaucratic standards for performance evaluation. They argued that being given more flexibility would make their jobs more difficult and would trouble the relationships they had with their people.

IT serves as a convenient whipping boy at BritArm precisely because of its impersonality. For example,

> Faced with rumored accusations of incompetence and pedantism by lending managers, the securities center's team leaders started inviting the assistants of these managers for a half-day visit to the center and lunch. I knew several of those assistants, and unanimously they came away with a higher regard for the team leaders and Doers 2 whom they met but no fewer complaints about the performance of the center. "They're good people and they're working hard," one said, "but the teams have too much to do, they are understaffed, and the technology falls down. Typical BritArm, really."

The shift of focus of complaints away from individuals is a dialectical move whereby the contradictory opinions of complainants and defendants are merged into the higher truth of TecSec being at fault. Relationships between ASC staff and their former colleagues in the branches, strained by process changes and performance problems, are rebuilt through shared deprecation of TecSec. This is the remedial ritual of deprecation. Rather than being separated by complaints and accusations, all parties come together in shared suffering of the bank's inadequacies in the area of IT.

It would be an exaggeration to say that all deprecation of TecSec served this remedial function. Formal complaints about TecSec were submitted by staff to the center manager, who would pass the complaints to the IT department if he believed that they were warranted. During my eight months at BritArm, TecSec was updated to reflect a change in bank policy regarding the necessity of getting all customers to sign a waiver form if they declined to seek independent legal advice before charging security to the bank—one of the most egregious cases in which doers had to lie to the system to produce the necessary forms for the customers to sign—and a problem that made the system hang periodically was addressed, as were several other issues. The TecSec users' group, however, had a list of dozens of other changes deemed necessary by center managers and agreed to in principle by IT; some had been on the list as long as a year but had not yet been scheduled to be implemented. Deprecation of TecSec might someday lead to its improvement, then, but more immediately it led to the improvement of relations between ASC and its internal customers. The ritual is repeated in interactions between TecSec users and developers. Complaints about IT people who are "second rate" and who have "no clue about what we do here" morph, when those IT people are met, into complaints about the system of prioritizing IT projects; planned improvements to TecSec were prioritized below other IT work and had been downgraded twice to make room for other work.

There are limits to the ritual effectiveness of deprecation. A common complaint at the bank—and one that is more common the higher one goes in the hierarchy—is that there is too much complaining at the bank and too much resistance to change. This is well-known, and there is a stigma attached to the label of *complainer* or, worse, *Luddite*. A complainer is "not on board" and "not a team player"; a Luddite is "deadwood" and an "old dog" who cannot be taught new tricks—attributes that no (secretly) ambitious organizational man or woman can afford to acquire.

> "I speak my mind too much to get on in this bank," a manager with a reputation
> for blunt speaking told me. "Actually, I never thought I'd get as far as I have. I
> won't get further."

Even when invited by a senior figure to complain, reservation is warranted. BritArm's main newsletter features an interview in each issue with some member of the bank's staff. The interviewees routinely are asked what is the greatest problem they perceive at the bank, and interviewees typically provide answers such as the following (from the April 1994 issue): "If I had to point to any frustrations, I suppose I would say working for a very large organization sometimes brings constraints which are, perhaps, necessary." Derogation and deprecation are a regular part of the BritArm day, but knowing where to draw the line is important.[18] Just as Kunda (1992, p. 107) describes a prescribed role distance in the strong culture of Tech—a token cynicism that was to be expressed as a sort of ritual exception that proves the official ideology to be the rule—so there is a prescribed role distance of earnest positivity and optimism that must be shown from time to time in the unpopular culture of BritArm. The review that found TecSec to be perceived by its users as "good" and "useful" came as no surprise to culturally aware staff at BritArm; that is just how they would have responded if they had been asked by executives or their consultants.

CONCLUSION

It is well documented that information technologies often allow uses beyond those intended by their designers. What I have tried to show in this chapter is that users, in addition to adapting IT in unexpected ways, can adapt *complaints* about IT in unexpected ways. When expressed by the culturally competent, ritual complaints about IT at BritArm can be tactics of strengthening group bonds and repairing relationships strained by organizational transformation. Given the enormous amount of complaining going on, there is little of the direct deprecation at BritArm that would provoke change. But complaint about IT may nevertheless facilitate transformation, not by causing it but rather by mitigating its side effects. What is more, the constancy of complaint can lend a sense of permanence—recall the received wisdom that the bank has not really changed in 300 years—to an organization facing increasingly rapid and radical changes. In the unpopular culture, it seems that the more things change, the more unpopular they become.

But to identify the function of a ritual is not to explain it. The Panglossian (Voltaire 1759, p. 4) formula—that all is for the best in this best of all possible worlds—is untenable. The culture of complaint has costs associated with it, namely, a cynicism and negative attitude that have been identified by people at all levels of the bank as being undesirable but that defy organizational efforts to change them. Multiple extensive and expensive culture change programs have failed to do more than enforce a limited lip service of positivity and optimism about the bank's IT program. Therefore, it is unclear whether the unpopular culture is optimally rational for BritArm or the result of strategic design. I described examples of Japanese and American banks where BritArm's unpopular culture could find no foothold in legitimacy. BritArm is a product of the wider British culture in which it is set. More accurately, it a product of interpreted borrowings from that wider culture. The bank is not so much British as it is *stereotypically* British in its self-deprecation[19] and strictures of tact.

It is beyond the scope of this chapter to examine the origins of the culture of complaint at BritArm. The purpose here is different, and the point perhaps is more general. When analyzing attitudes toward IT, we need to examine not only the *causes* of complaint (what it is about the system that makes people dissatisfied) but also the *consequences* of complaint (what social functions it might perform). The employees and managers of BritArm find themselves with plenty to complain about, in the conventional sense, regarding the bank's IT. Indeed, the complaints I have described would not be legitimate if there was not consensus that BritArm's technology is as relatively unspectacular as Britain's weather. What I have argued, however, is that the ritual functions of complaint are institutionalized in the bank in such a way that even if current problems with the IT were solved, other problems likely would be found to complain about in their stead. To understand complaint as situated rhetoric, we must understand it as an interaction ritual. If we consider ourselves too sophisticated to laugh at why the chicken crossed the road, then the joke might be on us.

NOTES

1. Specifically, it is by definition of *The Oxford English Dictionary* (Little et al. 1991, p. 383).

2. The definitions of *derogation* and *deprecation* come from *The Oxford English Dictionary* (Little et al. 1991, pp. 526, 523, respectively).

3. By way of methodological note, over the course of 18 months, I spent 8 months full-time at BritArm U.K. and 4 months full-time at the bank's U.S. subsidiary. In each case, the research was designed as a "T" whereby a long period of time was spent in a single part of the bank, followed by shorter periods of time in many other parts. In England (the focus of this chapter), I spent 3 months in a back-office processing center called the securities center. Following my time there, I spent 2 weeks shadowing a chief manager (in charge of 10 branches and of the lending to larger business customers), 2 weeks each in 3 branches of different sizes (large, medium, and small, each of which is said in the bank to have a different feel to it), 1 week each in another securities center and 3 other back-office units, 1 week in another branch, and 1 week in a regional office. I also spent a scattered 5 days at the bank's training college attending a course and a number of end-of-course dinners, where I had the opportunity to meet managers and staff from all over the bank. I spent 3 days with managers whom I met in this way, then spent 3 weeks in various parts of the head office in London, and finally had a week-long visit after my time at the U.S. bank to meet again with many of my informants. In the United Kingdom in particular, and to a lesser extent in the United States, I attended many private dinner parties, pub lunches, one beer breakfast, and every bank party to which I could get myself invited. During the early stages of the fieldwork, I tried taking notes while in the bank but found that, except in formal interview situations, this attracted too much attention and even suspicion. Therefore, outside of interviews, I kept a small notebook in my coat pocket and jotted down what reminders I could to be fleshed out that evening either on my laptop computer or into a tape recorder on my commute home. In addition, as insecure field-workers are wont to do, I picked up all manners of paperwork. There was not a brochure or report too insignificant to escape my collection. I did, however, sign a confidentiality agreement with the bank as a condition of my access, and this restricted the documents I could take away. Despite this, I was able to amass a large filing cupboard of materials to accompany my roughly 1,500 pages of notes.

4. The speaking notes acknowledged that pretax profits for the first six months of the year had risen to £767 million, an 83% increase over the £419 million from the previous year. Bad debt provisions had fallen by 47%, and the bank was reporting a 14% increase in its dividend.

The speaking notes explained why, despite superficial appearances to the contrary, these results were troubling. The argument can be summarized as follows. The results announced were for the BritArm Group as a whole, not just BritArm U.K. Branch Banking (UKBB). Much of the increase in profits derived from the group's international banking and investment banking businesses rather than from branch banking. Within UKBB, the increase in profits was attributable to a decrease in bad debt provisions. Operating income actually declined slightly (£3.45 billion vs. £3.47 billion from the previous year) and had been flat or falling for some time. Advances (lending) had fallen to £81.7 billion from the previous year's figure of £85.7 billion. The bank's cost-income ratio was higher than those of competitors. Further belt-tightening was in order. To say that the bad news interpretation of the interim results is a product of the unpopular culture is not to say that anything was fabricated; the bank's official explanation was a legitimate factual interpretation of an equivocal reality. The point is that, in other cultural contexts and with other ends in mind, other interpretations of the results also would have been possible.

5. The well-known problem is that there is little agreement about what *culture* actually means. As Alvesson (1993) notes, as a term it is economical: "One word signifies a broad range of intangible societal and organizational phenomena" (p. 3). With more than 250 anthropological definitions of *culture* from which to choose—Kroeber and Kluckhohn (1952) famously catalog 164 of them, Keesing's (1974) review adds 86 to that list, and I discuss Hannerz's (1992) definition in this chapter—in addition to numerous sociological ones, management scholars have chosen to invent scores of their own. As Van Maanen (1984) quips, "Those of us who are the culture vultures of organization studies are a fairly contentious lot and do not frequently adopt one another's definitions" (p. 216). This is only partly out of spiteful obstinacy. Van Maanen (1988) argues, "The ends of fieldwork involve the catch-all idea of culture, a concept as stimulating, productive, yet fuzzy to field-workers and their readers as the notion of life is for biologists and their readers" (p. 3). Concrete descriptions of particular cultures, then, are best served by vague definitions of culture in general. Ethnography, after all, is an inductive endeavor. Keeping culture imprecise in the abstract encourages each ethnographer to inductively arrive at a conception of culture appropriate for the context studied. Of course, with so many definitions available, the chances of inductively arriving at a conception of culture already articulated by someone else are increasing.

6. I am referring to the distinction that Berger and Luckmann (1967, p. 130) make between *primary* socialization and *secondary* socialization. Primary socialization starts during childhood; it is the process through which an individual becomes a member of society. Secondary socialization is a subsequent process that inducts an already socialized individual into a new sector of society such as the bank. In primary socialization, significant others, imposed on the individual, are in charge of his or her socialization. Their definitions of his or her situation are posited for the individual as objective reality. Secondary socialization seldom is as powerful except in cases where it is consistent with the already formed self and the already internalized world of primary socialization (pp. 131, 140).

7. I use the acronym ASC to specify this particular securities center without revealing its actual name.

8. Unfortunately, I was not able to ascertain the securities center's total budget figure so as to compare it to the overrun. Some indication of the magnitude of the overrun can be gleaned from the fact that the original business case for the center was based on estimated savings of £4.4 million over 10 years by perfecting security in a centralized unit instead of each branch doing it individually. The savings were expected mainly from being able to replace senior clerical staff with more junior staff because of TecSec. The cost overrun came primarily in the form of roughly 35 more employees working in the center than had been envisioned when the budget was drawn up.

9. In this sense, it is similar to the ritual of a host telling guests to makes themselves at home. This is meant to convey certain rights to the guests but is not meant literally (e.g., rummaging through drawers as if one were at home might be out of line). Likewise, I was being granted the right to hear derogations normally not for public consumption, but it was not clear whether it would have been acceptable for me to join in the good-natured fun at the bank's expense. I have more to say about this later.

10. Interestingly, although Japanese bankers clearly are less comfortable with self-mockery than are their British counterparts, the Japanese bankers described by Rohlen (1974) seem quite comfortable in joining the Brits in mocking England. Rohlen quotes a New Year's letter to employees in which the bank's president cautions, "Those who are misled by momentary prosperity into loosening the reins are destined to become, as England has, a sorrowful spectacle of decline" (p. 51).

11. I use the convention of setting off long examples drawn from my field notes in the same indented format as block quotes. This is simply to make them easier to read and is not an indication of their being verbatim quotes from my notes or from anywhere else.

12. In the securities centers, documents are not stored in file folders but rather are stored in A4-sized envelopes slit open across the top. These are called "pods," and on the way to retrieve the files on this day, I asked Cutler why they were called that. "I don't know," he told me. "Stupid, isn't it?" Derogation can be used not only as ice-breakers to get conversations started but also as deflections to bring conversations—and inquiry—to an end.

13. It was mild, too, compared to the conditions faced by English bank clerks during Victorian times who, as the social commentator Thackrah observed in 1831, "suffered from the confined atmosphere [of the counting house], a fixed position, and often from long days. Their muscles are often distressed by the maintenance of one posture, and they complain frequently of pains in the side of the chest. The digestive organs suffer most, a fact apparent even from the countenance and tongue. The circulation is imperfect; the head becomes affected, and though urgent disease is not generally produced, yet a continuance of the employment in its fullest extent never fails to impair the constitution and render the individual sickly for life" (quoted in Anderson 1976, p. 17).

14. This is not to say, as we shall see later, that no complaints about TecSec ever were addressed by the IT department.

15. *Whinge* is a term used more in England than in America. A whinge is a whine, that is, a peevish complaint.

16. More specifically, confusion is avoided so long as Hannerz's (1992) formula—"I know, I know that everybody else knows, and I know everybody else knows that everybody else knows" (p. 68)—holds.

17. This definition of *tact* comes from *The Oxford English Dictionary* (Little et al. 1991, p. 2232).

18. For example, as part of one of the bank's many culture change programs, psychometric tests were performed to evaluate executives' enthusiasm for the bank's vision. A league table of scores was produced so that each executive could see where he or she stood, but much to the disgust of the change agent, scores never were previously used in promotion decisions. But the message of the unacceptability of executive derogation or deprecation of the vision was clear.

19. Given the definitions of *derogation* and *deprecation* that I use in this chapter, *self-deprecation* might be a confusing label. *The Oxford English Dictionary* (Little et al. 1991) notes it as an anomaly, explaining that in the term self-deprecation, *deprecation* is taken to be synonymous with *depreciation* (i.e., "the action of speaking slightly of someone or something" [p. 523]) and, therefore, similar to *derogation*.

REFERENCES

Adams, D. (1985), *The More Than Complete Hitchhiker's Guide*. New York: Wings Books.

Alvesson, M. (1993), *Cultural Perspectives on Organizations*. Cambridge, UK: Cambridge University Press.

Anderson, G. (1976), *Victorian Clerks*. Manchester, UK: Manchester University Press.

Argyris, C. (1954), *Organization of a Bank*. New Haven, CT: Yale University, Labor and Management Center.

Baba, M. L. (1989), "Organizational Culture: Revisiting the Small-Society Metaphor," *Anthropology of Work Review*, 10, 7-10.

Berger, P. L. and T. Luckmann (1967), *The Social Construction of Reality*. New York: Doubleday.

Evans-Pritchard, E. E. (1940), *The Nuer*. Oxford, UK: Oxford University Press.

Goffman, E. (1971), *Relations in Public: Microstudies of Public Order*. New York: Basic Books.

Hannerz, U. (1992), *Cultural Complexity: Studies in the Social Organization of Meaning*. New York: Columbia University Press.

Keesing, R. M. (1974), "Theories of Culture," *Annual Review of Anthropology*, 3, 73-97.

Kroeber, A. L. and C. Kluckhohn (1952), *Culture: A Critical Review of Concepts and Definitions*. Cambridge, MA: Harvard University Press.

Kunda, G. (1992), *Engineering Culture: Control and Commitment in a High-Tech Corporation*. Philadelphia: Temple University Press.

Little, W., H. W. Fowler, and J. Coulson (Eds.) (1991), *The Shorter Oxford English Dictionary on Historical Principles*. Oxford, UK: Clarendon.

Malinowski, B. (1992), *The Argonauts of the Western Pacific*. London: Routledge and Kegan Paul.

Mills, C. W. (1963), *Power, Politics, and People*. New York: Ballantine.

Orlikowski, W. J. (1992), "The Duality of Technology: Rethinking the Concept of Technology in Organizations," *Organization Science*, 3, 398-427.

Rohlen, T. P. (1974), *For Harmony and Strength: Japanese White-Collar Organization in Anthropological Perspective*. Berkeley: University of California Press.

Roy, D. F. (1960), "Banana Time: Job Satisfaction and Informal Interaction," *Human Organization*, 18, 158-168.

Schein, E. H. (1992), *Organizational Culture and Leadership: A Dynamic View* (2nd ed.). San Francisco: Jossey-Bass.

Smith, V. (1990), *Managing in the Corporate Interest: Control and Resistance in an American Bank*. Berkeley: University of California Press.

Trice, H. M. and J. M. Beyer (1985), "Using Six Organizational Rites to Change Culture," in R. H. Kilmann, M. J. Saxton, and R. Serpa (Eds.), *Gaining Control of the Corporate Culture*. San Francisco: Jossey-Bass, 370-399.

Van Maanen, J. (1984), "Doing New Things in Old Ways: The Chains of Socialization," in J. L. Bess (Ed.), *College and University Organization*. New York: New York University Press, 211-247.

——— (1988), *Tales of the Field*. Chicago: University of Chicago Press.

Voltaire, F. M. A. (1759), *Candide*. Franklin Center, PA: Franklin Library.

Weeks, J. R. (1997), *Unpopular Culture: The Cult of Bureaucracy in a British Bank*. Paper presented at the Academy of Management meetings, Boston.

Whyte, W. F. (1955), *Street Corner Society: The Social Structure of an Italian Slum*. Chicago: University of Chicago Press.

Wood, V. (1991), *Victoria Wood*. London: BBC Radio Collection.

PART III

THE PRACTICE OF INFORMATION TECHNOLOGY AND
ORGANIZATIONAL TRANSFORMATION

Part III is the concluding portion of this volume, and the authors of the chapters that follow look at the uses that a particular information technology (IT) is put to as it becomes a part of the day-to-day work context of organizational members. The writings concentrate on what might be called "cultures of reception"—the collective patterns of thought and action that form wherever and whenever new ITs are introduced to the workplace. The perspective represented is primarily that of IT users. This perspective inevitably differs, often quite substantially, from that of designers as well as managers charged with implementing new technologies. As sociologists and anthropologists have argued for years, the workplace always is a location of struggle and contest. New elements are unpredictable, absorbed in a variety of ways in which learning new things or learning to do old things in new ways brings forth a wide range of often deeply interested and felt responses. Few people affected by a potential change in their established work routines are neutral toward what they see as the rhyme and reason for such change.

People do not become competent users of a new technology—be it the use of an electronic spreadsheet in an accounting firm or the use of a mobile digital terminal in a police squad car—by fiat, by reading about it, or by attending a training class or two. Learning how to be a competent user—how to act as one, talk as one, and be recognized as one—means sharing the practice (and the concepts of use that underlie such practice) that emerges in a particular place and time among others with whom one regularly interacts. These matters are highly contextual and are as likely to be implicit as explicit. Such learning comes from daily experiences shared with others such that practice is informed, shaped, monitored, stabilized, and changed within a community of users. What connects members of a work community is not some warm and cozy glow of fellow feeling but rather the sharing of the same tasks, the same obligations, and roughly the same goals. Interpersonal relationships form around ongoing shared practice and are likely to be as restrictive as open, as hierarchical as egalitarian, as internally divided as unified, and as resistant to new technology as accepting of it.

The five chapters that make up this part of the volume all take up the question of how a particular IT—ranging from e-mail to laptops, from cell phones to geographic information systems—is interpreted and taken up (or, in some cases, rejected) by those for whom the technology presumably is designed. The first chapter, by Brian T. Pentland, examines an initiative that began with the massive acquisition and dissemination of laptop computers for use by Internal Revenue Service field agents—the first step of a multi-billion-dollar "Tax System Modernization" program that never reached the second step. "Big Brother Goes Portable: End-User Computing in the Internal Revenue Service" details some of the ironies, contradictions, and (at best) quite modest organizational transformations that occurred when an identical piece of office equipment was made available to agents who ostensibly all shared the same task, organization, occupation, and training. Regional offices varied greatly in their acceptance and use of the standard-issue laptops. Some offices embraced the laptops as useful new devices, whereas other offices more or less ignored the new machines.

These differences in use are explained by Pentland in terms of the shared yet office-bound meanings that the laptops generate for potential users. These meanings are not readily apparent, however, without delving into the ordinary and altogether routine work problems that revenue agents face (then and now) in dealing with taxpayers, with each other, and with their superiors in the offices within which they work. The laptops were embraced when they offered agents an opportunity to better manage impressions with all these groups. The laptops were rejected when they proved to be embarrassing on numerous occasions. But as the author makes clear, the status-enhancing or status-diminishing characteristics attributed to the laptops do not take hold in isolation. Meanings are collective matters always linked to social circumstance. The laptops came to be appreciated or defiled only through the social interaction occurring among agents within an office as stories of use and non-use developed over time and were incorporated into the agents' understandings of how their work was best accomplished. In the end, we are given a tale in which the computer plays a very limited role. Nothing much changed in the Internal Revenue Service, the transformational project was halted, and certainly no major organizational changes resulted. Pentland's message is nonetheless an important one, for he shows us just how a new technology was thoroughly assimilated (and ignored) by agents going about their business as usual and how the inability or unwillingness on the part of the agents of change to consider this business—"to audit the taxpayer, not the return" (p. 188)—led to a most serious (and expensive) implementation failure.

If laptops have become familiar in many office settings (and at home), so too have cellular phones. Indeed, the inexpensive, mobile, plastic phone has become an almost taken-for-granted feature of modern life. Like laptops, they seem to be a simple extension of an existing technology, a new convenience that has quickly entered our world without great controversy or problem. But as Peter Manning argues and demonstrates in the second chapter in this part of the volume, "Information Technology in the Police Context: The 'Sailor' Phone," the simplicity and convenience of cellular phones may have wide-reaching practical implications and considerable symbolic significance when slipped into organizational settings. Using American police agencies as an example, the author shows how cellular phones augment and perhaps enhance traditional communication devices and, therefore, carry a latent (and sometimes realized) potential to reshape work processes and authority patterns in an organization. The analytic perspective illustrated in the chapter is that of dramaturgy—an approach that "uses the metaphor of the theater to explore how the communication of messages to an audience conveys information and creates impressions that shape social interactions" (p. 206). This is an apt lens for viewing the introduction of any new technology as both tool and symbol because it usefully focuses attention on the differentiated cultural meanings and on the uses such technology has for members of the organization. Specific meanings and uses are, however, unsettled for a time (perhaps a long time); therefore, the story of cell phones in police agencies still remains an open-ended, contested, highly variable tale.

In the third chapter in this part of the volume, Wanda J. Orlikowski, like both Manning and Pentland, also is attentive to the local concerns and practices of organizational members whose established work routines seemingly are disrupted by the introduction of new technology. "Improvising Organizational Transformation Over Time: A Situated Change Perspective" provides a close look at the activities of technical support employees in a large U.S. software firm over a two-year period during which their work becomes increasingly collaborative, documented, responsive to customers, accountable to management, and (by most measures) productive. This is a success story, but one told with a good deal of subtlety, for the shifts over time are attributable not to managerial or technological imperatives but rather to the informal ways in which support employees themselves fashion their uses of the new technology. The focus is on the always-situated practices of employees as they go about their everyday tasks in the face of increased demands, mandated shifts in the work structures, and occasional but not unexpected technical breakdowns. Getting the job accomplished—and accomplished with skill, pride, and dispatch—requires more than a little improvisation and mutual accommodation. The accumulation of these small, subtle, nearly imperceptible changes in individual and group practices results in what can properly be called a transformation—albeit an unplanned one—of the customer support organization. And, as the author makes clear, this improvisational and gradualist view of transformation contrasts sharply with current theories of organizational change: "The research discussed here questions the beliefs that organizational change must be planned, that technology is the primary cause of technology-based organizational transformation, and that radical changes always occur rapidly and discontinuously" (p. 226).

Like Orlikowski's account of transformation, the fourth chapter in this part of the volume, "Transforming Work Through Incremental Technology: A Comparative Case Study of Geographic Information Systems in County Government" by Daniel Robey and Sundeep Sahay, supports an incremental, continuous vision of technical and organizational change. Using an interpretive approach that focuses on socially constructed meanings, the authors contrast the implementation of the same geographic information system (GIS), Arc/Info, in the governments of North County and South County. This comparison reveals a much greater perceived organizational transformation in North County, where it followed previous generations of mapping technologies and where knowledge about its use was widely diffused through the organization during its implementation. By contrast, its implementation in South County, which had not used earlier generations of this technology and which implemented the change through a centralized data-processing department, was not seen as leading to any organizational transformation. The comparison focuses on four overlapping implementation stages (or, more precisely, social processes): initial positioning, transition to Arc/Info, deployment of GIS, and spread of knowledge. Particularly striking is the contrast between North County's broad dissemination of conceptual knowledge about the GIS throughout the organization by a group of geographers and South County's dissemination of minimal procedural knowledge by members of the centralized data-processing unit. This contrast in breadth and depth of organizational learning is pivotal to the story line developed in this tale of two counties and is downright crucial to what users regarded as an organizational transformation. Based on this comparison, the authors suggest that theories of organizational learning might profitably inform future studies of IT and organizational transformation.

The final chapter in this part (and in this volume) is by Susan Leigh Star and Karen Ruhleder. Echoing Gregory Bateson, it is titled "Steps Toward an Ecology of Infrastructure: Design and Access for Large Information Spaces." This chapter offers a detailed ethnographic account of the results of an effort to build and bring into daily use a dedicated (and highly specific) information system called the Worm Community System (WCS) that would link and support the work of a large, geographically dispersed research community of biological scientists. To date, the effort has not been successful by designer or user standards, as the studied laboratory scientists increasingly turn to less sophisticated but easier to use information systems such as the World Wide Web. This chapter, like Pentland's look at laptops in the Internal Revenue Service, addresses the failure of IT-related organizational transformation (or, at least, of the transformation desired). Star and Ruhleder tell us why in a theoretically novel fashion. Developing, first, an elaborate definition of infrastructure, the authors show how a variety of quite common conditions in local laboratories produced levels of complexity and contradiction that made WCS access and use relatively unattractive to the studied scientists. Three levels of problematic communication are postulated and illustrated by a set of particular difficulties faced by users (and would-be users) of the WCS. The levels and problems are quite general and represent enormous design challenges faced whenever the social and technical demands for standardization and customization meet. The authors conclude that infrastructure evolves only competitively and slowly (if at all) as " 'formal' planned structure melds with or gives way to 'informal,' locally emergent structure" (p. 340).

The chapters on practice and IT put forward in this part of the volume illustrate an array of organizational changes—from the slight to the significant, from the small to the large. A common theme running through these writings is that although organizational transformation is going on all the time, when examined ethnographically—up close, on the ground, and in detail—it might not appear as dramatic, as rapid, or as technologically driven as often is assumed. The methodological approaches taken by the authors of these chapters all stress the perspectives of those organizational members who are asked by others—usually managers—to put a new IT into routine use. These perspectives are informed most crucially by the nature of the work that the targeted organizational members believe is central to the proper performance of their jobs. IT then is assessed by practitioners largely in terms of whether it aids or hinders their performance as collectively and historically defined. If technology is to be taken up by members of a given work community, then it must "fit" the work context or risk considerable redefinition, if not outright rejection.

IT, like any other artifact that is a part of the social and material environment of a work organization, is subject to individual and collective actions that can circumvent the uses intended by designers and can alter—dramatically in many cases—the outcomes expected by managers charged with the implementation of IT innovations. Those who bring the laptops, the cell phones, or the "new-and-improved" software system to the organization often suppose that the primary status of the technology to organizational members will be task specific. They ignore the importance that members quite understandably attach to their relative authority in the workplace; their sense of honor, pride, and respect in (and bestowed on) their work; their internal and external lines of accountability built up over time; and their concern for the maintenance of face (both their own and that of others). Designers assume a model of the user and the situations of use in which the meaning and relevance of IT to particular users is unproblematic. This is the difficulty that all authors represented in this part (and in this volume) identify as central and unavoidable. When IT, no matter how simple or complex, moves into a setting populated by those who are unfamiliar with the use of such technology, problems of meaning inevitably come forth, and these are the problems that must be addressed when studying IT and organizational transformation. Because all meanings are contextual, theories of consequence must of necessity be informed by practice, sensitive to the past, highly situated, and invariably contingent. Some useful—indeed exemplary—examples are put forward in this part of the volume, but as all authors surely would attest, this is just a beginning.

7

Big Brother Goes Portable

End-User Computing in the Internal Revenue Service

BRIAN T. PENTLAND

> The Automated Examination System is the first substantive change in the way we
> do business in decades. First, it was quill and parchment, then 14-column paper
> and mechanical pencils, and now the computer.
>
> —Chief of Examination, midwestern Internal Revenue Service district

In July 1986, the Internal Revenue Service (IRS) launched Phase 1 of the
Automated Examination System (AES). Within 18 months, more than
14,000 revenue agents and their managers had been given laptop portable
computers, software, and training. I visited four IRS offices during the summer of 1987 and again during the summer of 1988. I discovered that in spite of
overall uniformity in organizational context, use of the laptops varied greatly
by organizational subunit. The laptops were revered in some offices and re-
viled in others. This finding was particularly striking given that the tasks,
technology, structure, and workflow appeared to be identical in all four locations. The question, of course, is why there were differences.

Although the data reported on here are more than 10 years old, the story
still is quite current. The AES was an early part of the Tax System Modernization program that has drawn ongoing criticism from Congress. The program
was halted a few years ago after expenditures of nearly $4 billion with little
tangible benefits (Crenshaw 1997). Although some new IRS computing

initiatives (e.g., electronic filing) have been moderately successful, most of
these efforts have either stalled completely or failed to deliver expected improvements (Anthes 1996). These failures have been particularly glaring, of
course, because the IRS is essentially an information processing organization; forms and checks go in, and forms and checks go out. According to some
estimates, this chronic inability of the IRS to manage its core technology has
cost U.S. taxpayers as much as $300 billion (Anthes 1996, citing a General
Accounting Office report), mainly in lost revenues but also in wasted expenditures such as the AES.

The purpose of this chapter is not, however, to diagnose the failure of the
AES or of other IRS technology efforts. Given the complexity of IRS systems
and the unrelenting changes in technology and tax laws, lack of success is not
especially surprising. The AES example still is interesting and instructive, I
think, because it demonstrates something that objectivist, mechanistic views
of technology lull us into forgetting: Even with the same technology, task,
organization, occupation, and training, one does not necessarily get the same
results. Theories that center on task and technology depend, implicitly, on the
relevant properties of the technology being objectively given rather than
symbolically constructed. In the case of the AES, there were significant and
surprising differences in the ways in which the technology was interpreted
and, consequently, how it was used or not used.

Thus, the goal of this chapter is to show how the meaning of a standardized
piece of office technology could vary so markedly from site to site within an
ostensibly homogeneous task and user environment. These variations suggest that any organizational transformation (or lack thereof) could take very
different forms in each of the sites. As we shall see, where the technology was
embraced, it opened the door to a variety of new work practices and the possibility of more extensive changes. It might be difficult to see these as "transformations," but they clearly were significant to the participants. Where the
laptops were rejected, however, the door remained closed. Because more
objective factors (e.g., task, technology) were constant across the entire organization, it suggests that any potential transformation hinged, to a great
extent, on the symbolic construction of the laptops in each location.

The perspective that informs this analysis has been called the "interactionist school" by information system researchers (Kling 1980; Lyytinen
1987). The interactionist view rests on assumptions that derive from
symbolic interactionism (Blumer 1969) and phenomenology (Berger and
Luckmann 1967). In this view, the meanings that actors attach to an object are
not inherent in that object but rather are produced by social interactions in the
organizational setting into which the technology is introduced (Barley 1987;

Frank 1979; Silverman 1970). For example, a given program might have a "bug" or a "feature" depending on how users come to know it and talk about it (Markus 1984). Likewise, the ambiguity inherent in the AES system provided ample room for constructing alternative beliefs.

The focus of this analysis is on the types of social interactions that revenue agents have and the significance of the laptops in the context of those interactions. The examples presented here reflect the meanings that seem to bear most directly on the use of the laptops. Because they depend so strongly on context, these meanings are specific to the practice of tax auditing and the details of the AES technology, making it difficult to argue that they are generalizable. Yet, the variety and intensity of interpretations constructed around the AES technology reminds us how much meanings matter.

DATA COLLECTION

The primary source of the data presented here is a series of unstructured interviews with revenue agents and managers in four IRS districts during May-June 1987.[1] The sites were selected by the IRS national office for geographical convenience; there was no special effort made, so far as I was aware, to pick "good" or "bad" sites or to showcase or hide any particular aspect of the implementation process. In all, I interviewed more than 80 persons, typically for one to two hours each. I also conducted follow-up interviews one year later, in June 1988, to verify that my initial findings were not strictly an artifact of the timing of the initial visits.[2] I spent a total of at least five days in each of the four sites. Strict regulations regarding the confidentiality of all taxpayer information have prohibited any firsthand observation of an actual audit. Admittedly, interviews are a limited and potentially biased source of data on social interaction. Nonetheless, I believe that the many "war stories" I have been told provide a useful glimpse of some of the basic features of the interactions that make up the world of revenue agents.

In addition to the interviews, a sample survey of revenue agents was conducted during February 1988. This survey enjoyed a response rate of 85 percent, resulting in 1,110 individual responses representing agents from all regions of the United States. In addition to collecting basic demographic data, the questionnaire focused on patterns of use, beliefs about computers and their use along a variety of dimensions, and various aspects of the training and implementation. Because these data have been analyzed and reported elsewhere (Pentland 1989, 1992), they are used here primarily to provide additional context and support for the interview data.

GETTING BEHIND THE NUMBERS:
WHAT REVENUE AGENTS DO

Revenue agents conduct field audits of corporations (Form 1120), partnerships (Form 1065), and sole proprietorships (Form 1040).[3] The term *field audit* derives from the fact that revenue agents visit the taxpayers' homes or businesses. Revenue agents are expected to spend as much as 80 percent of their time in the field, with the balance spent on office paperwork, legal research, and other activities. The emphasis on working in the field reflects the informal motto, "Audit the taxpayer, not the return" (Pentland and Carlile 1996). With the exception of large cases (which are handled by teams of specialists), revenue agents work alone on their cases.

The actual work of conducting a field audit is extremely varied because revenue agents cover the entire range of taxpayers present in the modern American economy, from investment banks to drug dealers. Every taxpayer has a unique set of books, circumstances, and tax issues. The incredible diversity of work pretty much guarantees that most agents will not specialize very much, if at all. According to one group manager, "Private accounting firms generally specialize; they get to know the details of certain lines of business. But [the] IRS doesn't have that luxury."

Agents are charged with auditing and understanding the tax implications of every transaction in a taxpayer's business, whether it appears in the taxpayer's books or not. In general, overstated deductions are easier to find than is unreported income, but both require considerable skill about where to look and how to interpret the data. As one senior agent explained,

> In revenue agent work, the idea is to look at which part of the return is giving the major tax benefit. There's usually something on the return that's real advantageous to a taxpayer, in terms of the timing of a loss, or the size of deduction, something like that. That's where you want to focus your attention. If it looks too good to be true, it probably is. That's the basic premise.

When an agent finds something amiss, it is called an *adjustment*. The agent must document the extent of the error or omission and write up his or her conclusions, citing the relevant sections of the Federal Tax Code, revenue rulings, or court cases that bolster the agent's position. Ultimately, a great deal of the agent's work is not so much adding up numbers and computing taxes as it is interpreting facts in light of the relevant law and writing up the analysis. The product of an audit is a case file, which includes (among other things) a set of work papers and supporting documents that explain the adjustments, and a revenue agent report (RAR), which informs the taxpayer of his or her adjusted tax liability.

Comparison of my observations of the IRS to other published accounts (Chommie 1970; Diogenes 1973; Surface 1967) shows that the basic structure, role, and daily life of the Examination division has remained largely unchanged for at least 20 years.

PHASE 1 OF THE AES:
THE LAPTOP PORTABLE COMPUTERS

Before discussing how computers affected the work of revenue agents, it is worth clarifying the scope of the AES as it initially was implemented. Although the ultimate goal of the AES was to make tax examination as near as possible a paperless process, that goal was a long way off at the time of this study, and little progress has been made during the intervening 10 years. The concept was to have electronic "work centers" for each occupation throughout the IRS; the work center for the revenue agent was one of dozens envisioned. When the whole system finally was in place, the paper flow between steps in the audit process could be reduced to electronic flows. The distribution of laptop portable computers was only the first of several phases that ultimately was planned to include a nationwide network of minicomputers and mainframes, online access to taxpayer records, online legal research, and artificial intelligence for classification and selection of returns.

In short, the scale of the proposed system was mind-boggling, especially given the state of the art in 1988. Almost by definition, the technology used during one phase would be outdated by the time the next phase could be implemented. Indeed, the Phase 1 laptops already were perceived by many revenue agents as obsolete by 1988, when I returned to do my second round of interviews. At that time, Phase 2 was officially "on hold" pending an evaluation of Phase 1 and was cancelled in early 1990 (Burnham 1990). In retrospect, given that each phase would need to be tightly interdependent with the others for the system to function as a whole, the AES would have been destined to a vicious cycle of obsolescence, incompatibility, and disappointment. At the time, however, the future looked bright and the laptops were intended to be the first of many important innovations on the way toward a paperless Examination division.

Although the overall goals were ambitious, Phase 1 was quite modest; it was limited to laptop portable computers and software for use in field audits. As I have argued elsewhere (Pentland 1989), the laptop portable computer seemed to be the ideal tool for the job given that revenue agents crunch numbers; write spreadsheets, forms, and reports; and are out of the office most of the time. They spend roughly 80 percent of their time out of the office. Laptop portable computers make sense for them. Better still, they portrayed an image of professionalism and power; revenue agents now would be armed with technology to match that of their clients. So, during Phase 1, each agent and manager was issued a Zenith 171 laptop portable, which was a standard MS-DOS computer with two $5\frac{1}{4}$-inch floppy disk drives but no hard drive (10-MB hard drives became available the following year, hence the rapid obsolescence of this particular model). It folded like a small, rather thick briefcase and weighed about 12 pounds. Although it had an internal modem and software for telecommunications, there was no way for agents to use these tools to access taxpayer data. Phase 1 of the AES was completely "standalone"—one agent, one computer. In addition, use of the computers was optional. As part of the agreement negotiated with the union representing the revenue agents, individuals could not be evaluated on their use or non-use of the computers in any way. During Phase 1, productivity was expected to rise only 2% to 3%, but it is not clear whether this gain ever actually was realized.

Indeed, it is striking how little of the revenue agents' work was affected by the laptop computers. Out of all the tasks that revenue agents perform, only the preparation of materials for the case file—forms, work papers, tax computations, document requests, correspondence, and the like—were potential candidates for the laptops. When asked whether he believed that the laptops changed the job, one manager explained,

> Somewhere down the road, when it's more than just a fancy calculator or typewriter. Things like direct access to the service center and legal research, those will be important. But for the time being, it does not really change the job.
>
> Once we get the final tax computation and the RAR, there's no difference between pre- and post-AES, as far as the agent goes. The paper trail stays the same from there on out. The case folders are assembled the same way, [and] the folder is ready to go from the manager's desk to review and ESP [examination support and processing] for final processing.

As these comments imply, a great deal of the work in the Examination division involves just moving paper—getting original returns and files from the regional service centers, assembling case files, sending them on for review and further processing, and then sending them back to the service centers for storage. This is the "mountain of paper" that everyone recognized as the central problem and that the AES was meant to attack. But the laptops did not even begin to make a dent in it because they provided no new access to data, no connectivity, and no way to store or retrieve electronic documents except on floppy disks. Everything ultimately still had to be done with paper.

It is worth noting that the implementation of the AES, unlike some instances of office automation, was not seen as deskilling the revenue agents'
job. Interviewees indicated very strongly that the computers did not in any
way deskill or deprofessionalize the job, and this result was strongly confirmed in the survey (with 79% of respondents saying that the laptops did not
diminish the value of professional judgment vs. only 9% who said that it did).
This result stems in part from the fact that the "real work" done by revenue
agents is not primarily adding up numbers and computing taxes (Pentland
and Carlile 1996). The extent of the "automation" during Phase 1 of the AES
was limited to those relatively minor parts of an agent's job that could be put
onto a simple personal computer. But even these minor changes take on great
significance to the revenue agent when viewed in the context of the social setting in which the technology is used.

SOCIAL INTERACTIONS IN A
FIELD AUDIT GROUP

Given this thumbnail sketch of the work and the tool, we can proceed to see
how the social interactions in the setting create the meanings attached to the
new technology. Following Goffman's (1959) distinction between "frontstage" and "backstage" social scenes, I divide the revenue agent's social
interactions into two categories. Frontstage, an agent has interactions with
taxpayers and their representatives (accountants and tax attorneys) that are
fundamentally adversarial and often rather tense and antagonistic. Pentland
and Carlile (1996) argue that these interactions are strategic (Goffman 1969)
in the sense that each party is attempting to present and maintain an appropriate front while the other party is trying to "uncover" it. From this perspective,
tax auditing is more like espionage than it is like accounting. Backstage,
within the IRS, an agent interacts primarily with his or her group manager and
other revenue agents. These interactions are naturally more cooperative but
nevertheless involve elements of competition, evaluation for promotion, and
impression management.

Frontstage: Interactions With Taxpayers

Revenue agents spend most of their time with taxpayers and the accountants and attorneys who represent them. Due to the difficult nature of the
interactions, meeting and dealing with the public is seen by many as the most
important part of an agent's job (Pentland and Carlile 1996). Naturally

enough, this interaction is the source of a variety of important meanings—both symbolic and substantive—for the laptops.

Laptops as a symbol of competence. Above all, the laptop brought a new credibility to revenue agents' work because it allowed them to replace the traditional handwritten reports with printed ones. It was not just that the reports were computer generated and presumed to be free of simple arithmetic errors (but not necessarily data entry or logical errors, of course). The important thing was simply that the reports looked better. Even people with terrible handwriting could produce clean, professional-looking documents, whereas before they could not.[4] This point was of enormous significance for agents in getting taxpayers to agree to their newly computed tax liabilities. Contrary to popular myth, a taxpayer is under no obligation to comply with IRS adjustments made at the time of an audit. Part of the job of the revenue agent is to get the taxpayer to sign the RAR (Form 4549), thereby agreeing that the adjustments made are correct and that the new tax should be assessed. If a taxpayer does not sign this form, then the case is designated "unagreed" and goes to the IRS appeals function, where it usually is settled. If it is not settled there, then it proceeds to federal tax court for trial. Cases that go unagreed create additional work for revenue agents because they must document the legal grounds for their positions more fully for use by appeals officers.

Strange as it might seem, agents perceive their job as "selling the adjustments to the taxpayer." As one group manager explained, the laptops helped in this process:

> An important thing to realize about the PC [personal computer] is that because it produces a better looking product—more legible, more comprehensible—it eases the selling job we have to do on the adjustments. You see, when you're out there doing an audit and it comes time to close the case, what you are really doing is selling your skills and image as a credible, competent examiner. Would you sign an agreement form prepared by someone you didn't trust to do it right? Probably not. That's part of why the PC is so important for agents, because a better looking product is easier to sell.

It is interesting to note that whereas there was a great deal of enthusiasm for the ability of the laptops to create a better looking product, the idea that they could facilitate a substantively better examination generally was rejected. The following viewpoints were typical:

> It [laptop] won't help with the audit plan. It won't look at the books and records. In general, it's just not going to make that much difference in how good an audit an agent can do.

It certainly isn't going to help you do an audit any better. The main part of the work involves judgment that can't be put into a computer. . . . Of course, it does give you a more professional-looking product.

The unique circumstances of revenue agents' work give rise to this peculiar finding. A key aspect of a computer's value to a revenue agent was its ability to facilitate a social interaction that often is antagonistic, acrimonious, and highly emotional—getting a taxpayer to agree to pay more taxes. The computers helped by providing better looking output without necessarily affecting the underlying quality of the work.

Laptops as a defense against procrastination. Taxpayers frequently wish to delay the assessment of new taxes, especially when confronted with a set of adjustments that is higher than expected. It is not unusual for a taxpayer to remember some additional piece of information at the last minute, which the agent is obligated to include in his or her calculations. Whether this information had been withheld deliberately or not, it is frustrating for the agent on the case. Without a computer, redoing the computations for a small return might involve only an additional one or two hours of work. But for a large case, it could be a nightmare:

It used to be that if they wanted to make a change in something after you'd done the computations, you just wanted to kill them. It could take days sometimes to redo the numbers and check them out, just for one little change. Now it's like, "Sure, how many? Make another. Who cares!"

By providing the ability to recompute taxes, interest, and penalties automatically, the laptops provided revenue agents with a degree of flexibility that was a very welcome addition to their set of tools and techniques. A group manager explained the benefits as follows:

Overall, the PC is seen as increasing the prestige of the job and shifting the balance of power in favor of the examiner. The tactic of holding receipts until the closing conference, which is actively pursued by some of the more cagey CPAs [certified public accountants] and taxpayers, used to result in several days to several weeks delay in closure. Now, [it] might only delay for several minutes.

In this respect, the laptops provided substantive benefits to the agents. Dealing with procrastinators is a valued skill at the IRS, so much so that it is considered to be an aspect of the official requirements for the job—called "critical elements."[5] To the extent that the laptops could help agents to close cases effectively and to forestall procrastination, it not only gave them an advantage over the taxpayers, it also tended to help them in their careers (a subject I consider later in terms of the backstage interactions). Thus, the general notion that users will adopt technology to the extent that it has some differential value in use takes on a particular meaning in the context of tax examination.

Laptops as an embarrassment. Not all agents saw the laptops as an advantage in the field. In particular, agents working in large urban areas reported feeling embarrassed by using the laptops in the field in front of accountants or attorneys. Having to change disks frequently was cited as the source of embarrassment:

> A key problem with the laptop is that people are afraid to be embarrassed in front of taxpayer representatives. They'd look like a fool with all those floppies. (manager in a northeastern city)

> I would never take that thing into the field and embarrass myself in front of some attorney by playing "floppy swappy." No way. I don't see how anyone can use it the way it is now. (revenue agent in the same site)

From a technical viewpoint, the problem here arose from the fact that the computers had no hard disks and the programs involved required several floppy disks to run.[6] But this strong sense of embarrassment and anxiety was reported in only one of the four districts visited. It is interesting to note that the preceding quotes were taken from the first round of interviews, before the revenue agents had much experience actually using the laptops. It is not clear whether there had been some early incident that shaped opinion on this matter or whether this anxiety was prospective. In any case, if the problem were purely technical, then it should have appeared everywhere given that all agents received the same computers and software.

The significance of this straightforward operational problem stems from the interactions that revenue agents in large urban areas have with accountants and attorneys. Consider the following remark from another agent in the same site, near a large city in the Northeast:

> We're dealing with a more sophisticated kind of taxpayer here. They're aggressive about pushing the limits, taking risks. They know there's a limited chance of getting caught. And when we go out to audit them, it's like they assume we're stupid until proven otherwise. Sometimes, you can get their respect in the initial interview if you ask the right questions, things they know are right on point. So, it's really hard to go out there with your laptop and risk embarrassing yourself by not knowing what you're doing.

This view was fairly typical in that location. The basic problem here was that the competence of the agents seemed to be in question from the start. Unless they were completely comfortable using the computers, as some of the agents were, they would tend to avoid that risk.

Although it is difficult to isolate the reason for this presumption, a large part of it rests on the labor market in these areas. In 1986, the IRS was offering accounting graduates between $3,400 and $6,800 less to start than the national average.[7] A uniform wage structure nationwide makes this problem particularly acute in urban areas. Justified or not, there seemed to be a perception among accountants and other taxpayer representatives that people working for the IRS must not be able to get better jobs elsewhere.[8] With this presumption working against them, it is easy to see why agents who are uncertain about the computers would avoid using them unless absolutely necessary. Although it is difficult to pinpoint the causes or effects of these types of attitudes, they clearly affect the relationship that agents have with the public, which in turn can affect the meanings attached to the new technology.[9] In this case, the anxiety caused by the potential for embarrassment served as a disincentive for use of the computers.

Backstage: Interactions With Managers and Peers

The interactions that agents have with managers and peers form the basis for a variety of career-related meanings for the laptops. The field audit function is organized into groups of 12 to 14 agents with a group manager. These immediate contacts comprise the most significant interactions that agents have within the service. Without more extensive research, it is difficult to assess the relative importance of peer interaction. However, many interviewees indicated that other agents are an important source of technical advice, moral support, and computer tips, among other things.

Laptops as a time saver or a time sink. Time is a central part of IRS culture. Unlike most parts of the federal government, the IRS earns money. As a result, there is a tremendous emphasis on how to complete a given analysis as quickly as possible. Agents and managers are constantly making judgments about the value of pursuing particular issues in a given audit. As one manager put it, "The main question is always whether there's any potential tax liability there." Implicit in that question is the idea that if there is not, then the time could be better spent elsewhere and the issue should be dropped.

The process of learning to use the laptops puts a strain on this cultural norm by asking agents and managers to take extra time now so as to save time later. According to an AES instructor in the Midwest,

It's pounded into their heads from the very beginning—time on case, time on case, keep it low, keep it low. So it's really hard for the agent to accept that it's okay for them to take time. But I don't think anyone has had any trouble for time. Nobody has been criticized. I've said it over and over, it's okay to take time. This is a major issue, and I've tried to stress it as much as possible.

A genuine effort was made to encourage people to take the time they needed to learn. But local conditions vary among districts, and the pressure to work cases sometimes has outweighed the desire to invest time in learning a new tool. A group manager explained his problem this way:

Time is not a luxury that people have [here in this district]. There have been a lot of people leaving, retiring, and so on, so their inventories have to get spread around to the other people in their groups. That creates an additional pressure to work the cases. Usually, cases are not moved between groups. There was a long period when [the] IRS could not do as much hiring as they wanted to do, so now when they finally can hire, they have to put all of their experienced people into training jobs, and that reduced the manpower devoted to actually working cases.

An agent in the same group described the sense of pressure about time that was created as a result of interacting with this manager (about three months after initial training):

They tell you that you have all the time in the world to do these exams with the PC, but in practice it doesn't work out that way. After the exam is over, they'll ask, "Why all the hours on that exam?" and it doesn't really help to say, "Because I used the PC." The pressure is always on to keep the hours down and the yield up.

Time pressure is also created by frontstage interactions with the taxpayer. Some taxpayers procrastinate, but others are interested in getting their audits over as quickly as possible. This is especially true when they are paying by the hour for attorneys or accountants to represent them.

The pressure to work cases efficiently created a type of catch-22 for revenue agents who wanted to use the laptops, a hurdle they somehow had to clear before they could integrate the machines into their work. They needed time to learn, but they did not have any to spare. Unless they invested substantial amounts of time, their skills would not improve. In fact, the skills learned in training tended to atrophy with disuse, thereby raising the hurdle. Agents who did not start immediately and use the laptops regularly were at a distinct disadvantage when they finally did start to use them.

In terms of the meanings that the laptops had for revenue agents, they depended on where the agents sat on the learning curve and where their managers sat in terms of backlogged cases. If the time pressure was high and the agents were just learning, then the laptops meant trouble—lots of hours and nothing to show, a time sink that had to be avoided. But for agents who were fully up to speed or who were working in groups with relatively light inventory, the laptops could become a time saver, a highly valued tool that they could not do without.

Laptops as a way in which to get ahead or fall behind. The implications of the laptops for time are part of a larger question involving the ability of the agents to get ahead in the organization. The pay structure for revenue agents is such that promotions are essential to maintaining adequate salaries. Promotions are dependent on completing the appropriate training and on group managers' annual evaluations of agents' work. An important question for revenue agents is how the laptops can help them in their efforts to make the next grade.

A peculiar feature of the introduction of the computers at the IRS was that use of the computers was made optional. Officially, managers could not even mention computer use, positively or negatively, in the evaluations of employees. This had been negotiated with the union representing the revenue agents, which wanted to make sure that the new technology did not unfairly disadvantage any of its members. Unofficially, various districts have created very different impressions among their agents regarding the importance of using the computers. Compare these remarks from agents in the Northeast and the Midwest, which were typical of interviewees in those regions:

> It may be required some time in the future, but we really can't predict when that might be. We certainly don't expect it next year. (Northeast)

> I'm absolutely positive that 18 months after training, the laptop can be used as a basis for evaluation. (Midwest)

This difference is accounted for by the fact that AES instructors in the Northeast apparently told trainees that laptop use might be required "sometime in the future." In the Midwest, one AES instructor reported, "We told trainees that it was going to be a critical element within a year after they got their laptops." When I said I thought that it was optional, the instructor laughed and replied, "Yeah, and your job is optional, too. Like you can come in if you want to, right? No, we expect them to use it."

Ultimately, the content of the critical elements that define the revenue agent position could be set only at the national level. Districts can interpret certain aspects of them but cannot change them. Consequently, the notion that computer use would be required at a particular time really was just a prediction—more rumor than reality.

The effect of this rumor on the meanings of the laptops for revenue agents was not very surprising. For those agents who believed that the laptops would be required for them to keep their jobs or to gain promotions, mastering the laptops was a necessity. They had to do so. For those who saw them as optional, the laptops were somewhat of an enigma. The following was a typical comment: "Why did the government spend all that money on computers and not require us to use them?" There was minimal incentive for these agents to invest the time needed to become proficient at using the computers.

Overall, the backstage significance of the laptops touched on two core concerns for the revenue agent: the use of time and organizational advancement. Revenue agents are expected to manage their time effectively, and this feeds directly into the issue of advancement. Promotions improve one's compensation, but they also lead to better working conditions given that higher grade agents tend to do a smaller number of large corporate audits rather than a large number of individual taxpayer and/or small business audits. Large audits are more "professional," they are more "technical," and the people involved are less likely to take it personally if the auditors make adjustments. Large audits are less emotionally charged and less stressful overall. To the extent that the laptops were seen as affecting (positively or negatively) time on case or one's chances for promotion, they were a highly significant thing for the revenue agents.

DISCUSSION

The interactionist perspective taken here provides a way of interpreting the meaning of automation to its users. Starting from the premise that the meaning of a new technology stems from the social context in which it is used, I have shown how the particular conditions in an IRS field audit group give meaning to the AES. In many ways, the unique set of circumstances described here make it difficult to generalize to other settings. Even though the IRS is the world's largest accounting practice, it also is a government agency involved in testing and enforcing tax compliance, so it probably has more in common with police organizations than with accounting firms (although police organizations and accounting firms have quite a lot in common, as Van Maanen and Pentland [1994] note). Even within the realm of white-collar service professionals, IRS agents are a unique breed; nobody else examines federal taxes. Nonetheless, there are some conclusions to be drawn.

Analyzing Meaning

The analysis here adopts the position that the value of a technology to its users must be assessed from the users' point of view. This general idea is quite well established, of course, and is built into models such as Davis's (1989) Technology Adoption Model (TAM), which includes a term for subjective assessment of utility. But what might be missing from these models is that subjective assessments are formed in the context of ongoing interactions. Revenue agents, for example, value the computers for reasons that are not readily apparent without delving into the day-to-day problems they face in dealing with taxpayers and with each other. Methodologically and theoretically, understanding these day-to-day problems would entail a shift from a variable-centered to a more narrative mode of analysis. Rather than asking what variables affect use and estimating the parameters of a model such as the TAM, a narrative mode of inquiry centers on stories about use (or non-use) that unfold over time. By analyzing the stories directly, as I have done here, one can understand not just the positive or negative assessments that may surround a new technology but also the reasons why those assessments are formed. This, in turn, may provide a bit more practical leverage on what might be done to influence them.

In analyzing meaning, one must start with the social context in which users will be operating and the norms, values, and assumptions of that context. The idea that culture matters also is a well-accepted part of sociotechnical analysis, but this case suggests that specific interactions matter as well. As illustrated here, it might be helpful to break the context down into the major domains of interaction. I used Goffman's (1959) dramaturgical divisions (frontstage and backstage), but any scheme that isolates socially meaningful and distinct spheres of activity would be helpful. This is especially true where the prospective users of the technology operate across boundaries or have contact with more than one type of audience for whom they need to manage impressions. For each audience, one might ask, "How does this technology contribute to, or detract from, the ability of this actor to stay in role, to manage impressions, or to preserve an appropriate front?" These questions are relatively easy to answer; one can get concrete examples of how a technology fits into (or fails to fit into) an ongoing social scene. By contrast, a direct focus on culture might lead one to ask how organizational values or assumptions affect artifacts such as technology. Although these questions are interesting, they are somewhat diffuse and difficult to pin down reliably. Thus, it often may be easier to focus on interactions (and the stories that are embodied in them) as a window onto values and assumptions.

What is missing from this story, however, is an explanation of why some agents adopted the technology and others did not. In principle, the symbolic benefits (e.g., more professional-looking reports) were available to all, and based on my data, nearly every revenue agent would appreciate such benefits. Yet, not all agents realized the benefits. This is where a predictive model, such as the TAM, is likely to be more helpful. As the situations described here illustrate, revenue agents have complicated jobs. Because of the practical necessity of completing audits as quickly as possible, they must constantly make trade-offs between getting the job done quickly and getting it done better. Depending on how they perceive the role of the laptop computers in that basic equation, they may or may not choose to use them. Those perceptions, of course, are shaped by the types of interactions outlined and analyzed here.

Organizational Transformation

One might ask what, if anything, was "transformed" by Phase 1 of the AES. Clearly, it was not the structure, mission, or basic policies and procedures of the organization, all of which were fixed. And during Phase 1, even the workflow of the audit process was held constant. The great expectations of computing and automation were limited to a very narrow sphere of work practice. But although it is narrow, that sphere—the tax audit itself—is highly symbolic of the IRS and its mission for both the revenue agents and the public. Transformation of the audit would be highly significant, even if it had limited impact on either efficiency or effectiveness. Goffman's (1959) dramaturgical framework leads us to ask, "Significant for whom, and in what context?" As I have argued, the frontstage and backstage have somewhat different casts of characters. Each carries its own distinctive needs and generates its own meanings. The public frontstage side of the audit could be transformed without necessarily having much effect on what goes on backstage. The great emphasis that revenue agents placed on creating professional-looking documents, "selling adjustments," and avoiding embarrassment seems to suggest that frontstage transformation was a highly desirable goal. And to a limited extent, that goal was achieved in some of the districts. But backstage, it was more or less business as usual. The laptops posed a new set of problems and opportunities concerning time on case and promotions but did not fundamentally restructure anything about the structure, processes, practices, or culture of the organization.

If one subscribes to the view that structure is produced and reproduced through routinized interactions of the type described here (Giddens 1984), then the possibility may exist, in theory, for these interaction-level effects to result in larger structural changes. We begin to see some evidence of this with the IRS. Because the process of meaning creation is social, whole groups—not just isolated individuals—tended to gravitate toward particular interpretations. This phenomenon was one of the most striking things about the AES implementation. In one district in the Northeast, nearly all agents interviewed indicated that neither they nor their peers used the computers on a regular basis. In another district in the Northeast, only a few agents seemed to be making regular use of the computers. By contrast, agents in the two midwestern districts reported using the laptops "at every opportunity." One year later, during follow-up interviews, the same general pattern persisted. Agents in the Northeast reported that they used the computers primarily for computing final taxes and penalties (the RAR report) and routine correspondence (e.g., form letters to request documents) but for little else. Agents in the midwestern districts, on the other hand, reported in follow-up interviews that they "couldn't work without" the computers and used them for a wide range of purposes including spreadsheets and database applications. These differences generally were supported by the survey data as well. It is difficult to attribute these variations to anything other than the subjective constructed meanings of the technology given that the objective conditions were nearly identical throughout the organization.

So, although Phase 1 could hardly be called transformational, it is interesting to speculate about what would have happened if the IRS had attempted to implement the subsequent phases of the AES. The paperless audit, if it had been achieved, would have been a major transformation of the work and the organization, linking revenue agents and their laptops to a network of minicomputers and mainframes. These systems would have significantly changed workflows, internal reporting, training, interactions with taxpayers, security procedures, and much more. But for these network-based applications to work, revenue agents had to be conducting computerized audits. Unless the laptop technology was integrated into their work practices, it is hard to imagine how subsequent phases could have been successful. The day-to-day work practices of the revenue agent in the field are the core activity without which the examination division cannot function. The field audit is, in that respect, the foundation on which the rest of the system needed to be built and without which the rest of the system would have no purpose. Seen from this perspective, meanings matter a lot. The strong positive associations that emerged around the laptops in some districts would have made more significant transformations possible. The strong negative associations constructed around the laptops in other districts would have made such transformations impossible.

Finally, as a study of the automation of professional work, this case provides an example in which the computers had a very limited impact on the knowledge, skills, and professional judgment required to do the job. The core of the revenue agents' job, of course, is to audit taxpayers, not their returns; the important work concerns judgments about people and their veracity, not numbers and their accuracy (Pentland and Carlile 1996). The assumption that a portable computer would be a perfect tool rests partly on a misinterpretation of just what revenue agents really do. The work of an IRS revenue agent involves face-to-face social interaction and judgment, and in this respect, it is much like that of other professionals doing knowledge-intensive work in highly social settings. Although there are a variety of ways in which computers can assist in such work, it is hard to imagine how this work ever could be automated. For the time being, most of the new computerization initiatives are on hold at the IRS. But elsewhere, organizations are charging ahead with portable computing of all types. It will be interesting to see how the meanings of these machines will emerge and change as well as what types of transformation (if any) will occur as organizations continue to deploy these portable assistants.

NOTES

1. The IRS has 64 districts nationwide. In many cases, a district corresponds to a state. In large urban areas (e.g., New York City), there often are multiple districts. A district may consist of several sites, called *posts of duty*. Two of the districts I visited were in the Midwest, and two were in the Northeast.

2. The initial visits were during May-June 1987, three to nine months after agents had first been given their computers and training. The follow-up visits were completed during June-August 1988. It was not possible to interview all of the same people on the follow-up visits due to promotions, vacations, and special assignments. When an original interviewee was not available, another agent or manager was substituted on an ad hoc basis.

3. In fact, revenue agents examine other types of tax returns as well such as excise taxes, employment taxes, and estate and gift taxes. Agents working in those areas are referred to as *specialists,* whereas the interviewees in this study are called *general program agents.*

4. Clerical support is very limited in field audit groups, so before the introduction of the computers, virtually all work was handwritten. Agents could choose to type something themselves, but that was not commonly done.

5. The following six critical elements are used in annual performance appraisals for revenue agents: (1) inventory management, (2) planning and scheduling, (3) examination techniques, (4) tax law interpretation and application, (5) preparation of work papers and reports, and (6) taxpayer relations. Of course, critical elements have subelements as well. For example, "minimizes delays caused by procrastination of taxpayers and/or representatives" is a subelement of planning and scheduling.

6. Revenue agents had two main programs that they used. One was a general-purpose integrated package (word processing, spreadsheet, database, and communications) called *Enable,* which required four disks. The other was the *1040 Workcenter,* which was written especially for IRS field agents. In its initial version, this program required 18 disks (although agents might use only 5 or 6 during a given audit). A revised 1040 workcenter, released in 1988, required only 7 disks, and most audits could be completed with only 2 or 3. Thus, although some disk swapping certainly was required, there is objective reason to believe that it would not have interfered with the conduct of the work.

7. Revenue agents starting at GS-5 (General Service–5) were offered $14,390 in 1988; those starting at GS-7 were offered $17,824. By comparison, private firms offered an average starting

salary of $21,216 at that time. The decision to hire at GS-5 versus GS-7 was based primarily on academic performance. GS-13 is the highest level revenue agent; in 1988, the GS-13 pay scale ranged from $38,000 to $50,000 based on tenure and merit.

8. I was not able to confirm this independently, but the sense of being "one down" was a frequent undercurrent in my discussions with revenue agents. Those agents with whom I discussed the subject explicitly had often held other accounting jobs and chose to work for the IRS for a variety of reasons including shorter hours, more job security, more interesting work, and greater independence and responsibility on the job. The fact that they needed to justify their decisions in this way, however, helps to support the overall point.

9. It is interesting to note that these types of contextual differences can occur for a variety of reasons, some of which are rooted in American history. Consider the experiences of one midwestern agent who explained, "There's a lot of differences in how people see the IRS, even right here in this district. I used to be stationed up north of here along the [Mississippi] river. Up there, they just loved the government; they even liked the IRS. They'd work with you to help you get your job done. . . . But if you go south of here, down near Arkansas, that's rebel country. They hate the government, and they especially hate the IRS. They don't want anything to do with you. So it's like night and day, really."

REFERENCES

Anthes, G. H. (1996), "IRS Project Failures Cost Taxpayers $50 Billion Annually," *Computerworld,* October 14, p. 1.

Barley, S. (1987), "Technology, Power, and the Social Organization of Work: Towards a Pragmatic Theory of Skilling and Deskilling," in S. B. Bacharach and N. DiTomaso (Eds.), *Research in the Sociology of Organizations* (Vol. 6). Greenwich, CT: JAI.

Berger, P. and T. Luckmann (1967), *The Social Construction of Reality.* Garden City, NY: Doubleday.

Blumer, H. (1969), *Symbolic Interactionism.* Englewood Cliffs, NJ: Prentice Hall.

Burnham, D. (1990), "The IRS's Bumbling Efforts to Update Its Computers," *The New York Times,* April 8, p. C12.

Chommie, J. C. (1970), *The Internal Revenue Service.* New York: Praeger.

Crenshaw, A. B. (1997), "IRS Moves to Update Computers: After Several Failures, a Cautious Approach," *The Washington Post,* May 16, p. G2.

Davis, F. D. (1989), "Perceived Usefulness, Perceived Ease of Use, and User Acceptance of Information Technology," *MIS Quarterly,* 13, 319-342.

Diogenes (1973), *The April Game: Secrets of an Internal Revenue Agent.* Chicago: Playboy Press.

Frank, A. W., III (1979), "Reality Construction in Interaction," *Annual Review of Sociology,* 5, 167-191.

Giddens, A. (1984), *The Constitution of Society.* Berkeley: University of California Press.

Goffman, E. (1959), *The Presentation of Self in Everyday Life.* New York: Doubleday.

——— (1969), *Strategic Interaction.* Philadelphia: University of Pennsylvania Press.

Kling, R. (1980), "Social Analyses of Computing: Theoretical Perspectives in Recent Empirical Research," *ACM Computing Surveys,* 12 (1), 61-110.

Lyytinen, K. (1987), "Different Perspectives in Information Systems: Problems and Solutions," *ACM Computing Surveys,* 19 (1), 5-46.

Markus, L. M. (1984), *Systems in Organizations: Bugs and Features.* Boston: Pitman.

Pentland, B. T. (1989), "Use and Productivity in Personal Computing: An Empirical Test," in *Proceedings of the Tenth International Conference on Information Systems,* Boston, December, 211-222.

———(1992), "Organizing Moves Software Support Hot Lines," *Administrative Science Quarterly,* 37, 527-548.

Pentland, B. T. and P. Carlile (1996), "Audit the Taxpayer, Not the Return: Tax Auditing as an Expression Game," *Accounting, Organizations, and Society,* 21, 269-287.

Silverman, D. (1970), *The Theory of Organisations: A Sociological Framework.* London: Heinemann.

Surface, W. (1967), *Inside Internal Revenue.* New York: Coward-McCann.

Van Maanen, J. and B. T. Pentland (1994), "Cops and Auditors: The Rhetoric of Records," in S. B. Sitkin and R. J. Bies (Eds.), *The Legalistic Organization.* Thousand Oaks, CA: Sage, 53-90.

8

Information Technology in the Police Context

The "Sailor" Phone

PETER K. MANNING

While the media celebrate the growing impact of personal computing, the Internet, and the "information highway," much modern work is still done without electronic assistance. The core technology of policing, for example, remains people talking to people, officers trying to persuade people by various interactional strategies to comply with requests, threats, and commands (Bittner 1990; Reiss 1992). However, even policing has been affected and shaped by the introduction of new information processing technologies (Manning 1992a, 1992b; Reiss 1992). One of these new tools is the mobile cellular telephone (or, as some police officers call it, the "sailor" phone[1]).

This chapter examines the use of the cellular phone (CP) in police agencies as an example of a relatively "low-tech" innovation in information technology. I draw on qualitative data, including interviews, focus group discussions, and firsthand observations conducted over the years in a number of American police agencies, to illustrate the impact of CPs on the social organization of police work in the early 1990s.[2] Dramaturgical analysis—the study of the selective use of messages to communicate to an audience—frames this study (Burke 1962; Goffman 1959). Dramaturgy reveals how the emergent meanings of technology arising from changes in communication and symbolization shape work processes and authority patterns (Weick 1988).

The chapter proceeds as follows. I first consider why technology is "dramatic." I next take up certain contextual features of policing, focusing in particular on the discretion that obtains for police officers of the lowest rank and other more or less special organizational features associated with what Lipsky (1978) calls "street-level bureaucracies." This sets the stage for an examination of how the drama of technology is played out in police agencies using CPs as the example of choice. The chapter concludes with a brief consideration of the consequences for policing (and police organizations) of information technology generally.

DRAMATURGY

Dramaturgy is a theoretical perspective that uses the metaphor of the theater to explore how the communication of messages to an audience conveys information and creates impressions that shape social interactions (Goffman 1959, 1974, 1983). Dramaturgical sociology sees social life as if it were a kind of theater. It studies the ways in which patterns of communication *selectively* sustain definitions of situations (a coded or schematic picture). This process of selective presentation constitutes *drama*. *Actors* (persons, groups, and organizations) perform using *fronts* (appearance, manner, and props) and *settings* (places in which behavior takes place) to convey realizations and idealizations to audiences. Through drama, individuals, groups, organizations, and societies imagine, constitute, and speak to themselves about themselves. Communication is produced by actors in various roles and settings, using various genres, to achieve audience compliance with a performance. Interaction shapes conduct by conferring meaning on physical objects, perspectives, or attitudes toward them and definitions of their capacities.

Within organizations, messages are encoded and decoded by communicants, and a working consensus on meaning is sought as teams of fellow communicants emerge relative to a given audience. The interaction order so shaped is the basis for understanding "what is happening here" and thus guides definitions of situations within an organization. Communications serve to mark both the instrumental and expressive features of exchanges. Once an actor takes a position or a line, others are bound to honor it, to defer to the performer, unless disruptions, role conflicts, or team management problems emerge. Interaction is then both an information exchange and a character contest.

Message presentation is often strategic, intended to *either* over- or under-emphasize some aspects of the communicational package and thus produce an impression. As a result, strategic organizational interaction often involves contests and power as various actors struggle to create, maintain, or dismantle a definition of a situation. Since communication is the basis for legitimation of commands and deference to authority, dramaturgy reveals potential conflicts and organizational dynamics. Yet patterns of interaction within which message presentations occur are not constantly negotiated or rediscovered. Interaction patterns tend to become routinized within a community of practice (Brown and Duguid 1991). This interaction order is marked and made visible by a ritual order, a set of known routines that connect patterns of deference, self-esteem, and organizational position.

ORGANIZATION AND TECHNOLOGY

General features of organizational response to technology are known. New technology (i.e., the means by which work is accomplished within a bounded, authoritatively ordered social system) is usually introduced by management to increase production and maintain control over workers and work processes (Thomas 1992). While the managerial assumption appears to be that power and authority relations will remain unchanged, it is well known that relationships between workers, supervisors, and top management are frequently altered by new technologies (Barley 1986; Roethlisberger and Dixon 1939; Thomas 1994). Changes in technology also make a symbolic statement about current technologies; about social roles, status, and authority; and about the distribution of power and decision making. Those with control over work processes may find such control at risk as new means to accomplish that work are introduced (Zuboff 1988).

Information processing technology, perhaps best seen as a "family" of related technologies of varying complexity and capacity, shapes communication within an organization both literally and figuratively. Recent ethnographic studies of the impact of information technology on work (and workers) focus on the organizational context within which the meaning of new information systems develops (e.g., Barley 1986, 1988; Orlikowski and Robey 1991; Orlikowski and Yates 1994; Zuboff 1988). These studies suggest that new technologies often destabilize the power balance between organizational segments by altering communication patterns, roles relationships, the division of labor, established formats for organizational communication, and taken-for-granted routines.

A drama of technology framework offers a natural history approach that is sensitive to time. A liminal period foreshadowing changes in power relations follows the introduction of new technology during which various segments of an organization negotiate (through statement and counterstatement) the meaning of the technology. In due course, reconstitution and redefinition of the technology occurs as work tasks and authority relations again become more or less stabilized. The dramaturgic study of technology sees changes in work process as carrying the potential to shift meaning and thus alter action patterns in an organization. Consider, for example, the kinds of changes the introduction of the CP makes possible in police agencies:

1. The CP changes physical settings because it occupies space and displaces other material objects in the work environment. The CP occupies the center console of the patrol car and thus forces a rearrangement of standard radio equipment, the storage of shotguns, the placement of a patrol officer's writing surface (typically, an attaché case), notepads, flashlight, nightstick, and other work tools.

2. The CP (re)shapes sociotechnical interactions (work-related talk) surrounding organizationally directed tasks. Officers can communicate to other officers without being monitored, arrange meetings, express meta-comments on other communications, and talk with friends while on duty.

3. The CP alters patterns of organizational authority if workers and work routines come under new forms of supervision or if the technology reduces face-to-face supervision. The CP permits direct, unmonitored communications with the public.

4. The CP introduces new and amplifies old modes of uncertainty in work processes. It provides an additional communication channel and may be used to call for assistance or request information. To the extent that the radio is used by officers to monitor each other's tasks and movements, communications on the CP make colleagues' actions less predictable.

5. The CP introduces a new symbol in the organization which is (initially) status enhancing for some and status reducing for others. In many police organizations, only top management [officials] have car phones. Only in a few cities are patrol vehicles so equipped. The CP connotes status in this context. More generally, the CP itself conveys a statement about the nature and content of previous work processes as well as the means through which work responsibilities are to be communicated and controlled.

6. The CP alters patterns of trust in the organization and introduces equivocality as messages are passed back and forth via a new communication channel (Manning 1988; Weick 1979). A new channel raises questions: How

trustworthy is this channel (to interception, monitoring)? How trustworthy is the sender? The receiver? The message?

7. The CP alters certain work routines and helps shape new norms. A routine traffic stop, for example, is altered when officers have the ability to directly call a tow truck, an ambulance, emergency medical services, fire services, or record checks without broadcasting over the police radio.

These alterations offer some intriguing tales and can potentially sharpen our understanding of technological innovation and organizational transformation. They can do so, however, only if the social and historical context within which a new technology enters an organization is also understood. To this end, a quick but highly focused sketch of the police world, past and present, is presented below. Particular attention is directed to (1) the social organization of policing, (2) police technology generally, and, to anticipate the analysis of the CP that follows, (3) the drama of technology as typically played out in police agencies.

The Social Organization of Policing

Centralized command and control in police organizations operates via the radio, phone, computers, behavioral routines, procedures, rules and regulations, and close supervision (Bordua and Reiss 1966). The guiding conceit is that communication with the dispatcher links patrol officers to a single voice of authority, produces official records of decision making, makes the police more accountable, and permits civilian review and audit, especially of major incidents. All communications theoretically are monitored and recorded. In practice, however, recording and monitoring reflects both rank and status within the organization. Most emphasis is on control of the lower participants: telephone operators (usually "civilians"), dispatchers (usually lower ranking uniformed officers), and patrol officers. To the extent that traces, electronic or paper, remain of communications, they form part of a reconstructed record used in internal affairs investigations, departmental hearings, media inquiries, or legal proceedings.

Police organizations are inspectorial bureaucracies. They are low-hierarchy organizations with more than 80 percent of their personnel at the lowest rank (the majority in the patrol division). Most information is generated and filtered by patrol officers, and they determine the quality, amount, and content of most of the information that rises to middle and top management. Patrol officers are relatively unskilled and begin (and often end) their careers on patrol. They are given little training for the job, nor are they provided advancement on the basis of educational achievement. They are promoted by mastering a series of written and oral examinations based largely on their knowledge of departmental rules and regulations. The organization tends to be rule bound and emphasizes strict discipline. Some argue that police agencies are "paramilitary organizations," although the widespread dispersal of officers obviates close immediate supervision (Jermier and Berkes 1979).

As a result of rank hierarchy, ecological segregation of patrol officers, and high discretion and value on immediate decision making, three segments exist within policing: patrol, middle management (sergeants and lieutenants), and top management (ranks above lieutenant) (Manning 1993). Occupational themes that help shape activities in the patrol and middle management segments of the organization such as defining "real police work" as on-the-street decision making contrast with themes held by top management such as the importance of public service and accountability. Members of each segment believe they are doing the same job but see the work quite differently (Manning 1977, chap. 3).

Police patrol practices exaggerate the importance of rule-oriented activities and reward the myriad skills of deviance and punishment avoidance (Kapeler et al. 1994). Patrol officers cultivate sophisticated means to produce the appearance of rule following (Bittner 1990; Fielding 1988; Rubinstein 1972, Van Maanen 1977). These include the routinization of actions, such as communication "by the numbers" over the radio, "ritualism," or filling out forms and doing paperwork to "cover one's ass" and reduce liability, and overt adherence to formal procedures combined with a covert disdain for authority and the command and middle management segments.

"Real policing" for patrol officers is construed as actions taken in the "here and now," and the core of "real police work" is thought to be revealed by the rapid resolution of an ongoing problem, often employing threats and force if seen as necessary (Bittner 1990). Information is personalized, often retained in memory rather than written, and embedded in the preference for secrecy characteristic of policing (Westley 1970). Abstract rules, policies, and procedures, as well as computerized information, *contrast* sharply with traditional modes of patrol decision making as well as with the ex post facto nature of most police first-line supervision (Van Maanen 1981). Officers spend long periods out of direct contact with the organization except through the radio. Their discretion is high, loosely coupled to the communication center (Manning 1988). Patrol officers get minimal feedback on the results of their work activities, are socially isolated from the dispatchers and operators, write brief and elliptical reports summarizing actions taken while on duty (written records are very short and highly formatted, and officers are not fond of the paperwork requirements of the job [Manning 1979, pp. 220-224]), and cling to secretive, personalized information. Police organizations are integrated by formal rank and are punishment oriented but also facilitate and encourage individual initiative and decision making.

Organizational controls on the worker (primarily the lower participants) and the forms of resistance they elicit are manifest in police agencies. Many patrol practices can be seen as strategic acts in the drama of work control, acts that require tacit teamwork to sustain an impression of propriety to various audiences (the public, colleagues, sergeants, command officers). Some collusive actions arise because policing is believed to be risky and highly uncertain. It is occasionally very dangerous, creating work-related anxiety and stress. But these—perhaps inherent—anxieties and uncertainties are amplified by a police ideology which positively values danger and is especially strong in the patrol segment. Police teamwork reveals a pattern of adhering to rigid procedures in the face of risk, work uncertainty, and the need to exercise authority (Skolnick 1966; Van Maanen 1977). Patrol officers see themselves as unsupported by "management" and at risk of punishment for complex decisions made on the street. Antagonisms and conflict between those at the top and bottom of the organization are heightened by the belief prevalent among the lower ranks that, while all officers share the same basic experience and conception of the work, management does not act in a supportive fashion when shootings, accidents, beatings, and mistakes arise.

This setting can be glossed as an organizational culture of distrust, punishment, and secrecy. The introduction of new technology signals new routines, rules, and contingencies and possible organizational change. Change symbolizes risk. Historically, new technology has served to increase information, surveillance, and risk of discipline and punishment for those at the bottom of the police hierarchy.

Police Technology

Technology has always held out tantalizing promise to the police. They have sought it and frequently advanced claims to professional status based on their technology (Colton 1979). Information technologies in particular are attractive to police agencies. More information is assumed to be better than less, although the primary emphasis is on increasing applied, useful, and succinct information. Large American urban police departments, in spite of evaluations showing the minimal impact of computer technology on crime control, efficient record keeping, and improved resource allocation (Manning 1992a, 1992b; Tien and Colton 1979), are now introducing a second and third generation of large mainframe computers and complex, expensive information software such as geocoding, automatic vehicle locators, and computerized fingerprint files. The organizational structure, strategy, and tactics of policing, however, remain largely unchanged (Sparrow 1993).[3]

Broad technological change shaping the means of policing proceeds apace, but the most important changes have been in the introduction of computer-based dispatching (and the related 911 system) and management information systems. In the last 15 years, however, federal funding for police innovation and research (apart from the Clinton Crime Bill of 1994) has been sharply reduced. Local funding has replaced large federal grants, and as a result, innovations such as CPs, laptop computers and mobile digital terminals (MDTs, which combine radio, telephone, and a monitor that displays data directly from computer files to a screen located in a police car) are funded by local authorities.

New information technologies have long been welcomed by top management in police organizations as "breakthroughs" in scientific policing and seized on as tools for the enhanced coordination among and discipline of patrol officers (Stead 1977). Innovations have been aimed toward increasing supervisory control of patrol officers, facilitating more rapid responses to reported incidents, improving the quality of police response to calls, upgrading the record-keeping process, and integrating various databases (Tien and Colton 1979). Information technologies such as computer-aided dispatch (CAD) and management information systems have been used for strategic planning, information storage and retrieval, and on-line responsive capacities (Tien and Colton 1979). These innovations have been widely adopted by police agencies and have reduced both response and record-keeping time while increasing the visibility and organizational traces of a patrol officer's activities. Ironically, such changes also have increased the workload of the police in urban areas. Although officers still enjoy large blocks of uncommitted time, the number of radio-dispatched calls handled and the amount of externally obligated patrol time have increased as distant, computerized modes of organizational control have been put in place (Greene and Klockers 1991). These technologies extend the supervisory potential of command over patrol activities, although it remains the case that little face-to-face supervision occurs (Reiss 1992; Van Maanen 1981).

These changes suggest a slow erosion of traditional policing practices. As officers have become increasingly oriented to the radio and computerized information, they have withdrawn from observation, interaction with citizens, and the pursuit of self-initiated investigation and activity (Reiss 1992). One consequence of this shift is a reduction in the quality and character of police supervision—the subtle substitution of computer records, on-screen data, and radio-telephone interaction for face-to-face supervision and on-the-street guidance (Reiss 1992).

The Drama of Technology

Recall that the dramaturgic framework suggests a liminal period follows the introduction of new technology. This period features negotiations over meanings among relevant parties and foreshadows potential changes in power relations. In due course, a reconstitution or redefinition of technology occurs, and a new integration of work and authority, now embedding the technology, follows. Consider this pattern in general form as it is applied to the introduction of new information technologies in police agencies.

Management, by introducing a new technology, makes the first gesture—a thesis. They may phase it in gradually or bring it on suddenly. Changes in work routines result, and tacit meanings brought to the work by those whose work routines are disrupted create both tensions and protean responses. Efforts are made to reduce the incongruity between the new traces and records of assignments and current activity made possible by the information technology and the valued, personalistic *craftwork of policing* tradition of police agencies that emphasizes self-monitoring, personal knowledge, decisiveness, and calling for assistance from others only when needed. Police management asserts that the technology increases the personal safety of officers by monitoring their assignments and movements, increases the information available to patrol officers, and reduces the time required for record inquiries and record keeping. Facets of the new technology are emphasized differentially across segments of the organization. Thus technology is given an organizational shape and placed on a symbolically defined, but contentious, social stage.

Normalization efforts are followed by adaptive responses, resistance, antitheses, or, most generally, *symbolic counterstatements*. These counterstatements compete for definitional hegemony within the organization. Responses to new technology take at least three forms (Pfaffenberger 1992). Each form or counterstatement generates context-specific meanings of technology and competes for dominance in defining the situation.

Countersymbolization. Some organizational members may both undervalue and underuse or eschew a new technology. They publicly assert its irrelevance and thus dramatize the power of the nonusing segment. Command and middle management rarely carry (or listen to) police radios. Few skillfully use computers. Investigators generally do not listen to the patrol radio channel, nor are they much guided by its directions, requests, and implications. These organizational segments can choose to devalorize the technology to symbolize their discretion and mark their autonomy from controlling devices. Conversely, the radio and related recording and monitoring modes are symbolically associated with the lowest status work of the police, uniform patrol, where the introduction and physical placement of technology in a patrol vehicle is accomplished by management decree (Manning 1988, chap. 2). In general, the level of supervision is inversely related to the responsibility of police employees. For example, in a large midwestern police department, 911 operators and dispatchers were monitored by far more devices such as written records, computer records, audiotapes, and personal supervision than were patrol officers (Manning 1988).

Counterappropriation. This form of symbolic counterstatement refers to the secret or modified use of a technology to undermine dominant meanings. It is an index of ambivalence. Counterappropriation is illustrated by patrol officer use of scanners, radar detectors, second guns, sap gloves, brass knuckles, drop knives, and other illegal weapons. One patrol officer reported that he slept in an out-of-the-way parking lot and turned on his radar detector to alert him to any vehicular movements nearby. He called it his "sergeant detector." Technologies may substitute illegitimate means for legitimate means and serve to maintain officers' control over their work and even increase police power vis-à-vis the policed.

Counterdelegation. Some organization members may overvalue a technology. Counterdelegation refers to the granting of excessive power and significance to a particular technology, thus elevating its potential to shape work. This attitude signifies resistance, although ironic consequence may sometimes occur. In a medium-sized city in Michigan, the head of the patrol division uses e-mail messages to supervise officers. To measure compliance with his supervisory requests, he checks to see if the e-mail messages have been received. Counterdelegation is illustrated also when radios or pagers are turned off, never turned on, or simply not carried or when a seat-belt buzzer is rendered inoperable by locking belts together and sitting on them. Officers in one medium-sized city turn off the sound on their video cameras or do not insert videotapes into the machines at the beginning of a shift. Claims that the radio malfunctioned or could not be heard are often used by patrol officers to avoid calls. Similarly, dispatchers are given false locations and current activity descriptions by patrol officers. Dispatchers, too, manipulate patrol officers in knowing ways. Quite common is the ploy used by patrol units who hear a call assigned over the radio and then arrive at the call as an unassigned but self-announced "backup" unit and, as such, remain "out of service" until the paperwork is completed by the unit assigned the call. This teamwork, collusion among officers, is designed to maintain an impression and sustain a collective "front" or "line" for a given audience, in this case, dispatchers and supervisors (Goffman 1959).

As statements and counterstatements (of various types) take place across ranks and time, a *technological reconstitution and integration* may gradually occur in the organization. Management makes the effort to embed the new technology within current authority patterns and organizational aims while those subject to the technology work out their own response to such efforts. The resultant organizational change is thus a matter of time, segment, and kind of response (and counterresponse) occasioned by the new technology.

CELLULAR PHONES AND THE POLICE

CPs highlight particular aspects of the drama of technology in police agencies. CPs are rapidly growing in use and popularity. Since 1985, the number of CPs has risen from some 340,000 to about 8 million in the United States ("Cops Who Kill Themselves" 1994). There were perhaps as many as 92 million in use in 1999. The number used by the police is unknown.

The CP was introduced in several departments to facilitate community policing in the mid-1980s and continues to grow in popularity. CPs allow community police officers a direct means of communicating with people in neighborhoods. But use of CPs extends well beyond community policing experiments. In Lansing, Michigan, and Madison, Wisconsin, the CP is in patrol cars and also is used by management-level police up to the rank of chief. Auburn Hills and Warren, Michigan, provide all patrol vehicles with MDT consoles containing built-in phones. The CP is standard equipment of the patrol cars in Dallas and widely used in Houston, Texas. CPs are spreading rapidly in Texas among supervisory personnel and in specialized units such as vice and narcotics (e.g., Midland, Waco, Amarillo). In short, CPs represent an innovation in police departments whose time has apparently come.

CPs are used in many ways. They are used officially by patrol officers to check on details of a police call with callers, to verify assignments, to discover if an incident remains ongoing, to discuss jobs with other officers, and to check information with the communications center. Officers can call other agencies such as social welfare agencies, other police departments, or emergency medical services rather than request police operators in the communication division to place such calls. They are also used unofficially for informal officer-to-officer communication, for pizza delivery, and for personal calls. In East Haven, Connecticut, the chief of police announced that CPs were being removed from police cruisers because they were being used to call 900 numbers that offer sexually explicit conversations with women ("Cellular Phones" 1992). A Federal Bureau of Investigation (FBI) informant reports that phones used by several federal law enforcement agencies in a large midwestern city were altered to block the capacity to make 900 calls. Thus was a scandal avoided.

At the supervisory level, CPs are used to coordinate field actions if radio channels are crowded or useless because the radio frequencies of participating agencies are incompatible, by vice and specialized (e.g., SWAT, TACT) units to communicate secretly about a raid or surveillance (i.e., members of such units often assume that police radio channels are being monitored, although it is also recognized by them that CPs can be scanned as well), and by top-level police officers to inquire about or offer advice on in-progress incidents as reported by middle-level officers and sergeants.

By 1995, it [was] clear that the CP [had] stimulated a variety of organizational responses. In its early guise, it was a communication channel outside the bureaucratic controls that applied to the use of the police radio. Countersymbolization was minimal. Top police command did not undervalue CPs, nor did patrol officers. CPs were used at both the top and the bottom of the command structure. Counterappropriation did occur as officers used the phones to call friends, avoid supervision, reduce work by handling complaints by phone, and, more generally, avoid work where possible. Counterdelegation seems to be emerging now as departments bring MDTs into patrol vehicles rather than CPs alone. MDTs are regarded by patrol officers as management tools. A supervisor can check when the microphone of the MDT is converted to a CP and view numbers called on the monitor. Moreover, supervisors can obtain printouts of patrol unit activities—of inquiries, vehicular and pedestrian stops, arrests, and so forth. Such output from MDTs is used to monitor and assess patrol officer "productivity."

It appear[ed] that the CP in late 1995 [was] entering the routinization phase. The dramaturgic perspective introduced earlier suggests that new technologies elicit different responses in organizational segments over time and will therefore have specific or "distributional" meanings assigned to them as well as general meanings. What changes can be discerned in authority patterns, collegial relations, and the police role itself as a result of the introduction of the CP?

The CP reduces the capacity of the command segment to anticipate, monitor, supervise, and control the actions of field officers. The segmentalized character of police work sustains a gap between patrol officers and sergeants and both of these segments with the command segment. The CP may increase or decrease these gaps over time, but it remains a device that buffers intersegment relationships within the organization and relationships between the organization and its environment. Presently, in cities such as Dallas, where all patrol units are equipped with CPs, officers can avoid central command structure and recording devices by directly communicating with the public or colleagues via the CP. In Dallas, CP communications are not recorded and therefore cannot be retrieved for use in disciplinary hearings or used by the courts in liability cases or by news agencies or citizens to reconstitute events. If this pattern prevails, communication via CP will further weaken the supervision of officers.

Officer-to-officer private communication at a distance by CP alters the nature of accountability and serves to maintain officers' teamwork or frontwork with regard to superior officers. Collusion is thus facilitated as when CPs are used to conceal police action. In Dallas, patrol officers developed a counter-appropriation strategy, the "Alamo Run." An on-duty patrol officer would wager that he or she could drive a patrol car from Dallas to San Antonio (some 250+ miles), have a Polaroid picture taken at the Alamo, and return inside an eight-hour shift. Fellow officers pledged to alert the officer via CP of anything untoward in the officer's assigned territory and to cover the calls.

On the other hand, if phone records are obtained for CPs, they can be used to monitor and hold officers accountable. Phone scanners can be used to locate and listen in to private conversations among officers. The integration of the CP and MDT produces an organizational record of calls and thus changes the potential for organizational supervision and sanction for improper use. It also means that, rather than being an alternative means by which to dramatize a counterstatement, the CP becomes yet another source of potentially controlling surveillance.

The availability of the CP changes expressive games (Goffman 1967, 1969). Deference to a line and a face, and the expressive order that lies behind it, can be privately orchestrated via the CP. Officers can talk about matters officially restricted or considered improper on the radio such as off-color jokes, racist and sexist remarks, atrocity tales, and blustering personal opinions. Moreover, the CP widens the range of communicational deceptions possible that permit the evasion of institutionalized rules and procedures about reporting, feedback, and legal liability. Widespread use of the CP creates new communication routines and partially decentralizes (and decenters) power.

The CP also disconnects a channel from the official organizational memory. A "comprehensive computer record" of patrol activities based on monitored radio communications no longer reproduces the sequence of decisions and actions made by officers in the field. Although such disconnections have always occurred when officers talked face-to-face off the air, it is now possible to rapidly collude at a distance via an unmonitored CP. Because information is essential to resource allocation, feedback is required from officers to sergeants and to top command. If no traces of decisions are to be located in organization memory, it reduces feedback and the police capacity to tailor new and more flexible or innovative responses to complex, unfolding events.

Routines created by officers to cope with new technologies are often secret and invisible (at least initially) to command officers. For example, using the CP to conceal one's location and activities from other officers is a learned routine. The semiprivate nature of CP communications makes it unlikely that such a routine will be widely known (or shared) by management. This routine is not part of the daily experience of management, nor did [those in management] experience it while in the lower ranks themselves, for the technology is new. While the supervisory use of CPs is an extension of command activities, patrol use of CPs is quite often a modification of accepted procedures.

The CP also allows changes in intraorganizational role relations with colleagues and in interorganizational role relations with members of the public. Unlike radio requests, using the CP permits record checks to be done without the knowledge of other officers. This heightens the isolation of officers. Decisions to act communicated by (or inferred from) the CP are not overheard by colleagues. At the same time, however, the CP alters teamwork opportunities and tightens some colleague relations while loosening others. Direct calls to colleagues via phone can stimulate mutual cooperation. Moreover, they allow officers to communicate directly and privately with other officers across political space (e.g., precinct, city, county, state, and national boundaries). Officers can alter political jurisdictional boundaries through personal decisions (e.g., calling for assistance from officers from other police agencies). This is, of course, an organizational and occupational benefit and may increase officer safety since radio communication across police departments is often impossible currently because radio channels are not shared. It also changes the relationship between patrol officers and specialized units, who can be alerted directly without the use of the main communications center, and between patrol officers and first-line supervisors, who can be reached privately.

Finally, it is worth noting that the communicational processes made possible by the CP could eventually draw officers closer to the public by facilitating direct communication and direct verification of calls. This pattern of communication between patrol officers and the public mimics the community policing movement's emphasis on police officers developing interpersonal skills and being in contact with citizens in non-crime-generated encounters. At present, however, the police seem little interested in such possibilities beyond those officers specifically assigned to community policing tasks.

CELLULAR PHONES, TIME, AND ORGANIZATION CHANGE

The CP represents a seemingly modest innovation that is, for the most part, embedded within the existing vertical and horizontal authority structures of policing. When used alone, the CP is a source of organization change, for it expands (slightly) police officer discretion. The CP then has the potential to elaborate characteristic dilemmas of inspectorial bureaucracies. Whether it will reshape patterns of authority remains to be seen. Since officers already have considerable discretion to "work the system" and already are at varying risk of punishment for errors and delicts that become known to management, the eventual impact of the CP is not easily predicted. More critically perhaps, the decentralized character of policing (viewed always by management as a problem) and the increasing availability of multiple-use information packages for police vehicles (and officers) such as MDTs may well obviate discussion of the impact of the CP alone.

The form of drama put forth here suggests that time is perhaps the most important variable in the study of the meanings of technology. Technology has a life within organizations, and those in policing who did not learn or use a given technology as a patrol officer—the first assignment of virtually all officers—will not grasp the meaning of the technology in the context of its use. Differential knowledge of the uses of new technology characterizes police cohorts and segments within the organization. Length of time in the organization as well as time in rank or position divides those at the top and middle from those on the bottom. The old days are not what they used to be (and may never have been). Change seems to be accelerating in succeeding organizational cohorts. But the learning capacity of the police suffers if the official memory of the organization is disconnected from those actions linked partially or fully to the use of CPs—although an unofficial memory will surely accumulate within and across agencies (and levels) in the form of an oral lore of stories surrounding episodes like the Alamo Run. It does seem likely, however, that police organizations will soon closely monitor CP use and thus incorporate data from CPs into formal records. Counterstatement begets counterstatement, and the drama continues.

This discussion of police technology suggests the utility of the dramaturgic perspective for the analysis of technological innovation in organizational contexts. Significant variation in the pattern of adaptation and resistance is to be expected and can be accounted for only when patterns of meaning are understood in terms of the impressions members of the organization wish to convey to particular audiences. Technology is shaped by organizational routines and structures, but it also serves to modify these routines and induce learning within and occasionally across organizational segments. A natural history approach, combined with a concern for deeply embedded work routines, perspectives, interests, and traditions, is thus needed to specify further studies of organizational adaptation to changes in information technology.[4]

NOTES

1. "Sailor" is a Texas pronunciation of "cellular." I was mystified when I first heard police officers in a seminar refer to "sailor phones" and thought that they were discussing naval communications. I finally worked out that the string of consonants in "cellular" is a mouthful for these men and that they were referring to mobile CPs.

2. My methods of collecting and organizing systematic field data on police uses of information technology are detailed at length in Manning (1977, 1979, 1988). Police organizations studied include a large midwestern police force, the metropolitan police force of London, and a large constabulary in the English midlands. The field materials have been used to examine (comparatively) the role of information in policing generally, drug policing specifically, and the call dispatch systems in use in these agencies. Additional—but less systematic—materials were gathered at law enforcement management institutes held in Lubbock and San Antonio, Texas, in 1991 and 1992, respectively. Four focus groups on work conditions were conducted by the author and a colleague, Jane White, with top command officers, inspectors, and sergeants in a very large midwestern police department in May 1994. Empirical materials presented in this [chapter] come from the American studies.

3. Police technology has advanced in the last 20 years. Some examples include developments in forensic technologies such as DNA typing from computer databases, biochemical assays and accident reconstruction, refinement of weapons including semiautomatic weapons, development of force-application techniques, and training in the use of noncoercive persuasive techniques. Since 1970, however, the most important changes in policing have been in computer-assisted information technology. The police now possess sophisticated data-gathering and environment-scanning capacity that includes management information systems, computer-assisted dispatching, and enhanced 911 (showing a caller's address and telephone number on an operator's screen). The automation of records and computer linkages among various databases (e.g., motor vehicle registration, driver's licenses, state and local criminal records, the FBI's National Criminal Information Center for criminal records and outstanding warrants) is ongoing. Other inventions, many quite popular in suburban departments, include in-car video cameras for filming traffic stops; fax systems for warrant approval; geocoded software to combine sets of information based on spatial distribution of city streets, services, risks, crime patterns, and calls for service; computer-based fingerprint files, mug shots, and records and the integration of these databases on a network or regional basis; and the use of mobile digital terminals that transmit information direct from the dispatcher to a screen in the patrol car. I am grateful to Steve Mastrofski (personal correspondence) for many items on this list.

4. Variations of this chapter were presented at an informal seminar at the University of Michigan School of Business Administration, Ann Arbor, MI, in July 1992 and to the Interdisciplinary Organization Studies Seminar at the University of Michigan in October 1992. Carole K. Barnett at the University of Michigan and John Van Maanen as the coeditor of this issue provided very helpful comments and editorial suggestions on earlier drafts.

REFERENCES

Barley, S., "Technology as an Occasion for Structuring," *Administrative Sci. Quarterly,* 31 (1986), 78-108.
———, "Technology, Power, and the Social Organization of Work," in N. Tomaso (Ed.), *Research in the Sociology of Organizations,* Vol. 6, JAI, Greenwich, CT, 1988, 33-80.
Bittner, E., *Aspects of Police Work,* Northeastern University Press, Boston, MA, 1990.

Bordua, D. and A. J. Reiss, "Command, Control, and Charisma: Reflections on Police Bureaucracy," *American J. Sociology,* 72 (1966), 68-76.

Brown, J. S. and P. Duguid, "Organization Learning and Communities of Practice," *Organization Sci.,* 2 (1991), 40-57.

Burke, K., *A Grammar of Motives and a Rhetoric of Motives,* Meridian Publishing, Cleveland, OH, 1962.

"Cellular Phones," *Law Enforcement News,* September 9, 1992, p. 7.

Colton, K., *Police Computer Technology,* D. C. Heath, Lexington, MA, 1979.

"Cops Who Kill Themselves," *Newsweek,* September 26, 1994, p. 58.

Fielding, N., *Joining Forces,* Routledge, London, 1988.

Goffman, E., *The Presentation of Self in Everyday Life,* Doubleday, New York, 1959.

————, *Interaction Ritual,* Aldine, Chicago, 1967.

————, *Strategic Interaction,* University of Pennsylvania Press, Philadelphia, 1969.

————, *Frame Analysis,* Harvard University Press, Cambridge, MA, 1974.

————, "The Interaction Order," *American Sociological Review,* 48 (1983), 1-17.

Greene, J. and C. Klockers, "Police Workloads," in C. Klockers and S. Mastrofski (Eds.), *Thinking About Police,* McGraw-Hill, New York, 1991.

Jermier, J. and L. Berkes, "Leader Behavior in a Police Command Bureaucracy: A Closer Look at the Quasi-Military Model," *Administrative Sci. Quarterly,* 24 (1979), 1-23.

Kapeler, V., R. Sluder, and G. Alpert, *Forces of Deviance,* Waveland, Prospect Heights, IL, 1994.

Lipsky, M., *Street-Level Bureaucrats,* Russell Sage, New York, 1978.

Manning, P. K., *Police Work,* MIT Press, Cambridge, MA, 1977.

————, *The Narc's Game,* MIT Press, Cambridge, MA, 1979.

————, *Symbolic Communication,* MIT Press, Cambridge, MA, 1988.

————, "Technological Dramas and the Police," *Criminology,* 30 (1992a), 327-346.

————, "The Police and Information Technologies," in M. Tonry and N. Morris (Eds.), *Modern Policing,* University of Chicago Press, Chicago, 1992b, 349-398.

————, "The Police Occupational Culture," unpublished paper, Michigan State University, 1993.

Orlikowski, W. and D. Robey, "Information Technology and the Structuring of Organizations," *Information Systems Res.,* 2 (1991), 143-169.

———— and J. Yates, "Genre Repertoire: The Structuring of Communicative Practices in Organizations," *Administrative Sci. Quarterly,* 39 (1994), 541-574.

Pfaffenberger, B., "Technological Dramas," *Science, Technology, and Social Values,* 7 (1992), 10-35.

Roethlisberger, F. J. and W. J. Dixon, *Management and the Worker,* Harvard University Press, Cambridge, MA, 1939.

Rubinstein, J., *City Police,* Farrar, Straus, and Giroux, New York, 1972.

Skolnick, J., *Justice Without Trial,* John Wiley, New York, 1966.

Sparrow, M., "Information Systems and the Development of Policing," Perspectives on Policing Series, No. 16, National Institute of Justice, Harvard University, 1993.

Stead, J. (Ed.), *Pioneers in Policing,* Patterson Smith, Montclair, NJ, 1977.

Thomas, R. J., "Organizational Politics and Technological Change," *J. Contemporary Ethnography,* 20 (1992), 442-477.

————, *What Machines Can't Do,* University of California Press, Berkeley, 1994.

Tien, J. and K. W. Colton, "Police Command, Control, and Communications," in Law Enforcement Assistance Administration, *What Works?* Government Printing Office, Washington, DC, 1979.

Van Maanen, J., "Working the Street," in H. Jacobs (Ed.), *Prospects of Reform in the Criminal Justice System,* Sage, Beverly Hills, CA, 1977, 83-130.

————, "The Boss," in M. Punch (Ed.), *Control in the Police Organization,* MIT Press, Cambridge, MA, 1981, 227-250.

Weick, K., *The Social Psychology of Organizing,* 2nd ed., Addison-Wesley, Reading, MA, 1979.

————, "Technology as Equivoque: Sense-Making in New Technologies," in P. S. Goodman and L. Sproull (Eds.), *Technology and Organizations,* Jossey-Bass, San Francisco, 1988, 1-44.

Westley, W., *Violence and the Police,* MIT Press, Cambridge, MA, 1970.

Zuboff, S., *In the Age of the Smart Machine,* Basic Books, New York, 1988.

9

Improvising Organizational Transformation Over Time

A Situated Change Perspective

WANDA J. ORLIKOWSKI

Organizational transformation—substantially changing an organization's structure and practices—has always been of interest to researchers and practitioners. For decades, however, questions of transformation remained largely backstage as organizational thinking and practice engaged in a discourse dominated by questions of stability. Oriented around the organizing principles of mass production and bureaucracy, such a discourse emphasized routinization, standardization, control, and automation. Today, however, many organizations face an altered economic, political, and technological world, a world in which flexibility, customization, and learning are the watchwords and visions of agile manufacturing, virtual corporations, and self-organizing teams are prominent. In such a world, stability is out, change is in.

As the backstage becomes increasingly center stage, it seems appropriate to examine the kinds of models that currently inform our understanding of organizational transformation and to consider their adequacy in the light of this new organizational stage. A range of perspectives on organizational transformation have developed over the past few decades (see Pettigrew [1985] and Wilson [1992] for extensive reviews). However, many of these perspectives—grounded as they are in the prior discourse of stability—are often poorly suited to a world where change is no longer a background activity but rather a way of organizational life. These perspectives embody assumptions about agency, context, technology, and change which may be inappropriate given the different social, technological, and economic conditions emerging today. To illustrate, consider three perspectives that have influenced studies of technology-based organizational transformation—planned change, technological imperative, and punctuated equilibrium.

Planned change models presume that managers are the primary source of organizational change and that these actors deliberately initiate and implement changes in response to perceived opportunities to improve organizational performance or "fit" with the environment. Such models have dominated the organizational change and development literatures and include force field analysis (Lewin 1951), contingency frameworks (Burns and Stalker 1961; Dunphy and Stace 1988; Galbraith 1973; Miles and Snow 1984), innovation theories (Hage and Aiken 1970; Meyer and Goes 1988; Zaltman et al. 1973), and practitioner-oriented prescriptions for organizational effectiveness (Deming 1986; Hammer and Champy 1993; Peters and Waterman 1982). This perspective has been criticized for treating change as a discrete event to be managed separately from the ongoing processes of organizing and for placing undue weight on the rationality of managers directing the change (Pettigrew 1985). From the vantage point of the new organizing discourse with its presumption of frequent change, learning, and self-organizing, such disembedding of change from the ongoing stream of organizational action and heavy reliance on foresightful managerial action are problematic.

In opposition to the voluntarism of planned change models, the *technological imperative* perspective affords little discretion to managers or any other organizational actors. Technology is seen as a primary and relatively autonomous driver of organizational change, so that the adoption of new technology creates predictable changes in organizations' structures, work routines, information flows, and performance (Blau et al. 1976; Carter 1984; Huber 1990; Leavitt and Whistler 1958). These organizational notions of a "technological imperative" echo a broader strain of technological determinism evident in sociohistorical studies (Winner 1986), economic analyses (Heilbroner 1967), and contemporary culture (Smith and Marx 1994) where the seduction of a "technological fix" is largely taken for granted. The absence of any significant role for agency in this perspective undermines possibilities for proactive organizational change, which is problematic for the new organizing discourse where assumptions of agility and flexibility require actors to explore, learn, and innovate new alternatives for working and organizing over time and in different circumstances. In addition, the deterministic logic of the technological imperative is incompatible with the open-ended nature of many new technologies which assume considerable user customization (Malone 1995) and thus user construction of capabilities and effects.

Punctuated equilibrium models arose in opposition to gradualist models which posit that organizational change is slow, incremental, and cumulative (Meyer et al. 1993). In contrast, punctuated equilibrium models assume change to be rapid, episodic, and radical. Gersick (1991, p. 12) writes that "relatively long periods of stability (equilibrium) [are] punctuated by compact periods of qualitative, metamorphic change (revolution)." Punctuated discontinuities are typically triggered by modifications in environmental or internal conditions, for example, new technology, process redesign, or industry deregulation. Such punctuated models have informed macro studies of long-term shifts in various industries (Abernathy and Clark 1985; Romanelli and Tushman 1994; Tushman and Romanelli 1985), while elaborations of this perspective have proposed a hybrid of the punctuated equilibrium and gradualist logics (Miller and Friesen 1984; Mintzberg 1987; Pettigrew et al. 1992; Tushman and Anderson 1986). Both the punctuated equilibrium perspective and its hybrids raise difficulties for the new organizing discourse because they are premised on the primacy of organizational stability. Whether improving an existing status quo or shifting to a new one, the assumption underlying these models is that the preferred condition for organizations is some sort of steady state or "equilibrium" (Mintzberg 1987). This presumption of stability (which is also shared, although more implicitly, by the planned change and technological imperative perspectives) begs questioning in a context of organizations experimenting with essentially nonstable organizational forms, processes, and technologies (e.g., self-organizing, flexible, customizable).

All three of the perspectives reviewed above also neglect what—following Mintzberg's (1979, 1987) distinction between deliberate and emergent strategies—may be termed "emergent change." Where deliberate change is the realization of a new pattern of organizing precisely as originally intended, emergent change is the realization of a new pattern of organizing in the absence of explicit, a priori intentions. Such emergent change is realized only in action and cannot be anticipated or planned (Mintzberg and Waters 1985). Because they are abstracted from the ongoing and grounded activities of organizational actors, the three perspectives on technology-based organizational transformation do not easily account for emergent change. Yet the notion of emergence is particularly relevant today as unprecedented environmental, technological, and organizational developments facilitate patterns of organizing which cannot be explained or prescribed by appealing to a priori plans and intentions. The variety of economic and social activity that has appeared on the World Wide Web in the past few years is just one recent and powerful example of such emergence.

The current discourse on technology-based organizational transformation thus embodies assumptions which are problematic in the light of an organizing discourse emphasizing emergence, flexibility, and self-organization. A perspective that posits change rather than stability as a way of organizational life may offer a more appropriate conceptual lens with which to think about change in contemporary organizations. I outline such an additional perspective in this chapter, suggesting that it affords a particularly powerful analytical strategy for examining and explaining technology-based organizational transformation.

A SITUATED CHANGE PERSPECTIVE

The new perspective proposed here is premised on the primacy of organizing practices in organizational change. While earlier practice-based research challenged the conventional wisdom that incremental changes always occur gradually (Tyre and Orlikowski 1994), the research discussed here questions the beliefs that organizational change must be planned, that technology is the primary cause of technology-based organizational transformation, and that radical changes always occur rapidly and discontinuously. While recognizing that organizational transformation can be, and often is, performed as a deliberate, orchestrated main event with key players, substantial technological and other resources, and considerable observable and experiential commotion, I want to explore another kind of organizational transformation here, one that is enacted more subtly, more slowly, and more smoothly, but no less significantly. Such organizational transformation is grounded in the ongoing practices of organizational actors and emerges out of their (tacit and not so tacit) accommodations to and experiments with the everyday contingencies, breakdowns, exceptions, opportunities, and unintended consequences that they encounter. March (1981, p. 564) notes,

> Because of the magnitude of some changes in organizations, we are inclined to look for comparably dramatic explanations for change, but the search for drama may often be a mistake. . . . Change takes place because most of the time most people in an organization do about what they are supposed to do; that is, they are intelligently attentive to their environments and their jobs.

Barley (1988, p. 51), similarly writes,

> Because forms of action and interaction are always negotiated and confirmed as
> actors with different interests and interpretations encounter shifting events . . . ,
> slippage between institutional templates and the actualities of daily life is prob-
> able. In such slippage resides the possibility of social innovation.

In this perspective, organizational transformation is not portrayed as a
drama staged by deliberate directors with predefined scripts and choreo-
graphed moves, or as the inevitable outcome of a technological logic, or as a
sudden discontinuity that fundamentally invalidates the status quo. Rather,
organizational transformation is seen here to be an ongoing improvisation enacted by organizational actors trying to make sense of and act coherently in
the world.

Invoking the notion of improvisation to understand organizational transformation owes much to Weick's (1993) claim that our ideas about organization design are based on an inappropriate architectural metaphor which por-
trays it as "a bounded activity that occurs at a fixed point in time," focusing on
"structures rather than processes . . . [where] structures are assumed to be stable solutions to a set of current problems" (p. 347). Instead, Weick proposes
the metaphor of theatrical improvisation, where organization design

> tends to be emergent and visible only after the fact. Thus the design is a piece
> of history, not a piece of architecture. . . . Design, viewed from the perspective
> of improvisation, is more emergent, more continuous, more filled with surprise,
> more difficult to control, more tied to the content of action, and more affected
> by what people pay attention to than are the designs implied by architecture.
> (pp. 348-351)

The notion of change as ongoing improvisation resonates with the focus on
situated action taken by practice researchers (Hutchins 1991; Lave 1988;
Suchman 1987). In contrast to the classical view of change as a process of
managerial planning, design, and intervention, Hutchins (1991), for example, argues that "several important aspects of a new organization are achieved
not by conscious reflection but by local adaptations" (p. 14). In research on
information technology, Rice and Rogers' (1980) concept of "reinvention"
and Ciborra and Lanzara's (1991) notion of "designing-in-action" similarly
echo some of the situated and improvisational ideas invoked here.

The kind of change process I intend with the notion of situated change is
well illustrated by Escher's *Metamorphose* series (Figure 9.1), where, as the
artist explains, through the passage of time, "a dynamic character is obtained
by a succession of figures in which changes of form appear gradually"

(Escher 1986, p. 120). Each variation of a given form is not an abrupt or discrete event, nor is it, by itself, discontinuous. Rather, through a series of ongoing and situated accommodations, adaptations, and alterations (that draw on previous variations and mediate future ones), sufficient modifications may be enacted over time that fundamental changes are achieved. There is no deliberate orchestration of change here,[1] no technological inevitability, no dramatic discontinuity, just recurrent and reciprocal variations in practice over time. Each shift in practice creates the conditions for further breakdowns, unanticipated outcomes, and innovations, which in their turn are responded to with more variations. And such variations are ongoing; there is no beginning or end point in this change process.

A view of organizational transformation as situated change is grounded in assumptions of action, not stability. Organizations are enacted. They are constituted by the ongoing agency of organizational members and have no existence apart from such action (Giddens 1984). Every action taken by organization members either reproduces existing organizational properties or alters them. Through sustained adjustments in organizing practices—however unintentional and unacknowledged—social changes can be enacted. Change is thus inherent in everyday human action. This basic premise of the situated change perspective echoes March's (1981) observation that "in its fundamental structure, a theory of organizational change should not be remarkably different from a theory of ordinary action" (p. 564). Informed by Giddens' (1984) notions of structuring, Weick's (1993) improvisational metaphor, and the insights of practice research, this chapter outlines a perspective on change as inherent in everyday practice and as inseparable from the ongoing and situated actions of organizational members. Such a perspective emerged as central to my analysis of an organization implementing and using new information technology.

In the research study described in this chapter, I examine how subtle shifts in action by organizational actors transformed—over a two-year period—aspects of their work practices, organizing structures, and coordination mechanisms, and I explore the implications of such shifts for the organization. My analysis laid the groundwork for a practice-based perspective, which offers a conceptual lens with which to focus on types of transformations not discernible to the perspectives of planned change, technological imperative, and punctuated equilibrium. The situated change perspective is offered as a complement to, not a substitute for, the existing change perspectives. In most organizations, transformations will occur through a variety of logics. Indeed, the study discussed reveals elements of planned and punctuated change triggered by managerial action around the implementation of new technology. More significantly, however, the study reveals the critical role of situated change enacted by organizational members using the

Figure 9.1. Metamorphosis

technology over time. Such a practice logic has been largely overlooked in studies of organizational transformation and appears to be particularly relevant to contemporary concerns of organizing; hence, it is the focus of my attention here.

RESEARCH SETTING AND METHODOLOGY

Site

Zeta Corporation[2] is a software company headquartered in the Midwest, with sales and client service field offices throughout the United States and the world. Zeta is one of the Top 50 software companies in the United States, with $100 million in revenues and about 1,000 employees. The company produces and sells a range of powerful software products, which run on a variety of computing platforms. These products provide capabilities of decision support and executive information analysis and are used by thousands of corporations around the world.

The focus of my study was the Customer Support Department (CSD), which is part of the Technical Services Division headed by a senior vice president. The CSD is a 53-person department run by a director and two managers which has traditionally had a very cooperative culture, reflecting a collegial management style and a shared interest in solving customer problems. The mission of the CSD is to provide technical support via telephone to all users of Zeta's products including clients, consultants, Zeta field service representatives, and other Zeta employees. This technical support is provided by customer support specialists (hereafter referred to as specialists), all of whom have been extensively trained in Zeta's products and in techniques of technical support. The department has grown from 10 specialists in 1990 to its current high of 50 specialists. All the specialists have college degrees, mostly in computer science, engineering, and business information technology. Many of the specialists view their current position as an entry point into the high-tech industry, and few intend to make technical support a career. Although turnover of specialists in the CSD is high (as in other companies), the rate has declined over the past few years. When specialists leave the CSD, many stay within Zeta, moving laterally into departments such as product management and field service.

Customer support at Zeta, as is often the case in technical support (Pentland 1992), is a complex activity. Customer calls are rarely resolved with a brief answer. They typically require several hours of research and include searches of reference material, review of program code, and attempts to replicate the problem. Some incidents will require interaction with members of other departments such as development and quality assurance. Problems identified by specialists as bugs are sent on to product development, where they will be assessed for criticality and, if appropriate, scheduled for correction. The volume of calls to the CSD has increased significantly in recent years due to new product introductions and the growing range of operating platforms supported. Currently, the department receives an average of 100 calls a day, although volumes fluctuate by time of month, season, and maturity of product. Specialists, working in four-hour shifts, rotate their time "on the phones," so that in any one day about 20 specialists will take calls from customers.

In January 1992, an initial purchase of the Notes technology (from Lotus Development Corporation) was made to explore the feasibility of using Notes as a technological platform for tracking customer calls. At the time, the CSD was using a homegrown system (Inform), but significant problems with its use made replacement a priority. On the acquisition of Notes, an implementation team including a developer newly assigned to the Technical Services Division, one of the CSD managers, and several specialists designed and tested a trial call-tracking system within Notes. By mid-1992, the Incident Tracking Support System (ITSS) had been developed, and evaluations of its use in practice began. Two phases of this evaluation were conducted: an experimental pilot from July to September 1992 and an expanded pilot from September to December 1992. By the end of 1992, the decision was made to commit to the use of Notes as the platform for tracking all customer calls, and additional licenses for Notes were bought. This set the stage for a full rollout of ITSS to all members of the CSD and the enactment of the organizational changes which are the focus of this discussion.

Data Collection and Analysis

Data collection at Zeta was conducted in two phases. Phase I (Gallivan et al. 1993) took place at the time of the two pilots (August-December 1992), while Phase II occurred two years later (July-December 1994). Both phases involved the use of unstructured and semistructured interviewing, observation, and document review. Fifty-one interviews of 60 to 90 minutes in length were conducted across the two phases. All interviews were recorded and transcribed. Participants spanned vertical levels and functional groupings and included specialists from the CSD; both CSD managers; the CSD director; the Technical Services senior vice president; the technologists responsible for the new technology; and members of the product development, product management, and quality assurance departments (Table 9.1 shows a breakdown by function, level, and phase). Observation took the form of sitting with specialists when they were on and off the phones and taking notes on their

TABLE 9.1   Numbers and Types of Interviews in Zeta Corporation in Phases I and II

	Phase I	Phase II	Total
Senior management (division and department)	2	3	5
Group management	4	4	8
Specialists	7	20	27
Technologists	1	6	7
Other members (developers, quality assurance, etc.)	—	4	4
Total	14	37	51

work practices, particularly their use of the Inform and ITSS technologies. Specialists were encouraged to talk aloud about what they were doing, and these descriptions were supplemented with questions probing particular issues. Materials reviewed included the set of user manuals for Notes and ITSS (which provided detailed information on the design and functionality of the technology), the report documenting the feasibility of acquiring a new incident tracking system (which revealed the intentions underlying the implementation of ITSS), management reports generated in ITSS (which showed the kinds of resource and output tracking conducted by the CSD managers), and samples of the ITSS database records (which allowed an examination of the types of documentation being generated by specialists).

I used qualitative techniques to analyze the data (Eisenhardt 1989; Miles and Huberman 1984; Pettigrew 1990; Strauss and Corbin 1990), informed by the overall focus on practices, change, and structuring and a more detailed attention to grounded concepts. I first read all the interview transcripts, observation notes, and documentation to identify issues and topics that related to work practices and change. After analyzing and aggregating these to arrive at a set of common or recurring themes, I then reexamined the data in terms of the new set of common themes, paying particular attention to the enactment of change, the role of technology, and the passage of time. The feasibility report completed in 1991 and the Phase I data collected during 1992 allowed me to distinguish between deliberate and emergent organizational changes and to determine the timing of deliberate changes. The timing and order of emergent changes were more difficult to establish but were assessed from participants' interviews and the schedule of technology updates. I shared my preliminary findings with the specialists and managers of the CSD, and they provided helpful comments which confirmed and elaborated the identified issues and themes.

The focus of analysis in this study was the everyday practices of the specialists and their managers, and while work practices were observed during on-site data collection, the ongoing changes enacted over the two years were not observed firsthand. Ideally, a study of such changes would involve the sorts of extensive and intensive participant observation enabled by techniques of organizational ethnography (Van Maanen 1979, 1988). This was not possible in the current study, but the data collected proved adequate to distinguish five different situated changes.

RESULTS

My analysis suggests that the organizing practices and structures of Zeta's CSD changed considerably over the two years following implementation of the ITSS technology. The transformation, while enabled by the technology, was not caused by it. Rather, it occurred through the ongoing, gradual, and reciprocal adjustments, accommodations, and improvisations enacted by the CSD members. As will be detailed, their action subtly and significantly altered the organizing practices and structures of the CSD workplace over time, transforming the texture of work, nature of knowledge, patterns of interaction, distribution of work, forms of accountability and control, and mechanisms of coordination. Five metamorphoses may be distinguished during the two-year period, and while this analytical division provides a convenient way of anchoring a discussion of the CSD's transformation, it is conceptually imprecise because the organizational changes were (and continue to be) fluid and ongoing, so that any sharp partitioning of change is misleading. The process of gradual transformation in the CSD was practically enacted in a much less discrete and organized fashion than can be suggested textually. Depiction of the overlapping and ongoing nature of this transformation is attempted in Figure 9.2, which shows the situated changes as enacted through a structuring process over time.

The structuring process underlies the ongoing production and change of social practices. It posits a recursive relationship between the everyday actions of human agents and the social structures which are both medium and outcome of those actions. Figure 9.2 depicts the social structures focused on here, the organizational properties of Zeta and the CSD. These included authority relations, division of labor, strategies, incentive systems, evaluation criteria, policies, work culture, and the like, which represented the institutionalized aspects of the Zeta and CSD social systems. These constrained and enabled the production of ongoing practices by members of the CSD while also being changed over time by those practices, as suggested by the variation in shading of Figure 9.2. Technology is not specifically depicted in

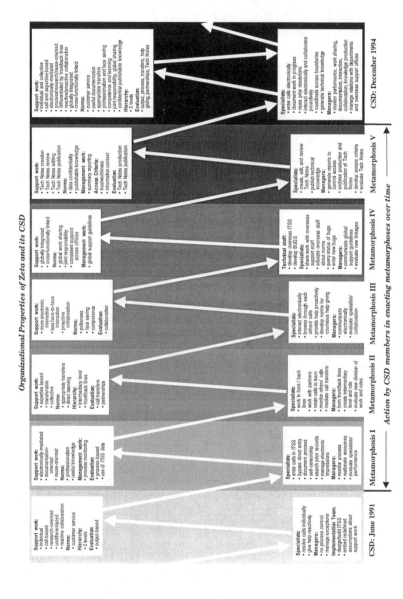

Figure 9.2. Practice-Based Model of Organizational Transformation at the CSD

Figure 9.2, but it played a critical role in mediating the changes in practices and structures. The conceptualization of technology drawn on here is informed by structurational analyses of technology in organizations (DeSanctis and Poole 1994; Orlikowski 1992) and posits technology not as a physical entity or social construction but rather as a set of constraints and enablements realized in practice by the appropriation of technological features (Orlikowski 2000). Information technology in the CSD plays a role similar to that of organizational properties—shaping the production of situated practices and being shaped by those practices in turn.

Each of the CSD's five metamorphoses can be characterized by (1) an analysis of the practices which enacted the changes including the organizational properties which influenced and which were influenced by those changes, (2) the specific technological features which were appropriated in use, and (3) the unanticipated outcomes which resulted from the changes and which influenced further changes. The following metamorphoses are discussed:

Metamorphosis I: the organizational changes associated with the shift to electronic capture, documentation, and searching of call records in the ITSS database

Metamorphosis II: the organizational changes associated with the redistribution of work from individual to shared responsibility

Metamorphosis III: the organizational changes associated with the emergence of a proactive form of collaboration among the specialists

Metamorphosis IV: the organizational changes associated with expanding into a global support practice and with creating interdepartmental and cross-functional linkages

Metamorphosis V: the organizational changes associated with controlling access to and distributing extracts of the knowledge contained within the ITSS database

A brief overview of the work practices within the CSD before the arrival of the new technology is useful background for the subsequent discussion of metamorphic changes.

Work in the CSD Before Implementation of the New Technology

The acquisition of the Notes technology and the creation of an incident tracking system within it marked a significant technological and ultimately organizational change for the CSD. There was no division of labor within the department. Specialists who had been in the CSD for at least a year were

PROBLEM REPORT
_____

Problem Number: 9871457   User Problem Number:

Bug/Enhancement Number:
_____

Name: JENNY   Date: 10/31/90   Time: 11:00AM

Others: Duane King
_____

Client Name: John Doe   PHONE: 999-000-1234

Company: Acme Co.   STATUS:

Time Spent: 30-45 min.   Answered Date: 10/31/90   Time: 11:30AM

Product: Omni   Version No: 3.0   Operating System:
_____

Description: READ DIF FILE INTO WORKSHEET UNRAVEL INTO VARIABLE UPDATE
                REORGANIZE RECEIVED: SYSTEM ERROR ARGET01 PROBLEM HAS
                OCCURED. EXPORT/IMPORT DATABASE

Solution: TOLD HIM THIS WAS NOT GOOD! SHOULD EITHER 1) RESTORE FROM
                BACKUP AND CHECK DB OR 2) EXPORT/IMPORT DB.

Problem Category:
_____

Figure 9.3. Sample Record From the Inform Database

informally regarded as "senior specialists" and recognized as being more knowledgeable and experienced. All specialists took calls, scribbling problem descriptions on slips of paper and then working on the problems individually until they were resolved. The process of work was not documented or reviewed in any way. Problem solving was the central activity of customer support. While specialists were expected to record their call resolutions in the Inform database, entry was haphazard at best. The records actually entered typically exhibited limited detail and questionable accuracy, and as a result, searching in this database was often unproductive. Figure 9.3 displays a sample record from the Inform database.

Managers performed no monitoring of the specialists' work process, evaluating them essentially on output. They were frustrated by their inability to track calls, analyze the status of particular calls, assess the department's workload, balance its resources, and identify issues and problems before they became crises. Managers' motivation in acquiring a new incident tracking system was influenced by these frustrations. As one manager recalled,

> We were totally unable to produce any type of weekly reporting or any statistics about who called us and why. We weren't quickly able to categorize any of our

problems. We had a system, but you questioned the data that was in there because it was cumbersome to get the data in there. . . . [Also,] if a month had gone by, I had no clue what had gone on. So, I would have to go and find the specialist who had worked on the problem and ask [him or her] to either remember what had happened or try and find some piece of paper [on which it] might have been written down.

ITSS Design and Implementation

In contrast to Inform, ITSS was designed so that specialists would create an incident record in the ITSS database as each call was received and then regularly update the incident record with the progress being made on the incident. They were to enter not just the problem description and its resolution but also all the steps taken in the process of resolving the incident. Because ITSS was implemented in Notes, which allows databases stored on a server to be accessed from distributed, networked personal computers, the incident records in the ITSS call database were designed to be accessible by all members of the CSD. The design of ITSS was accompanied by procedural redefinitions of customer support work, and these modifications were introduced to the specialists through a series of training sessions that included hands-on use of ITSS during which specialists directly entered calls into the ITSS database and updated ITSS records by documenting their process of resolving customers' problems.

Once trained, specialists began to use ITSS to do their support work, and as they responded to the modifications in their work and appropriated the technological features of ITSS, they enacted some of the changes intended by the implementation team. Other changes emerged as specialists and their managers accommodated issues and breakdowns in the use of ITSS and improvised techniques and norms to effectively utilize the new technology in their changing work practices.

Metamorphosis I

Figure 9.4 depicts the first set of metamorphic changes enacted with ITSS in the CSD. As indicated in the figure, these changes were both deliberate and emergent, involved specialists' and managers' work practices, were associated with some unanticipated outcomes, and involved particular features of the ITSS technology. The changes involved those specifically intended by the implementation team: electronic recording of all customer calls taken by the CSD, electronic documentation of work done on those calls, electronic reuse of prior call resolutions to avoid duplication of effort, and electronic monitor-

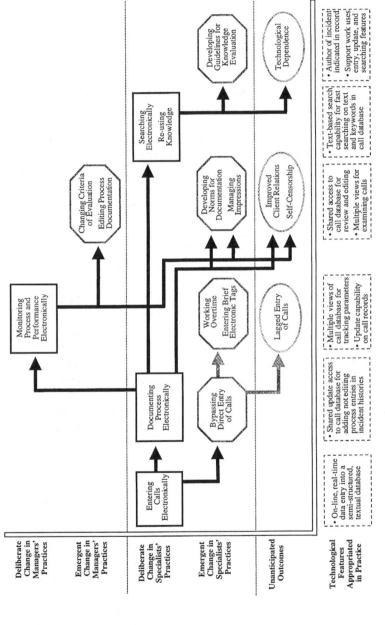

Figure 9.4. Metamorphosis I: Changes in Support Work and Management Enacted With Use of ITSS Over Time

ing of process and performance to facilitate process tracing and resource management.

Electronic entry of calls. One of the premises underlying the design of ITSS was that specialists should enter incidents directly into the ITSS database while on the phone with customers. The ITSS technology, designed to operate as an on-line, real-time database system, facilitated such direct entry with its "Compose New Incident" feature which provided a structured data entry screen for recording the new call. Specialists were trained to invoke this feature on receiving a new call and enter the customers' data in the structured and free-form fields when talking to them on the phone. While this feature enabled direct entry, some aspects of its design were also constraining, sufficiently so that most of the specialists continued to use paper to record their phone interactions with customers, entering these calls into ITSS at a later time. This practice of bypassing direct entry persisted despite ongoing urging by managers and despite a recognition by specialists of the advantages of direct entry (e.g., being able to give customers an incident number as a reference, being able to get an early indication of the day's workload, being able to record the time calls are received, avoiding the risk of misplacing calls by misplacing the paper on which they were noted).

The specialists had a number of reasons for choosing to retain their original work practice of recording calls on paper. For some, limited typing proficiency inhibited direct entry of calls:

> If you're not confident in your typing skills, there's just no way you're going to put a call in on-line. Because you're going to have typing mistakes, you'll be trying to fix them, and then you can't read what you've typed.

> When calls come in, I just jot them down first. I mean, I tried both ways, by killing two birds with one stone by entering and listening, but my typing skills, I guess, aren't fast enough, so I can't obtain all the information if I type.

Specialists further noted that the navigation of ITSS's structured data entry screen was incompatible with how information was provided by customers. Consequently, specialists found the mechanics of manipulating the ITSS data entry screen distracting when they were trying to understand customers' often complex problems:

> I'm not comfortable typing in the incident as they're telling it. I find it's more of a distraction. I'm trying to figure out what piece of the form to fill in, and they're talking rapidly about a problem. So, my concentration is split, and I find myself not being able to ask the right questions or forgetting some piece of information.

> When I get a call, I personally write it down first. I think that is because I'm trying to pay attention more to what the client's talking about and trying to understand the problem. And I think that if I were actually trying to type in that information into ITSS, I would lose something. . . . It's not like, "I've heard this before, I know what this is." I really need to understand what they're doing because in order for me to either try and recreate it or try and fix it, I really need to make sure I fully understand exactly what they're doing. It's different every time.

In addition, specialists were aware that the ITSS technology and underlying network might fail occasionally. As a result, many of them utilized paper as an improvised (manual) backup system:

> When I take a call, I always write it out. . . . [So,] if the network goes down, I've got their phone number on a piece of paper.

This improvisation allowed specialists to continue working on their calls even when the technology became unavailable.

Specialists' continued manual recording of calls (and avoidance of direct entry into ITSS) sometimes created problems when they received many calls in a day and their subsequent electronic entry lagged behind. Most specialists improvised ways of dealing with backlogged data entry, for example, working after hours to get caught up or entering brief information initially to tag the call and enter it into ITSS and then elaborating the description when they had more time.

Specialists' practice in working around the direct electronic entry of calls suggests, to invoke Heidegger (1977), that the ITSS technology is not as "ready-to-hand" as pen and paper. Both the structured nature of the technology's data entry screen and the act of typing interjected an interface into the activities of listening, interacting, comprehending, and articulating the problem. Specialists ended up focusing on the interface and on manipulating it accurately, an explicit concentration which does not arise when writing free-form with pen on paper. For the specialists (as for most of us), writing with pen and paper in an unstructured manner has been familiar since grade school and, hence, simply part of the background, taken for granted. In contrast, use of the ITSS technology required typing and screen manipulation skills which diverted concentration from customers and their problems. The occasional unpredictability of the technology at the time of a call (whether slow or inaccessible) further raised barriers to the feasibility of direct electronic entry. All of these elements served to increase the "unreadiness-to-hand" of the ITSS technology, so that to specialists it appeared as a distinct object and interface that had to be attended to consciously. To avoid such cognitive diversion and concentrate on interacting intelligently with customers while on the phones, specialists had improvised various practices to bypass direct entry and compensate for the time lag when they fell behind.

Electronic process documentation. ITSS was deliberately designed to enable users to record, chronologically, the work being done on each incident as it was being done. Figure 9.5 shows a sample record from the ITSS database. The top half shows the structured fields in which specialists had to enter specific information (aided by the provision of "pick lists" where the system offers a menu of acceptable values), and the lower section contains the unstructured "Incident History" field in which narrative descriptions of work in progress could be entered to create a chronological trace of the work process over time.

Specialists were now required to record the progress being made on each call in the Incident History field of that call's ITSS record. This change in specialists' job requirements was enabled by the edit feature in ITSS which allowed specialists to update incident records previously entered. When specialists completed some activity on a customer's incident, they updated that incident's record in the ITSS database by noting the kind of work done and the steps to be followed next. ITSS was designed to allow this process documentation to be open-ended. The Incident History field in which specialists made their progress updates was unstructured, allowing entry of free-form text. ITSS automatically appended information identifying the time, date, and person making the update, and it arranged the updates in reverse chronological order. The ITSS edit feature, however, was restricted in that specialists could only add new entries to the Incident History field; they could not edit any previous entries made. Once an item had been added to the Incident History field, it remained there permanently. This history could not be rewritten, and as we shall see, the permanent nature of this recording led to some self-censorship on the part of the specialists.

An interesting unanticipated outcome of electronic process documentation within ITSS was that it altered the CSD's relationship with its customers:

> It has dramatically changed communications with customers. We are no longer guilty until we can prove we're innocent. We have all the facts at hand. So, when customers call up and say, "I called two weeks ago and nobody ever called me back," either a specialist or a manager can just immediately say, "Well, let me look at the database. I see that you called last Tuesday at 4:13 p.m. and we called you back at 5:06 p.m. and closed your call." We get countless calls like that, people ranting and raving without any specifics, and the minute we can get specific and tell them what we did or didn't do for them, they immediately retract their statements and start being nice. . . . It's a great shield for the support people; their butts are covered. That's not something we anticipated.

Incident Form

Incident: XX-1-0999

Owner: Gillian Smith   Opened: 11/28/94 09:45 AM

Company: Acme Co.

Caller: **John Doe**   Title:

Location: 444 Science Park   Rel:
             Vista City, MA 02139

Phone: 999-000-1234   Fax: 999-000-9999

Call Back: Phone:

Product: DSX 4.13 {4.1700}

Platform: PC STANDALONE - 486   Environment: DOS 5.0

Module: N/A   Workstation: N/A

Incident Description

Title: In DSX 4.x, how do you populate insample for each mrentry?

Description: Insample is dimensioned by geog, time, and mrentry. Doe wants to populate insample differently
              for different mrentries, but doesn't know how. He wants to know how.

Res. Type: General Question

Resolution:

Incident Management

Assignee: Tom Brown

Status: Work in Progress   Close Date:

Time Now: 10   Time Total: 50 minutes

Bug Number: Severity: 4

Interoffice #:   T/O Assignee:

Other #s: Transfer Date:

Reviewed: Not Reviewed

Review Date: Reviewer:

Incident History

***** 12/06/94 09:27:25 AM Jenny Jones (US) {Total Time = 50} (Work in Progress) (S4)
    [Tom Brown = Assignee] [Gillian Smith, Tom Brown = MailTo]

"INSAMPLE is a keyword in the control file; you can set it as follows:
    ControlfileKeyword   ControlFileValue
    INSAMPLE   INSAMPLE 01011
    INSAMPLE   INSAMPLE 01013
Can be set with however many measures you want.
I've tried to reach Doe at the above #, but unable to. If he calls back we can give him this info. "

***** 12/02/94 12:41:43 PM Tom Brown (US) {Total Time = 40} (Work in Progress) (S4)
    [Tom Brown = Assignee] [Gillian Smith = MailTo]

"Not sure if this is possible. Will consult with Jenny and see .... might have to wait for Arthur ? We'll see.
Searched GROUCHO for some details. Nothing like this found for 4.13 - only references to the DOS DataServer."

***** 12/02/94 11:59:21 AM Martha Robinson (US) {Total Time = 20} (Work in Progress) (S4)
    [Tom Brown = Assignee] [Tom Brown, Gillian Smith = MailTo]

"Tom, can you please take a look at this call? Apparently Doe called back and would like an answer soon.
If you can't take it please let me know. Thanks, Martha."

***** 11/29/94 10:11:06 AM Gillian Smith (US) {Total Time = 10} (Open) (S4)

"Talked to Arthur. He has worked with this issue before, and explained that it's complicated. He will refresh his
memory and get back to me."

Figure 9.5. Sample Record From the Incident Tracking Support System Database

Process documentation, electronic or other, had not previously been part of specialists' work practices. The definitions of support work had been changed to reflect the requirement to document process electronically, and evaluation criteria had been adjusted accordingly. These new organizational conditions (communicated via intensive training on the use of ITSS) changed specialists' understanding of their jobs, and once ITSS was fully deployed, all proceeded to appropriate ITSS to document their work process. In this action, the specialists enacted the deliberate change intended by the implementation team, thereby generating the audit trail deemed necessary to make specialists and their managers more accountable for the work of the CSD. Through such ongoing enactment, specialists reinforced and eventually institutionalized a new set of work practices, substantially mediated by information technology and expanded to include documentation. In the process, specialists had also become accountable, institutionally, not just for their output but also for their work in progress.

Electronic monitoring. With specialists producing electronic process documentation of their work in progress, managers were able to use the ITSS technology for dynamic monitoring of call load, work process, and individual performance. In this, they were strongly influenced by the institutionalized properties of Zeta, which required them to provide various statistics on departmental workload to justify their headcounts to show that they were utilizing their resources and new technology effectively and which held them accountable for providing quality technical support to customers. To conduct their monitoring, the three CSD managers appropriated various features of ITSS, particularly the "View" feature which facilitated the presentation of ITSS data in multiple ways. The ITSS technology was also constraining in that there was not a strong statistical capability, so that only straightforward counts and categorized reports could be obtained. Anything more complex required the data to be extracted into another system and manipulated there.

In monitoring specialists' process documentation through ITSS, managers changed their work practices to reflect the window they now had on specialists' ongoing performance, a view that had not been possible before. This deliberate change in managers' practices occasioned an emergent change in how they evaluated specialists. They now assessed technical competence and problem-solving strategies (at least as these were documented):

> We evaluate their technical skills. Notes is part of the way we do that: looking at the calls they close and how well they resolve them. Where did they go to look for help? Do they get in and get their hands dirty? . . . I also look at problem-

solving skills . . . , reviewing their calls and seeing what history and thought process they've gone through.

In addition, managers began to evaluate the process documentation itself, not
merely using it as an indicator of actions and strategies. In this way, they reinforced the new definition of the customer support job as comprising both
problem solving and documentation. Indeed, keeping process documenta-
tions up to date was presented as just as critical, or even more important than,
problem solving, as one manager observed:

> I explain to [the specialists] that it's more important that they document the call
> than solve it quickly. And I give the example of the executive vice president of
> development walking into my office and asking me what's wrong at a particular
> site. And I can double-click, and I've got the information right there. And if
> that's up to date, we're golden, and we look good. And if it's not, and I have to
> go chase somebody down to get the most recent information, we don't look
> good, and that database all of a sudden isn't valid. He'll never trust it again.

In their on-line and ongoing examination of the ITSS database, managers
occasionally entered comments or edits to improve the quality of the documentation or to communicate with specialists. For example, a specialist I was
observing received electronic mail notification that one of his incidents had
been updated. On accessing the record, he found that one of the managers had
made the following entry in the record's Incident History field:

> Milt, is this one closed out? Please update. Thanks, Isobel.

Specialists responded to this electronic monitoring by developing norms
about what and how to document and managing impressions of themselves
through their electronic text.

Norms for process documentation. While the requirement of process documentation had been well established, the precise nature and representation of
this documentation was left largely unspecified. As noted above, the technology imposed few restrictions in the Incident History field, allowing the entry
of free-form text of unspecified length. The implementation team members
indicated that they had also not provided any documentation guidelines, pre-
ferring "to keep things voluntary and democratic." This technological "freedom" was both enabling (allowing a variety of expressions and formats) and
constraining (allowing inconsistency and ambiguity). As a result, documentation during the early period of ITSS use was characterized by considerable
variability in quality and detail as the specialists experimented with different

styles and details in their descriptions of process. Over time, however, a number of informal norms about effective process documentation emerged, influenced by the occasional comments or edits made by managers in the ITSS records and by the experience of specialists who realized in practice the value of documenting well and consistently. A vivid illustration of the latter was the story, recounted many times, of the specialist who was working on one of her calls, searched in ITSS, and located an incident which exactly matched the error message she was researching. Delighted, she accessed the Incident History field, only to find that "it was, like, totally nothing. I mean, it was useless." Frustrated and angry at the creator of the incident, she looked at the field indicating authorship, only to discover it was herself. This story, as another specialist commented,

> makes you realize that it's really going to benefit people if, you know, if even your thought process and everything can get into the incidents.

The norms that emerged from specialists' use of ITSS reflected their recognition that the database was a shared resource and that value lay in making the content of incident records reusable, whether by other specialists in the group or by themselves at a future time:

> In my incidents, I try to be very specific, even though I find sometimes it's boring to do that. . . . I mean, I'm really tired of typing [all the details] in, but I figure some poor sap in another year is going to be trying to solve this problem he's never seen before, so I still need to write all that down.

> You need to be a little more thoughtful about how you present information so that it's useful for other people. . . . You have to have the description in there in such a way that you've made sure you've used key words that other people might search on. . . . There's a lot more thought involved rather than just kind of a scratch pad situation.

These norms, once shared and practiced within the CSD for some time, became reinforced and established as important cultural norms about the representation of work process within electronic documentation. Norms also emerged about the representation of self within this electronic text.

Impression management. Specialists were very aware that as they worked with the ITSS technology, their use reflected, very visibly and immediately, on their work practices and on themselves as support specialists. The boundary between private work and public space had shifted significantly as specialists used ITSS to produce an ongoing electronic text of their work process, which was available for future use and served as the basis on which managers had begun to evaluate them. Before their use of ITSS, specialists had tended to do much of their research work in private, making public only their questions to colleagues and their problem resolutions to customers. With ITSS, specialists now made public most aspects of their research work through their own documentation of their ongoing work in progress. They participated in making their work (and thereby themselves) electronically visible and accountable. While specialists retained some discretion over what, how, and when to make their work visible, they had changed the nature of their work from being largely off-line (done privately in one's own space and never recorded) to being largely on-line (done privately but recorded publicly in a shared space). The transparency of the electronic text ensured that specialists' work lives were now more "on display," or at least potentially so, through the medium of ITSS.

Many specialists were acutely aware of their new visibility—some of them referred to it as "big brother"—and responded by improvising some informal guidelines about what they would and would not articulate within the electronic text. In so doing, they began to appropriate the features of ITSS to manufacture a virtual or "electronic persona" of themselves by consciously engaging in impression management (Goffman 1959). Goffman's (1959) distinction of front and back regions is useful here to explain specialists' use of such impression management. The "front region" is where the performance takes place and where individuals strive to maintain and embody certain standards of politeness and decorum (p. 107), while the "back region" is where the impression managed by a performance is openly constructed, rehearsed, and contradicted (p. 112). The ITSS records represented the (electronic) front region of the specialists' back region work. It was here that they expressed the activities they had performed backstage in terms that were compatible with the norms of frontstage behavior. In this public recounting of private work, there occurred an accounting of effort in a manner designed (whether deliberately or not) to create a particular professional representation of self:

> I am definitely more careful about how I say things now. If I want to say some guy was a real jerk to me, I might phrase that a little differently and say that he was not very nice. . . . We have to be more careful about entering information. We have to be more diplomatic.

> There is, like, a general rule that you've got to be courteous and use the right language. You have to use the correct and politically correct language. You don't want to use any slang. You just want to be professional about it.

In representing their work publicly, specialists were conforming to the standards of the front region by their impression management, the unanticipated result of which was self-censorship, limiting what was documented within the ITSS database. For example,

> The accessibility of the database is something that I'm always aware of, and I think I'm very guarded in what I put into the database. I am always concerned about being politically correct, professional, diplomatic.

> It's kind of like, if you don't want anyone to read this, don't write it, you know. What I may do is vent by just typing something and then erasing it.

What was interesting about this electronic impression management was that it was not actual electronic scrutiny within the front region that compelled "political correctness" but rather the possibility of such scrutiny—inherent in the notion of a front region—that focused specialists' attention on what impression of themselves was being conveyed in electronic text:

> It's not obvious if they're watching the numbers. There is an undercurrent of scrutiny; big brother is there, but it's below the surface.

Such self-regulation is a form of "participatory surveillance" (Poster 1990) and an interesting electronic example of Foucault's panoptic discipline (Orlikowski 1991; Zuboff 1988). As Foucault (1979, pp. 202-203) notes, "He who is subjected to a field of visibility, and who knows it, assumes responsibility for the constraints of power; . . . he becomes the principle of his own subjection."

While some specialists felt the electronic exposure provided by their and their managers' use of ITSS as vulnerability, others saw some advantages:

> I know that it's kind of like big brother watching over you, but it really doesn't bother me in that way. It's good because . . . you get so many calls that you forget what's going on . . . and that you should have alerted these people. And by having the managers look at our database and say, "Oh, this is this client and we need to alert this, that, or the other," it helps. I think it's more of a team approach.

> It's a record of what we're doing, and . . . it's a number that we can point to [so as to] show how we are working and how well we are working.

In particular, those specialists who felt that they were "high performers" welcomed the electronic scrutiny as it made their accomplishments more visible:

[ITSS] is a working database of what I'm doing. . . . It's my brag record. I have
more calls in there than anybody else.

For a while, I had taken an incredible number of calls. And [ITSS] sort of vali-
dated the fact I am very busy, I am taking a lot of calls, I am really contributing
to the group effort.

Thus, for some specialists, the use of ITSS created a forum in which to showcase their efforts, occasions to manage impressions of themselves as highly
productive. Indeed, the electronic text provided opportunities for individuals
to "make-work" (Goffman 1959) by fabricating or embellishing work in their
documentation of work in progress. Specialists continually engaging with
and contributing to such a transparent electronic text changed how they represented themselves to others, engaging in the construction of professional
electronic personae. Such constitution of self was facilitated by the cognitive
and normative awareness of how different their work practices were when
they were mediated by the technology:

There's more of a record. It's more of an on-line mentality. . . . It's a different
mental attitude. . . . It's a mind-set of everything being on-line and everything
being accessible to everybody and recording everything in the computer, as
opposed to, you know, presenting a report to your boss at the end of the month.
The ongoing thing. The idea that anybody can read your words if you want them
to, or if they have the right access, and that some people can get in there and read
your notes even if you haven't given them access.

With the expansion of support work to include process documentation and
the adjustment of evaluation criteria to reinforce that change, the boundaries
of public and private work space have shifted. Both managers and specialists
have become much more attentive to the process of customer support. However, this change masks another more subtle shift in the texture of work
within the CSD—a focus less on process per se than on the process as documented in incident records within ITSS. This is a technologically mediated
process orientation, where the interest is less in the execution of work than in
the symbolic artifacts that describe the execution of work and which are immediately and continually available through the technology. The text has
become central. Poster (1995, p. 85), drawing on Foucault's analysis of discourse, suggests that "databases are discourse" because they "effect a constitution of the subject." Such a constitution of specialists is present in the
creation, examination, and monitoring of the ITSS electronic text, where the
incident records serve as symbolic surrogates for the specialists, traces of and
testaments to their work. To retain some discretion in this discourse, specialists developed norms for the construction and manipulation of the text, strate-

gies for managing impressions and expressions within it, and an awareness of some of the political and personal consequences—intended and other—of its use.

Electronic searching. The ITSS database of calls with its documentation of process and resolutions soon contained enough prior incidents to make searching the database a useful step in researching problems. Specialists expanded their appropriation of ITSS features by beginning to use the powerful search engine available to quickly scan the ITSS database on specified keywords or text. By including such searching as part of their problemsolving activities, specialists enacted a deliberate change in their work practices intended in the original design of ITSS. Searching the ITSS database became increasingly valuable over time, as the number of incident records grew from some 4,000 in December 1992 to 35,000 in December 1994. Searching ITSS located possibly reusable problem resolutions that often saved time and effort and offered insight into approaches and strategies for resolving various problems. Specialists reported resolving up to 50 percent of their problems through electronic searching, an accomplishment that had not been possible without the mediation of support work by the ITSS technology.

As specialists depended increasingly on searching to do their problem solving, the reliability of the knowledge in ITSS became a central concern. The ITSS technology itself offered no indicators or guarantees of the reliability or relevance of the data contained within it. Such a concern led specialists to develop some social heuristics for assessing the quality of knowledge in the ITSS records. The ITSS technology was designed to automatically assign a unique number to each incident entered into the database. This number included a code which identified the particular specialist who had documented the incident. Specialists learned each other's identifying codes and enacted an emergent change in their work practices when they began relying on this identifier to gauge the likely quality of potentially reusable incidents:

> You tend to evaluate information differently from different people. So, if you see
> 40 items from a search, you go to the incidents of those folks you've gotten good
> information from in the past.

> I know certain people in the department, and I know that Arthur has a reputation
> for writing short novels as resolutions. I mean, he's a wonderful source of infor-
> mation and when he has an incident, he really spends the time to put a lot of
> detail in it. And it's extremely helpful. So, when I get an incident from him, I'm
> very comfortable with that information. Whereas, some of the other people in the
> department . . . for example, Beavis has a reputation that he doesn't do much
> research.

Thus specialists in the CSD improvised techniques for judging the quality of the electronic texts they chose to use in their own work.

The change in specialists' work practices to include electronic searching led, over time, to the unanticipated outcome of technological dependence, which seems almost an inevitable result of mediating work practices through technology. Technological dependence within the CSD has both a physical and a psychological referent. Dependence resulted from the ever-increasing use of the ITSS technology. Thus, when the system broke down, the specialists lost their ability to execute much of their ongoing work:

> We had a power outage last week because of the thunderstorm, and there was virtually nothing I could do. Almost everything I needed to do was on the networks. So, we were pretty much paralyzed.

> You must have heard, we lost part of our searching capability for, like, two days. Monday, Groucho died. [Note: Groucho is the name of one of the file servers used to store the ITSS database. The others are Chico, Moe, and Curley.] . . . I mean, we came in Monday morning and it's dead. And we didn't have it for two days. . . . It was really actually very crippling. It was very hard to do your job because so much depends on it. You know, you get a call and your first resource is to search in ITSS, and it was like, "My resources aren't here!"

Some specialists were less dependent than others and managed to devise ways of working around technological breakdowns:

> I would say we're very dependent on ITSS as a whole . . . and we sort of work around it when it's down. We pull out a sheet of paper and just start writing. . . . The other side of that is the searching tool. Certainly, when it's down, you become a little crippled because the information that you could pull up in a matter of seconds now might take a little longer because you have to find the right person.

Not all specialists, however, were able to fall back on other forms of working when the technology was not available. In particular, junior specialists who had learned support work in the context of ITSS had no cognitive and behavioral resources for working without the technology:

> We're extremely dependent on these databases. Without them, I feel underconfident. I feel I can't do this. I would be much more stressed out without them . . . because I would feel like more calls are coming in that I can't answer than I can. So, psychologically, it would be difficult.

Such dependence was also reflected in junior specialists' behavior. While I was observing a junior specialist at work, he kept issuing searches within ITSS to try to find an incident that resembled a problem he was researching. His remarks while doing so reflected the expectation that "all the answers" are in the database:

> Hmm, why can't I find anything here? There's got to be something in here. I'll keep trying.

And he did, for quite a while, until eventually abandoning his search and moving on to another incident.

Metamorphosis II

The second set of metamorphic changes enacted with ITSS in the CSD is displayed in Figure 9.6, which shows the emergent changes in work practices that evolved from the previous deliberate changes in electronic entry of calls and process documentation. These changes comprised a redistribution of work and responsibility within the CSD from being primarily individual and undifferentiated to being more collective and involving new roles and hierarchical levels.

Sharing work via partners. After about a year of using ITSS, the managers and senior specialists initiated an emergent change in how work was distributed within the CSD. This change had not been planned prior to the implementation of ITSS, but the growing reliance on ITSS and the communication capabilities of the Notes technology created an opportunity for the CSD to redistribute call loads. In particular, the informal distinction between "junior" and "senior" specialists was formalized in the structural division of "front-line" and "back-line" support levels. Junior specialists were designated as on the front line, where they were expected to take all calls, resolve as many as they could by searching the ITSS database, and then electronically transfer those calls they felt they could not manage to the senior specialists assigned to the back line. A manager noted,

> We call it "partners," and the way it works is that newer members of the group spend an average of 40 to 50 percent of their time taking incoming calls, and they're partnered with a more senior member of the group during their shift. . . . The partner gets assigned problems that the junior member doesn't need to worry about.

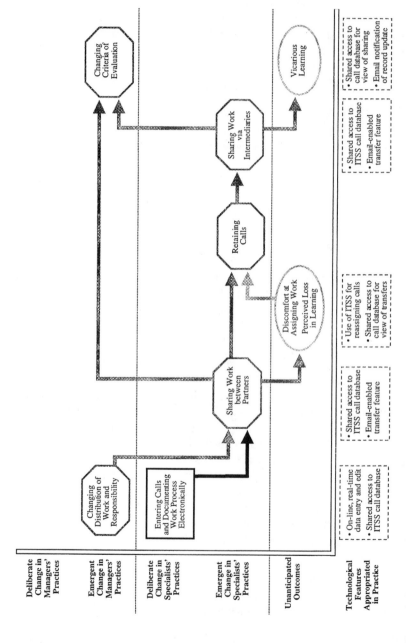

Figure 9.6. Metamorphosis II: Changes in Distribution of Work Enacted With Use of ITSS Over Time

Deliberate
Change in
Managers'
Practices

Emergent
Change in
Managers'
Practices

Deliberate
Change in
Specialists'
Practices

Emergent
Change in
Specialists'
Practices

Unanticipated
Outcomes

Technological
Features
Appropriated
in Practice

Changing
Criteria of
Evaluation

Changing
Distribution of
Work and
Responsibility

Entering Calls
and Documenting
Work Process
Electronically

Sharing Work
between
Partners

Retaining
Calls

Sharing Work
via
Intermediaries

Discomfort at
Assigning Work
Perceived Loss
in Learning

Vicarious
Learning

- On-line, real-time
data entry and edit
- Shared access to
ITSS call database

- Shared access to
ITSS call database
- Email-enabled
transfer feature

- Use of ITSS for
reassigning calls
- Shared access to
call database for
view of transfers

- Shared access to
ITSS call database
- Email-enabled
transfer feature

- Shared access to
call database for
view of sharing
- Email notification
of record update

The new distribution of work shifted responsibility for a call from being the sole purview of the individual who initially took it to being the shared responsibility of the individual and his or her partner. When enacted by the specialists, this shift changed the organizing structure and work practices of the CSD. A new role, the partner, had been introduced and the department had become hierarchically differentiated by expertise, experience, and status. The change in organizing structure had not been intended prior to the implementation of ITSS, but ongoing experience with ITSS created an awareness among managers and specialists of its feasibility and advantages. The key features of the technology that enabled the structural change were the capability for all specialists to share access to the ITSS database, the capability within ITSS for calls to be reassigned to other specialists (via a simple "Assign To" button on the ITSS Edit screen), and the capability for the system to automatically issue electronic mail messages to specialists notifying them that they have been assigned calls. Use of the ITSS technology over time and increased knowledge of its capabilities had thus enabled the CSD to institute a new division of labor.

As specialists began to enact their new organizing structure by changing their work practices, realization of the new division of labor ran into difficulties. Many specialists refrained from assigning calls to their designated partners as instructed, retaining their old practice of handling all the calls they took themselves. Two reasons cited by specialists seem to account for such action. One, they were uncomfortable assigning work to senior colleagues:

> You can just assign a call to a partner, but I don't. I only assign the call if he offers to take it. That way you're not really dumping on the other person.

> My rule of thumb is if I really don't know anything about the product or the issue and I know it's definitely not my area of expertise, then I would send e-mail and ask [my partner], "What do I do? Do you have any suggestions?" But I keep ownership of the incident because it takes the pressure off of that person.

Two, some junior specialists preferred to solve their own problems, seeing such action as both a sign of competence and a learning opportunity. For example,

> I don't like passing off calls; . . . it's kind of like a cop-out for me because I want to learn more about things and it would be kind of a way of not learning. It wouldn't be a learning process.

Sharing work via intermediaries. Managers reacted to this unanticipated reluctance to transfer calls by creating a new role—that of an intermediary—to facilitate the distribution and transfer of work between the front and back lines. Two senior specialists were designated as intermediaries, and their work practices changed significantly. From taking calls and solving problems, they now electronically monitored the incidents entered into ITSS by junior specialists and ensured that assignments to senior specialists, where they felt appropriate, took place. One intermediary described her role:

> I monitor the incoming calls to make sure that the people that are taking incoming calls can either handle the call or else refer the call to someone else. Because we have support set up with front and back lines, we have people that take incoming calls, and if they can't answer them in an [appropriate] amount of time, then we transfer the call to someone who is more experienced, maybe more expert in that type of problem.

While junior specialists did lose direct experience with solving certain problems, they did not give up all opportunities for learning. The technology included a feature that enabled them to be notified whenever any action was taken on a record. Thus, a junior specialist, having assigned a call to a partner, could request that the system send electronic mail each time the partner updated the record. This way, junior specialists could follow the progress of calls and learn vicariously at least.

The sample ITSS record shown in Figure 9.5 illustrates some of the shared responsibility for work that the specialists had enacted with ITSS and the creation of partner and intermediary roles. The call was originally taken by Gillian Smith, a front-line specialist, who entered the call into the ITSS database on November 28, 1994. The next day, she updated the incident's history (see bottom entry of history field), indicating that she had talked to Arthur, a senior specialist and the local expert on the DSX product, and was waiting for his recommendation. No further documented work took place on this call until December 2, 1994, when an intermediary, Martha Robinson, stepped in and reassigned the call to Tom Brown, a senior specialist and Gillian's designated partner. This reassignment was indicated under the Incident Management section of the record and was prompted by the fact that a number of days had passed without activity and that the customer had called back requesting a response. The e-mail-enabled feature of the technology is visible under the entry on December 2, 1994, where both Tom and Gillian are designated as "MailTo," which means they were sent electronic mail notifying them of any subsequent update to this record. Tom responded to the newly assigned call within the hour and indicated that he had unsuccessfully searched the ITSS database for clues and that he would consult with Jenny Jones, another senior specialist knowledgeable about DSX. On December 6, 1994, Jenny, the senior specialist consulted by Tom, updated the record with a possible solution.

In response to the new distribution of work, managers adjusted their evaluation criteria to reflect the changed responsibilities and roles within the CSD. This involved browsing the ITSS database to determine how senior specialists helped their junior partners resolve their calls and the extent to which the intermediaries stepped in to reassign calls when necessary. This emergent change in managers' practices further reinforced the structural change by distinguishing the roles of partner and intermediary and differentiating the evaluation of front- and back-line specialists.

Metamorphosis III

The third set of metamorphic changes enacted with ITSS in the CSD is presented in Figure 9.7. Again, the changes were mainly emergent, being occasioned by specialists' responses to the first two metamorphic changes: the deliberate changes in electronic entry, process documentation, and on-line searching as well as the emergent changes in work sharing and call reassignment. Here, the situated changes involved a shift toward more electronic interaction among the specialists and the development of a new, technology-enabled form of collaboration which was proactive rather than reactive and which offered unexpected benefits in problem-solving activities.

Electronic interaction. The increased use of ITSS to accomplish much of support work led specialists to spend considerably more time interacting electronically, an emergent change in their work practices. Specialists began to use the ITSS technology not only to enter, document, research, and reassign calls but also to communicate with each other via the electronic mail facility available in the underlying Notes system. They sent messages seeking technical advice, distributing departmental announcements, and sharing humor. This increased use of ITSS as a medium of interaction had the unanticipated consequence of decreasing specialists' face-to-face interaction, shifting the CSD's strongly oral culture toward one that was more written and electronic:

> I've noticed stretches of two to three days where I'm at my desk trying to resolve my calls as quickly as possible, and I haven't talked to anyone. . . . It's like, if Lotus Notes has the answers, why should I go talk to anyone?

Some specialists compensated for this shift in interaction medium by creating occasions for getting together with colleagues, either at lunch or at informal meetings:

256

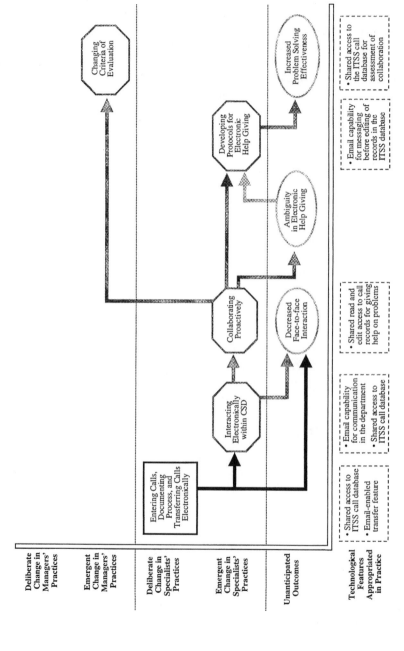

Figure 9.7. Metamorphosis III: Changes in Interaction and Collaboration Enacted With Use of ITSS Over Time

If I thought something important enough came up that everybody in the XSS group [should know]—and there's only four of us—I would say, all right, let's get together and discuss this, even if it was for a half an hour. We'd just kind of sit down and go back and forth.

The increased use of electronic interaction also set the stage for an interesting emergent change in specialists' collaboration.

Proactive collaboration. With specialists interacting more through ITSS and sharing access to all calls in the ITSS database, an electronic form of collaboration emerged in their work practices. Shared commitment to customer service had been a strong norm in the department since its inception, and it had recently been reinforced by the structural shift to partners and intermediaries. Nevertheless, before ITSS, collaboration was essentially reactive. Because all calls were held individually, specialists could only provide help on each other's problems when asked to do so. The technology of ITSS provided all specialists with access to everybody's problems, essentially a window on the problems currently being worked on within the department. Specialists discovered that with this virtual window into the workload of their peers, they could browse through each other's calls to locate those they could provide help on. Then, using the technology to send electronic mail or enter comments in a record's Incident History, specialists could provide suggestions or solutions to each other. In this way, they improvised a form of proactive help giving where they actively sought problems in the electronic database that they had solutions for rather than waiting to be asked if they had a solution to a particular problem. This emergent change in collaboration implicitly acknowledged specialists' awareness of their shared responsibility for calls received by the CSD.

Specialists—both junior and senior—changed their work practices so that they routinely engaged in electronic help giving, whether solicited or not:

We all help each other out, you know. Like, if I see Martha's gotten 15 calls and I've only gotten 3, I'm going to go in and I'm going to help her, whether she feels she needs it or not. I'm going to do some research for her. She does the same for me. And it's because, you know that one day you'll get killed, [and] the next day you don't get killed. So, you're going to help whoever's getting hit the hardest that day.

Sometimes if I see something that's open on somebody's calls which I've seen before, I may put a note in the incident and say, "Hey, I think I've seen this before; this might be this and this." . . . I found a couple of times that's really been helpful for me.

Proactive electronic help giving, however, was not simply a straightforward matter of providing knowledge or suggestions. It also involved a social interaction with particular issues of "courtesy." The appropriate etiquette for giving or receiving unsolicited help was, at least initially, quite ambiguous. Specialists were concerned about being rude or intrusive, and so they evolved a set of social protocols over time:

> Sometimes if I don't have a lot open, I may check around and see if anybody else has something that they need done to, you know, help around. I would go in and see who looked overwhelmed, and I'd say, "Boy, you looked like you had quite a day yesterday; do you need some help?" I would do that in person. It would be very rude to go in and resolve their call.

> A lot of times, I'll see something that's similar to what I may have already worked on. And I might be able to save them some time from even having to search by telling them what call I resolved this in. I'll send them Notes mail with my resolution. I won't close the call for them, but I'll give them what resolution I've used.

They also qualified their comments and descriptions so as not to mislead colleagues:

> [When] I put a note in Duane's call, I said, "I'm not sure, but it looks like it might be this and this." And I was very careful to say, you know, "I don't want to lead you astray here, but . . ."

Specialists also had norms for acknowledging the help received from colleagues. For example,

> We all welcome whatever help we can get . . . [and] we always send back a note [saying], "Thanks, you just saved me some time. I appreciate your help."

I observed one specialist writing in the Incident History of her own call, "This could be a nightmare," which, she explained, was intended "to warn anyone who might be interested in helping out," so that they knew what they were getting into before they began working on it.

Specialists also attempted to maintain a sense of collegiality in their electronic collaboration. See, for example, some of the comments entered in the ITSS record displayed in Figure 9.5. During my observation, I noticed one senior specialist entering comments in junior specialists' call records by addressing them by name and signing her own name. She explained,

I'm mucking around in their calls, so I do [use first names]; otherwise, it's so impersonal. It takes the formality out of it. It takes the edge off of it. So, if I'm being somewhat critical, it doesn't come across negatively.

An unanticipated consequence of the emergence of proactive collaboration was an increase in the effectiveness with which problems were solved. Managers responded by changing their evaluation criteria of specialists to take such unsolicited and courteous help giving into account:

When I'm looking at incidents, I'll see what help other people have offered, and that does give me another indication of how well they're working as a team.

The use of ITSS facilitated proactive help giving by specialists which included, but also transcended, the formal division of labor into front and back lines. This unexpected innovation in work practices and the emergence of norms around the courteous and diplomatic giving of unsolicited help reflected both the cooperative culture of the CSD and its shared focus on solving customer problems.

Metamorphosis IV

Figure 9.8 shows the fourth set of metamorphic changes enacted with ITSS in the CSD. Here, both emergent and deliberate changes were enacted by specialists and managers to facilitate a global support practice and an interdepartmental coordination mechanism.

Electronic linkages with overseas support offices. During 1993 and early 1994, the senior vice president of the Technical Services Division authorized the implementation of the ITSS technology in the three main overseas offices that had customer support departments—United Kingdom, Europe, and Australia. In addition, the technology was configured so that the four support departments shared copies of each other's ITSS databases, which were replicated every two to three hours. This meant that all four of the support offices had access to each other's databases, increasing the sources of knowledge that specialists could draw on in their research. This linkage of the four ITSS databases facilitated a global distribution of work, with overseas support specialists using the ITSS technology to transfer calls they could not solve to the U.S. support office, which was larger and had more expertise. Previously, overseas support staff would have transferred incidents to the United States via faxes and phone calls, but such exchanges were often ambiguous, necessitating lengthy clarification dialogues, and complicated by time zone differences, which made synchronous telephone conversations difficult to

260

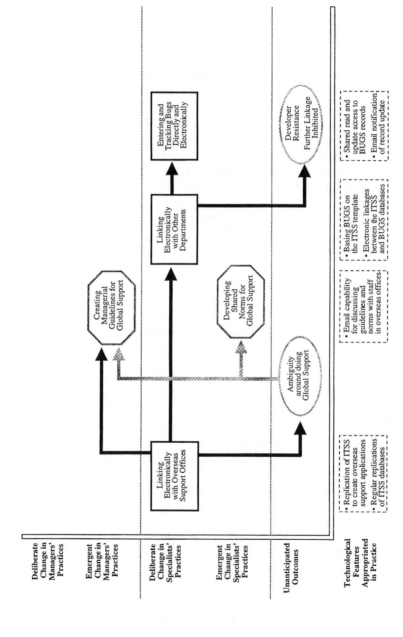

Figure 9.8. Metamorphosis IV: Changes in Interdepartmental Coordination Enacted With Use of ITSS Over Time

schedule. Use of ITSS as a transfer medium overcame the synchronicity constraint and ensured that more information about each incident was included.

Integrating the various support offices into a global support practice, however, did not just require a technological linkage. Social norms and expectations about call responsibility and workload were also necessary to facilitate cooperation across the remote offices. Initially, different customs and expectations generated ambiguity and created breakdowns in communication among the support staff across the various offices. The U.S. specialists, for example, resented what they saw as the tendency by overseas specialists to "just throw things over the wall," a sense exacerbated by the asynchronicity and impersonality of the ITSS-based electronic transfers. Such apparently noncollaborative behavior violated the CSD specialists' norms about support, which they had come to regard as a collective and shared activity:

> A lot of times, it's almost as though we're getting the problem without any analysis or testing on the part of the other office. . . . If we ask for details on a certain piece of it or ask them to clarify a certain point, it may be days—sometimes it's weeks—before a response will come through, . . . and then they say we talk down to them.

> I would say there is a fair amount of [calls] that, if they bothered to search in the database, they would have found the answer and it wouldn't have generated the transfer to us. It's just very frustrating because here you are, working with somebody, you work for the same company, you're on the same team, and you get attitudes back and forth.

Research has pointed to the importance of developing shared assumptions and expectations about use of a new technology (Orlikowski and Gash 1994), and the U.S. specialists' frustrations suggest that the overseas specialists have a different understanding of the division of responsibility among support offices. Used to the collaborative problem-solving norms that have developed within the CSD, the U.S. specialists expected a similar relationship with their overseas colleagues. Overseas specialists, in contrast, had just started using the ITSS technology and had not had time to develop norms of collaborative problem solving around incidents. They may have understood the relationship with the U.S. office as one of assigning responsibility for incidents. Responding to these breakdowns, the CSD managers contacted their overseas counterparts by phone and electronic mail, and together they generated a set of guidelines that explicitly articulated the procedures and expectations associated with a global support practice. Similarly, specialists began to send electronic mail to their overseas counterparts to clarify their expectations around joint responsibility for calls and offered specific suggestions for how their collaboration could be facilitated.

Electronic linkages with other departments. Based on the success of the ITSS expansion into overseas offices, the senior vice president of the Technical Services Division authorized the development of a number of Notes-based bug tracking systems (one for each Zeta product) for installation within Zeta's product development, product management, and quality assurance departments. These bug systems (BUGS), modeled on the ITSS system and linked directly to it, were motivated by the CSD's interest in being able to report and track bugs more efficiently and hence were initiated, developed, and paid for by the Technical Services Division.

The bug tracking systems were built to allow a direct linkage from the ITSS database to the BUGS database. For example, if a specialist working on an incident discovered that the problem was due to a bug, he or she could directly access the appropriate BUGS database to report the bug. The reference number assigned to that bug would appear in the original incident record (see the "Bug Number" field under Incident Management in Figure 9.5). Later, if the specialist was curious about the status of that bug, he or she could open the original incident in ITSS, click on the bug field, and be directly connected to the appropriate BUGS record for determining the progress to date on that bug. Thus specialists changed their work practices of reporting and querying bugs. They now electronically transferred bugs that they had found directly into the appropriate bug tracking system, and they electronically queried the status of various bugs simply by calling up those records directly. This eased the task of reporting bugs to product development (previously a manual process) and gave specialists up-to-date information on the status of bugs when they needed it. By using the e-mail-enabled notification feature, they could have the system notify them whenever someone updated a particular record in one of the bug databases. Specialists found these interdepartmental electronic linkages useful:

> The bug system provides a way to keep track of the work between the QA [quality assurance] department finding the bug, the development fixing the bugs, and the status of the fix. But what's great is that we've actually hooked it into our incident system so that when a call comes into support and it turns out that it's a bug, we just click on a field and boom, it merges into the bug system, and so now we can keep track of it. Before, that was really frustrating; we really went into a black hole.

> Whenever someone goes in and makes a modification to that bug from development, we're notified immediately. So, we're not hanging around, you know,

having to go in and check every couple of days or every couple of months to see when our bugs get fixed. . . . We're notified every time they do something.

An unanticipated consequence of this interdepartmental expansion of ITSS use was the resistance it evoked from the Zeta product developers. They were reluctant to change their work practices to use BUGS, in part because they saw use of these systems as unimportant given that bug fixing represented only a small aspect of their work responsibilities:

> It's probably a sense that [bug tracking] isn't the real work. This is a little bit outside. We're trying to produce a product. [BUGS] is only a tool that helps us maintain a product, but it's not really part of the product itself.

In contrast, use of ITSS by the CSD specialists was central to most of their work practices. Developers also worked under significant time constraints to get the next release of their product out and hence were reluctant to take the time to learn to use a new system to facilitate their fixing of the old product. Their attention and interest were clearly focused elsewhere. The unanticipated outcome of developer resistance to use the Notes technology in their work or to change their work practices consequently inhibited future attempts by the CSD to more closely integrate the activities of the support and development departments.

Metamorphosis V

Figure 9.9 depicts the fifth set of metamorphic changes realized in the CSD with use of ITSS. It shows the deliberate and emergent changes that specialists and managers enacted in response to an increasing demand for access to the knowledge generated and archived within ITSS.

Electronic access control. With the ITSS database emerging as an increasingly valuable knowledge archive through the work practices of the specialists, others in Zeta began to demand access to this database, either to assess trends in customer problems or to directly obtain resolutions to specific problems. Because of the level of detail in the ITSS database, CSD managers and specialists were concerned about who had access to the ITSS database and how the accessed information would be used. For example, they feared information would be used against the department or individual specialists:

> There are people in the company who say, "Well, I just want a copy of this entire database so that I can use it to research problems for my customers and I won't have to call you." But sure as shooting, they'll look at it and say, "Well, I don't

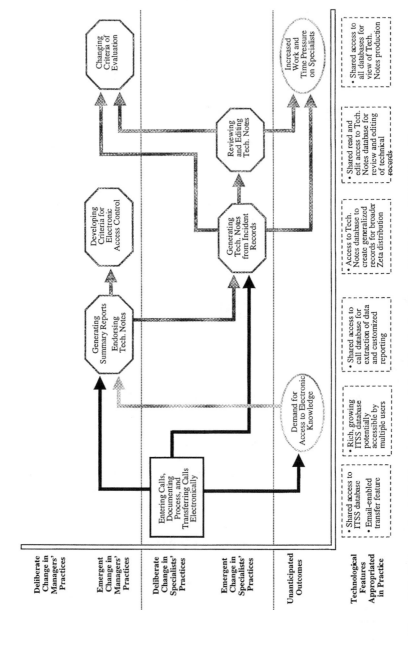

Figure 9.9. Metamorphosis V: Changes in Knowledge Distribution Enacted With Use of ITSS Over Time

264

agree with that answer, and why did it take two days to get that answer?" . . .
[Our] fear is that finger-pointing is an outcropping of access. It's not everybody's
motivation going in, but it happens.

Since we use this database all day long and pretty much everything we do is in
here, you're under the microscope. And there's a lot of people in the company
who could essentially look at this database and start criticizing.

They also feared that the ITSS information would be taken out of context and
used inappropriately:

[ITSS] isn't really a knowledge base, it's a history of all the problems we take in.
And just because one incident might tell you to do something one way doesn't
necessarily mean that it's going to solve [every] problem. . . . Somebody in the
sales group is not going to understand that. . . . They will read it and take it as
gospel, and it's not.

All we attempt to do in support is answer the question to the best of our abilities.
There's no guarantees that it's right. . . . I don't think we want a situation where
somebody passes something onto a client, and it ends up being a big problem for
the client, and then everybody turns around to us and says, "Well, we got it from
your database, so what's going on?"

Over time, the CSD managers developed various mechanisms for dealing
with this unanticipated demand; at the same time, norms around electronic
access control gradually emerged, being improvised through a process of
learning and experience in use. As a manager observed,

Initially, I knew why I didn't want them to have it, and that was that it could be
used against me. But at the point, I wasn't secure in being able to articulate that,
maybe because I didn't have enough knowledge. I couldn't have looked [the
president of Zeta] in the face and told him that that data could be used against
me and felt strongly enough about it. I guess I had to experience [it]; I had to go
through a couple of years with that system knowing [and] experiencing different
situations and say to myself, "Gee, if they had access to my data, I'd be dead
right now." . . . And now, I just have a much better perspective, and I'll go up
against anybody when it comes to access of this data.

At first, managers established a strong position of refusing ITSS access to
anyone outside of the CSD. For individuals seeking information on customer

trends, they offered as an alternative customized, summary reports. A manager described a specific example:

> The western region heard about this great database that we had, and they were particularly interested in finding out what their clients call us about. . . . So, as a way to pacify them, I got a copy of a client list from them, and I would on a weekly basis go in and just highlight the week's activity in view of those clients . . . and fax it to them.

For individuals seeking technical information, managers referred them to a mechanism improvised by the specialists and known as "Tech. Notes," which disseminated sanitized extracts of ITSS data throughout Zeta (see next section). Only after some time did managers relax their strong position on "no access to ITSS," although they still allow access only to selected individuals:

> We have given access to a few product management-type people on the basis of whether we felt we could trust them with the information. If other people were to move into [those positions,] we'd take the access away.

The CSD also communicated its position on ITSS access in the on-line ITSS users' guide:

> ITSS is, for the most part, the backbone of technical support. It has become so valuable that other groups are requesting access to it for everything from account management to client addresses. Reasonable requests for access to ITSS information will be considered, but let the users beware!!! ITSS is intended as a call tracking application, not a technical notes database or a client tracking database. The information in ITSS is provided "as is," with no guarantees. It represents the best efforts of technical support specialists working in a very complex support environment under serious time constraints. *Any use of ITSS that negatively impacts Support will not be allowed, and all offenders will have their access revoked immediately.* [emphases in original, highlighted in red]

Electronic knowledge dissemination. After many months of using ITSS and realizing the benefit of the ITSS knowledge base, the specialists began to generate sanitized summaries of information about particularly common or difficult problems. They shared these summaries among themselves and disseminated them to other Zeta departments. This practice, which had started informally among the specialists, received a big boost when the CSD managers used it to justify denying requests for direct access to ITSS. Zeta had in place a number of company-wide electronic bulletin boards known as Source

Zeta (implemented in the cc:Mail software package). Different departments (e.g., customer support, product management) used these bulletin boards to announce information or distribute knowledge about various products. Specialists proposed the idea of taking common or important customer problems from ITSS, documenting them with clear descriptions and appropriate solutions, and then disseminating them via Source Zeta to the rest of Zeta (including the many field service representatives who represented up to 30 percent of the CSD's callers).

The transfer of knowledge from the ITSS database to Source Zeta took a few steps. First, individual specialists voluntarily wrote up sanitized and generalized "position papers" as Tech. Notes on specific technical issues. These Tech. Notes were entered into the Tech. Notes Review database (within the Notes technology), where they were reviewed by a (volunteer) committee of specialists whose comments triggered corrections and elaborations by the original author. This review cycle was facilitated by the shared access to databases provided by the technology. After iterating a few times through the review cycle, a Tech. Note would be published on the Source Zeta bulletin board and thus disseminated throughout the firm. The initiative for producing Tech. Notes lay with the specialists. While not a mandatory part of their job, many specialists included this activity in their work practices, motivated by an interest in reducing calls from field service representatives and a desire to increase their personal visibility within Zeta:

> The incentive is more or less trying to save somebody else time. You document something that you spent a lot of time on so that somebody else doesn't have to spend the time later on.

> It is a very visible note of productivity. . . . The primary author's name is associated with it, and it's distributed in a way that indicates it came from support. So, I suppose it has both personal and group recognition.

The practice of generating and reviewing Tech. Notes was applauded by the managers, who modified their evaluation criteria to include such activity in their assessments of individuals' performance. An unanticipated outcome of the use of Tech. Notes as access control, however, was that it increased specialists' workload. Converting the electronic knowledge in ITSS from its situated, specific form to a more generic, abstract, and accurate form more suitable for broader dissemination was time-consuming, and at the time of my final interviews, specialists were finding that this voluntary activity had begun to add to their sense of time pressure. Presumably, further metamorphoses will occur as responses to these pressures.

IMPLICATIONS

Almost 20 years ago now, March (1981) called for theoretical developments that explain "how substantial changes occur as the routine consequence of standard procedures or as the unintended consequence of ordinary adaptation" (p. 575). The practice-based perspective outlined in this chapter attempts to take this call seriously. By focusing on change as situated, it provides a way of seeing that change may not always be as planned, inevitable, or discontinuous as we imagine. Rather, it is often realized through the ongoing variations which emerge frequently, even imperceptibly, in the slippages and improvisations of everyday activity. Those variations that are repeated, shared, amplified, and sustained can, over time, produce perceptible and striking organizational changes.

Such situated changes were associated with the implementation and use of new technology in the customer support department of Zeta. The appropriation of this technology by members of the CSD, and the adaptations and adjustments they enacted over time, facilitated the slow, sometimes subtle, but surprisingly significant transformation of the organizing practices and structures of the CSD. In particular, we saw changes in the following areas: the nature and texture of work (from tacit, private, and unstructured to articulated, public, and more structured), patterns of interaction (from face-to-face and reactive to electronic and proactive), distribution of work (from call based to expertise based), evaluation of performance (from output focused to a focus on process and output as documented), forms of accountability (from manual and imprecise to electronic and detailed), nature of knowledge (from tacit, experiential, and local to formulated, procedural, and distributed), and mechanisms of coordination (from manual, functional, local, and sporadic to electronic, cross-functional, global, and continuous).

Figure 9.2 depicts these transformational changes in the CSD as emerging out of the ongoing practices of organizational actors. The theoretical premise is that these practices are generated through a structuring process, where the everyday actions of organizational members produce, reproduce, and change their organizing structures. Changes in the CSD's organizing practices (and hence its structures) were initially triggered by the design and installation of a new information technology to mediate support work. In contrast to the technological imperative perspective, however, this new technology did not cause particular predetermined organizational changes. Rather, it was designed and constructed by the CSD implementation team to provide a set of features which both constrained and enabled the ITSS users in ways anticipated and unanticipated by the implementation team. The ITSS technology enabled specialists and managers of the CSD to allow the representation and storage of structured and free-form data about each call entered into the database, provide shared access to networked users, support fast searching of records in the database, facilitate communication and call transfers, allow replication of distributed databases, and afford direct links to related databases. But the ITSS technology also constrained the practice of support work by formalizing and encoding particular procedures for conducting support work; providing only particular structured views of the data in the form of fixed entry and edit screens (manipulation of which required careful attention); restricting structured fields to only certain values, thus legitimating only certain meanings; presenting a strictly chronological trace of work in progress that endorses documentation, not action; preventing the alteration of incident histories; making work process visible and measurable; providing few cues or clues about communication and collaboration norms; offering little statistical capability; and mediating work so that when the technology breaks down or exhibits errors, breakdowns arise in user routines.

As members of the CSD attempted to make sense of and appropriate the new technology and its embedded constraints and enablements, they enacted—through the structuring process—a series of metamorphic changes in their organizing practices and structures. These changes were grounded in members' daily actions and interactions as they responded to the expected and unexpected outcomes, breakdowns, and opportunities that their technological sensemaking and appropriation afforded. While some of the changes were deliberate and intended, others were emergent and unanticipated. In contrast to the planned change perspective, thus, many of the changes realized by the CSD were not planned a priori, and neither were they discrete events. Rather, they revealed a pattern of contextualized innovations in practice enacted by all members of the CSD and proceeding over time with no predetermined end point. A comparison of CSD practices and structures in June 1992 and December 1994 (Figure 9.2) reveals significant changes in work, norms, structure, coordination mechanisms, evaluation criteria, and technology use. These changes were not all implemented with the initial deployment of the technology (Metamorphosis I) but emerged and evolved through moments of situated practice over time. These findings suggest—contrary to the punctuated equilibrium prediction that organizations do not experience transformations gradually—that local variations in practice can, over time, shade into a set of substantial organizational metamorphoses.

The five metamorphoses in Zeta's CSD provide one instance of situated organizational change. Considerable further empirical research is necessary. As indicated earlier, the current research is limited by the retrospective nature of much of the data. Studies that allow long-term observation of ongoing practices would clearly deepen and extend the analysis, begun here, of organizational change as situated in moments of practice. Further empirical research is also needed to determine the extent to which a practice-based perspective on transformative change is useful in other contexts and how different organizational and technological conditions influence the improvisations attempted and implemented. While the changes in the CSD were relatively effective, one may imagine, for example, that in a more hierarchically organized or more rigidly controlled workplace, the sorts of workarounds, adjustments, and innovations enacted by Zeta actors may not have been tolerated or successful. Organizational inertia and resistance to change—often seen in organizations and predicted by a number of change theories—were not apparent within the CSD. Members of the CSD appeared to be open to exploring alternative ways of working and of learning from and changing with the new technology. The CSD managers initiated and encouraged such experimentation and learning, thus providing a legitimating context for ongoing improvisation. Indeed, these ongoing changes continue within the CSD, and as the research study ended, there was no sense of a transformation completed. Metamorphosis continues, as one manager observed:

> We've had ITSS for two years. I'm surprised that the enthusiasm hasn't gone away. . . . I think it's because it's been changed on a regular basis. And there's always some new feature, or we think about . . . other things that we can do with it. Knowing that they're going to get implemented keeps you wanting to think about it and keep going.

Similarly, more research is needed to investigate how the nature of the technology used influences the change process and shapes the possibilities for ongoing organizational change. Had a more rigid, more fixed-function technology been used, the pattern of use and change realized within the CSD would have been different. The specific ITSS technology was built within a general technological platform (the Notes groupware system) which is more open-ended, generic, and user-customizable than are traditional transaction processing or single-user computer systems. Such technological capabilities represent a new class of organizational computing, which Malone and colleagues (1992) aptly refer to as *radically tailorable tools*. The distinguishing capability of such tools is that they enable users to construct or customize specific versions and local adaptations of the underlying technological features. This capability has two important implications for practice. One, it allows for easy ongoing changes to the technology in use, in contrast to more rigid, fixed-function technologies which are difficult and costly, if not impossible, to change during use. Two, because customization is required for effective use, ongoing learning in use and consequent technological and organizational changes are encouraged. As Orlikowski and colleagues (1995) suggest, because new customizable technologies are so general, local adaptations and ongoing accommodations of such technologies and their use are necessary to make them relevant (and keep them relevant) to particular contexts and situated work practices. Such adaptations and accommodations cannot be known upfront and typically have to be enacted in situ. The practice-based logic of change followed by the CSD would appear to be a particularly useful process for implementing and using such new technologies.

The particular kinds of metamorphoses identified in Zeta's CSD— increased documentation, accountability, visibility, and differentiation; shared responsibility; proactive collaboration; distributed and cross-functional coordination; and knowledge dissemination—are clearly specific to one unit (CSD) within one organization (Zeta). This is appropriate in a perspective of situated change, which by definition assumes context specificity. However, the *process* of change outlined here—ongoing local improvisations in response to deliberate and emergent variations in practice—is potentially generalizable and is offered as a stimulus for further research. Of particular interest is the general usefulness of this perspective in those organizations embracing calls for flexibility; experimenting with ongoing learning; or investing in open-ended, tailorable technologies.

The dominant models of technology-based organizational transformation—planned change, technological imperative, and punctuated equilibrium—each make a number of assumptions about the nature of agency, context, technology, and change which are appropriate to an organizing practice premised on stability. Contemporary demands for organizations to be flexible, responsive, and capable of learning require organizing practices to deal with ongoing change. I have proposed an additional perspective on organizational transformation that avoids the strong assumptions that have characterized prior change perspectives because it focuses on the situated micro-level changes that actors enact over time as they make sense of and act in the world. In its presumption of ongoing action, a practice lens allows for the possibility of ongoing change. It conceives of change as situated and endemic to the practice of organizing. It affords an analysis of technology-based organizational transformations that is ongoing, improvisational, and grounded in everyday, knowledgeable agency. As such, it may offer a unique and especially appropriate strategy of interpretation for the new organizing discourse becoming increasingly common today.[3]

NOTES

1. While Escher, as artist, clearly orchestrated the metamorphoses exhibited, he has depicted the transformation process as driven by a situated momentum.

2. Names of the organization and its departments, members, products, and technology applications have all been disguised.

3. This research was supported by the Center for Coordination Science at the Massachusetts Institute of Technology.

REFERENCES

Abernathy, W. J. and K. B. Clark, "Innovation: Mapping the Winds of Creative Destruction," *Research Policy,* 14 (1985), 3-22.

Barley, S. R., "Technology, Power, and the Social Organization of Work," in N. Tomaso (Ed.), *Research in the Sociology of Organizations,* Vol. 6, JAI, Greenwich, CT, 1988, 33-80.

Blau, P., C. McHugh-Falbe, W. McKinley, and T. Phelps, "Technology and Organization in Manufacturing," *Admin. Sci. Quarterly,* 21 (1976), 20-40.

Burns, T. and G. M. Stalker, *The Management of Innovation,* Tavistock, London, 1961.

Carter, N. M., "Computerization as a Predominate Technology: Its Influence on the Structure of Newspaper Organizations," *Academy of Management J.,* 27 (1984), 247-270.

Ciborra, C. U. and G. F. Lanzara, "Designing Networks in Action: Formative Contexts and Postmodern Systems Development," in R. Clarke and J. Cameron (Eds.), *Managing Information Technology's Organisational Impact,* Elsevier Science, Amsterdam, 1991, 265-279.

Deming, W. E., *Out of the Crisis,* MIT Press, Cambridge, MA, 1986.

DeSanctis, G. and M. S. Poole, "Capturing the Complexity in Advanced Technology Use: Adaptive Structuration Theory," *Organization Sci.,* 5, 2 (1994), 121-147.

Dunphy, D. C. and D. A. Stace, "Transformational and Coercive Strategies for Planned Organizational Change," *Organizational Studies,* 9, 3 (1988), 317-334.

Eisenhardt, K. M., "Building Theories From Case Study Research," *Acad. Management Rev.,* 14, 4 (1989), 532-550.

Escher, M. C., *Escher on Escher: Exploring the Infinite,* Harry N. Abrams, New York, 1986.

Foucault, M., *Discipline and Punish,* Vintage Books, New York, 1979.

Galbraith, J. R., *Designing Complex Organizations,* Addison-Wesley, Reading, MA, 1973.

Gallivan, M., C. H. Goh, L. M. Hitt, and G. Wyner, "Incident Tracking at InfoCorp: Case Study of a Pilot Notes Implementation," Working Paper No. 3590-93, Center for Coordination Science, Sloan School of Management, Massachusetts Institute of Technology, 1993.

Gersick, C. J. G., "Revolutionary Change Theories: A Multilevel Exploration of the Punctuated Equilibrium Paradigm," *Acad. Management Rev.,* 16, 1 (1991), 10-36.

Giddens, A., *The Constitution of Society: Outline of the Theory of Structure,* University of California Press, Berkeley, 1984.

Goffman, E., *The Presentation of Self in Everyday Life,* Doubleday/Anchor, New York, 1959.

Hage, J. and M. Aiken, *Social Change in Complex Organizations,* Random House, New York, 1970.

Hammer, M. and J. Champy, *Reengineering the Corporation,* HarperCollins, New York, 1993.

Heidegger, M., *The Question Concerning Technology* (W. Lovitt, Trans.), Harper & Row, New York, 1977.

Heilbroner, R. L., "Do Machines Make History?" *Technology and Culture,* 8 (1967), 335-345.

Huber, G. P., "A Theory of the Effects of Advanced Information Technologies on Organizational Design, Intelligence, and Decision Making," *Acad. Management Rev.,* 15, 1 (1990), 47-71.

Hutchins, E., "Organizing Work by Adaptation," *Organization Sci.,* 2, 1 (1991), 14-39.

Lave, J., *Cognition in Practice,* Cambridge University Press, Cambridge, UK, 1988.

Leavitt, H. J. and T. L. Whistler, "Management in the 1980s," *Harvard Business Rev.,* 36 (1958), 41-48.

Lewin, K., *Field Theory in Social Science,* Harper & Row, New York, 1951.

Malone, T. W., "Commentary on Suchman Article and Winograd Response," *Computer-Supported Cooperative Work J.,* 3, 1 (1995), 36-38.

———, K. Y. Lai, and C. Fry, "Experiments With OVAL: A Radically Tailorable Tool for Co-operative Work," in *Proceedings of the Conference on Computer-Supported Cooperative Work,* Association of Computing Machinery/Special Interest Group on Computer and Human Interaction and Special Interest Group on Office Information Systems, Toronto, 1992, 289-297.

March, J. G., "Footnotes to Organizational Change," *Admin. Sci. Quarterly,* 26 (1981), 563-577.

Meyer, A. D. and J. D. Goes, "Organizational Assimilation of Innovations: A Multilevel Contex-tual Analysis," *Acad. Management J.,* 31, 4 (1988), 897-923.

———, ———, and G. R. Brooks, "Organizations Reacting to Hyperturbulence," in G. P. Huber and W. H. Glick (Eds.), *Organizational Change and Redesign,* Oxford University Press, New York, 1993, 66-111.

Miles, M. B. and A. M. Huberman, *Qualitative Data Analysis: A Sourcebook of New Methods,* Sage, Beverly Hills, CA, 1984.

Miles, R. E. and C. C. Snow, "Fit, Failure, and the Hall of Fame," *California Management Rev.,* 26, 3 (1984), 10-28.

Miller, D. and P. H. Friesen, *Organizations: A Quantum View,* Prentice Hall, Englewood Cliffs, NJ, 1984.

Mintzberg, H., "An Emerging Strategy of 'Direct' Research," *Admin. Sci. Quarterly,* 24 (1979), 582-589.

———, "Crafting Strategy," *Harvard Business Rev.,* July-August (1987), 66-75.

——— and J. A. Waters, "Of Strategies: Deliberate and Emergent," *Strategic Management J.,* 6 (1985), 257-272.

Orlikowski, W. J., "Integrated Information Environment or Matrix of Control? The Contradic-tory Implications of Information Technology," *Accounting, Management, and Informa-tion Technology,* 1, 1 (1991), 9-42.

———, "The Duality of Technology: Rethinking the Concept of Technology in Organizations," *Organization Sci.,* 3, 3 (1992), 398-472.

——— and D. C. Gash, "Technological Frames: Making Sense of Information Technology in Organizations," *ACM Trans. Information Systems,* 12 (1994), 174-207.

———, J. Yates, K. Okamura, and M. Fujimoto, "Shaping Electronic Communication: The Metastructuring of Technology in Use," *Organization Sci.,* 6, 4 (1995), 423-444.

———, "Using Technology and Constituting Structures: A Practice Lens for Studying Technol-ogy in Organizations," *Organization Sci.,* 11, 4 (2000), 404-428.

Pentland, B. T., "Organizing Moves in Software Support Hot Lines," *Admin. Sci. Quarterly,* 37 (1992), 527-548.

Peters, T. J. and R. H. Waterman, *In Search of Excellence: Lessons From America's Best-Run Companies,* Harper & Row, New York, 1982.

Pettigrew, A. M., *The Awakening Giant,* Blackwell, Oxford, UK, 1985.

———, "Longitudinal Field Research on Change: Theory and Practice," *Organization Sci.,* 1, 3 (1990), 267-292.

———, E. Ferlie, and L. McKee, *Shaping Strategic Change: Managing Change in Large Orga-nizations,* Sage, Newbury Park, CA, 1992.

Poster, M., *The Mode of Information: Poststructuralism and Social Context,* University of Chicago Press, Chicago, 1990.

———, *The Second Media Age,* Polity, Cambridge, UK, 1995.

Rice, R. E. and E. M. Rogers, "Reinvention in the Innovation Process," *Knowledge,* 1, 4 (1980), 499-514.

Romanelli, E. and M. L. Tushman, "Organizational Transformation as Punctuated Equilibrium: An Empirical Test," *Acad. Management J.,* 37, 5 (1994), 1141-1166.

Smith, M. R. and L. Marx (Eds.), *Does Technology Drive History? The Dilemma of Technological Determinism,* MIT Press, Cambridge, MA, 1994.

Strauss, A. and J. Corbin, *Basics of Qualitative Research: Grounded Theory, Procedures, and Techniques,* Sage, Newbury Park, CA, 1990.

Suchman, L., *Plans and Situated Action,* Cambridge University Press, Cambridge, UK, 1987.

Tushman, M. L. and P. Anderson, "Technological Discontinuities and Organizational Environments," *Admin. Sci. Quarterly,* 31 (1986), 439-465.

———— and E. Romanelli, "Organizational Evolution: A Metamorphosis Model of Convergence and Reorientation," *Res. Organizational Behavior,* 7 (1985), 171-222.

Tyre, M. J. and W. J. Orlikowski, "Windows of Opportunity: Temporal Patterns of Technological Adaptation in Organizations," *Organization Sci.,* 5, 1 (1994), 98-118.

Van Maanen, J., "The Fact of Fiction in Organizational Ethnography," *Admin. Sci. Quarterly,* 24 (1979), 539-550.

————, *Tales From the Field,* University of Chicago Press, Chicago, 1988.

Weick, K. E., "Organizational Redesign as Improvisation," in G. P. Huber and W. H. Glick (Eds.), *Organizational Change and Redesign,* Oxford University Press, New York, 1993, 346-379.

Wilson, D. C., *A Strategy of Change: Concepts and Controversies in the Management of Change,* Routledge, London, 1992.

Winner, L., *The Whale and the Reactor: A Search for Limits in an Age of High Technology,* University of Chicago Press, Chicago, 1986.

Zaltman, G., R. Duncan, and J. Holbek, *Innovations and Organizations,* John Wiley, New York, 1973.

Zuboff, S., *In the Age of the Smart Machine,* Basic Books, New York, 1988.

10

Transforming Work Through Information Technology

A Comparative Case Study of Geographic Information Systems in County Government

DANIEL ROBEY

SUNDEEP SAHAY

It is commonly assumed that information technologies have the potential to transform social organizations. Through their capacity to gather, store, manipulate, and transmit information efficiently, information technologies may support more effective forms of organizational coordination and control and render traditional structures obsolete. Transforming organizations with information technologies is an important business objective because traditional structures are often ineffective in producing desired levels of productivity, customer service, employee welfare, and shareholder value. Scott Morton (1991) has argued that, in the future, all organizations will need to be transformed with computer-based technologies to be effective.

Yet the literature on information systems contains many reports of unfulfilled potential, even where transformation is a formal organizational objective (e.g., Davenport and Stoddard 1994; Pinsonneault and Kraemer 1993; Robey et al. 1995; Zuboff 1988). These recent studies are consistent with earlier reviews of the literature on the organizational impacts of information

From "Transforming Work Through Information Technology: A Comparative Case Study of Geographic Information Systems in County Government," by Daniel Robey and Sundeep Sahay, 1996, *Information Systems Research,* Vol. 7, No. 1, pp. 63-92. Copyright © 1996, Institute for Operations Research and the Management Sciences. Reprinted with permission.

technology, which have consistently identified mixed and contradictory findings (Attewell and Rule 1984; Huber 1984; Kling 1980; Markus and Robey 1988; Nelson 1990; Robey 1977; Swanson 1987). From all such accounts, it is safe to conclude that organizational transformation is not accomplished through the mere installation of new systems with greater computational powers. Rather, the success of technology-enabled organizational change depends upon a combination of technical and social influences that are only partially controllable. New information systems must meet demanding technical requirements and high performance standards, and the existing social context must be receptive to attempts to change it. As technical and social influences interact, a diversity of consequences may be realized; intended transformations may occur, older forms may persist, or unanticipated combinations of new and old practices may emerge.

This research adopts an interpretive approach to examine the implementation of geographic information systems (GISs) in two local county governments in the United States. Interpretive research assumes that social reality is subjectively understood, both by participants in the organization and by researchers (Burrell and Morgan 1979; Hirschheim and Klein 1989; Orlikowski and Baroudi 1991; Walsham 1993). Like all human artifacts, applications of information technology are open to interpretation by their developers, users, and other actors. We assume that the understandings and meanings which actors ascribe to information technology affect the technology's actual design, deployment, use, and consequences. Accordingly, we do not treat a GIS as an object capable of effecting social change independently of actors' interpretations.

GEOGRAPHIC INFORMATION SYSTEMS

Among the applications of information technology with transformational potential are GISs. A GIS is a type of computer-based system that captures, stores, displays, analyzes, and models natural and artificial environments using data referenced to locations on the earth's surface. Spatial data are usually described in a GIS by geographic position and other attributes in computer-readable form. Regulatory pressures, scarce resources, and public involvement in environmental decisions have led both public and private organizations to adopt GISs as a tool for modeling complex spatial problems. GIS technologies continue to advance with improvements in computer graphics, database management technologies, and the incorporation of satellite images. These advances have made more sophisticated, accurate, and cost-effective GIS applications available to support decisions and inform policies in areas such as environmental resource management, land-use planning, and law enforcement, among others.

GIS applications have transformational potential because they inform decisions about resources that are distributed across space. In the context of government organizations especially, a GIS has the potential to consolidate the work of departments that deal with different resources within a defined geographic area. By providing a common technical base for spatial analysis, a GIS has the potential to integrate tasks involving surveying, mapping, designing, planning, and other related activities normally performed in separate departments. Thus, a GIS provides the capability for reducing structural differentiation by cutting across existing organizational boundaries and for creating new work procedures related to spatial analysis. GIS applications have become extremely popular, particularly in the public sector. Fletcher and colleagues (1992) described GISs as the technology with the biggest impact on the thinking of county managers in local governments in the United States.

Despite their potential, information technologies have not been associated with transformations of government organizations in previous research. To the contrary, the weight of evidence favors the persistence of existing formal structures and political alignments when computers are introduced in local governments (Danziger et al. 1982; Danziger and Kraemer 1985; Kraemer 1991; Pinsonneault and Kraemer 1993). In summarizing the findings of an extensive research program on the effects of computers in government, Kraemer (1991) concluded that computing reinforced existing power structures and played little role in changing organizational structures:

> For the most part, computing has had no discernible effect at all on organization structure. Where it has had a discernible effect, it has led to slightly greater centralization of already centralized organizations. Thus, computing has clearly reinforced existing organizational arrangements. (p. 172)

While GISs were not common at the time of these studies, Kraemer expressed doubt that reforms in public administration would ever be directly associated with newer technologies: "Technology is not the driver; it is rarely even the catalyst; at most, it is supportive of reform efforts decided on other grounds" (p. 178).

In this [chapter], our objective is to advance understanding of the relationship between applications of information technology (GISs particularly) and organizational changes in the public agencies that use them. Our approach is to take a detailed empirical examination of how the technology is interpreted by social actors engaged in its development and use. By understanding the subjective sense that participants make of GISs, we believe that their role in organizational transformation can be better understood.

SOCIAL INTERPRETATIONS
OF INFORMATION TECHNOLOGY

Recent approaches to research on the organizational consequences of information technologies emphasize the importance of the social context of implementation and the subjective meanings ascribed to information technologies. As actors propose, design, develop, implement, and use information systems, they endow them with social meanings or interpretations. These interpretations help to shape the subsequent use of the technology, somewhat independently of technology's material properties (Hirschheim and Newman 1991; Prasad 1993; Robey and Azevedo 1994; Walsham 1993). The study of social interpretations can yield insight into the "social construction" of both information technology and organizations (Berger and Luckmann 1967; Bijker et al. 1987). Research that focuses on social interpretation can also potentially explain why similar or identical technologies often produce different social consequences even in comparable organizational settings (Barley 1986; Orlikowski 1993; Orlikowski and Gash 1994; Robey and Rodriguez-Diaz 1989). An interpretive study of information systems, for example, might reveal why users in one organization fail to exploit a technology with transformational potential while it is fully exploited in another. An interpretive study might also reveal why technologies with more modest transformational potential might occasion significant changes in a particular organization.

Key Assumptions

Two key assumptions underlie interpretive research on information technology. First, neither human actions nor technologies are assumed to exert direct causal "impacts" on organizations. Deterministic causal assumptions are replaced by the assumption of emergent causality, wherein consequences result from the interplay among computing infrastructures, conflicting objectives and preferences of different social groups, and the operation of chance (Markus and Robey 1988; Pfeffer 1982; Slack 1984). Emergent causality assumes that social consequences are not conditioned by any particular set of predictor variables. Rather, any number of influences may operate within a given social context to produce social interpretations and outcomes. The consequences of a technology like GISs, therefore, are assumed to be indeterminate. This assumption directs researchers' attention away from the multivariate contingency models designed to explain greater variance in the social consequences of information technology (e.g., Attewell and Rule 1984), while it draws attention to the complex social processes by which those consequences are enacted. Through detailed contextual analyses of the interactions between human actors and technology, social consequences can be traced, understood, and eventually managed. The interpretive approach eschews general "imperative" arguments about information technology and favors a particularistic, contextual orientation.

The second guiding assumption is that technology is conceived as a material artifact that embodies human purposes but that it remains open to interpretation during implementation and use. Information technology is produced through human action; it does not and cannot occur naturally. The material properties of technology may be the result of social compromises and fallible knowledge during design and construction, so the exact purposes of its designers may not be faithfully rendered in the resulting product. Furthermore, information technologies are prone to adaptations of use, sometimes called reinventions or workarounds (Fulk 1993; Johnson and Rice 1987; Kraut et al. 1989). They may be socially reconstructed through use, producing consequences different from those initially imagined. These assumptions of interpretive research reduce the temptation to regard information technology as capable of producing social results directly.

Explaining Technology-Enabled
Organizational Transformation

The results of a growing number of studies show the value of the assumptions used in interpretive research on information technologies. Several studies have focused upon the social context and processes that produce the meanings of technology, thereby offering potential explanations for the social outcomes. For example, Orlikowski's (1993) comparison between two organizations adopting computer-aided software engineering (CASE) tools revealed a diversity of outcomes not explained by the characteristics of CASE alone. Differences in competitive conditions, corporate strategies and structures, and arrangements for managing information technologies were all linked to differences in the consequences of adopting and using CASE tools. Radical changes, or reorientations, in both the products and processes of system design were targeted (and partially achieved) in one organization, whereas incremental variations were targeted and achieved in the other, using essentially the same technology. From this study, the importance of specific aspects of context and process were established.

Other studies support the general conclusion that organizational context influences the consequences of information technology. Robey and

Rodriguez-Diaz (1989) reported that differences in organizational cultures were partially responsible for the divergent experiences encountered by an implementation team installing the same information system in different offices of a multinational organization. In several case studies reported by Zuboff (1988), the political processes surrounding implementation were linked to failed attempts to transform organizations using information technology. Walsham (1993) employed a scheme based on structuration theory to examine the effects of context and process on interpretations of information technology in several organizations. In each of these studies, the researchers focused on the social meanings of information technology as a basis for explaining its organizational consequences. In turn, social interpretations of technologies were linked to the organizational context and social processes surrounding implementation.

While these studies amply demonstrate the source of social interpretations and their role in the implementation of information systems, they leave unanswered many questions about the processes through which information technology affects organizations. More recent studies illuminate some of the dynamics of organizational changes accompanying information technology. For example, it is clear that the implementation of technical changes can frequently deviate from a rational sequence designed to mesh technical and strategic objectives. Technologies may be acquired first, followed by changes in skill requirements, organizational structure, and, lastly, competitive strategy (Yetton et al. 1994). Moreover, Sauer and Yetton (1994) explored the effects of simultaneous, contradictory changes in technical systems and concluded that multiple implementations (of a Kanban ordering system and a Material Requirements Planning system) in a single organization could impede one another. Additionally, the timing of social adaptations to technological change appears to affect subsequent use and consequences of a variety of technologies. Tyre and Orlikowski (1994) detected "windows of opportunity," occurring soon after new technologies were introduced, in which most successful adaptations were likely to occur. Adaptations after the initial window period were far less frequent or consequential than those occurring immediately after implementation. This finding suggests that, if the window of opportunity is missed, technologies with transformational potential may not be used to change existing organizational structures and patterns of work. Together, these studies have focused needed attention on the timing and sequence of events in the process of technical change.

Recent research has also begun to reveal the importance of different rates of technical changes in organizations. Although a distinction has been established in the organizational literature between radical (revolutionary) change and incremental (evolutionary) change (Dewar and Dutton 1986; Tushman and Romanelli 1984), empirical studies have produced contradictory findings regarding the relative effectiveness of radical and incremental change (e.g., March 1981; Miller 1982; Miller and Friesen 1982; Romanelli and Tushman 1994). In one of the first studies to examine the dynamics of radical changes involving information technology, Gallivan and colleagues (1994) proposed a distinction between the nature of change (radical vs. incremental) and the pace of change (rapid vs. gradual). Their report of one firm adopting CASE tools revealed a paradoxical pattern in which radical changes were effectively implemented at a gradual pace rather than rapidly, as might be expected. This finding suggests that both rapid and gradual rates of change may be associated with organizational transformation, although little is known about the relative effectiveness of implementation processes that proceed at these different rates.

Studies such as these stimulate further inquiry into the implementation processes for information technologies that purportedly enable organizational transformation. The present study is designed to contrast the experiences of two organizations with GIS technology and uses an interpretive approach to detect and explain differences in GIS processes of implementation and the related organizational consequences.

METHOD

The research method employed in this study was to conduct interviews with a large number of respondents in two organizations. Analysis was aided by a comparative research design, which allowed contrasts between interpretations of the same GIS technology in the two organizations. By studying the same technology in comparable organizations, this design directed attention to the contrasts between implementation processes as potential explanations of divergent interpretations and social outcomes.

Research Design and Sampling

The research was conducted in two neighboring county government organizations that were in the process of implementing GISs. The two organizations used the same GIS software (called Arc/Info) for similar purposes. In one organization, given the pseudonym North County here, two user groups (Planning Department and Land Management Department), one GIS coordinating group (Technical Services), and two persons outside of these three departments were studied. In the second county, given the pseudonym South County, two user groups (Planning Department and Environmental Management Department) and one GIS coordinating group (Office of Computer Services) were studied. Within each organization, the sampling plan was flexible

TABLE 10.1 Research Design and Sampling Plan

	Department				
Research site	Technical Support Group	User Department	User Department	Others	Total Respondents
North County	Technical Services (6)	Planning (12)	Land Management (11)	Legal (1) and Regulation (1)	31
South County	Office of Computer Services (14)	Planning (3)	Environmental Resource Management (12)	0	29
Total respondents	20	15	23	2	60

NOTE: Numbers of respondents are in parentheses.

and evolved with the research needs. Key respondents were initially identified from the selected departments based on their involvement in GIS implementation. Discussions with these key people provided a deeper understanding of the social networks within and across departments, and additional respondents were selected from these networks.

A total of 32 interviews were conducted in North County with 31 different people (1 respondent was interviewed twice, the second interview serving to verify certain issues). Of the 31 respondents, 29 belonged to one of the selected departments, and 2 belonged to departments not previously identified (Legal and Regulation). In South County, a total of 29 people provided 28 interviews (in one case, 2 people were interviewed together). Table 10.1 shows the organizational locations of all respondents in the study.

The primary method for gathering data was through semistructured personal interviews. Questions about the features and limitations of the GIS were asked first, followed by questions about both the implementation of the GIS and its consequences. Implementation questions asked whether the GIS was deployed as a distributed or centralized system, which department originated the technology, and how the organizational structure was established to oversee GIS implementation. Interview reports for this information were supplemented with documents and archival sources such as the organization's business plan. Questions about organizational consequences sought respondents' reactions to changes in their work and the organization as a result

TABLE 10.2 Summary of Coding Schemes

North County	South County
1. *Initiation*	1. *Initiation*
1.1 Need	1.1 Capability
1.2 Capability	1.2 Software selection
1.3 Software selection	
2. *Implementatio n*	2. *Implementation*
2.1 Organization	2.1 Intraorganization
2.2 Technology	2.2 Interorganization
	2.3 Technology, intraorganization
	2.4 Technology, interorganization
3. *Impacts*	3. *Impacts*
3.1 Current	3.1 Current
3.2 Future	3.2 Future

of GIS implementation. Information about each respondent's education, training, and experience with technology was also obtained in the interviews.

Data Analysis

Interview data were analyzed in four distinct steps: (1) coding and splitting the transcribed texts, (2) integrating the split data to form themes, (3) aligning themes with relevant social groups, and (4) contrasting the themes between the two sites.

Coding and splitting. All interviews were transcribed and coded according to the scheme shown in Table 10.2. The coding scheme was developed through an iterative process whereby the two authors first established preliminary categories, then independently read sample transcripts and coded text into those categories, and then compared their classifications and discussed discrepancies. The preliminary categories were modified, and other sample texts were again coded independently. At each iteration, the rules for assigning segments of text to each category were articulated and refined. The iterations eventually produced the coding categories shown in Table 10.2; the detailed rules used to assign text to these categories are available in Sahay (1993, Appendix 3.3). The iterative process ensured consistency in the method by which text was coded, which is comparable to the notion of interrater reliability as required in positivist research (Hirschman 1986).

Using this scheme, all remaining interview texts were split into coded segments by one of the authors.

Formation of themes. Themes were formed by defining a unifying idea that represented the interpretations found in multiple coded segments. Conceptual labels were assigned to describe the common thread among these ideas, and similarly labeled segments were combined into themes and assigned more general labels. A computer program was written to assist in the location and grouping of similarly coded segments of text. No specific number of themes was sought, although a conscious attempt was made to avoid the generation of too many themes with similar ideas underlying them.

Alignment of themes with relevant social groups. As used in research on the social construction of technology, the concept of relevant social group refers to the sets of people who are capable of influencing the implementation and use of technology (e.g., Bijker 1987; Fulk 1993; Mackenzie and Wajcman 1985). These groups were identified by detecting commonalities among the respondents connected with the coded segments that made up each theme. Thus, members of the relevant social groups were defined as those who subscribed to the same themes. Relevant groups formed around departments (e.g., the Planning Department in North County), organizational levels (e.g., managers), disciplines (e.g., geographers), and functions (e.g., initiators of the GIS in North County).

Contrasting themes between sites. To take advantage of the comparative research design, contrasts between sites were studied carefully to see how groups in the two organizations differed in their interpretations of GIS technology. Themes were compared directly and associated with differences in the reported consequences of technology.

RESULTS

Using the method of analysis described above, 44 themes were generated and associated with nine relevant social groups in North County, and 39 themes associated with eight groups were generated in South County. In the present analysis, only those themes directly relevant to explaining the organizational consequences of the GIS are drawn upon; an exhaustive analysis of themes and groups derived from the study is reported elsewhere (Sahay 1993). Select themes were grouped into five categories representing four distinct processes of implementation (initiation, transition, deployment, and spread of knowledge) and the organizational consequences of GIS. These categories are related to the interview schedule insofar as they reflect the researchers' concern with capturing interpretations related to the implementation and consequences of the GIS. However, the specific categories are derived from analysis of similarities among themes detected in the data. Categories were used to organize a narrative description of the implementation and consequences of the GIS in each site. Representative excerpts from specific interviews were used to illustrate the consequences and processes. The results are organized to provide, first, an overview of GIS implementation and the consequences reported by respondents in each site. Then, the four specific processes are presented as a means of explaining the differences in consequences between sites.

North County

Overview of GIS implementation. The implementation of Arc/Info in North County began in October 1989 with the preparation of a 72-page planning document that included a business case justifying the need for Arc/Info. A team of senior officials, drawn largely from the Geographic Sciences Department (GSD) and headed by a senior geographer, defined the overall implementation strategy. The planning document was prepared with the assistance of a well-known consultant who worked closely with the team. The selection process consumed three months, culminating in the choice of Arc/Info based on its technical and functional superiority over two competing packages. A distributed technical environment was chosen for implementation, with users holding primary responsibility for developing applications, maintaining different coverages, and controlling the quality of individual data sets. The functions of archiving and indexing were retained by the GSD, which had become a clearinghouse for the analysis and maintenance of spatial data in the years prior to the introduction of Arc/Info. The GSD had previously included a core group of five technicians, primarily using earlier computer systems for spatial analysis (i.e., Computer Vision and PC Arc/Info). When Arc/Info was introduced (on Sun workstations), the GSD was disbanded, and the technicians were redistributed over five user departments.

Implementation of the GIS in North County was governed by a three-tier committee structure. At the top level was the GIS sponsor's group, which included representatives from top management. The second tier of the structure included GIS coordinators who were responsible for ensuring that their departmental GIS activities adhered to organizational procedures and data standards. The coordinators were closely linked to the GIS sponsor's group through some overlapping membership. A subcommittee of the second tier, the GIS Technical Advisory Committee (GTAC) included GIS professionals drawn from each department represented by the GIS coordinators. Most members of the GTAC were geographers, and the committee exercised considerable influence in shaping the technical future of the GIS through such tasks as design of the data dictionary, repair of software bugs, and development of procedures for archiving data. The third tier of North County's governance structure was the users group, which existed to enhance user awareness and to provide feedback from users to top management. A group of GIS professionals, called the GIS Support Group, was responsible for operational matters such as keeping the system running, loading the software, configuring the workstations, maintaining the data sets, managing the archiving of data, assisting users with backups, solving user problems, and conducting training.

The geographers in the GSD subscribed to an integrative and holistic philosophy of GIS technology's role and function, which seemed consistent with their academic discipline. They assumed users to be mature enough to appreciate a distributed system, and they favored a high degree of user training. The geographers' extensive experience with mapping programs equipped them with the capability to absorb new spatial technologies. Although most of the other groups (technicians, surveyors, and managers) were more familiar with data represented in digital form, they also understood spatial concepts and mapping systems in general. Consequently, it was easy for user groups to negotiate contracts for data conversion with GIS vendors. The implementation of the GIS in North County had gathered a great deal of momentum, and by the second year of its three-year implementation program, more than 50 workstations had been installed compared to the 12 originally budgeted.

Impacts of the GIS in North County. Despite the fact that the system was only partially implemented, it was widely expressed that Arc/Info had already produced changes in departmental structure and in the conduct of North County's business. Seven members of the social group identified as "managers" considered the GIS to have redefined key aspects of work and organization. One commented that the GIS has forced decision makers to restructure most systems because "it can't be a distributed system with centralized support." Another remarked that "people have had their responsibilities redirected to perform functions that involved [the] GIS." These managers also concurred that individual departments interacted with each other to a greater extent than previously because they were required to maintain shared standards on common data. This produced new channels of communication between departments and forged links that had not existed before. With the redistribution of the five technicians from the GSD group within Technical

Services to the user departments, users' control over GIS applications was further reinforced.

Interviews revealed that Arc/Info was regarded as the cause of these organizational changes. For example, a technical supervisor in the Planning Department, and one of the heaviest GIS users, reported that the technology "increases the trust between different departments and divisions. . . . I think it has helped a lot with the environment here where everybody had put up walls around themselves. These walls have come down." Another manager in Technical Services supported this reasoning with the comment, "[The] GIS basically forces a stronger union. [Departments] have to depend on each other. It is kind of like you all win together or fail together." Another GIS user in the Planning Department reported, "The resources are a lot better now because [the] GIS relates all of the agencies together so you can get more information." The ability to "jump over on somebody else's computer," which referred to the sharing of applications and integrated databases, was mentioned by a technician in Land Management as a great new capability.

Arc/Info was also seen to have changed the variety, efficiency, and accuracy of spatial analyses conducted in North County. A diverse range of applications had been made possible because of Arc/Info, from monitoring permit violations over time to examining socioeconomic shifts in the population. Individual spatial analyses also involved more detail than before. For example, while users might previously have developed and consulted one land-use map, Arc/Info now permitted various subclassifications with land use. A GIS planner reported, "I can sit and run several classifications of the area just like that. We used to take a day to do a classification on a small area." Several respondents supported the idea that the GIS allowed much faster and superior analyses. This had already led, in their view, to an escalation of the demand for GIS analyses, even when they were not always necessary. The same GIS planner mentioned that "overkill" sometimes occurred when, for example, an engineering model was performed with the GIS when it did not have to be. A director in Technical Services noted that "the downside [to] all this technology is that sometimes we over-analyze things, and we don't use our experience and gut-level feelings." The groups subscribing to these themes included seven technicians and six different managers, almost half of the respondents interviewed in North County.

Such changes were accompanied by differences of opinion on the matter of job security. A group of five technicians feared that managers, engineers, and other professionals would become self-sufficient users of the GIS and that the jobs of any technicians reluctant to learn GIS-related skills were potentially threatened. Other respondents felt that jobs had become more secure and that there was little danger that current skills would become obsolete. On the contrary, skills were being upgraded as Arc/Info provided the opportunity for users to learn the skills needed to meet the need for more geographical information. A technical supervisor reported that "jobs are very secure because the demand for information is going to be 100 times more than before."

South County

Overview of GIS implementation. The GIS was initiated in South County in 1987 through the efforts of a small group of people, including the director and the Technical Support supervisor, at the Office of Computer Services (OCS). South County's government was organized into independent agencies, and OCS was the central unit that provided data processing services to all other agencies in the county. With the introduction of Arc/Info, the GIS was added to the services provided by OCS. Funding to acquire the GIS and other new systems was generated from contributions by the different departments to a common pool. In the first year, OCS obtained financial support from several larger user agencies including Police, Zoning, Waste, and Elections.

As a centralized "data processing shop" in a large governmental organization, OCS ran most of its applications for its client agencies on an IBM mainframe computer. OCS favored traditional controls and standards for system development and had resisted the deployment of distributed computer systems. OCS personnel generally lacked experience dealing with spatial information, and the transition to Arc/Info raised some important manpower issues for South County's OCS. In contrast with most of its data processing applications, which were designed to run on the mainframe, OCS implemented Arc/Info on a Digital Vax computer system. A centralized technical configuration was adopted, with OCS maintaining the central databases, providing application development and support services, and conducting training programs for users. OCS's centralized Application Development and Technical Support groups were made responsible for developing specific GIS applications for users on a contractual basis.

The GIS was introduced into two departments studied in this research: Environmental Resource Management (ERM) and the Planning Department. Federal programs and agencies such as the Storm Water Utility and Federal Emergency Management Agency mandated that maps for storm water outfall and flood protection layers be prepared by the GIS. ERM decided to develop a data management system prior to any real GIS applications. The Planning Department's interest in the GIS took place through a chance encounter with members of North County's GIS group. This led to further meetings in which ideas were exchanged regarding the use of the GIS to support different planning activities. As mandated by South County's governance mechanisms, all user departments contracted with OCS to develop their respective GIS applications.

Impacts of the GIS in South County. Among the respondents in the two agencies studied in South County, Arc/Info was reported to have made limited impact. A user in ERM, who had worked with the GIS applications being developed by OCS, reported bluntly, "I don't see any organizational change because we have [the] GIS." The Planning Department had not made a firm commitment to the GIS, and the three users interviewed there had not experienced any consequences. Their position was to "wait and see" what effects the GIS might have before proceeding with more serious financial commitments. In addition, there were few impacts on work and manpower requirements. A biologist noted that in ERM the extra work that had been generated due to the GIS involved only data entry, and that was accomplished using temporary interns. Since most GIS work at ERM was conducted through the OCS analysts, the in-house development of GIS skills for the ERM analysts was limited. Three OCS staff members shared the belief that surveyors were apprehensive about losing their jobs, but the majority of users indicated that GIS technology would not displace anyone. Because new skill requirements were focused narrowly around data entry, impacts of the GIS on job skills were seen as negligible in South County.

Overall, consequences were limited to the GIS's use as a device to produce attractive maps while supporting a small amount of spatial analysis and database management. Some managers in the two user agencies feared that people might indulge in geographical analysis just because the tools were available, not because a project required it. These managers were pessimistic about the possible consequences of the GIS, and they expected that any changes would come slowly given budget and manpower restrictions and the functioning of South County's bureaucracy.

Explaining the Contrasts Between Counties

It is clear that the consequences of GISs in the two county organizations studied were very different. North County's experience was considered a "transformation" by the respondents, and the organizational and work changes that they perceived were readily attributed to the GIS technology. Thus, the respondents in one organization considered the GIS to be responsible for transforming their work and organizational structure. The GIS was also seen to have simultaneously elevated skill requirements and provided an opportunity for employees to improve their skills, thereby securing their jobs for the future. By contrast, none of these consequences was reported by respondents in South County. Although the GIS technology being used was the same as that employed by North County, respondents in South County perceived little impact and forecast only moderate use of the GIS despite its admitted potential.

Explaining these divergent experiences can help to illuminate the more general question of information technology and organizational transformation. In the remainder of the results section, we examine specific contrasts between the *initiation* of the GIS at each site, the *transition* from older technology to new, the manner in which the GIS was *deployed* at each site, and the *spread* of *knowledge* about the GIS. These processes were formed by organizing selected themes generated from the coding of text segments into larger categories. The labels used represent the common activities apparent (to the researchers) in the group of themes. These four aspects of the implementation process help to explain the differences in organizational consequences of the technology. Table 10.3 summarizes the differences between organizations on each of these four processes as well as the reported organizational consequences.

Initial positioning. In North County, Arc/Info GIS was positioned as a state-of-the-art technical response to the organizational need for new methods for conducting spatial analysis. The inefficiencies of previous systems and the organizational structure were mentioned expressly by five different respondents. According to a technician in Land Management, "Whenever you wanted maps or information, you requested it from [the GSD], and they put it in their stack of priorities and gave it back to you whenever they could get to it." The GSD was frequently referred to as a "closed shop," even in the formal implementation plan for Arc/Info where the closed shop was described as inefficient and an impediment to the spread of GIS knowledge.

The proposal to acquire Arc/Info represented it as a new order of spatial analysis and positioned the acquisition as a total organizational effort rather than a departmental one. A manager in Land Management said, "We had to build a business case. What is the payoff of converting, establishing a GIS system, [and] getting people to buy into it, especially the upper management?" A user in the Planning Department added, "We are not building any kingdoms. We want this to be an organizational initiative." To effect this organization-wide effort, the initiating group sought representation from different departments in the software selection process, prepared the 72-page document detailing objective criteria and benchmarks, selected the criterion of demonstrated functionality, and employed the consultant to develop the business case. All these factors supported the Arc/Info initiative in North County and helped to produce the shared understanding that the GIS was

TABLE 10.3 Summary of Comparisons Between Sites

Basis for Comparison	North County	South County
Consequences of GISs	The GIS was widely acknowledged as responsible for transforming the conduct of work and the relationships among departments. Centralized GSD group within Technical Services was disbanded, and technicians were reassigned to user departments.	The GIS was slowly implemented with little consequence for users. Minor increases in staffing in the Office of Computer Services were attributed to the GIS.
Implementation processes		
Initial positioning	The GIS was positioned as an organization-wide response to shared needs. Initiating group was geographers with holistic view of organization and application systems.	The GIS was positioned as a revenue-adding service provided by the Office of Computer Services. Initiating group was focused on marketing service to user departments.
Transition to Arc/Info	Transition to the GIS was smooth and continuous due to prior experience with spatial technologies.	Transition to the GIS was abrupt and discontinuous due to lack of prior capability with mapping systems.
Deployment of GISs	The GIS was deployed in a distributed technical configuration supported by a central group. Users had primary responsibility for developing and maintaining applications.	The GIS was deployed in a centralized technical configuration controlled by the Office of Computer Services. Data processing personnel had responsibility for developing applications for users.
Spread of knowledge	Conceptual knowledge about the GIS was spread among users through training conducted by the initiating group of geographers.	Procedural knowledge was conveyed to users through training conducted by the Office of Computer Services.

NOTE: GIS = geographic information system.

selected using objective criteria and that, indeed, "Arc/Info was the right choice."

By contrast, Arc/Info was introduced in South County with little explicit mention about the need for the software and the methods used for its selection. Arc/Info was primarily positioned as a revenue-generating product that OCS had added to its existing range of data processing services, to be marketed to the rest of South County. Acquiring Arc/Info was a relatively isolated effort by a small group of OCS staff headed by the Technical Support supervisor, who had had no prior experience with mapping systems. The participation of users was limited to attendance at fund-raising seminars. According to a technical supervisor in OCS, cost was the primary criterion for choosing Arc/Info over two competing systems. This perception was shared by at least seven OCS staff members and comprised a clear theme in the analysis.

A central pool of funds to support GIS development in South County was established. Some of the departments in the county, including Police and Elections, were regarded as "richer" because they had larger budgets, and they made substantial contributions to this fund. Other users had relatively limited budgets and did not make any significant contributions. The director of the Planning Department, for example, commented, "Right now, we are hoping that the land use [contribution] will allow us to participate without having to make an out-of-pocket contribution." By waiting to see how the GIS succeeded before they made significant financial commitments, such users admitted a disparity wherein GIS development did not correspond to the actual need for GIS products. While smaller departments had to refrain from developing applications, the funding formula used by OCS allowed the richer departments to "move ahead like gangbusters," according to one respondent. Other users supported this interpretation by referring to the funding of the GIS by a "handful of departments," in contrast to the practice of taking county money "out of the general fund every year to fund this thing."

Transition to Arc/Info. Prior experience and demonstrated capability in working with spatial technology enabled a smooth transition to Arc/Info in North County. The interviews revealed that at least half of the respondents in North County had prior experience with spatial mapping programs like Computer Vision and Autocad or with image processing software like ERDAS. A number of respondents also had academic training in disciplines that emphasized spatial analysis such as geography, urban planning, and architecture. Also contributing to the smooth transition was the relatively long employment of people working with the GIS in North County. Many had progressed through several transitions, from paper maps to various computer-based systems. As a technician remarked, "We already know about calibrating and geo-referencing and real-world coordinates. Xs and Ys, lats and longs, and all those things were already familiar to me." Another technician said, "Making use of digital mapping equipment was part of the culture of the district. Most people got used to the idea of digital maps instead of paper maps."

By contrast, the transition to Arc/Info in South County was regarded as abrupt because of the inexperience of OCS's personnel in working with spatial systems. South County had for 20 years functioned as a traditional "IBM shop" which served the data processing needs of as many as 50 county agencies but which had never worked with any mapping programs. A GIS programmer in OCS described her situation as follows:

> I have been in IBM all my career. I've never dealt with graphics before. I was strictly a number cruncher. So, there was that other stumbling block I had to overcome. . . . I keep comparing it with a different universe in itself. You go through this black hole and you are in the Arc/Info world, and everything within Arc/Info is like a different galaxy.

Six different members of the OCS staff shared this theme, reflective of their traditional data processing backgrounds; few had any experience or training in GISs. Moreover, the director of the GIS had 16 years of data processing experience, and the Technical Support supervisor had worked more than 10 years in this area. Thus, the transition to spatial concepts in South County was considered by its initiators in OCS to be radical and discontinuous.

Deployment of GISs. In North County, geographers assumed responsibility for planning and executing the deployment of Arc/Info as a distributed system in which users shared data and applications. A senior geographer reflected the shared view of nine geographers, technicians, and managers in using the analogy of a football game to describe the arrangement for the GIS. The distributed deployment of the GIS was compatible, in their view, with this team-based, integrative approach in which the success of the team depends on the performance of its individual members. The preference of geographers for distributed deployment is also reflected in the comments of a respondent who had degrees in both geography and computer science:

> Maybe it is the geography part in me which says you need to distribute certain things, and then there is the computer science part in me that says that certain things need to be centralized. . . . The smartest move we did was getting [the] GSD disbanded. It is not an IS [information systems] or GSD thing. This is really . . . an unselfish posture.

As stated in the business case, the distributed deployment of Arc/Info was to ensure user participation in development and to spread the responsibilities for database maintenance among those with the greatest interest in individual data sets.

By contrast, in South County, OCS assumed centralized control over the development, support, and training functions for the GIS. Both the users and OCS analysts perceived certain technical advantages to centralization: the reduction of data redundancy, improved quality control, and speedier access. However, opinions varied regarding the organizational benefits of centralizing responsibility for the GIS. The OCS analysts believed that centralization would enable a rapid growth of GIS capabilities among users and preserve the enforcement of standards in developing new systems. For example, the OCS supervisor responsible for setting up the GIS users group in South County expressed the view, "There is a need to step back and get more into traditional data processing methodologies than we have in the past." Another OCS manager commented, "The problem arises when departments try to do things which are not part of their mission."

The users disagreed with this view and said that centralization inhibited the growth of GIS applications. A user in ERM remarked, "If anything, the centralized GIS has inhibited growth because of the problems in product development with people seeing it as more trouble than it is worth." Users suspected OCS of keeping them in a dependent relationship, restricting training, controlling purchases of all computer equipment in the county, and restricting users' access to the system. One user at ERM described OCS's "hardware lock" which prevented users from getting command-level access to their own systems, and another viewed much OCS time as wasted on unimportant mapping details like "[spending 90 percent of their time] making the black line that goes around the border thicker." Another ERM manager questioned whether the centralized arrangement was conducive to supporting the work of the departments: "It contributes to the perception that their motivations were different from supporting our needs. Sometimes they make [us] feel that we exist in order to support them in the development of [the] GIS."

Spread of knowledge. North County's geographers emphasized the cultivation and spread of conceptual knowledge about GISs, Arc/Info in particular. Their training programs were designed to facilitate spatial thinking rather than getting people bogged down in detailed software procedures and commands. Training taught users to visualize problems in spatial terms and to translate the need for geographical products into workable GIS solutions. This involved understanding relatively advanced concepts such as topology, geo-referencing, and geo-coding. The trainers believed that the users should become self-reliant with the software because a distributed environment could be effective only when a mature user community understood how to meet its own needs. "We try to make the training more useful and make more sense to the users," said one geographer involved with training. Another commented, "I think the biggest issue in terms of human resources is to train the people."

Other means for spreading knowledge about GISs in North County were the efforts of the GTAC, a group dominated by geographers, and the GIS user group, which included at least 50 active users. The user group provided greater visibility to GIS technology, which further enabled the spread of knowledge. Informal learning also occurred and was reinforced by the widespread use of common geographical language among users, who comfortably spoke in terms of latitude, longitude, geo-coding, and other geographical concepts.

In contrast to the emphasis upon spreading conceptual knowledge in North County, the training conducted by OCS for South County agencies emphasized operational or procedural knowledge. For example, users were shown how digitizing was performed and how information about outfalls was entered into the database. While these users admitted that they learned to generate reports from a menu-driven system, they did not develop a conceptual understanding of the system. One user commented on her experience in training: "I have not worked with [the] GIS before this project, and I have not learned a whole lot about it other than how to enter data into the system." Other users called the OCS stance a "closed-shop" attitude because OCS was not willing to transfer much knowledge about the system. The members of the OCS staff who were interviewed, however, shared the belief that the training provided to users was adequate. One OCS staff person commented, "Well, in most cases, if we design a menu-driven system for a department which will maintain a map, we provide a level of training such that the user can pull up the menu." From the users' perspective, such operational training did not include building more general knowledge about spatial concepts or GIS technology.

DISCUSSION

The findings of this study consist of interpretations provided by respondents in two organizations where the same basic applications of information technology were implemented. Intersite comparisons revealed distinct differences in interpretations about the consequences of GISs and the processes wherein the technology was introduced. North County's respondents regarded Arc/Info as a causal agent that both transformed their ways of conducting business and removed organizational barriers between departments.

GIS expertise spread widely in North County, creating pressure on technicians and surveyors, among others, to upgrade their skills. By contrast, the GIS was reported to have had little organizational impact in South County, where it was controlled and operated by a central data processing department. South County's respondents acknowledged the potential of the GIS to change their work processes and organization, but they had yet to experience such change at the time of this research.

These contrasts provide useful information for those interested in information technology's role in organizational transformation. Because the same technology (Arc/Info) was experienced differently during its introduction in the two counties, the results reported here strongly support the idea that information technology's consequences are socially constructed, that is, that technology's social consequences depend upon its social meanings more than on its material properties. Beyond confirmation of this particular insight, the results reported here add to knowledge about the dynamics of implementation and contribute to a theoretical understanding of how implementation and transformation are related. Two points are raised in the remainder of the discussion. First, because the differences in outcomes were associated with reported differences in the initiation, transition, deployment, and spread of knowledge about GISs, these results provoke discussion about the *continuity of technical change and organizational transformation.* Second, our findings suggest that *organizational learning,* with its emphasis on spreading knowledge and empowering technology's users, be adopted as a theoretical perspective for future research on organizational transformation.

Continuity of Technical Change and Organizational Transformation

By most accounts, the concept of organizational transformation is associated with radical, discontinuous change in structures and processes. Whether part of a reengineering effort that begins with obliterating existing structures (Hammer and Champy 1993) or conceived as revolutionary, quantum change (Miller 1982; Miller and Friesen 1982; Romanelli and Tushman 1994), transformation is typically not seen as incremental, piecemeal, and continuous. Nonetheless, our results identified a gradual and continuous process of change in North County, where earlier generations of computerized mapping products had been used for several years. The change process culminated in the acknowledged transformation of work even before Arc/Info was fully implemented. In South County, neither data processing personnel nor users were familiar with technologies for spatial analysis, and the implementation of Arc/Info did little to provoke radical change. To the contrary, the discontinuity of technical change seemed to work against the technology's potential to affect work practice. On the basis of these results, we conclude that organizational transformations, paradoxically perhaps, may result from continuous experience with potentially transformational technologies. Discontinuous experience with technologies, while conceptually consistent with the idea of radical change, may not be conducive to organizational transformation.

On close examination, this conclusion is not as contradictory as it may first appear. Radical transformations in the way that work is performed and organized may be more easily accomplished by continuous, rather than discontinuous, changes in technology because changes that proceed gradually enhance the existing competencies of users. Therefore, these technologies have more chance of acceptance and use. Where information technologies, in particular, are counted upon to enable transformations, the acceptance and cooperation of those people who ultimately interact with the technologies enhance the prospect that transformation will actually occur. Gradual transformational efforts that leverage existing user knowledge may succeed where rapid implementation of unfamiliar technologies may fail to attract support and acceptance. When unfamiliar technologies are employed as enablers of radical organizational change, we should expect users to resist the ensuing, competence-destroying disruptions to their worlds of work.

This reasoning is consistent with Tushman and Anderson's (1986) study of the introduction of new technology at the industry level of analysis. Where new technology is interpreted as a continuation of existing technological capabilities, as in North County, it is more likely to be seen as "competence enhancing." Where new technology is interpreted as a departure from existing technological capabilities, as was evident from comments made by South County's OCS staff, it can be perceived as "competence destroying" (Tushman and Anderson 1986). Competence-enhancing technologies build upon an established base of knowledge, whereas competence-destroying technologies require the creation of new knowledge before the transformation can occur. The spread of new technology is easier in a competence-enhancing environment because social interpretations of technology are allowed to evolve slowly. By contrast, technological discontinuities disrupt the spread of new technology because new competencies must be developed.

Organizational Transformation
Through Organizational Learning

Quite frequently, researchers and practitioners have operated without the benefit of theory to understand the variables, conditions, and processes that enable organizational transformation (Scott Morton 1991). Where theory has informed research and practice, a wide variety of theoretical perspectives has been employed. As a result, there is no one orthodox theoretical perspective from which to view the phenomenon of organizational transformation as enabled with information technology. On the basis of the research reported in this [chapter], it is suggested that the theoretical perspective of organizational learning might profitably be exploited in future research on the transformation of organizations, especially where information technology is involved. Organizational learning places emphasis on the acquisition and use of shared knowledge and the need to overcome barriers to acquiring new knowledge (Attewell 1992; Huber 1991). It also utilizes the concept of "organizational memory" (Walsh and Ungson 1991) to convey the idea that older practices might be difficult to obliterate, even in the most radical change efforts. Organizational learning emphasizes controlled experimentation and the spread of knowledge throughout an organization rather than the impassive decomposition and reassembly of tasks suggested by advocates of reengineering (Robey et al. 1995). Acquiring and spreading knowledge about GISs emerged as a major process describing common themes in both counties. In North County, such knowledge acquisition was part of the implementation strategy of the initiating group; by contrast, the processes of deployment and spread of knowledge in South County effectively restricted users from learning what the GIS might have been able to offer them. Moreover, the technicians in South County's OCS found it difficult to master the new skills of spatial analysis because the GIS was such a great departure from their traditional "data processing" culture.

The interpretation of the experiences in North County and South County as organizational learning is consistent with the recent evidence on implementing information technology reported by Gallivan and colleagues (1994). While they focused on no single body of theoretical work to support their analyses, their findings support an interpretation using organizational learning. They concluded that "significant benefits in learning, participation, and flexibility may be afforded by a gradual pace, whereas such benefits may be forfeited in the rush to implement rapidly" (p. 336). The research results reported here support the claim that gradual changes benefit learning and potentially lead to significant transformations in work and organization that are both understood and accepted by organizational members.

Organizational learning may be facilitated by decentralized structures that promote initiative, experimentation, and spread of knowledge (Cohen and Levinthal 1990; Fiol and Lyles 1985; Levitt and March 1988). Clearly, the decentralization of many GIS functions in North County, following the breakup of the centralized GSD, enhanced organizational transformation by placing more initiative in the hands of the users. Information technologies like GISs can become transformational only if they are used to their potential, and decentralized management encourages more widespread knowledge and acceptance of technology. When users are involved with selecting hardware and software, developing applications, implementing them, and training each other in their use, overall knowledge increases. In North County, geographers promoted the GIS's deployment as a distributed system that both empowered users and required them to become literate in the new spatial technology. Users also had the primary responsibility for developing and maintaining coverages and applications, and users comprised most of the coordinating unit, which provided technical and administrative support. South County's more centralized computing environment gave OCS the responsibility for maintaining data and building applications, and users expressed mistrust and apprehension toward the central unit. Thus, structural differences were associated with different degrees of organizational learning and different social consequences of the same technology.

CONCLUSION

This research applied interpretive methods within a comparative research design to examine the relationship between information technology and organizational transformation in two county government organizations. The results obtained reaffirm the value of an interpretive approach to research on technological change in organizations by showing how nearly identical technologies occasioned quite different social meanings and consequences in comparable organizational settings. This study contributes to the general argument that information technologies are socially constructed and that shared meanings within a particular social context influence their organizational consequences. The material properties of GISs, and Arc/Info software in particular, appeared to be less influential in shaping those consequences than the social interpretations of GISs. Thus, we concur with Barley (1986) that technology is an *occasion for*, not a determinant of, organizational change. Similar technologies may be introduced in different organizations to support similar kinds of work, but the social processes and contexts surrounding their implementation may be so different as to occasion divergent outcomes. The assumption of emergent causality employed in this study increases the researcher's sensitivity to the social processes contributing to transformation.

Moreover, this research has provided evidence on the dynamics of organizational transformation. In North County, respondents reported their work and organization to be transformed by information technology, which was implemented by users with previous experience with related mapping and spatial systems, who deployed the technology as a distributed system and who actively encouraged the spread of conceptual knowledge about the technology. The transformation, therefore, was associated with gradual and continuous technical change. In South County, where no transformation was reported, changes were introduced abruptly and controlled by a central data processing department that restricted all but the necessary procedural knowledge to operate the system. These findings suggest that the pace of implementation is influential in effecting organizational transformation.

To help make sense of these findings, the theoretical perspective of organizational learning was proposed. While rarely applied to issues of information technology and organizational change, organizational learning focuses directly upon the processes of generating, distributing, and accessing shared knowledge in an organization. Because the effective use of new information technologies often requires that substantial knowledge barriers be overcome (Attewell 1992), many efforts to transform organizations with new technologies may meet resistance or produce confusion. Although a relatively immature and imprecise theoretical approach (Huber 1991), organizational learning focuses directly on the issues revealed by the present study. In one site, barriers to understanding the GIS were not substantial, and efforts were made to decentralize organizational structure and disseminate GIS knowledge widely. By contrast, users in the other site reported restrictions on their knowledge of and access to the GIS. Organizational learning also provides a logical explanation for the observation that gradual technical changes were associated with organizational transformation. A gradual pace of technical change facilitates learning, which in turn dissolves potential resistance and encourages the development of useful applications. It can be argued that, unless applications of information technology are understood and used, they have little chance of transforming work.

Because they are drawn from a study of two organizations, these results should not be generalized to other contexts. Each context is different, so we should expect different contextual elements to interact with technical initiatives to produce different consequences. The findings should not even be extended to other settings where a GIS, or even Arc/Info, is implemented. What is true for GISs in the two local county governments studied may be untrue for GISs in other governmental units or in private enterprises.

However, the conclusions of this study may have more general applicability to understanding information technology's role in the transformation of work and organizations. Any potential enabler of radical organizational change needs to be understood and accepted by those using it before it can be expected to play a transformational role. Accordingly, an implementation process that facilitates organizational learning may enhance the transformational potential of GISs and other information technologies.[1]

NOTE

1. We acknowledge the support provided by the Judge Institute of Management Studies, University of Cambridge.

REFERENCES

Attewell, P., "Technology Diffusion and Organizational Learning: The Case of Business Computing," *Organization Sci.,* 3 (1992), 1-19.

———— and J. Rule, "Computing and Organizations: What We Know and What We Don't Know," *Comm. ACM,* 27 (1984), 1184-1192.

Barley, S., "Technology as an Occasion for Structuring: Evidence From Observations of CT Scanners and the Social Order of Radiology Departments," *Admin. Sci. Quarterly,* 31 (1986), 78-108.

Berger, P. L. and L. Luckmann, *The Social Construction of Reality: A Treatise in the Sociology of Knowledge,* Doubleday, New York, 1967.

Bijker, W. E., "The Social Construction of Bakelite: Towards a Theory of Invention," in W. E. Bijker, T. P. Hughes, and T. Pinch (Eds.), *The Social Construction of Technological Systems,* MIT Press, Cambridge, MA, 1987, 159-190.

————, T. P. Hughes, and T. Pinch (Eds.), *The Social Construction of Technological Systems,* MIT Press, Cambridge, MA, 1987.

Burrell, G. and G. Morgan, *Sociological Paradigms and Organization Analysis,* Heinemann, London, 1979.

Cohen, W. M. and D. Levinthal, "Absorptive Capacity: A New Perspective on Learning and Innovation," *Admin. Sci. Quarterly,* 35 (1990), 128-152.

Danziger, J. N., W. H. Dutton, R. Kling, and K. L. Kraemer, *Computers and Politics,* Columbia University Press, New York, 1982.

———— and K. L. Kraemer, *Computers and People,* Columbia University Press, New York, 1985.

Davenport, T. H. and D. B. Stoddard, "Reengineering: Business Change of Mythic Proportions?" *MIS Quarterly,* 18 (1994), 121-127.

Dewar, R. D. and J. E. Dutton, "The Adoption of Radical and Incremental Innovations: An Empirical Analysis," *Management Sci.,* 32 (1986), 1422-1433.

Fiol, C. M. and M. A. Lyles, "Organizational Learning," *Academy of Management Review,* 10 (1985), 803-813.

Fletcher, P. T., S. I. Bretschneider, and D. A. Marchand, *Managing Information Technology: Transforming County Governments in the 1990s,* Center for Science and Technology, School of Information Studies, Syracuse University, Syracuse, NY, 1992.

Fulk, J., "Social Construction of Communication Technology," *Acad. Management J.,* 36 (1993), 921-950.

Gallivan, M. J., J. D. Hofman, and W. J. Orlikowski, "Implementing Radical Change: Gradual Versus Rapid Pace," in J. I. DeGross, S. L. Huff, and M. C. Munro (Eds.), *Proceedings of the Fifteenth International Conference on Information Systems,* Association of Computing Machinery, New York, 1994, 325-339.

Hammer, M. and J. Champy, *Reengineering the Corporation: A Manifesto for Business Revolution,* HarperCollins, New York, 1993.

Hirschheim, R. and H. K. Klein, "Four Paradigms of Information Systems Development," *Comm. ACM,* 32 (1989), 1199-1216.

———— and M. Newman, "Symbolism and Information Systems Development: Myth, Metaphor, and Magic," *Information Systems Res.*, 2 (1991), 29-62.

Hirschman, E. C., "Humanistic Inquiry in Marketing Research: Philosophy, Method, and Criteria," *J. Marketing Res.*, 23 (1986), 237-249.

Huber, G. P., "The Nature and Design of Post-Industrial Organizations," *Management Sci.*, 30 (1984), 928-951.

————, "Organizational Learning: The Contributing Processes and the Literatures," *Organization Sci.*, 2 (1991), 88-115.

Johnson, B. M. and R. E. Rice, *Managing Organizational Innovation: The Evolution From Word Processing to Office Information Systems*, Columbia University Press, New York, 1987.

Kling, R., "Social Analyses of Computing: Theoretical Perspectives in Recent Empirical Research," *Computing Surveys*, 12 (1980), 61-110.

Kraemer, K. L., "Strategic Computing and Administrative Reform," in C. Dunlop and R. Kling (Eds.), *Computerization and Controversy*, Academic Press, San Diego, 1991, 167-180.

Kraut, R., S. Dumais, and S. Koch, "Computerization, Productivity, and Quality of Work-Life," *Comm. ACM*, 32 (1989), 220-238.

Levitt, B. and J. G. March, "Organizational Learning," *Annual Rev. Sociology*, 14 (1988), 319-340.

Mackenzie, D. and J. Wajcman, *The Social Shaping of Technology*, Open University Press, Milton Keynes, UK, 1985.

March, J. G., "Footnotes to Organizational Change," *Admin. Sci. Quarterly*, 26 (1981), 563-577.

Markus, M. L. and D. Robey, "Information Technology and Organizational Change: Casual Structure in Theory and Research," *Management Sci.*, 34 (1988), 583-598.

Miller, D., "Evolution and Revolution: A Quantum View of Structural Change in Organizations," *J. Management Studies*, 19 (1982), 131-151.

———— and P. M. Friesen, "Structural Change and Performance: Quantum Versus Piecemeal-Incremental Approaches," *Acad. Management J.*, 25 (1982), 867-892.

Nelson, D. L., "Individual Adjustment to Information-Driven Technologies: A Critical Review," *MIS Quarterly*, 14 (1990), 79-98.

Orlikowski, W. J., "CASE Tools as Organizational Change: Investigating Incremental and Radical Changes in Systems Development," *MIS Quarterly*, 17 (1993), 309-340.

———— and J. J. Baroudi, "Studying Information Technology in Organizations: Research Approaches and Assumptions," *Information Systems Res.*, 2 (1991), 1-28.

———— and D. C. Gash, "Technological Frames: Making Sense of Information Technology in Organizations," *ACM Trans. Information Systems*, 12 (1994), 174-207.

Pfeffer, J., *Organizations and Organization Theory*, Pitman, Boston, 1982.

Pinsonneault, A. and K. L. Kraemer, "The Impact of Information Technology on Middle Managers," *MIS Quarterly*, 17 (1993), 271-292.

Prasad, P., "Symbolic Processes in the Implementation of Technological Change: A Symbolic Interactionist Study of Work Computerization," *Acad. Management J.*, 36 (1993), 1400-1429.

Robey, D., "Computers and Management Structure: Some Empirical Findings Re-examined," *Human Relations*, 11 (1977), 963-976.

———— and A. Azevedo, "Cultural Analysis of the Organizational Consequences of Information Technology," *Accounting, Management, and Information Technologies*, 4 (1994), 23-37.

———— and A. G. Rodriguez-Diaz, "The Organizational and Cultural Context of Systems Implementation: Case Experience From Latin America," *Information and Management*, 17 (1989), 229-239.

————, N. A. Wishart, and A. G. Rodriguez-Diaz, "Merging the Metaphors for Organizational Improvement: Business Process Reengineering as a Component of Organizational Learning," *Accounting, Management, and Information Technologies,* 5 (1995), 23-39.

Romanelli, E. and M. L. Tushman, "Organizational Transformation as Punctuated Equilibrium: An Empirical Test," *Acad. Management J.,* 37 (1994), 1141-1166.

Sahay, S., *Social Construction of Geographic Information Systems,* unpublished doctoral dissertation, Florida International University, 1993.

Sauer, C. and P. Yetton, "The Dynamics of Fit and the Fit of Dynamics: Aligning IT in a Dynamic Organization," in J. I. DeGross, S. L. Huff, and M. C. Munro (Eds.), *Proceedings of the Fifteenth International Conference on Information Systems,* Association of Computing Machinery, New York, 1994, 41-50.

Scott Morton, M. S. (Ed.), *The Corporation of the 1990s: Information Technology and Organizational Transformation,* Basic Books, New York, 1991.

Slack, J. D., *Communication Technologies and Society: Conceptions of Causality and the Politics of Technological Intervention,* Ablex, Norwood, NJ, 1984.

Swanson, E. B., "Information Systems in Organization Theory: A Review," in R. J. Boland and R. A. Hirschheim (Eds.), *Critical Issues in Information Systems Research,* Wiley, Chichester, UK, 1987, 181-204.

Tushman, M. L. and P. Anderson, "Technological Discontinuities and Organizational Environments," *Admin. Sci. Quarterly,* 31 (1986), 439-465.

———— and E. Romanelli, "Organizational Evolution: A Metamorphosis Model of Convergence and Reorientation," in L. L. Cummings and B. M. Staw (Eds.), *Research in Organizational Behavior,* JAI, Greenwich, CT, 1984, 171-222.

Tyre, M. J. and W. J. Orlikowski, "Windows of Opportunity: Temporal Patterns of Technological Adaptation in Organizations," *Organization Sci.,* 5 (1994), 98-118.

Walsh, J. and G. R. Ungson, "Organizational Memory," *Academy of Management Review,* 16, 1 (1991), 57-91.

Walsham, G., *Interpreting Information Systems in Organizations,* Wiley, Chichester, UK, 1993.

Yetton, P., K. D. Johnston, and J. F. Craig, "Computer-Aided Architects: A Case Study of Strategic Change and IT," *Sloan Management Rev.,* Summer (1994), 57-67.

Zuboff, S., *In the Age of the Smart Machine: The Future of Work and Power,* Basic Books, New York, 1988.

11

Steps Toward an Ecology of Infrastructure

Design and Access for Large Information Spaces

SUSAN LEIGH STAR

KAREN RUHLEDER

An *electronic community system* is a computer system which encodes the knowledge of a community and provides an environment which supports manipulation of that knowledge. Different communities have different knowledge, but their environment has great similarities. The community knowledge might be thought of as being stored in an electronic library.

—Bruce Schatz (1991, p. 88)

Does virtual community work or not? Should we all go off to cyberspace, or should we resist it as a demonic form of symbolic abstraction? Does it supplant the real, or is there, in it, reality itself? Like so many true things, this one doesn't resolve itself to a black or a white. Nor is it gray. It is, along with the rest of life, black/white. Both/neither.

—John Perry Barlow (1995, p. 56)

From "Steps Toward an Ecology of Infrastructure: Design and Access for Large Information Spaces," by Susan Leigh Star and Karen Ruhleder, 1996, *Information Systems Research,* Vol. 7, No. 1, pp. 63-92. Copyright © 1996, Institute for Operations Research and the Management Sciences. Reprinted with permission.

WHAT IS INFRASTRUCTURE?

People who study how technology affects organizational transformation increasingly recognize its dual, paradoxical nature. It is both engine and barrier for change, both customizable and rigid, both inside and outside organizational practices. It is product and process. Some authors have analyzed this seeming paradox as *structuration* (after Giddens); technological rigidities give rise to adaptations, which in turn require calibration and standardization. Over time, structure-agency relations re-form dialectically (Davies and Mitchell 1994; Korpela 1994; Orlikowski 1991). This paradox is integral to large-scale, dispersed technologies (Brown and Duguid 1994; Star 1991a, 1994). It arises from the tension between local, customized, intimate, and flexible use, on the one hand, and the need for standards and continuity, on the other.

With the rise of decentralized technologies used across wide geographical distance, both the need for common standards and the need for situated, tailorable, and flexible technologies grow stronger. A lowest common denominator will not solve the demand for customized possibilities; neither will rigid standards resolve the issue (Trigg and Bodker 1994). It is impossible to have "universal niches"; one person's standard is in fact another's chaos. There are no genuine universals in the design of large-scale information technology (Bowker 1993; Star 1991a).

Furthermore, this simultaneous need for customization and standardization is not geographically based or based on simple group membership parameters. An individual is often a member of multiple communities of practice which use technologies differently and which thus have different demands on their flexible-standard requirements. There is no absolute center from which control and standards flow and, as well, no absolute periphery (Hewitt 1986). Yet some sort of infrastructure is needed.

We studied the building of a geographically dispersed, sophisticated digital communication and publishing system for a community of scientists. The system-building effort, which was itself an attempt to enhance and create infrastructural tools for research, took place during a period of immense, even radical change in the larger sphere of electronic information systems (1991-1994). One purpose of the development effort was to transform local laboratory organization and minimize inefficiencies of scale with respect to knowledge and results. The vision was of a kind of supra-laboratory stretched over the entire scientific community. The needs for both standards and customizable components were equally strong. The system development process also became an effort to bring together communities of practice with very different approaches to computing infrastructure. Designers and users faced two sorts of challenges in developing the system: communicating despite very different practices, technologies, and skills and keeping up with changes occasioned by the growth of the Internet and tools like Gopher and Mosaic. Trying to develop a large-scale information infrastructure in this climate is metaphorically like building the boat you're on while designing the navigation system *and* being in a highly competitive boat race with a constantly shifting finish line.

This [chapter] is about that experience and about its ultimate failure to produce the expected organizational and infrastructural changes. It offers an analytic framework and vocabulary to begin to answer the question: What is the relationship between large-scale infrastructure and organizational change? Who (or what) is the changer, and who changed? We begin with a definition of infrastructure and then focus on two aspects of the system development effort: communication and mutual learning between designers and users.

When Is an Infrastructure?

> What can be studied is always a relationship or an infinite regress of relationships. Never a "thing."
>
> —Gregory Bateson

Yrjö Engeström (1990), in his "When Is a Tool?," answers the implied title question in terms of a web of usability and action. A tool is not just a thing with pre-given attributes frozen in time—but a thing becomes a tool in practice, for someone, when connected to some particular activity. The article is illustrated by a photo of a physician working at a terminal covered with yellow post-it notes, surrounded by hand-scribbled jottings, talking on the phone—a veritable heterogeneous "web of computing" (Kling and Scacchi 1982). The tool emerges in situ. By analogy, infrastructure is something that emerges for people in practice, connected to activities and structures.

When, then, is an infrastructure? Common metaphors present infrastructure as a substrate: something upon which something else "runs" or "operates" such as a system of railroad tracks upon which rail cars run. This image presents an infrastructure as something that is built and maintained and which then sinks into an invisible background. It is something that is just there, ready-to-hand, completely transparent.

But such a metaphor is neither useful nor accurate in understanding the relationship between work/practice and technology. It is the image of "sinking into the background" that concerns us. Furthermore, we know that such a definition will not capture the ambiguities of usage referred to above. For example, without a Braille terminal, the Internet does not work to support a blind person's communication. And for the plumber, the waterworks system in a household connected to the city water system is a target object, not background support. Rather, following Jewett and Kling (1991), we hold that infrastructure is a fundamentally relational concept. It becomes infrastructure in relation to organized practices. Within a given cultural context, the cook considers the water system a piece of working infrastructure integral to making dinner; for the city planner, it becomes a variable in a complex equation. Thus we ask, *when*—not *what*—is an infrastructure?

Analytically, infrastructure appears only as a relational property, not as a thing stripped of use. Bowker (1994) calls this "infrastructural inversion," a methodological term referring to a powerful figure-ground gestalt shift in studies of the development of large-scale technological infrastructure (Hughes 1983, 1989). The shift deemphasizes things or people as simply causal factors in the development of such systems; rather, changes in infrastructural relations become central. As we learn to rely on electricity for work, our practices and language change, we are "plugged in," and our daily rhythms shift. The nature of scientific and aesthetic problems shift as well. As this infrastructural change becomes a primary analytic phenomenon, many traditional historical explanations are inverted. Yates (1989) shows how even so humble an infrastructural technology as the file folder is a central factor in changes in management and control in American industry. In the historical analysis, the politics, voice, and authorship embedded in the systems are revealed—not as engines of change but rather as articulated components of the system under examination. Substrate becomes substance.

With this caveat, infrastructure emerges with the following dimensions:

- *Embeddedness.* Infrastructure is "sunk" into, or inside of, other structures, social arrangements, and technologies.

- *Transparency.* Infrastructure is transparent to use in the sense that it does not have to be reinvented each time or assembled for each task but invisibly supports those tasks.

- *Reach or scope.* This may be either spatial or temporal; infrastructure has reach beyond a single event or one-site practice.

- *Learned as part of membership.* The taken-for-grantedness of artifacts and organizational arrangements is a sine qua non of membership in a community of practice (Lave and Wenger 1992; Star 1996). Strangers and outsiders encounter infrastructure as a target object to be learned about. New participants acquire a naturalized familiarity with its objects as they become members.

- *Links with conventions of practice.* Infrastructure both shapes and is shaped by the conventions of a community of practice, for example, the ways that cycles of day-night work are affected by and affect electrical power rates and needs.

Generations of typists have learned the QWERTY keyboard; its limitations are inherited by the computer keyboard and thence by the design of today's computer furniture (Becker 1982).

- *Embodiment of standards.* Modified by scope and often by conflicting conventions, infrastructure takes on transparency by plugging into other infrastructures and tools in a standardized fashion.

- *Built on an installed base.* Infrastructure does not grow de novo; it wrestles with the "inertia of the installed base" and inherits strengths and limitations from that base. Optical fibers run along old railroad lines, new systems are designed for backward compatibility, and failing to account for these constraints may be fatal or distorting to new development processes (Monteiro et al. 1994).

- *Becomes visible upon breakdown.* The normally invisible quality of working infrastructure becomes visible when it breaks; the server is down, the bridge washes out, or there is a power blackout. Even when there are backup mechanisms or procedures, their existence further highlights the now visible infrastructure.

The configuration of these dimensions forms an "infrastructure," which is without absolute boundary on *a priori* definition (Star 1989a, 1989b). Most of us, in speaking loosely of infrastructure, mean those tools which are fairly transparent for most people we know about, wide in both temporal and spatial scope, embedded in familiar structures—like power grids, water, the Internet, airlines. That loose talk is perfectly adequate for most everyday usage but is dangerous when applied to the design of powerful infrastructural tools on a wide scale such as is now happening with "national information infrastructures." Most importantly, such talk may obscure the ambiguous nature of tools and technologies for different groups, leading to de facto standardization of a single, powerful group's agenda. Thus it contributes to Kraemer and King's (1977) "politics of reinforcement" in computerization. Such talk may also obscure the nature of organizational change occasioned by information technology development.

If we add these dimensions of infrastructure to the dual and paradoxical nature of technology, our understanding deepens. In fact, the ambiguity and multiple meanings of usage marks any real functioning system. *An infrastructure occurs when the tension between local and global is resolved.* That is, an infrastructure occurs when local practices are afforded by a larger scale technology, which can then be used in a natural, ready-to-hand fashion. It becomes transparent as local variations are folded into organizational changes and becomes an unambiguous home—for somebody. This is not a physical location or a permanent one but rather a working relation—since no home is universal (Star 1996).

The empirical data for this chapter come from our work as ethnographers/ evaluators of a geographically dispersed virtual laboratory or "collaboratory" system meant to link the work of over 1,400 biologists (Star 1991b). The system itself appeared differently to different groups; for some it was a set of digital publishing and information retrieval tools to "sit upon" already existing infrastructure, for others it supported problem solving and information sharing, and for yet others it was a component of an established set of practices and infrastructural laboratory tools. The target users had vastly differing resources and computing skills and relationships, and these in turn were sharply different from those of the designers.

This development effort took place at a moment of rare, widespread infrastructural change. With the growth of the Internet and World Wide Web and their utility software (such as Mosaic, Netscape, Gopher, and WAIS), as well as the myriad of e-mail uses, electronic bulletin boards, and listservs, the boundaries of system implementation are embedded in the eye of an informational and organizational hurricane of change. For a few of our respondents, the system became a working infrastructure; others, however, turned to Gopher and Mosaic and other Internet tools. And of course, the skill base and learning curve, as well as other factors such as support networks in organizations which help users with such tools, is itself constantly changing. This changing environment, combined with the complexities of implementation from the user's perspective, contributed to the system's ultimate failure in achieving its original goal of becoming the central information resource and the primary communication conduit within a particular scientific community.

THE WORM COMMUNITY SYSTEM:
BACKGROUND

The Worm Community System (WCS) is a customized piece of software meant to support the collaborative work of biologists sequencing the gene structure and studying other aspects of the genetics, behavior, and biology of *Caenorhabditis elegans,* a tiny nematode (Pool 1993; Schatz 1991). It is one example of a new genre of systems being developed for geographically dispersed collaborative scientific work. WCS is a distributed "hyperlibrary," affording informal and formal communication and data access across many sites. It incorporates graphical representations of the physical structure of the organism; a periodically updated genetic map; formal and informal research annotations (thus also functioning as an electronic publishing medium); directories of scientists; a thesaurus of terms linked with a directory of those interested in the particular subtopic; and a quarterly newsletter, the *Worm*

Breeder's Gazette. It also incorporates an independently developed database, *acedb.* Many parts of the system are hypertext-linked.

Its principal designers were computer scientists, some with backgrounds in biology. However, WCS was developed with the close cooperation of several biologists; user feedback and requests from those biologists were initially incorporated into the system over the years of development. Its development was part of a broader project to both construct and evaluate the implementation and impact of a scientific collaboratory. Two ethnographers, [the present authors], were members of the project team but not part of the technical development effort per se. The ethnographic component of the project is described in more detail below.

The community consists, as we have stated, of about 1,400 scientists distributed around the world in some 120 laboratories (as of 1994). They are close-knit and consider themselves extremely friendly, as indeed we found them to be. Until recently, most people were first- or second-"generation" students of the field's founders. *C. elegans* was chosen as the "model organism" for the Human Genome Initiative (HGI), said to be the largest scientific project in history. "Model organism" means that the actual findings from doing the worm biology and genetics will be directly of interest to human geneticists, for example, when homologues are found between oncogenes (cancer-causing genes) in the worm and in the human (although worms do not get cancer as such, there are developmental analogies). In addition, the tools and techniques developed in the *c. elegans* mapping effort will be useful for the human project.

Senior biologists are concerned that the impact of the HGI and increasing interest in the worm will adversely affect the close, friendly nature of relationships in the community. Viewing this community as a loosely coupled organization whose members often work in and interact with more formal organizations, these new constraints and opportunities threatened to upset traditional linkages and a collaborative culture heavily dependent on apprenticeship and continued personal contact. Members of the community themselves were willing to become a "model organism" for the ethnographers because they hoped the system would help maintain the community's strong bonds and friendly character in the face of rapidly increasing visibility and growth. In that sense, the goal was not only organizational transformation in terms of available resources and information-sharing opportunities but also the retention of desired characteristics in the face of transformation for the worse.

The work of *c. elegans* biologists can be captured by the notion of solving a jigsaw puzzle in four dimensions across considerable distance. (The labs we studied were located in the United States and Canada; input comes from Europe, Japan, and Australia as well.) In addition to the four dimensions, the data are structured differently and must be mapped across fields; for example, a behavioral disorder linked with one gene must be triangulated with information from corresponding DNA fragments. Labs working on a particular problem (e.g., sperm production) are in frequent contact with each other by phone, fax, and e-mail, exchanging results and specimens.

The worm itself is remarkable both as an organism and as a component of a complex pattern of information transfer integral to the biologist's work. It is microscopic and transparent (thus easier to work with than opaque creatures such as humans). It is a hardy creature and may be frozen, mailed to other labs via UPS, thawed out, and retrieved live for observation. Worms and parts of worms travel from one lab to another as researchers share specimens. Worm strains with particular characteristics, such as a mutation, may be mailed from a central stock center to labs requesting specimens. Tracking the location and characteristics of organisms thus is an important part of record keeping and information retrieval.

Computing use and sophistication in the labs varies widely. In the labs most active in trying out WCS, there are one or two active, routine WCS users. In many, computing is confined to e-mail, word processing, or the preparation of graphics for talks. In most labs, there is one "computer person," often a student, who is in charge of ordering new programs and designing databases to keep track of strains and other information.

Our role in the project as ethnographers has been to travel to worm labs; interview about and observe both the use of computing and WCS and other aspects of routine work; and ask questions on topics including careers in the community, competition, routine information-sharing tasks, how computing infrastructure is managed, and so on. We did semistructured interviews and observations at 25 labs with more than 100 biologists over a four-year period (1991-1995)[1] and fed back to designers both specific suggestions ("so-and-so found a bug") and general observations ("such-and-such would violate community norms"), several of which were incorporated into development.

Sociological analysis to support computer design is relatively new (Bucciarelli 1994). The participatory design approach developed in Scandinavia paved the way for workplace studies which inform design (Anderson and Crocca 1993; Bødker 1991; Ehn 1988), usually using a combination of a case study approach and action research, with rapid feedback from users of computing systems. Where possible, we adapted those principles. At the same time, trying to cover a geographically distributed community in aid of complex systems development also meant that neither a strict case study nor rapid prototyping was possible. We covered as much territory as possible with traditional interviewing and observational techniques. The analysis of the data was conducted with a grounded theory approach, beginning with a substantive description of the community and moving to more abstract analytical frameworks as our comparative sites grew in number (Strauss 1986).

Most respondents said they liked the system, praising its ease of use and its understanding of the problem domain. On the other hand, most have not signed on; many have chosen instead to use Gopher and Mosaic/Netscape and other simpler net utilities with less technical functionality. Obviously, this is a problem of some concern to us as system developers and evaluators. *Despite good user prototype feedback and participation in the system development, there were unforeseen, complex challenges to usage involving infrastructural and organizational relationship.* The system was not widely adopted, nor did it have an immediate impact on the field as the resources and communication channels it proffered became available through other (often more accessible) means. However, WCS itself continues to change and adapt; the latest version is based entirely on Web technology, and the Web will shortly have enough functionality to reproduce the custom software WCS.[2]

SIGNING ON AND HOOKING UP

Those working in the emergent field of computer-supported cooperative work (CSCW), of which the collaboratory is a subset, have struggled to understand how infrastructural properties affect work, communication, and decision making (Kraemer and King 1977; Malone and Olson, forthcoming; Schmidt and Bannon 1992).

One of the classic CSCW typologies has distinguished important task differences for synchronous/asynchronous systems, proximate/long-distance use, and dedicated user groups/distributed groups with fluctuating membership (Ellis et al. 1991). This was useful for characterizing an emerging group of technologies; however, it offers no assistance in analyzing the issues associated with implementation or integration (Schmidt and Bannon 1992). It also does not analyze the relational aspects of computing infrastructure and work, either real-time "articulation work" or aspects of longer term, asynchronous production tasks. We encountered many such issues in the worm community in the process of "signing on" and "hooking up" to WCS—tasks related to finding out about the system, installing it, and learning to use it. For most of the worm biologists we interviewed, the tasks involved in signing on and hooking up had preoccupied them, and they had not gotten over the initial hurdle and into routine use.

Consider the set of tasks associated with getting the system up and running. WCS runs on a Sun workstation as a stand-alone or remotely; on a Mac with an ethernet connection remotely over the NSFnet; or, with less functionality, on a PC over the Net. Prior to using WCS, one must buy the appropriate computer, identify and buy the appropriate Windows-based interface, use a communications protocol such as telnet and/or FTP, and locate the remote address where one "gets" or operates the system. Each of these tasks requires that people trained in biology acquire skills taken for granted by systems developers. The latter have interpersonal and organizational networks that help them obtain necessary technical information and also possess a wealth of tacit knowledge about systems, software, and configurations. For instance, identifying which version of X Windows to use on a workstation means understanding what class of software product X Windows is, installing it, and then linking its configuration properly with the immediate or remote link. Following instructions to "download the system via FTP" requires an understanding of file transfer protocols across the Internet, knowing which issue of the *Worm Breeder's Gazette* lists the appropriate electronic address, and knowing how FTP and X Windows work together.

These common issues of shopping, configuration, and installation are faced in some degree by all users of computing. But solving these "shopping" and informational issues will not always suffice to get work done smoothly. For instance, deciding to buy a SPARC station (one popular UNIX-based workstation) and run it on a campus which has standardized itself on DOS machines may bring you into conflict with the local computer center and its attempts to limit the sorts of machines it will service. Or, there may be enough money to buy the computer but not enough to support training for all lab staff; in the long term, this disparity may create inequities.

We discovered many such instances, common to a variety of system development efforts and types of users and all interesting for the design of collaborative systems. With the advent of very large scale systems such as the U.S. National Information Infrastructure, they become pressing questions of equity and justice as well as questions of organizational formation, *trans*formation, and demise. They simultaneously enact technological infrastructure and social order. We encountered a myriad of contexts and tasks surrounding system use. These varied in complexity and consequences, and we borrowed a metaphor from learning theory to characterize these variations.

LEVELS OF COMMUNICATION AND
DISCONTINUITIES IN HIERARCHIES OF INFORMATION

The "tangles" encountered in signing on and hooking up occur in many venues and may inhibit desired organizational transformation; at the least, they inform its character and flavor the growth of infrastructure. We turned to

Gregory Bateson as a theorist of communication for a more formal under-standing of the ways in which communicative processes are entangled in the development of infrastructure. We rely on his *Steps to an Ecology of Mind* (Bateson 1978). The term *ecology,* as adapted to our analysis here, refers to the delicate balance of language and practice across communities and parts of organizations; it draws attention to that balance (or lack of it). It is not meant to imply either a biological approach or a closed, functional systemic one.

Bateson's Model

Bateson (1978), following Russell and Whitehead, distinguishes three levels in any communicative system. At the first level are straightforward "fact" statements, for example, "The cat is on the mat." A discontinuous shift in context occurs as the statement's object is changed to "I was lying when I said 'the cat is on the mat'." This second-order statement tells you nothing about the location of the cat but only something about the reliability of the first-order statement. In Bateson's words,

> There is a gulf between context and message (or between metamessage and mes-sage) which is of the same nature as the gulf between a thing and the word or sign which stands for it or between the members of a class and the name of the class. The context (or metamessage) *classifies* the message but can never meet it on equal terms. (p. 249)

At the third level, the gulf appears in evaluating the context itself: "There are many conflicting approaches to evaluating whether or not you were lying about the cat and the mat." In this sentence, the listener's attention is forced to a wider and deeper range of possibilities; again, it may classify the message about lying but is of a different character.

Theorizing the gulf between levels, Bateson and others have gone on to classify levels of learning with similar distinctions and discontinuities. There is a first- and second-order difference in learning something and learning about learning something, and between the second and third are even more abstract differences between learning to learn and learning about theories of learning and paradigms of education. As the epigraph to an earlier section indicates, of course the regress upward is potentially infinite.

For our purposes, we identify three levels (or "orders") of issues that appear in the process of infrastructure development and discuss each with respect to the worm community and WCS. As with Bateson's levels of com-munication or learning, the issues become less straightforward as contexts change. This is not an idealization process (i.e., they are not less material and more "mental") or even essentially one of scope (some widespread issues may be first order) but rather questions of *context*. Level 1 statements appear in our study: "UNIX may be used to run WCS." These statements are of a different character than Level 2 statements such as "System developers may say UNIX can be used here, but they don't understand our support situation." At Level 3, the context widens to include theories of technical culture: "UNIX users are evil; we are Mac people." As these levels appear in developer-user communication, the nature of the gulfs between levels is important.

First-order issues may be solved with a redistribution or increase of extant resources including information. Examples would be answers to questions such as: What is the e-mail address of WCS? How do I hook up my SPARC station to the campus network?

Second-order issues stem from unforeseen or unknowable contextual effects, perhaps from the interaction of two or more first-order issues. An example here is given above: What are the consequences of my choosing a SPARC station instead of a Mac if my whole department uses Macs? If I invest my resources in learning WCS, are there other more useful programs I am neglecting?

Third-order issues are inherently political or involve permanent disputes. They include questions about schools of thought of biological theory for designing the genetic map of the organism for WCS. They raise questions such as whether competition or cooperation will prove more important in developing systems privacy requirements and whether complexity or ease of use should be the main value in interface design. Such questions may arise from an interaction of lower order issues such as the choice of computer system and the trade-offs between scientific sophistication and ease of learning.

In this sense, infrastructure is context for both communication and learning within the web of computing (Kling and Scacchi 1982). Computers, people, and tasks together make or break a functioning infrastructure. In Bateson's (1978) words,

> It becomes clear that the separation between contexts and orders of learning is only an artifact. . . . The separation is only maintained by saying that the contexts have location outside the physical individual, while the orders of learning are located inside. But in the communicational world, this dichotomy is irrelevant and meaningless. . . . The characteristics of the system are in no way dependent upon any boundary lines which we may superimpose upon the communicational map. (p. 251)

Information infrastructure is not a substrate which carries information on it, or in it, in a kind of mind-body dichotomy. The discontinuities are not between system and person, or between technology and organization, but rather between contexts. Here, we echo recent work in the sociology of technology and science which refuses a "great divide" between nature and artifice, human and nonhuman, technology and society (e.g., Latour 1993).

These discontinuities have the same conceptual importance for the relationship between information infrastructure and organizational transformation that Bateson's work on the double bind had for the psychology of schizophrenia. If we, in large-scale information systems implementation, design messaging systems blind to the discontinuous nature of the different levels of context, we end up with organizations which are split and confused, systems which are unused or circumvented, and a set of circumstances of our own creation which more deeply impress disparities on the organizational landscape.

We apply this typology below within the context of "signing on" and "hooking up." Following that application, we discuss the implications of this typology for other forms of information systems development and the broader implications for understanding the impact of new computer-based media and their integration into established communities.

First-Order Issues

First-order issues are often those which are most obvious to informants, as they tend toward the concrete and can be addressed by equally concrete solutions (more money, time, training, or support). The first-order issues in this setting center around the installation and use of the system and include finding out about it, figuring out how to install it, and making different pieces of software work together. First-order issues, however, are not limited to "startup" but rather recur over time as work patterns and resource constraints shift (they also may be a byproduct of second- or third-order changes).

Informational issues. Potential users needed to find out about the system and determine the requirements for its installation and use. "Shopping" for the system involved decisions about hardware and software and sometimes also involved agreements with other departments to share resources or funding. At one major lab, the "worm" people had WCS loaded onto a server owned by the "plant" people on the floor above them. Establishing this agreement involved finding out about WCS resource needs and the local availability of these resources. This agreement negated the need to find out about system building and maintenance since the worm people were piggybacking off the original efforts of the plant people to purchase and put the server in place.

Issues of access. In some labs, physical access was critical. WCS might be located in an overcrowded and noisy room, stuck in the corner of a lounge on a different floor of the building altogether, or accessible only during certain hours. This was the case in the deal cut between the worm and plant people above: "The WCS and *acedb* are really on a machine upstairs; it belongs to the plant genome project people. . . . We can only use it evenings, weekends" (Brad Thomas, PD[3]).

Other labs experienced time limitations and physical inconveniences: "You can access *acedb* through the Suns downstairs, but it's not convenient. You can only do it after-hours. People just won't use it" (Eliot Red, PD). "Our computing is good compared to other labs. I finished up a Ph.D. at UCLA; they had one VAX, some PCs, [and] you had to walk to another building to use the VAX" (Brad Thomas, PD).

When we asked whether lab notebooks would one day be replaced with small palmtop computers or digitized pads, researchers were dubious. Respondents at one cramped lab in an urban high-rise simply noted that there was no place to put another computer, even a small one. They shared their lab with another group and even lacked space for some necessary lab equipment. Such simple spatial or architectural barriers are crucial for the usability of any system, especially those conceived and designed as integral parts of someone's workflow.

Baseline knowledge and computing expertise. Computing expertise was unevenly distributed within the labs; much equipment seemed out of date or unsophisticated. One senior researcher was not aware that databases were available without fixed-length fields, and a principal investigator (PI) made a category error in discussing operating systems and applications (equating "a Mac" and "a UNIX"). In general, PIs thought that the level of knowledge was rising through undergraduate and graduate training, but empirically this did not seem to be the case. This might have constituted a learning-level gulf (equating the ability to use on-line applications with the ability to understand broader systems concepts). Although there were a few highly skilled people and one or two with advanced computing expertise, these were not clustered in either the graduate student or postdoctoral student category.

This sort of knowledge may be an access issue just as much as is space or location. First-order issues in this arena certainly include not only learning to use WCS software but also understanding the platform on which it runs. WCS itself is designed to be extremely user-friendly and can be effectively used without much difficulty. The typical user in our study was a graduate student, postdoctoral student, or PI with enough knowledge about both domain and community to read a genetic map and recognize the importance of the *Worm Breeder's Gazette.* One user commented, "I just turned it on, pushed buttons" (Ben Tullis, PD).

In fact, at demos and trials at conferences, most users found WCS to be fairly easy and intuitive once they were on it. However, the platform on which it is based was not transparent (to biologists). WCS runs under UNIX, and both the operating system and software such as X Windows or Suntools require expertise most biologists didn't have:

> UNIX will never cut it as a general operating system. Biologists won't use it; it's for engineers. [Someone in the lab] had a printing question, [and it] took him three months to get something to print. (Bob Gates, GS)

Furthermore, many respondents were unclear about carrying out other sorts of networked computer tasks such as uploading and downloading files from mainframe to terminal. This made it difficult for them to integrate WCS use with e-mail correspondence, word processing files, and other Internet information spaces.

Training often took place in a haphazard way, depending on everything from luck to personal ties:

> I learned by using it as an editor. The second time I learned the formatter. A lot of people are comfortable with e-mail, and a lot of people are now using GenBank and sequencing packages. . . . We get some on-the-job training. [Two of the graduate students in the lab] write up instruction sheets. The person who was the systems administrator until February was a good friend. [I] got a lot of push and shove from him, a lot of shared ideas. (Jeff Pascal, PD)

No lab offered special training in computing, although some students had taken classes at local computer centers. Several said that they only learn "exactly enough to suit what you have to do" (Carolyn Little, PI).

Addressing first-order issues. On the surface, these issues may be solved in a fairly straightforward fashion. Effective shopping requires appropriate information, gathered and evaluated by a technically knowledgeable individual. When expertise needed for making computing decisions doesn't reside in the lab itself, it can be brought in from the outside, perhaps by turning to a campus computing facility or hiring a savvy undergraduate in computer science. Proposals can be written for equipment purchases. Issues of physical access can be solved by making the case for additional space. Issues of technical access can be solved by additional training. For instance, just as departments in the humanities are starting to offer tutorials or even certificates in humanities computing, biology departments could offer similar tutorials tailored to the needs of their own communities.

However, first-order selection issues are often intermingled with or converge to form higher order issues. Shopping, for instance, is not *just* a matter of getting the right information to the right person but also requires information distribution channels that bridge several academic communities: worm biologists, tool builders, and local computing support centers. Similarly, when shopping and selection raise questions of standards, they become intermingled with questions of organizational and workplace culture ("UNIX is for engineers, not biologists"). This is a particularly salient issue in instances where multiple groups share computing or where computing support is available for only a limited set of technological choices.

Second-Order Issues

Second-order issues can be analytically seen either as the result of unforeseen contextual effects, such as aversion to UNIX by biologists, or as the collision of two or more first-order issues, such as uncertainty during shopping combined with lack of information about how to hook up the system. These sorts of combinations can mean the person is forced to widen the context of evaluation and link choices about software packages with best guesses about the direction of the organization. Included in this category are cultural influences on technical choices, paradoxes of infrastructure, "near-compatibility" and the "almost-user community," constraints becoming resources, and understanding the nature of baseline skills and their development. They are second order because they broaden the context of choice and evaluation of the straightforward first-order issues such as obtaining software and access to machines.

Technical choices and a clash of cultures. Shopping and selection interact not only with training and ease-of-use issues but also with organizational cultural issues. For example, five people independently mentioned being put off by UNIX, usually in the context of comparing it favorably with the Mac. One PI mentioned having no base of UNIX knowledge available from the local computer center, although he had taught himself enough to run a SPARC station (Joe White, PI). Others expressed similar sentiments: "As long as it's easy, we'll use anything, like the Macs. So, you can do like cut and paste, like you can on the Mac" (Eliot Red, PD). "We were previously using UNIX, but this is much easier. UNIX is impossible. It's a real pain. This is much easier—the Macs, you know" (Linda Smith, PI).

One person who defined himself as a "crossover" person (between biology and computing) said,

> It's a big problem. Biologists are Mac people, and UNIX is an evil word. Most people are afraid of it and refuse to use it: "If it's not on Mac, I don't want it." There are a lot of problems getting people to use it rather than delegate the use of it. (Harry Jackson, GS)

Yet UNIX, apart from forming a basis for WCS and the language of its design team, was often also the language of the computer scientists who supported and maintained the local university computing environment. This apparent gulf between user communities led some biologists to speculate that there are "two types of scientists—love or hate the computer" and that "the only way they'll ever [use] it is by force" (Jeff Pascal, PD). They attributed successful computer use to "some kind of natural affinity" (Eliot Red, PD). This divergence has important implications for training, as do some other basic "cultural" issues.

Paradoxes of infrastructure. The uneven spread of computing expertise and resources shows vividly how a simple increase, or lack, of first-order resources cannot fully explain a successful infrastructure. Differences of expertise and local organizational savvy between relatively rich and relatively poor labs may override first-order concerns. For example, one of the poorest labs, still running outdated IBM PC-XT equipment, actively used the system, had developed its own databases, and tracked strain exchange with a level of sophistication unparalleled in the community. The lab's PI loved to "play around" with software and hardware and loved the challenge of overcoming the limitations of his lab. Second-order problems were thus reduced to first order by his own skill and interest.

The richest lab, on the other hand, had just received a substantial grant from the HGI to completely "hook up" the entire biology infrastructure on campus. However, this rich lab was de facto unable to operate the system through a combination of "waiting for the ethernet" and "waiting for the Sun." The PI illustrated the dilemma:

> We applied for an ethernet in May. [laughs] It should be here [in a few years]. . . .
> They'll be independent of the building network, [the people] on the SPARC. The
> Macs will be on the building network. (Linda Smith, PI)

A graduate student continued the story:

> No one will put the wires in, though . . . we made a deal with the network people
> [network services] that we'd run wires and they'd connect it up. . . . They man
> age all the campus networks. [Someone else] has dealt with Sun, though. (Steve
> Grenier, GS)

At the time of the interview, they had strung their own cables and were waiting on the delivery of the SPARC stations. Linda Smith (the PI) then anticipated having to spend a lot of time to "get the software under way."

Even institutions with outstanding technical support had no organizational mechanisms for translating that expertise to highly domain-specific questions, applications, and issues. Campus computer centers were often neither knowledgeable about nor interested in application packages relevant to biologists and geneticists, nor was there support for independently purchased hardware or software:

> Computing support s***s at [research institution]. I called the center for help with installing WCS on the Sun, and they basically told me, find a UNIX guy [and] buy him some pizza. . . . If we have problems with the network or programs they support, they do it. If you didn't buy your hardware from them, forget it. If they don't support your software, forget it. It's handled on a department-by-department basis. Biology has no infrastructure. (Bob Gates, GS)

Who "owns" a problem or an application was locally determined, and attribution of ownership made a great difference in individuals' ability to get help. Some PIs developed on-campus linkages that would bring computing expertise to bear on their own problems. The PI of one small lab submitted a grant together with a computer science faculty member interested in the visualization of scientific data. Together, they planned to develop a tool for visual data representation and analysis; in the process, the PI will get not only a tool to support his research but also a UNIX-based workstation from which he can access WCS.

These issues were of great concern to postdoctoral students looking to start up their own labs with increasingly limited funds. WCS was seen as a tool of the "upper tier" of richer labs (Harry Markson, GS) and was described as "a rocket" when "we need a Model T" (Marc Moreau, GS). A postdoctoral student planning to start his own lab complained,

> Half a system for everyone is better than a really great system for just a few labs. . . . We had to hire [a computer specialist affiliated with another lab]. Even the computer guys here [two graduate students] worked on it three weeks, and they couldn't load the [WCS] system. It's oriented to big labs. (Jay Emery, PD)

He added, "If it's not on a Mac or IBM, it won't get to people," and suggested, "You need a modular system. You need to be able to have parts of the database running on the Mac—*reach the small labs*" (emphases added).

Tensions between a discipline in flux and constraints as resources. What might be seen as constraints that could be overcome with technology may become resources from a different perspective. We proposed that it would be trivially easy to make the *Worm Breeder's Gazette* available on a continual update basis. On the one hand, continual updates would have served the needs of a very fast-moving community:

> The faster the [WCS] update, the better. . . . You do it through the *Gazette,*
> you contribute regularly. You're competing [with other labs] on the same gene.
> (T. Jones, GS)

> You need frequent updating; shortly after each *Gazette* (i.e., within two weeks
> after a *Gazette*), there should be a new release. . . . The WCS *Gazette* could
> replace hard copies; it would be cheaper. (Brad Thomas, PD)

Yet other respondents objected strongly to this option, even though they worked in the same competitive environment. Objections centered around the utility of community-imposed deadlines on structuring work, both in terms of submitting and reading articles:

> I would run the newsletter exactly how it's run now. Just leaving it open-ended is
> not good. If there is infinity, there is never a time to review things—and no dead-
> lines. (John Wong, GS)

> If the WCS were used to publish *Gazette* articles, what would be optimal? Well,
> continual would not be so good. There is something to be said for deadlines.
> Even six times a year, and it becomes background noise. . . . It's hard to predict
> whether a frequency change will change the impact. (Gordon Jackson, PI)

The deadline was simultaneously constraint and resource.

The distribution pattern for the *Gazette* not only affected the work habits of individuals but also was integrally linked to communication and coordination within labs and across them:

> [*Do you think WCS will replace the* Gazette*?*] If it replaces it, then we won't read
> it. I mean, when the *Gazette* arrives, we split it up and each read a part. Then we
> use it to get into other people's work. (Ed Jones, GS)

> [*What kinds of information do you not keep on the computer?*] Well, you couldn't
> have the newsletter on electronically. The constant update would be a nightmare.
> There would be no referenceable archive. (Paul Green, PI)

This last point is an important one since the *Gazette* serves as a reference database containing pointers not only to work being carried out in various labs but also to protocols and so on. For newcomers to the discipline, it serves as an important teaching tool; the on-line version would make back issues available more easily. A continual update format would require a new way of referencing or indexing contributions. One person envisioned a different form of ongoing information service, "something in between a formal and informal database" where "if you have little write-ups you could put them in an annotation box" (Alan Merton, PI). As for the *Gazette,* he suggested, "You could put a more formal thing into an on-line *Gazette* format and keep it as it is" in terms of content, timing, and organization.

"Near-compatibility" and the "any day now" user. Sometimes the gulf between first and second orders appears as a sense that what is happening *should* be first order. So strong is this sense that it can lead to some seemingly odd behavior. We encountered a persistent idea among respondents that they were "just about to" be hooked up with the system and that the barriers to hooking up were in effect trivial. Sometimes this even caused them to say that they *were* using the system, whereas observations and interviews in fact showed that they were not. For instance, when trying to find a site to observe in a large city with several universities and several labs listed as user sites, one of the authors spent almost a week tracking down people who were actually using the system. No one she talked with was using it, but each person knew of someone else in another lab who supposedly was. After following all leads, she concluded that no one was really using the system, though they all "meant to" and figured that it would be available "any day now."

This is not difficult to observe ethnographically but presents a real difficulty in administering surveys about use and needs. It is clear that this representation is not mendacious but rather a common discounting of what seem, from a distance, to be trivial "plug-in" difficulties. The above observations of the difficulties associated with hooking up and getting started, coupled with infrastructural limitations, would suggest that these issues are not trivial at all. In fact, these issues turn out to be lethal as they become both chronic and ubiquitous in the system as a whole.

Addressing second-order issues. In principle, second-order issues can be resolved by combining an increase in resources with heightened coordination or cooperation between different technical and user communities such as installing a user support telephone line, hiring a "circuit rider" who can help with hooking up and integration difficulties, and increasing other skill resources locally. However, realistically, biologists are not among the richest of scientists, despite the influx of HGI money. Money for capital expenditures is especially scarce, and decisions made about the purchase of or commitment to a particular system often persist for a decade or more. Thus second-order issues in system use and development may become third-order issues: Why should this lab get resources? Which problem is the most important one?

These issues occur at the level of the broader community and transcend the boundaries of any particular institution.

Third-Order Issues

Third-order issues are those which have been more commonly identified by sociology of science in discussions of problem solving. They have the widest context, involving schools of thought and debates about how to choose among second-order alternatives. These permeate any scientific community for the reason that all scientific communities are interdisciplinary and contain different approaches and different local histories. They plague communities which are growing rapidly, working in uncharted areas, and exceptionally heterogeneous. Third-order issues may not be immediately recognized by members of the community as such, as they can be part of the taken-for-granted. Nevertheless, they have long-term implications. With respect to difficulties of signing on and hooking up, they include triangulation and definition of objects, multiple meanings of information, and network externalities.

Triangulation and definition of objects. Different lines of work in the worm community come together in sharing information including genetics, molecular biology, statistics, and so on. One person explained, "I came from [another lab] where I was working on frogs" (Brad Thomas, PD). Another person described himself as "really a developmental geneticist" and added that a few years ago "the field was smaller; . . . now, many people are coming from outside, from mammals, protein labs" (Harry Markson, GS). Many people moved into the worm community from other areas after graduate school. Differences sometimes fell along the classical lines of organismal biology versus molecular or genetic research: "I am more of a wormy person. That's true of the community in general. Sometimes you choose a system that's more organismal" (Jane Sanchez, PD).

Collaboration may take place across disciplinary or geographic boundaries:

> [*Are you collaborating with anyone?*] "I'm collaborating with people in the worm and non-worm community—mostly immunologists in the non-worm community, people interested in the immune system. In the worm community, I'm collaborating with [a person in another state] on [a particular gene]. (Harry Markson, GS)

Disciplinary origin and current area of work affected the kinds of information individuals needed and the tools and data sources with which they are familiar. Those studying the organism for its own sake differed in their information needs from those using it exclusively as a model organism. Many informants had very specific expectations for WCS data:

> You need more options, especially for sequencing. This will be especially important once the [HGI] gets under way. . . . We need to work with subsets of sequences, examine them in more detail. (Brad Thomas, PD)

> What you'd want is a parts list, a list of cells. . . . If it's a neuron, its connections with other neurons. . . . That's for neurobiologists. (Harry Markson, GS)

Identifying the system with a particular subline of work and not as a general utility increased the barriers to usage. System construction was further complicated by another layer of object definition in that some respondents felt that WCS represented "CS people [computer scientists] . . . building a system only for CS people" and that WCS "has a vision that isn't necessarily what biologists want."

Multiple meanings, data interpretation, and claim staking. The nature and character of the community were changing as more people entered the "worm world" from other disciplines. During the last decade, it grew from a few hundred to over 1,000 members: "It's neat that it's exciting now, but it's also strange to have so many people" (Jane Sanchez, PD).

One goal of WCS is to support communication in a scientific community known for its willingness to share information but the growth of which has exceeded the ability of informal communication networks to serve as a conduit for this information (Schatz 1991). The issues of developing a collaborative system, however, go far beyond the technical. The multiple meanings or interpretations of particular communications turn out to be important at all levels.

For example, suggestions that it might be useful to have a "who's working on what" directory in the system raised issues of competition and the role of secrecy. Some said they would hesitate to put in certain kinds of information or wanted announcements delayed until "they had findings":

> There's always a problem you're going to get scooped. You always walk a very fine line. There's a lot of people working on my problem. . . . If you publish in the *Gazette,* you can lay claim to it. People would respect it. There have been some clashes, some labs trying to glom on to how much they can. It's going to be a struggle from here on out. . . . It's complex with the claim staking. That's why you want to get into it far enough so you can get ahead—before you announce it. If you could preface it with "wild speculation" [laughs], . . . well, there's a lot of

times those can have a big payoff. But then again, if five people jump on it, and in the meantime you're scooped . . ., that's not so good! (Mike Jones, PD)

Different communication channels also implied different degrees of freedom: "You can be wrong with no stigma" in the newsletter, said one graduate student, and a PI explained, "People are reluctant to do annotations [to the newsletter]. . . . It's the fear of putting yourself on the line, making a commitment to what you're doing. It means being wrong in the eyes of your colleagues" (Joe White, PI). He suggested delayed publication of annotations, letting them sit locally for a month or so first, and a postdoctoral student at another lab suggested the implementation of a personal level and a public level of annotation (Brad Thomas, PD). Another PI, however, became angry at this idea. He felt that this would work directly against WCS's commitment to community-wide sharing of information and turn WCS into a local tool rather than a community resource.

Trust and reliability of information is a final concern worth noting; articles in the *Gazette,* annotations, and the like all carry some kind of implicit value with them. First of all, information ages; old data are superseded by new, problems are resolved, protocols are updated. Neither traditional sources nor the current WCS have any fixed way of marking the relative validity or trustworthiness of a set of data. Annotations with updates or the ability to "gray out" old data in the *Gazette* might present technical solutions to these problems, yet there are sometimes no clear-cut answers to these questions, especially in a community populated with multiple viewpoints. In general, says one postdoctoral student, "there is no right or wrong. . . . You have to reach consensus on things, [and] you have to look at labs, which labs you trust more" (Brad Thomas, PD). He wanted to use annotations as a means of raising alternate viewpoints: "I'm knowledgeable [in Area X]. Sometimes others who clone don't know as much; they write things that are wrong. I would feel entitled to make annotations." Under the scheme he proposes, it would still be up to the reader of the annotation to sort out and make sense of competing information. He noted wryly that people will cite you as a foil when you've said something incorrect in any event, however, and that there's no way to prevent this. All these instances of data meaning different things under different circumstances—who notifies whom and when, what medium is used, who makes an annotation, or why a particular citation is or isn't included—required knowledge of the community that wasn't captured in any formal system (Star 1989a).

Network externalities and electronic participation: Subtleties and cautions.
The notion of externalities originates in economics and urban planning; a city may be said to afford "positive externalities" of cultural resources. For an

artist, New York's externalities usually outweigh those available in Champaign, Illinois, although other amenities such as cost of housing and safety may be greater in the latter. A network externality means that the more actors actively participate in a system or network, the greater the potential emergent resources for any given individual; it is distinct from the notion of "critical mass," which focuses on the number of subscribers/users at which system use becomes viable. Externalities may be negative in that, eventually, not being "hooked up" may make it impossible to participate effectively within a given community of work or discourse. For instance, the telephone network became a negative externality for those businesses without telephones sometime in the early 20th century; electronic mail has recently acquired a similar status in the academic world. For some purposes, standards (as in information standards) form important aspects of network externalities; that is, users of nonstandard computing systems are at a disadvantage as network externalities become intertwined with particular operating systems and data interchange protocols (see David [1985] for a cogent analysis and example).

It is currently still difficult to understand the role of network externalities in the worm community, but as electronic access becomes the primary access mechanism for some forms of data, and as participation in all forms of electronic communication rises, they become increasingly important. Let us consider two examples: WCS as an element of democratization and, more generally, data repositories as both a means of maintaining openness in the community and a means of providing value to the community.

One goal of the system development is democratization of information—the facilitation of access to critical data through a uniform interface. Yet the more central WCS becomes to the community either as a whole or as defined by key labs, the more those who cannot sign on along with the others will suffer. The "politics of reinforcement" suggests that the rich labs—either in terms of extant computing infrastructure or in their ability to procure or develop it using internal resources—will get richer as network externalities become more dense (Kraemer and King 1977). This issue may be receding in importance as alternatives to WCS emerge via data available at FTP sites and through Gopher and Mosaic; much of the information available via WCS can now be "pulled from the Net." Nevertheless, WCS is superior in its possibilities for graphical representation, and some forms of data analysis require such tools.

Issues of participation persist in several venues. For instance, a key repository is the genetic map, which represents the relative positions of genes on the chromosomes; another is the physical map, which represents cloned fragments of worm DNA and how they overlap to form the chromosomes (Schatz 1991):

> There's a time problem. You want experts doing this, but you want to do your own stuff [and] you don't want to maintain a database. If you want this to serve a global community, you have to get the data properly defined. (Brad Thomas, PD)

> There are data that should be on the [physical] map, but they are buried in labs all over the world. . . . When it was fragmented, people sent in clones. Now it's filled in, more coherent. The need to communicate back broke down. There used to be a dialogue; now there's a monologue. They don't bother telling Cambridge they've cloned genes. . . . With the genetic map, there's still dialogue. (Ben Tullis, PD)

Some of this is an issue of time; two attempts at an electronic bulletin board for the worm community "died out within two weeks due to lack of contributions" (Bob Gates, GS). Annotation and updating take work, and "it's not of immediate profit" (Sara Wu, PD). However, other reasons were also cited. When asked why the dialogue broke down, the person quoted above replied,

> There's a communication pyramid. You've got approximately 600 to 700 people in the community [in 1991]. One third of the community arrived between when [the community] was fragmented and [when it was] cohesive. They know only the cohesive map. (Ben Tullis, PD)

Newcomers weren't there when these repositories were created and did not share commitment to their upkeep and growth. Competition was also cited as a factor and was linked to the issue of timing discussed above. Someone who overheard the question on dialogue breakdown contributed the following comment:

> Yeah, like [one very well-known] lab . . . not sending in a note [on X]. And [another well-known] lab, they don't publish things when [they] are close to a gene they're working on. (Kyle Jordan, PD)

A graduate student in the same lab echoed a similar view of data sharing:

> Instant updating won't go far. People who want an immediate result to be known only want a small number to know. It's more competitive; people are more careful. They don't want everything to be global. By the time it gets into the *Worm Breeder's Gazette,* it's not critical anymore. The people who really need to know already know. (Bob Gates, GS)

WCS does not maintain the databases or publications featured in these discussions, but it would provide uniform access and an easy-to-use interface to them (once the system is up and running). It derives a significant part of its own value from community participation in their upkeep and maintenance. Without community commitment to the maintenance and upkeep of these materials, WCS has neither value nor legitimacy as a system that fosters either communication or collaboration.

Furthermore, if WCS is to develop its own niche within the community, it will also have to develop its own role in terms of legitimating, documenting, and disseminating information. Currently, for instance, an annotation published in WCS has uncertain value within the community:

> Contributing to the WCS, it's not a real publication. You have to send stuff to the *Worm Breeder's Gazette* if you want to publish widely. (Jane Jones, PD)

> You get a better sense of contributing when you send to the *Gazette*. If you annotate the WCS, you don't know if it's being read. (Morris Owe, GS)

This is an issue that will face similar systems as they try to piggyback on established systems, repositories, and the like, especially when in competition with multiple other avenues for information retrieval and electronic communication. It is also important in the building of digital libraries and publishing systems. Will an electronic journal publication "count" as much as a printed one?

All of us, in addition, face paradoxes of efficiency or information overload and the danger of diverting a successful manual information tracking system over to the computer with a loss of productivity. Many economists have noted the so-called "productivity paradox" in firms with the introduction of information systems (productivity often declines with investment in information technology). Similar paradoxes are a real danger in science with its delicate funding processes, understudied task structures, and fuzzy means of measuring productivity.

Tool building and the reward structure in scientific careers. Finally, the role of tool building and tool maintenance may be undergoing a shift as computer-based tools become more prevalent. The tension between traditional notions of work and tool building (and new opportunities for the same) have been observed in other academic communities (Ruhleder 1991, 1995; Weedman 1995). One person was there in the early days of the database *acedb* and still contributed regularly, sending e-mail about bugs and suggestions for graphics. Others constructed local tools such as annotated gene lists (a project carried out part-time over the course of a year), using data from WCS. Yet another person, as mentioned above, planned to team up with a computer scientist to develop tools for data visualization. Many of our respondents could list tools (from techniques, to compilations of targeted information, to analysis software) that they would have liked to see added or perfected. The difficulty is that there are no clear rewards for this kind of work except for the contributions the tool makes to one's own work. The biologist working with the computer scientist doesn't get any "credit" for this within his or her own discipline (the biologist anticipated having tenure by the time this project would begin). As one postdoctoral student put it in a comment appropriate for both sides, "There are a hundred things that are useful, but you don't get a Ph.D. for [them]" (Jay Emery, PD).

Addressing third-order issues. Third-order issues are a feature of complex communities. They may become easier to observe during times of flux because they resist local resolution. Novel technologies, situations, and concerns create immediate resource requirements and gaps in learning that can be addressed locally. Over time, however, the interactions of these first-order and second-order issues combine to raise broader questions which push the magnitude of a "solution" out of the local realm and into the wider community.

Electronic access to data via WCS, for instance, calls into question not only local resource allocations but also broader institutional alliances and patterns of contributions at the disciplinary level. The resolution of these issues or conflicts (if, indeed, they are resolved) may result in the creation of new subspecialties, new requirements for a discipline or profession, new criteria for the conduct and evaluation of work, and new reward structures. Resolutions or "readjustments" will not only take place overtly (i.e., through a petition to a campus computing committee or a decision to reallocate travel funds to a lab computing fund). They may be played out on a political level by individuals with high stakes in maintaining stature or controlling resources, or they may be resolved serendipitously, even unconsciously. For instance, as mentioned above, questions of access to WCS and the maintenance of an open, democratic structure within the community may become moot as other forms of access through the Internet become easier.

DOUBLE BINDS:
THE TRANSCONTEXTUAL SYNDROME ON THE NET

Until now, we have simply followed Bateson's (1978) typology for learning in categorizing infrastructural barriers and challenges. Bateson's ideas about levels of learning originated in communication theory and cybernetics; more than a taxonomy, they are an expression of set of dynamics:

> Double bind theory is concerned with the experiential component in the genesis of tangles in the rules or premises of habit. I . . . assert that experienced breaches in the weave of contextual structure are in fact "double binds" and must necessarily (if they contribute at all to the hierarchic processes of learning and adaptation) promote what I am calling transcontextual syndrome. (p. 276)

The formal statement of the problem is expressed as a logical one, following (as we noted earlier) Russell and Whitehead's theory of classification. In "The Logical Categories of Learning and Communication," Bateson (pp. 279-308) notes that a category error such as confusing the name of a class and a member of that class will create a logical paradox. In the world of pure logic, this appears as a fatal error because such logical systems seem to exist outside of time and space. In the real world, particularly the behavioral world, however, people cope by working within multiple frameworks or "world-views" maintained serially or in parallel.

When messages are given at more than one level simultaneously, or an answer is simultaneously demanded at a higher level and negated on a lower one, there arises a logical paradox or "double bind," an instance of what Bateson (1978) terms the "transcontextual syndrome." While Bateson drew his examples from family contexts in the course of his work on schizophrenia, double binds occur in academic and business contexts as well. Middle managers in rapidly changing environments, for instance, are frequently caught between the goals and expectations articulated by senior management and the actions of senior management with respect to budget allocation and performance evaluation (Mishra and Cameron 1991). Companies may formally promote efforts toward "reengineering" and "empowerment" yet offer no mechanisms for employees to participate in decision making, or they may sanction employees for not being active learners while refusing to acknowledge modes of learning and experimentation that fail to conform to very specific models (Ruhleder et al. 1996). In the words of Bateson (1978), "There may be incongruence or conflict between context and metacontext" (p. 245). Over a protracted period of time, with many such messages, schizophrenia may result, either literally or figuratively.[4]

People attempting to hook up to complex electronic information systems encounter a similar discontinuity between message types. The rhetoric surrounding the Internet makes "signing on" and "hooking up" sound remarkably straightforward. Furthermore, the benefits sound instantaneous and far-reaching. Why, then, do so many problems arise when members of the worm community try to take a similar step? Why are there so many disappointments with accessing information, and how may we understand these?

We identify several varieties of double binds arising across two levels or orders from what we call *infrastructural transcontextual syndrome:*

1. The gap between diverse contexts of usage
2. The gap inherent in various computing-related discussions within the worm community itself
3. The gulf between "double levels of language" in design and use

The gap between diverse contexts of usage. What is simple for one group is not for the other, so what appears to be a Level 1 message to computer scientists posed a Level 2 problem for users, creating a double bind. For instance, when asked about getting onto the system, designers of WCS might say, "Just throw up X Windows and FTP the file down." The tone of the message is clearly Level 1, a simple "recipe" for the UNIX literate. For the relatively naive user, however, it requires him or her to move to a different contextual level and to figure out what type of a thing an "X Window" is and what it means to "FTP a file down." A Level 1 instruction thus becomes a complex set of Level 2 questions, closely related to the user's own level of expertise. These kinds of transcontextual difficulties will intensify as collaborative systems and groupware are developed for increasingly nonhomogeneous user communities (Grudin 1991, 1994; Markussen 1994).

Another part of this type of double bind is an infinite regress of barriers to finding out about complex electronic information systems (Markussen 1995). If you don't know already, it's hard to know *how* to find out, and it isn't always clear how to abstract knowledge from one system to another. What is obvious to one person is not to another; the degrees of obviousness continue indefinitely, forming complex binds. For example, there is no single book that can tell you from scratch about computers or networked computing; the only way in is to switch contexts altogether and work more closely with those who already know, becoming a member of some community (Suchman and Trigg 1991; Suchman et al. 1986). This may account for the power of the participatory design model popular in Scandinavia, in which designers and users work together to the point of developing a shared context at all levels of interaction (Ehn 1988). It may simultaneously account for the difficulty of explaining or popularizing the model outside of Scandinavia, the working context of which differs greatly from the United States or other parts of Europe.[5]

The gap inherent in discussions within the worm community. Within the worm community itself, there exists a Level 2/Level 3 double bind. Just as

Level 1 statements can engender Level 2 questions, so can Level 2 discussions open up higher order issues. Discussions about package or platform choice become discussions about resource allocation, data interpretation, and network externalities. Take, again, the case of "FTP-ing a file down." Talk of learning about FTP, about alternatives such as Gopher and the like, becomes questions of access across labs, of database maintenance and data reliability, and of norms and rewards within the community for contributions to the database.

These issues are particularly poignant ones for "older" members of a fairly new community who recognize that technical choices and decisions made at Level 2—evaluations of the options for responding to Level 1 signals—have the ability to dramatically affect third-order issues. In the worm community, the concerns involve changes in the composition of the community as "outsiders" join and what this means for data interpretation and tool construction. The concerns also center around the multiple roles that research on the organism plays: "end in and of itself" versus model organism for the HGI. Tools aimed at Level 2 problems deeply affect the options open to the discipline when addressing third-order questions and setting broad conceptual directions.

Double levels of language in design and use. There may be double binds in those aspects of the system which are self-contradictory, between formal system properties and informal cultural practices. The language of design centers around technical capacity, while the language of use centers around effectiveness. Robinson (1991) notes that for systems that provide electronic support for computer-supported cooperative work, only those applications which simultaneously take into account both the formal, computational level and the informal, workplace/cultural level are successful. This problem is not unique to this domain. Gasser (1986), for instance, identifies a variety of "workarounds" developed to overcome the rigidity (and limitations) of a transaction processing system, while users of an insurance claims processing system developed an elaborate and informal set of procedures for articulating alternatives and inconsistencies (Gerson and Star 1986). Other examples abound.

While none of these studies identifies the problems/solutions as evidence of a double bind, each may be expressed in these terms. The "language" of the designer is focused on the technical representation of a particular set of data (i.e., customer records) and the efficiency of processing them to meet a particular goal (i.e., claims processing). The "language" of the user is focused on the need to mediate between conflicting viewpoints (i.e., doctors vs. representatives for large customer groups) and the need to develop effective workflows within their own workplaces. Orlikowski (1993) discusses more narrowly the conceptualization of software design methods and tools as languages and, together with Beath, examines the consequences of nonshared languages or organizational barriers to full participation of users (Beath and Orlikowski 1994).

This double bind is also captured in the discussion of Mac versus UNIX and what it means in terms of a clash of cultures between biologists and computer scientists. On one level, it is a discussion about operating systems; on another, it is representative of two worldviews and sets of values with respect to the relationship between technology and work—the relationship between the tool and its user. In the case of WCS, designers focused on features of technical elegance and sophistication such as constructing a mechanism for continuous *Gazette* updating or fully exploiting hypertext possibilities. Yet constant information updating works against the biologists' informal mechanisms for information distribution, processing, and integration. And biologists were less interested in additional layers of complex hypertext linkages than in simple capabilities, like printouts of parts of the genetic map, which could be taken back to their lab benches, tacked up, pasted into a notebook, and easily annotated in the flow of work.

Summary and Recommendations for Addressing Double Binds

WCS—and the push for collaboratory development which set the stage for this and other projects (Lederberg and Uncapher 1988)—was driven by a desire not only to support collaborative scientific efforts but also to foster "ideal communities" of rich communication and seamless universal information access. WCS had the advantage of starting with a community in which many of those norms were already in operation and whose small size made it relatively cohesive. It had a dedicated design team with knowledge of the target domain. It had an interested user population. Yet it never achieved its original goals, and while it does serve as a platform for communication and information access for some, others have found the barriers locally insurmountable or the system itself superfluous.

When will WCS become infrastructure? The answer is, probably never in its original form, for the reasons outlined above. The development of the system and its integration into the community could not overcome the double binds that emerged within the context of system implementation and use. Nor could its development negate the impacts of other technologies such as Gopher and Mosaic. Constructed largely as a series of "building blocks" available from other sources, it was easy enough for those building blocks to assemble or duplicate themselves elsewhere. But WCS and other systems' development efforts based on this model of collaboratory *can* benefit from some of the lessons learned or newly illustrated through our analysis. And organizations interested in developing large-scale information and communication infrastructures (whether formal business organizations or loosely coupled academic communities) can become aware of the efforts required on their part to meet developers halfway. Having identified different instances of double binds that predicated the failure of WCS, we are left with the need to suggest positive action. We offer two recommendations below for addressing double binds.

The role of multidisciplinary development teams. One of the key difficulties with double binds is recognizing them in the first place; individuals involved in a situation may not be able to identify instances of this transcontextual syndrome. The other key difficulty, once a double bind is identified, is to articulate it such that the other party will recognize it as a problem. Dynamics of power and authority are clearly important here. In family settings, a parent might reject affectionate behavior on the part of the child and then, when the child withdraws, accuse the child of not loving the parent. The child may not always have capacity for analyzing and correcting this inconsistency, just as employees may not really have the power to address problems in a business environment that overtly empowers them. Managers may even subtly sanction the "wrong" kind of empowered behavior. Users are often given computer-based tools that are either cumbersome or ill explained to them; when they fail to use them, they are labeled as being "resistant" to technology (Forsythe 1992; Markus 1983; Markus and Bjørn-Andersen 1987).[6]

A computing-related analog would be the denial on the part of developers or system administrators that technical difficulties really mask higher order conceptual problems centered around work practices and community standards and a failure on the part of users to recognize the complexity of their work domains, their hidden assumptions, and the various motivations of the stakeholders involved. If we expect designers to learn about the formal and informal aspects of the user domain, to learn to "speak the language," we must ask users to meet designers halfway by learning their language and developing an understanding of the design domain. If designers are at fault for assuming that all user requirements can be formally captured and codified, users are often equally at fault for expecting "magic bullets"—technical systems that will solve social or organizational problems.

The fault may really lie in neither camp. Often miscommunication resulting in the double binds of language and the context within which the process of design/use occurs are responsible. The emergence of multidisciplinary development teams may help to alleviate aspects of the transcontextual syndrome identified above, with ethnographers helping users and designers bridge the contextual divide. "You can FTP that from such-and-such a site" might well give way to "I can give you the FTP address, but the kind of data you'll get won't be detailed enough for what you want to do with it." By sharing an understanding of both the formal, computational level (traditionally the domain of the computer programming and systems analyst) and the informal level of workplace culture, double binds may be more easily identified as all members of the team learn to correctly identify the various orders or levels to which a message might belong. This sharing, however, requires institutional contexts that support and even reward this kind of collaboration.

The nature of technical user education. Many elements of the "computing infrastructures" emerging within the academic and business communities are not custom made. They consist of locally developed applications, off-the-shelf packages or tailored applications, local area networks and the Internet, commercial on-line services, and "shareware" such as Mosaic and Netscape. They vary greatly in terms of stability, maintainability, interoperability, and access to support. Yet in order to carry out their work effectively in increasingly computer-based environments, individuals must be able to negotiate complex configurations of technical resources. Pentland's (1997) analysis of software help lines attests to this complexity: "Software support is an activity that occurs on the 'bleeding edge' of technology, on the boundary between the known and the unknown." Support technicians and customers are often speaking from two disparate viewpoints, and successful support means recognizing and juggling this reality (Heylighen 1991). The emergence of local "tailors" (Trigg and Bødker 1994) and "technology mediators" (Okamura et al. 1994) may provide a bridge between relatively generic technologies and their local interpretation and application.

Individuals are being told that they must adapt to new technologies and become technically literate, yet the type of training and support offered to them rarely gives them the basis necessary to evolve along with the infrastructure. Training sessions, on-line tutorials, and user manuals focus on a set of skills limited to particular applications and occur outside of the context of actual work. Computer support centers may assist individuals in situ but tend to be reactive, imparting one solution at a time without any contextual connection to the kinds of technical problems the user has had before. To apply Bateson's (1978) framework, they are aimed at giving people the skills to address first-order technical issues, though broader issues—such as whether the implementation of a particular groupware technology is consistent with local, career, or global strategic direction—may require second- or third-order conceptual skills.

Frameworks for various levels of "computer literacy" already exist within the computer science and education communities. What are missing are institutional mechanisms—whether the "institution" is a business enterprise, a university, or a scientific discipline—to support individuals in two ways. First, they do still need to teach specific skills, but they need to place these skills within a technical context that enables users to apply them to the next application and the next. Second, they need to assist users in developing and maintaining the kind of computer literacy that will allow them to understand and address second- and third-order issues, especially as they unfold over time—a kind of learning that occurs through ongoing dialogue and experimentation. That literacy must thus be coupled with an understanding of emerging work practices (locally and more broadly within their organizations). Finally, organizations also need to develop mechanisms for legitimating and rewarding the work of local tailors and mediators.

These institutional mechanisms can be, in part, consciously constructed. But in order for them to grow dynamically along with emergent user expertise and an emergent base of computing technologies, they must be predicated on the notion that organizations function as complex communities and that learning takes place within local communities of practice (Lave and Wenger 1992; Star 1995). The creation and use of discrete technologies must occur within a broader context which is constantly reified by participants within and across the various communities of practice which define a particular organization. The success of systems developed to support their work is predicated on the creation of shared objects and practices, boundary objects, and infrastructures (Star 1989b; Star and Griesemer 1989). For instance, use of WCS was and continues to be predicated on the complex interaction between a variety of small and large communities: the WCS development team, a non-homogeneous target population (the worm community), local systems support groups, and remote data collection and distribution centers. All of these constitute extant, partially overlapping communities of practice. Discontinuities in these interactions, unequal participation, and the emergence and continued rise of competing technologies have contributed to the inability of WCS to emerge as boundary object or to fully submerge as infrastructure.

ORGANIZATIONAL ENVIRONMENT:
COMMUNITIES AND LARGE-SCALE INFRASTRUCTURE

Using the analysis put forward in the previous section, we would like to understand the nature of the claims about community and the Net as examples of the complex emergence of infrastructure. We see a number of ways in which the merging of medium and message in the talk about scientific electronic communities is problematic in addition to the double bind/ transcontextual syndrome issues. Scientists do not "live on the Net." They do make increasingly heavy use of it; participation is increasingly mandatory for professional advancement or even participation, with a rapidly changing set of information resources radically altering the landscape of information "user" and "provider" (Klobas 1994), and the density of interconnections and infrastructural development is proceeding at a dizzying rate. That development is uneven. It is an interesting mixture of local politics and practices and on-line and off-line interactions, and it is filled with constantly shifting boundaries between lines of work; cohorts and career stages; physical, virtual, and material culture; and increasingly urgent and interesting problems of scale.

The multiple meanings of WCS for different groups and individuals are useful as exemplars for understanding the challenges posed by "the Net." From one perspective, WCS fits well the cognitive map of the scientist with respect to information: links between disparate pieces, graphical representations, layers of detail, and so on. Yet relatively few worm biologists have "signed on" to WCS, even as the community itself is growing rapidly. The seeming paradox of why our respondents chose to use Gopher, Mosaic, and other simpler, public access systems rather than WCS involves a kind of double bind on a larger scale.

To take on board the custom-designed, powerful WCS (with its convenient interface) is to suffer inconvenience at the intersection of work habits, computer use, and lab resources. Its acquisition disrupts resource allocation patterns; ongoing use and support requires an investment in changes of habit and infrastructure. The World Wide Web, on the other hand, can be accessed from a broad variety of terminals and connections, and Internet computer support is readily available at most academic institutions and through relatively inexpensive commercial services.

Yet, even within the larger context of infrastructure, there are other ways in which WCS serves its community less well than alternate emerging infrastructures. Science is an integrative and permutable domain and requires a complementary infrastructure (Ruhleder and King 1991). The construction of WCS, while it integrates a large number of materials, does so in a constricted fashion. Lab notebooks, by way of contrast, are extremely open and integrative documents (Gorry et al. 1991). At the same time, computing infrastructures, including Gophers, FTP sites, and so on, while still at a very primitive level, fit more closely with this integrative model than relatively closed systems such as WCS, and these infrastructures are growing at a phenomenal rate. For these reasons, and despite frustrations over the lack of indexing and search capabilities, use of Gopher and Mosaic within the *C. elegans* world abounds.

CONCLUSION

Can an organizational support system be developed that allows people to coordinate large-scale efforts, provide navigational aids for newcomers, yet still retain the feeling of an informal, close-knit community or cohesive organizational culture? If structure is not incorporated a priori, then does it emerge, and how? Just as WCS was intended to bridge geographic and disciplinary boundaries within the worm community, groupware and related technologies are being constructed as technical infrastructures to support members of an organization in bridging physical, temporal, and functional boundaries.

Experience with groupware suggests that highly structured applications for collaboration will fail to become integrated into local work practices (Ruhleder et al. 1996). Rather, experimentation over time results in the emergence of a complex constellation of locally tailored applications and repositories, combined with pockets of local knowledge and elements of the formal infrastructure to create a unique and evolving hybrid. This evolution is facilitated by those elements of the formal structure which support the redefinition of local roles and the emergence of communities of practice around the intersection of specific technologies and types of problems. These observations suggest streams of research that continue to explore how infrastructures evolve over time and how "formal" planned structure melds with or gives way to "informal," locally emergent structure.

The competing requirements of openness and malleability, coupled with structure and navigability, create a fascinating design challenge—even a new science. The emergence of an infrastructure—the "when" of complete transparency—is thus an "organic" one, evolving in response to the community evolution and adoption of infrastructure as natural, involving new forms and conventions that we cannot yet imagine. At the same time, it is highly challenging technically, requiring new forms of computability that are both socially situated and abstract enough to travel across time and space (Eveland and Bikson 1987; Feldman 1987). Goguen (1994) and Jirotka and Goguen (1994) recently referred to these as "abstract situated data types" for requirements analysis and note that requirements engineering in this view in fact *becomes* "the reconciliation of technical and social issues."

In the end, it seems that organizational change and the resolution into infrastructure are usually very slow processes. Local and large-scale rhythms of change are often mismatched, and what it takes to really make anything like a national or global information space is at the very cutting edge of both social and information sciences. The mixture of close-in, long-term understanding gained by ethnography and the complex indexing, programming, and transmission tasks afforded by computer science meet here, breaking traditional disciplinary boundaries and reflecting the very nature of the problem: When is an ecology of infrastructure?[7]

NOTES

1. Names have been changed to preserve anonymity.

2. Personal communication between Susan Leigh Star and Bruce Schatz, September 28, 1995.

3. PI = principal investigator; PD = postdoctoral student; GS = graduate student.

4. The child insists on seeing the literal level and ignoring context or inappropriately seeing context literally. The often-noted poetry in schizophrenic language is a result of this refusal; good poets deliberately play with transcontextual double entendres. Formally, this ignores or transgresses the gulf between message and metamessage.

5. Participatory design has its own inherent difficulties (Markussen 1994; Nyce and Löwgren 1995).

6. There is an analogy here with medicine, namely, studies of "patient" compliance which overlook the infrastructural and political features of medicine itself. See, for example, Strauss (1979) and Strauss and colleagues (1985).

7. WCS was partially funded by the NSF under grants IRI-90-15047, IRI-92-57252, and BIR-93-19844; by grants to Star from the Program in Culture, Values and Ethics and the Advanced Information Technologies Group, University of Illinois; and by an NSF Professional Development grant. Additional support was provided by the University of Arizona and the University of Illinois. We would also like to thank Bruce Schatz and other WCS staff, Michael Elmes, Sam Politz, Marc Berg, Geof Bowker, Nick Burbules, Tom Jewett, Alaina Kanfer, Rob Kling, Jim Nyce, Stefan Timmermans, John Garrett, Tone Brattetieg, Pål Søregaard, Eevi Beck, Kari Thoresen, Ole Hanseth, Eric Monteiro and the Internet Project working group at the Institute for Infomatics, University of Oslo, Yrjö Engeström, Chuck Goodwin, and Dick Boland.

REFERENCES

Anderson, William L. and William T. Crocca, "Engineering Practice and Codevelopment of Product Prototypes," *Comm. ACM,* 36 (1993), 49-56.

Barlow, John Perry, "Is There a There in Cyberspace?" *Utne Reader,* 68, March-April (1995), 53-56.

Bateson, Gregory, *Steps to an Ecology of Mind,* Ballantine Books, New York, 1978.

Beath, Cynthia and Wanda J. Orlikowski, "The Contradictory Structure of Systems Development Methodologies: Deconstructing the IS-User Relationship in Information Engineering," *Information Systems Res.,* 5, 4 (1994), 350-377.

Becker, Howard S., *Art Worlds,* University of California Press, Berkeley, 1982.

Bødker, Susanne, *Through the Interface,* Lawrence Erlbaum, Hillsdale, NJ, 1991.

Bowker, Geoffrey, "Information Mythology and Infrastructure," in Lisa Bud-Frierman (Ed.), *Information Acumen: The Understanding and Use of Knowledge in Modern Business,* Routledge, London, 1994, 231-247.

―――, "The Universal Language and the Distributed Passage Point: The Case of Cybernetics," *Social Studies of Sci.,* 23 (1993), 107-127.

Brown, John Seely and Paul Duguid, "Borderline Issues: Social and Material Aspects of Design," *Human-Computer Interaction,* 9 (1994), 3-36.

Bucciarelli, Louis L., *Designing Engineers,* MIT Press, Cambridge, MA, 1994.

David, Paul, "Clio and the Economics of QWERTY," *American Economic Rev.,* 75 (1985), 332-337.

Davies, Lynda and Geoff Mitchell, "The Dual Nature of the Impact of IT on Organizational Transformations," in R. Baskerville, O. Ngwenyama, S. Smithson, and J. DeGross (Eds.), *Transforming Organizations With Information Technology,* North-Holland, Amsterdam, 1994, 243-261.

Ehn, Pelle, *Work-Oriented Design of Computer Artifacts,* Lawrence Erlbaum, Hillsdale, NJ, 1988.

Ellis, C. A., S. J. Gibbs, and G. L. Rein, "Groupware: Some Issues and Experiences," *Comm. ACM,* 34 (1991), 38-58.

Engeström, Yrjö, "When Is a Tool? Multiple Meanings of Artifacts in Human Activity," in Yrjö Engeström (Ed.), *Learning, Working, and Imagining,* Orienta-Konsultit Oy, Helsinki, Finland, 1990.

Eveland, J. D. and Tora Bikson, "Evolving Electronic Communication Networks: An Empirical Assessment," *Office: Technology and People,* 3 (1987), 103-128.

Feldman, Martha, "Constraints on Communication and Electronic Messaging," *Office: Technology and People,* 3 (1987).

Forsythe, Diana, "Blaming the User in Medical Informatics: The Cultural Nature of Scientific Practice," in David Hess and Linda Layne (Eds.), *Knowledge and Society: The Anthropology of Science and Technology* (Vol. 9), JAI, Greenwich, CT, 1992, 95-111.

Gasser, Les, "The Integration of Computing and Routine Work," *ACM Trans. Office Information Systems,* 4 (1986), 205-225.

Gerson, E. M. and Susan Leigh Star, "Analyzing Due Process in the Workplace," *ACM Trans. Office Information Systems,* 4 (1986), 257-270.

Gorry, G. Anthony, Kevin B. Long, Andrew M. Burger, Cynthia P. Jung, and Barry D. Meyer, "The Virtual Notebook System™: An Architecture for Collaborative Work," *J. Organizational Computing,* 1 (1991), 223-250.

Grudin, Jonathan, "Obstacles to User Involvement in Software Product Development, With Implications for CSCW," *International J. Man-Machine Studies,* 34 (1991), 435-452.

———, "Groupware and Social Dynamics: Eight Challenges for Developers," *Comm. ACM,* 37, 1 (1994), 92-105.

Goguen, Joseph, "Requirements Engineering as the Reconciliation of Technical and Social Issues," in M. Jirotka and J. Goguen (Eds.), *Requirements Engineering: Social and Technical Issues,* Academic Press, San Diego, 1994.

Hewitt, Carl, "Offices Are Open Systems," *ACM Trans. Office Information Systems,* 4 (1986), 271-287.

Heylighen, Francis, "Design of a Hypermedia Interface Translating Between Associative and Formal Representations," *International J. Man-Machine Studies,* 35 (1991), 491-515.

Hughes, Thomas P., *Networks of Power: Electrification in Western Society, 1880-1930,* Johns Hopkins University Press, Baltimore, MD, 1983.

———, "The Evolution of Large Technological Systems," in Wiebe E. Bijker, Thomas P. Hughes, and Trevor Pinch (Eds.), *The Social Construction of Technological Systems,* MIT Press, Cambridge, MA, 1989, 51-82.

Jewett, Tom and Rob Kling, "The Dynamics of Computerization in a Social Science Research Team: A Case Study of Infrastructure, Strategies, and Skills," *Social Sci. Computer Rev.,* 9 (1991), 246-275.

Jirotka, Marine and Joseph Goguen, *Requirements Engineering: Social and Technical Issues,* Academic Press, San Diego, 1994.

Kling, R. and W. Scacchi, "The Web of Computing: Computing Technology as Social Organization," *Advances in Computers,* 21 (1982), 3-78.

Klobas, Jane E., "Networked Information Resources: Electronic Opportunities for Users and Librarians," *Information Technology and People,* 7 (1994), 5-18.

Korpela, Eija, "Path to Notes: A Networked Company Choosing Its Information Systems Solution," in R. Baskerville, O. Ngwenyama, S. Smithson, and J. DeGross (Eds.), *Transforming Organizations With Information Technology,* North-Holland, Amsterdam, 1994, 219-242.

Kraemer, Kenneth L. and John L. King, *Computers and Local Government,* Praeger, New York, 1977.

Latour, Bruno, *We Have Never Been Modern* (Catherine Porter, Trans.), Harvard University Press, Cambridge, MA, 1993.

Lave, Jean and Etienne Wenger, *Situated Learning: Legitimate Peripheral Participation,* Cambridge University Press, Cambridge, UK, 1992.

Lederberg, J. and K. Uncapher, "Towards a National Collaboratory," in *Report of an Invitational Workshop at the Rockefeller University,* National Science Foundation, Washington, DC, 1988.

Malone, Tom and Gary Olson (Eds.), *Coordination Theory and Communication Technology,* Lawrence Erlbaum, Hillsdale, NJ, forthcoming.

Markus, M. Lynne, "Power, Politics, and MIS Implementation," *Comm. ACM,* 26, 6 (1983), 430-444.

―――― and Niels Bjørn-Andersen, "Power Over Users: Its Exercise by System Professionals," *Comm. ACM,* 30, 6 (1987), 498-504.

Markussen, Randi, "Dilemmas in Cooperative Design," in *PDC '94: Proceedings of the Participatory Design Conference,* Computer Professionals for Social Responsibility, Palo Alto, CA, 1994, 59-66.

――――, "Constructing Easiness: Historical Perspectives on Work, Computerization, and Women," in Susan Leigh Star (Ed.), *The Cultures of Computing,* Basil Blackwell, Oxford, UK, 1995.

Mishra, Aneil K. and Kim S. Cameron, "Double Binds in Organizations: Archetypes, Consequences, and Solutions From the U.S. Auto Industry," presentation at the Academy of Management annual meeting, Miami Beach, FL, August 13, 1991.

Monteiro, Eric, Ole Hanseth, and Morten Hatling, "Developing Information Infrastructure: Standardization vs. Flexibility," Working Paper 18 in Science, Technology, and Society series, University of Trondheim, Norway, 1994.

Nyce, James and Jonas Löwgren, "Toward Foundational Analysis in Human-Computer Interaction," in Peter J. Thomas (Ed.), *The Social and International Dimensions of Human-Computer Interfaces,* Cambridge University Press, Cambridge, UK, 1995.

Okamura, Kazuo, Masayo Fujimoto, Wanda J. Orlikowski, and JoAnne Yates, "Helping CSCW Applications Succeed: The Role of Mediators in the Context of Use," in *Proceedings of the Conference on Computer-Supported Cooperative Work,* ACM Press, Chapel Hill, NC, October 22-26, 1994.

Orlikowski, Wanda, "Integrated Information Environment or Matrix of Control? The Contradictory Implications of Information Technology," *Accounting, Management, and Information Technology,* 1 (1991), 9-42.

――――, "CASE Tools as Organizational Change: Investigating Incremental and Radical Changes in Systems Development," *MIS Quarterly,* 17 (1993), 309-340.

Pentland, Brian, "Bleeding Edge Epistemology: Practical Problem Solving in Software Support Hot Lines," in Stephen Barley and Julia Orr (Eds.), *Between Craft and Science: Technical Work in U.S. Settings*, ILR Press, Ithaca, NY, 1997.

Pool, Robert, "Beyond Databases and Email," *Science*, 261, August 13, 1993, pp. 841-843.

Robinson, Mike, "Double-Level Languages and Cooperative Working," *AI and Society*, 5 (1991), 34-60.

Ruhleder, Karen, "Information Technologies as Instruments of Transformation: Changes to Work Processes and Work Structure Effected by the Computerization of Classical Scholarship," Ph.D. dissertation, Department of Information and Computer Science, University of California, Irvine, 1991.

————, "Reconstructing Artifacts, Reconstructing Work: From Textual Edition to On-line Databank," *Sci., Technology, & Human Values*, 20 (1995), 39-64.

———— Brigitte Jordan, and Michael B. Elmes, "Wiring the 'New Organization': Integrating Collaborative Technologies and Team-Based Work," presented at the meeting of the Academy of Management, Cincinnati, OH, August 9-12, 1996.

———— and John Leslie King, "Computer Support for Work Across Space, Time, and Social Worlds," *J. Organizational Computing*, 1, 4 (1991), 341-356.

Schatz, Bruce, "Building an Electronic Community System," *J. Management Information Systems*, 8 (1991), 87-107.

Schmidt, Kjeld and Liam Bannon, "Taking CSCW Seriously: Supporting Articulation Work," *Computer-Supported Cooperative Work (CSCW): An International J.*, 1 (1992), 7-41.

Star, Susan Leigh, *Regions of the Mind: Brain Research and the Quest for Scientific Certainty*, Stanford University Press, Stanford, CA, 1989a.

————, "The Structure of Ill-Structured Solutions: Heterogeneous Problem-Solving, Boundary Objects, and Distributed Artificial Intelligence," in M. Huhns and L. Gasser (Eds.), *Distributed Artificial Intelligence 2*, Morgan Kauffmann, Menlo Park, NJ, 1989b, 37-54.

————, "Power, Technologies, and the Phenomenology of Conventions: On Being Allergic to Onions," in John Law (Ed.), *A Sociology of Monsters: Essays on Power, Technology, and Domination*, Routledge, London, 1991a.

————, "Organizational Aspects of Implementing a Large-Scale Information System in a Scientific Community," technical report, Community Systems Laboratory, University of Arizona, Tucson, 1991b.

————, "Misplaced Concretism and Concrete Situations: Feminism, Method, and Information Technology," Working Paper 11, Gender-Nature-Culture Feminist Research Network series, Odense University, Denmark, 1994.

———— (Ed.), *The Cultures of Computing*, Blackwell, Oxford, UK, 1995.

————, "From Hestia to Home Page: Feminism and the Concept of Home in Cyberspace," in Nina Lykke and Rosi Braidotti (Eds.), *Between Monsters, Goddesses, and Cyborgs: Feminist Confrontations With Science, Medicine, and Cyberspace*, ZED Books, London, 1996, 30-46.

Star, Susan Leigh and James Griesemer, "Institutional Ecology, 'Translations,' and Boundary Objects: Amateurs and Professionals in Berkeley's Museum of Vertebrate Zoology, 1907-1939," *Social Studies of Science*, 19 (1989), 387-420.

Strauss, Anselm, *Qualitative Methods for Social Scientists*, Cambridge University Press, Cambridge, UK, 1986.

———— (Ed.), *Where Medicine Fails*, Transaction Books, New Brunswick, NJ, 1979.

————, S. Fagerhaugh, B. Suczek, and C. Wiener, *Social Organization of Medical Work*, University of Chicago Press, Chicago, 1985.

Suchman, L. and R. Trigg, "Understanding Practice: Video as a Medium for Reflection and Design," in J. Greenbaum and M. Kyng, (Eds.), *Design at Work,* Lawrence Erlbaum, Hillsdale, NJ, 1991, 65-89.

————, Randy Trigg, and F. Halasz, "Supporting Collaboration in Note-Cards," in D. Peterson (Ed.), *Proceedings of the Conference on Computer-Supported Cooperative Work (CSCW-86),* ACM Press, New York, 1986, 1-10.

Trigg, Randall and Susanne Bødker, "From Implementation to Design: Tailoring and the Emergence of Systematization in CSCW," in *Proceedings of the Conference on Computer-Supported Cooperative Work,* ACM Press, New York, 1994, 45-54.

Weedman, Judith, "Incentive Structures and Multidisciplinary Research: The Sequoia 2000 Project," presented at the American Society for Information Science meeting, Chicago, October, 1995.

Yates, JoAnne, *Control Through Communication: The Rise of System in American Management,* Johns Hopkins University Press, Baltimore, MD, 1989.

Index

Abernathy, W. J., 225
Ackland, T. G., 56
Adam, N., 130
Adams, D., 168
Adjustment (IRS), 188-189
Adler, R. S., 118
AES. *See* Automated Examination
   System
Age of Unreason (Handy), 21
Aiken, M., 224
Aitken, H. G. J., 64
Allen, M., 313
Alpert, G., 210
Alvesson, M., 176n5
Anderson, G., 56n2, 177n13
Anderson, M., 36, 47, 53, 56
Anderson, P., 225, 297
Anderson, W. L., 312
Anthes, G. H., 186
Appelbaum, S. H., 20, 21, 28
Applegate, L., 7
Arc/Info. *See* Geographic information
   systems (GIS) two-county study
Argyris, C., 169-170
Arithmometer, 46-47, 48-49
Armstrong, R., 59, 78
Aronson, N., 98
ARPANET, 93, 103-104
Artisinal manufacturing, 15, 25, 29
Attelesey, S., 67
Attewell, P., 118, 276, 279, 298

Austrian, G., 47, 55
Automated Examination System (AES),
   185, 186, 187
   laptop computers in, 189-191
   scope of, 189
   See also Automated Examination
      System (AES) study
Automated Examination System (AES)
      study:
   conclusions, 199-202
   data collection, 187
   laptop computers
      advancement and, 197-198
      as embarrassing, 194-195
      symbolic benefits of, 192-194
      time use and, 195-197
   study sites, 187
   See also Automated Examination
      System (AES)
Avila, L., 75
Awerbuch, A., 105
Azevedo, A., 278

Baba, M. L., 158
Babbage, C., 45
Babbage Principle, 45, 54
Baldwin, R. B., 64
Bannon, L., 313
Barbash, F., 70
Barley, S., 186, 207

About the Editors

JoAnne Yates is Sloan Distinguished Professor of Management in the Sloan School of Management at the Massachusetts Institute of Technology. Her research, which includes both historical and contemporary studies, focuses on understanding how the use of communication and information within firms shapes and is shaped over time by its changing organizational, managerial, and technological contexts. Her *Control Through Communication: The Rise of System in American Management* (1989, 1993) looks at the evolution of communication systems in firms historically. She also collaborates with Wanda Orlikowski, of Sloan's Information Technology group, on studies of electronic communication in contemporary organizations. This work has been published in outlets such as the *Academy of Management Review, Administrative Science Quarterly,* and *Organization Science.* She currently is chair of the Organizational Communication and Information Systems division of the Academy of Management and serves on editorial boards of several journals.

John Van Maanen is Erwin Schell Professor of Organization Studies in the Sloan School of Management at the Massachusetts Institute of Technology. He has been a visiting professor at Yale University, the University of Surrey (United Kingdom), and INSEAD (France). He has published a number of books and articles in the general area of occupational and organizational sociology. Cultural descriptions figure prominently in his studies of the work worlds of patrol officers on city streets in the United States, police detectives and their guv'nors in London, and (most recently) park operatives at Disneyland. He is the author and editor of numerous books including *Organizational*

Careers (1977), *Policing: A View From the Street* (with Peter Manning) (1978), and *Tales of the Field* (1988). His most recent work is *Qualitative Studies of Organizations* (Sage, 1998).

About the Contributors

Charles Bazerman is Professor and Chair of Education at the University of California, Santa Barbara. He is interested in the social dynamics of writing, rhetorical theory, and the rhetoric of knowledge production and use. His most recent book is *The Languages of Edison's Light* (2000). Previous books include *Constructing Experience, Shaping Written Knowledge: The Genre and Activity of the Experimental Article in Science, The Informed Writer: Using Sources in the Disciplines,* and *Involved: Writing for College, Writing for Your Self.* Coedited volumes include *Textual Dynamics of the Professions, Landmark Essays in Writing Across the Curriculum,* and a special issue of *Mind, Culture, Activity* on "The Activity of Writing, the Writing of Activity." Current projects include a rhetorical theory of literate action and an investigation of environmental information.

Martin Campbell-Kelly is Reader in Computer Science at the University of Warwick, United Kingdom, where he specializes in computer history and human-computer interaction. His publications include *ICL: A Business and Technical History* (the official history of Britain's principal computer manufacturer) and the *Collected Works of Charles Babbage.* He recently completed a one-year Simon Senior Research Fellowship at the University of Manchester, where he conducted a study of Victorian data processing techniques.

Jonathan Coopersmith is Associate Professor of History at Texas A&M University. The present chapter is part of a larger history of the fax machine from its origins during the 1840s to the present. His first book was *The Electrification of Russia, 1880-1926* (1992).

Suzanne Iacono is Program Director for Computation and Social Systems (Information and Intelligent Systems Division, Computer and Information Sciences and Engineering Directorate) of the National Science Foundation. She received her Ph.D. in management information systems from the University of Arizona and received her M.A. and B.A. in social ecology from the University of California, Irvine. Previously, she held a faculty position at Boston University and was a visiting scholar in the Sloan School of Management at the Massachusetts Institute of Technology. She is an associate editor for *The Information Society* and the *MIS Quarterly* and conducts research on social informatics and electronic communication.

John L. King is Dean and Professor in the School of Information at the University of Michigan. His research focuses on the development of high-level requirements for information systems design and implementation in strongly institutionalized production sectors. The goal of this work is to improve the design of information technologies, for both organizational and institutional usability, through better articulating the processes of requirements analysis, specification, and prototype creation. His work also informs policy and strategy development at the firm, sectoral, and institutional levels. He served as editor-in-chief of the journal *Information Systems Research* from 1993 to 1998 and served as Marvin Bower Fellow and as a visiting professor at the Harvard Business School in 1990. From 1980 to 1999, he was a professor of information and computer science and management at the University of California, Irvine, where he received his B.A. in philosophy and Ph.D. in administration.

Rob Kling is Professor of Information Science and Information Systems in the School of Library and Information Science at Indiana University, where he also directs the Center for Social Informatics. He is editor-in-chief of *The Information Society* and recently wrote and edited the second edition of *Computerization and Controversy: Value Conflicts and Social Choices*. His research focuses on topics within social informatics such as the roles of digital libraries and electronic publishing in altering professional communication, social aspects of high-speed networking, and technology-based social movements.

Peter K. Manning is Professor of Sociology and Criminal Justice at Michigan State University. He received his Ph.D. from Duke University. He has published several books on policing and is the author of the forthcoming *A*

Communicational Theory of Policing as well as several articles on policing and technology. His current research involves a dramaturgical analysis of private security and loyalty, a book on aspects of postmodern ethnography (with Betsy Cullum-Swan), and fieldwork on crime-mapping in a large urban police department.

Wanda J. Orlikowski is the Eaton Peabody Chair of Communication Sciences and an Associate Professor of Information Technologies in the Sloan School of Management at the Massachusetts Institute of Technology. Her research focuses on technology and organizational change, with particular emphasis on the relationships between information technologies and organizing structures, work practices, culture, communication, and social cognition. She received her Ph.D. in information systems from New York University and has published in journals such as *Academy of Management Review, Administrative Science Quarterly, Information Systems Research, MIS Quarterly,* and *Organization Science.*

Brian T. Pentland is Associate Professor in the Department of Accounting at Michigan State University. Previously, he was a member of the faculties in the Anderson Graduate School of Management at the University of California, Los Angeles, and in the School of Business Administration at the University of Michigan. His primary area of interest is in the relationship between work and technology, although he also has been developing techniques for business process modeling and the sequential analysis of qualitative data. His publications have appeared in *Administrative Science Quarterly; Organization Science; Accounting, Organizations, and Society; Technology Studies;* and *Accounting, Management, and Information Technologies.* He currently serves on the editorial boards of *Administrative Science Quarterly; Accounting, Management, and Information Technologies;* and *Information, Technology, and People.* He holds degrees from the Massachusetts Institute of Technology (S.B., 1981, mechanical engineering) and the Sloan School of Management at MIT (Ph.D., 1991, organization studies).

Daniel Robey is John B. Zellars Professor of Computer Information Systems at Georgia State University. He teaches courses on qualitative research methods in information systems and information technology and organizational transformation. He received his doctorate in administrative science from Kent State University in 1973. He is editor-in-chief of *Information and Organization,* is senior editor of *MIS Quarterly,* and serves on the editorial boards of *Organization Science,* the *Canadian Journal of Administrative Science,* and the John Wiley series on Information Systems. He is the author of three books and numerous journal articles. His current research includes empirical examinations of the effects of a wide range of technologies on organizational structure and patterns of work. It also includes the development of theoretical approaches to explaining the development and consequences of information technology in organizations.

Karen Ruhleder is Assistant Professor of Library and Information Science at the University of Illinois, Urbana-Champaign. Her research is in the ethnography of information systems and the analysis of infrastructures to support distributed collaborative work. She has published in the information systems and sociology of science literature. A current project analyzes patterns of learning and collaboration around groupware (with Brigitte Jordan). She also is a member of the Illinois Research Group on Classification.

Sundeep Sahay is affiliated with the University of Oslo, Norway. Previously, he was a lecturer in the Information Technology Institute at the University of Salford, United Kingdom, where he lectured in the area of information technology and society. Before that, he worked on a three-year research project at Cambridge University, United Kingdom, with Geoff Walsham studying the implementation and use of geographical information systems in India and Malaysia. He received his Ph.D. in information systems from Florida International University in 1993.

Susan Leigh Star is Professor of Communication at the University of California, San Diego. She received her Ph.D. in sociology of science and medicine from the University of California, San Francisco. Previously, she was a professor of information science at the University of Illinois, Urbana-Champaign. She also has taught at the University of California, Irvine; Keele University, England; and several universities in Scandinavia as a guest professor. Much of her research has been on the social implications and design of large-scale technology, especially information technology. Among her publications are *The Cultures of Computing* (1995), *Regions of the Mind: Brain Research and the Quest for Scientific Certainty* (1989), and *Sorting Things Out: Classification and Its Consequences* (with Geoffrey Bowker) (1999). She is volume editor for Science and Technology for the forthcoming *Women's Studies International Encyclopedia* (edited by Cheris Kramarae and Dale Spender). Her current research concerns ethical and methodological practices in on-line research with human participants.

S. Lynne Taylor is Assistant Professor of History in the Department of History at the University of Waterloo, Canada. She holds a Ph.D. in history from the University of Michigan, an M.A. in history from the London School of Economics, and a B.A. in business administration from the University of

Western Ontario, Canada. She researches the social history of World War II and its immediate aftermath. Recent work has focused on black markets and the post-World War II refugee crisis.

John R. Weeks is Assistant Professor of Organizational Behavior at INSEAD, France. He specializes in issues of organizational culture and ethnography and is particularly interested in lay ethnography, the process by which organizational members come to reflect consciously about their own culture. His most recent work is a field study of the causes and consequences of the "unpopular culture" in a large British bank, where everyone from the chief executive officer to the most junior clerk agrees that a radical change of culture is necessary and desirable, yet they also agree that such change is practically impossible. He holds a Ph.D. in management from the Sloan School of Management at the Massachusetts Institute of Technology and an M.Phil. in management from Oxford University, United Kingdom.

Susan J. Winter is Assistant Professor in the College of Business at the University of North Carolina at Charlotte. She received her Ph.D. from the University of Arizona in 1992, her M.A. from Claremont Graduate University in 1989, and her B.S. from the University of California, Berkeley, in 1982. She previously served on the faculties of Florida Atlantic University; the University of Waterloo, Canada; and the University of Victoria, Canada. She has more than 15 years of international managerial and consulting experience. Recent research interests include the impact of technology on the organization of work and the symbolic aspects of information technology (particularly as related to the Internet and to entrepreneurial ventures). She has published in journals such as *Information Systems Research, Information & Management, Frontiers of Entrepreneurship Research,* and the *Journal of Vocational Behavior.* She has presented her work at the International Conference on Information Systems and at the Academy of Management. She also has contributed chapters to scholarly books.